Struggles for Recognition

The publisher and the University of California Press Foundation gratefully acknowledge the generous support of the Robert and Meryl Selig Endowment Fund in Film Studies, established in memory of Robert W. Selig.

Struggles for Recognition

*Melodrama and Visibility
in Latin American Silent Film*

Juan Sebastián Ospina León

UNIVERSITY OF CALIFORNIA PRESS

University of California Press
Oakland, California

© 2021 by Juan Sebastián Ospina León

Library of Congress Cataloging-in-Publication Data

Names: Ospina León, Juan Sebastián, 1984– author.
Title: Struggles for recognition : melodrama and visibility in
   Latin American silent film / Juan Sebastián Ospina León.
Description: Oakland, California : University of California Press,
   [2021] | Includes bibliographical references and index.
Identifiers: LCCN 2020044321 (print) | LCCN 2020044322 (ebook)
   | ISBN 9780520305427 (cloth) | ISBN 9780520305434 (paperback) | ISBN 9780520973411 (epub)
Subjects: LCSH: Melodrama in motion pictures—20th century. |
   Silent films—Latin America.
Classification: LCC PN1995.9.M45 O87 2021 (print) |
   LCC PN1995.9.M45 (ebook) | DDC 791.43/3098—dc23
LC record available at https://lccn.loc.gov/2020044321
LC ebook record available at https://lccn.loc.gov/2020044322

29 28 27 26 25 24 23 22 21
10 9 8 7 6 5 4 3 2 1

For M. and A.

Contents

List of Illustrations	ix
Acknowledgments	xi
Introduction: Melodrama and Visibility	1
1. "Filmdom" before and during the Great War	25
2. Buenos Aires Shadows: Urban Space, Fallen Women, and Destitute Men	54
3. Bogotá and Medellín: A Tale of Two Cities and Conservative Progress	80
4. Orizaba, Veracruz: Yesterday's Melodrama Today	109
5. South to North: Latin American Modernities	137
Conclusion: Struggles for Recognition	164
List of Abbreviations	173
Notes	175
Works Cited	217
Index	235

Illustrations

1. "Bill Posting Prohibited" / 5
2. "Babylon of Steel" / 7
3. Fox Film advertisement / 29
4. "The tempest takes down the oak tree" / 49
5. "Sinner" / 56
6. Picture of a cabaret dancer on cover of *Fray Mocho* / 58
7. Serial-queen melodrama advertisement / 64
8. Grand lobby of Gath & Chavez department store (1908) / 66
9. Organ grinder and "fallen" woman in advertisement for *El organito de la tarde* / 74
10. Blessing of Colombia Film studios / 81
11. Iris in/outs equate the suffering male lead with a bleeding Christ / 83
12. Scenes from *Alma provinciana* featuring Rosa's plight / 99
13. "In the hands of the vulture" / 101
14. A "censorship committee member" in a top hat ogles a woman's legs / 102
15. The filipichín gets ready for a date / 107
16. "A Wretched Passerby" / 117
17. Adolfo gets up in the nick of time / 120

18. Cover for *Nettles and Violets* (1920) / *124*
19. Orientalist depiction of drug use in *El Demócrata* / *131*
20. Ajuria and Francis X. Bushman on set of *Una nueva y gloriosa nación* / *141*
21. Monstrous Uncle Sam and Lady Justice / *154*

Acknowledgments

This book engages with melodrama as a dominant mode for making visible and intelligible multiple experiences of modernity in early twentieth-century Latin America. At the same time, it traces the global circulation of moving images that shaped, and was shaped by, Latin American markets during the period of silent cinema. The northbound journey this book embarks on, across multiple urban enclaves—from Buenos Aires to Los Angeles—stems to a great extent from the assistance, knowledge, and openness of the colleagues and friends I encountered in my travels. Many people and institutions supported me in the completion of this book. Archivists, administrators, professors, and friends helped me turn this project into a reality.

All translations from Spanish, French, Italian, and Portuguese are my own unless otherwise indicated. An earlier version of chapter 2 was published as "The Conventillo, the Department Store, and the Cabaret: Navigating Urban Space and Social Class in Argentine Silent Cinema, 1916–1929," *Journal of Latin American Cultural Studies* 26, no. 3 (2017): 377–91.

Archival institutions in Argentina, Colombia, Mexico, the United States, and Italy made this work possible. Not only did they open their doors to me; the human element in each of them actively shaped the questions and structure of this book. In Argentina, I would like to thank the staff of the Biblioteca del Congreso de la Nación; the Biblioteca Nacional; the Instituto Nacional de Estudios de Teatro; the

Museo de Cine Pablo Ducrós Hicken, particularly Andrés Levinson; and the Universidad del Cine Library. Special thanks to Adrián Muoyo, library director at the Escuela Nacional de Experimentación y Realización Cinematográfica, whose expertise in tango and early twentieth-century Buenos Aires—shared in the most affable chitchats—shines through chapter 2. My gratitude, in Colombia, to staff of the Biblioteca Luis Ángel Arango; the Biblioteca Nacional, particularly Lyda España Rodríguez; and the Fundación Patrimonio Fílmico Colombiano.

In Mexico, I would like to express my gratitude to the staff of multiple archives: the Archivo General de la Nación; the Biblioteca Miguel Lerdo de Tejada; la Hemeroteca Nacional—particularly the archivists who listened to my pleas and allowed me to look at some originals, not always the dreaded microfilm; the Cineteca Nacional; and the Filmoteca de la Universidad Nacional Autónoma de México. My special gratitude to Antonia Rojas Ávila, who introduced me to Esperanza Vázquez and, in so doing, radically changed what I foresaw as my fourth chapter. In the United States, special thanks to my editor Raina Polivka and editorial assistant Madison Wetzell at the University of California Press for their enthusiastic support and assistance. Thanks also to the staff at the UC Library system, Stanford Libraries, Carnegie Mellon University Libraries, the Library of Congress, and National Archives II. In Italy, my gratitude to Elena Beltrami of the Cineteca del Friuli who, despite the agitation *Le giornate del cinema muto* imply, found time to help me retrieve the materials I was looking for.

In the earliest stages of the project, generous grants, fellowships, and research funds allowed me to complete this book. Summer and travel grants as well as the Normative Time fellowship from the Graduate Division of the University of California, Berkeley, facilitated travel to Argentina and Colombia. A Dissertation Writing Fellowship supported my work when life took me to Istanbul for an extended period. In later stages, research funds provided by the School of Arts and Sciences of the Catholic University of America facilitated research in Mexico City as well as writing opportunities.

I am indebted to many colleagues and friends for their intellectual support. For their mentorship, I thank Natalia Brizuela, Francine Masiello, and Linda Williams. Their guidance went—and goes—above and beyond. At UC Berkeley, the attendees of the Visual Cultures Working Group pushed me to polish the very first drafts of this project. Thanks to my dear friends Krista Brune, Manuel Cuéllar, Camilo

Jaramillo, and Ivett López Malagamba. Their critiques and encouragement are the warp and weave of this book. Rielle Navitski deserves an acknowledgments section of her own. Thank you, Rielle, for your outstanding generosity and feedback. Most important, thank you for your friendship. Special thanks to Laura Isabel Serna, Mónica García-Blizzard, Camila Gatica Mizala, and Andrea Cuarterolo, who kindly shared their expertise and insights. My gratitude to colleagues who have read parts of this book, or "behind the scenes" matter: Jeff Hinkelman, Jennifer Alpert, Suleyman Dost, Daniel García-Donoso, and Chelsea Stieber.

In my travels, I was fortunate to encounter wonderful people who helped me intellectually and logistically. In Buenos Aires, David Oubiña, like a Virgil of sorts and despite his busy schedule, took me around the city, opening doors that would otherwise have been shut or left unknown to me. Luis Facelli graciously shared his unpublished work. Octavio Morelli, after some hesitation, opened up a trove of *Excelsior* at the ENERC (understandable, when the Biblioteca Nacional, unscrupulous researchers have cut out, and stolen, the articles and images they needed from rare illustrated early film periodicals). Alejandro Gómez, my childhood friend, happened to be in Buenos Aires at the time and hosted me. In Mexico City, Itzia Fernández and David M. J. Wood pointed me in the right direction. With her unique cordiality, Esperanza Vásquez shared with me her inspiring passion for restoring Mexico's moving-image patrimony. Carolina Cabello, thank you for giving me *posada* (and making me feel at times as if I was on vacation). My gratitude also to the Cabello family, as well as Larissa Bosch and her family. In Bogotá, I thank Leila El'Gazi and Diego Rojas, two pioneers of silent film research in the country, for their time and insights. No words of gratitude would be enough to thank my parents—this book being but a still-frame of their never-ending and unconditional support. In Istanbul, my gratitude to Izzettin and Zühal Güvenç. In Washington, DC, my gratitude to Manuel Cuéllar and to Juliana Martínez, whose company made more bearable the academic-market forces beyond my control, forces that for far too long have kept my family apart.

This book is dedicated to my wife and son. It took shape during his early childhood. Is he part of a generation gravitating again toward "attractions" over narrative? I do not know. But for sure, I will walk by his side as he explores the visual cultures awaiting him. (And perhaps tweak here and there, for the cause of melodrama!) Güzelim, *bu kitap aslında bir kitap değil. Bu beni sonunda sana yaklaştıracak bir anahtar. İnşallah bir daha asla ayrı kalmayacağız, asla. Seni seviyorum ve bu projeyi nihayete erdirmem adına yaptığın herşey için sana teşekkür ediyorum. Hayatımızın bu devresinin önümüzdeki hayat boyu sürecek hikayenin kısacık bir bölümü olması dileğiyle.*

Introduction

Melodrama and Visibility

Of a hundred proletarians, ninety ignore who is Karl Marx.
But ninety can tell you in what style Rudolph Valentino
gives a kiss.
—Roberto Arlt

Writing for *El Hogar* in 1928, the prolific short-story writer and journalist Horacio Quiroga condemned Buenos Aires film productions. In his view, local film, "in the best cases, [comprises] a melodrama handled with the least tact possible[;] a poem of unsophisticated sensibility equivalent to what is represented in many of our tango songs."[1] Ten years earlier, a journalist had deemed films produced in Santiago de Chile regressive because they were too melodramatic. "Modern cinematography excludes melodramatic themes," he contended.[2] For both critics, melodrama exceeded the boundaries of good taste. It did not accord with present times. And yet it abounded in film and other popular media. As these two examples show, early Latin American film critics lobbed the term *melodrama* at films in pejorative descriptions. Without truly giving melodrama its due, other critics would grant some qualities to this narrative mode. The year the renowned nineteenth-century Argentine novel *Amalia* premiered in film (1914), another *El Hogar* critic—referring to Ponson du Terail's popular serial novels—claimed: "Finally, Rocambolesque melodrama has been resuscitated." In his terms, melodrama "is interesting, moving, inspires passion"—but, as he makes clear, is—"for the imbeciles."[3] Such derisive columns sought to elevate film critics over films and readership, even as they hinted at tastemakers' earnest interest in the ubiquity of melodrama. Quiroga, for instance, later acknowledged that in barrio film theaters, "The taste for the naturalness of the scene [*la naturalidad escénica*], filtered now even to small newspaper vendors, is the greatest cultural conquest cinema has achieved among us."[4] There was something to be learned from melodrama after all, Quiroga suggests: through melodrama, spectators developed the ability to discern nuances in cinematic language and mise-en-scène.[5]

Southern Cone critics were not unique in chronicling melodrama's effects on spectatorial connoisseurship. Witty commentary regarding film formulae and spectatorial response could also be found in Bogotá, Colombia. In 1917, a critic observed that "the cinema public is domesticating itself."[6] Not without sarcasm, he stressed filmic melodrama's capacity to modernize local spectators, recording how, at first, spectators were astounded by on-screen kisses, "so intense they could straighten up the hairs of a peach," but then they quickly "learned the schools: Gaumont brand kisses, Pathé brand, Nordisk. Italian school embraces, sighs Bertini brand. . . . In brief, the whole range of twentieth-century loving [*amatoria*]."[7] This discriminating ability—the skill to single out erotic conventions specific to different production companies on a transnational level—reveals how the avid consumption of new mass cultural products, mainly the illustrated press and the cinema, led to an elaborate understanding of films. The critic also acknowledges how moving images registered changes in the public sphere, making new forms of sociability visible. According to these early critics, cinema naturalized new, hair-raising practices in the spectator's everyday life.

As these varied accounts of melodrama and modern change indicate, cinema spread unevenly throughout Latin America during the silent period. That filmmaking was an "artisanal" endeavor in certain regions,[8] while a thriving industry in others—and that film distribution and exhibition also varied considerably—complicates any overarching analysis aspiring to relate melodrama to diverse experiences of modernity in Latin America. The artisanal, "an important category of uninitiated and autodidactic culture-making,"[9] foregrounds the role of many filmmaking pioneers in Latin America: the "part who had no part" in the perceptual coordinates of their communities and who, through the cinema, entered the modern political pact, the pact of representation.[10] Contrasting examples—from different regions and cities—reveal how new ways of being and new practices sprung from radical changes gained visual saliency through filmic melodrama. In film, melodrama procured sites of intelligibility to both register and make sense of modern change. It recorded technologic and infrastructural achievements, signaled the emergence of new forms of sociability, and rearticulated private and public spheres. Of course, melodrama conferred visibility on certain aspects of Latin American modernities while concealing others. Such play between visibilities and invisibilities was not without complications. This book examines the heuristic function melodrama performed during the silent period and how it delineated ways to relate to—and inhabit—modern change.

Here, *melodrama* serves as the shorthand for *melodramatic regime*, a point of convergence for seeing and doing that yields a revelatory imperative.[11] By reading melodrama in terms of a visual regime—the historical rearrangement of subject matter and access to representation[12]—this book explores how it affected the mechanics of public participation and induced new forms of political subjectivity during the silent period, as it visualized and shaped the social arena of urban modernity. The case studies herein expound on the way Latin American silent films and silent film culture speak to the issues of visibility and invisibility for emergent social groups or actors. This question of representation has theoretical and political implications. The processes associated with modernity and cinema unfolded differently in each of the contexts under study. Cumulatively, the cases under scrutiny posit the ideological flexibility of melodrama and its textual maneuvers. As we shall see, melodrama can be—and has been—mobilized for both liberal and illiberal ends, as it reveals *and* conceals social inequities.

This book builds on recent work in film and media studies, particularly film history, that invites us to think transnationally.[13] Taking film culture as a key critical category for understanding the convergence of urban environments, the popular press, cinematic melodrama, and contested notions of urban space—within and across national contexts—this book proposes avenues of research germane for Latin American film studies and beyond. It draws connections between film cultures in the Americas and redeploys theoretical and methodological concepts relevant to film studies scholarship in diverse contexts. Traveling north through multiple cities—from Buenos Aires to Los Angeles—*Struggles for Recognition* explicates the complex relations melodrama established with differing processes of modernization. In so doing, it traces how established and emergent social actors harnessed melodrama to reshuffle their social positions in the contested sites of urban modernity. Studying multiple urban sites in which melodrama functioned in remarkably distinct ways allows for a productive historical reevaluation of both melodrama and modernity.

To study the relationships between melodrama and modernity in transnational contexts requires definitions of both terms, however. For, as Ben Singer duly notes, both modernity and melodrama belong "high up on any list of big, vague concepts that—despite their semantic sprawl, or perhaps because of it—continually reward critical inquiry."[14]

MEANINGS OF MODERNITY

In early twentieth-century Latin America, *modern* was a fraught term, to be sure. Flourished by diverse social actors—in public lectures, the press, and moving images—this new byword served diverse agendas. *Modernidad* (modernity) was not widely used in Latin America until the late twentieth century, when it consistently circulated in debates about postmodernity.[15] The adjective *moderno*, on the contrary, appeared often in the works of intellectuals throughout the nineteenth century and, at least in urban areas, "became ubiquitous" in printed media from the early twentieth century onward.[16] As early as 1900, illustrated periodicals such as *Caras y Caretas* (1898–1939) and *Revista Cromos* (1916–present) introduced photographic sections on the material progress of "Buenos Aires moderno" and "Bogotá moderno," respectively. Harnessing the novel technologies of the rotary press and the halftone printing process—which allowed for reproducing photographs—reflected radical changes proper to many Latin American urban spaces. Urbanization and commercialization caused a new density of downtown congestion, along with new social dynamics between city center and neighborhoods shaped by (inter)national migration. These new, heterogeneous societies lent a sense of fragmentation to urban space that was further complicated by the expansion of public transportation, city traffic, and new ways of visual marketing. Periodicals depicted a fast-paced daily life, a contemporary way of being that was both threatening and exciting (see figure 1). Catering to an ever-growing readership, newspapers and illustrated magazines pictured urban experience as overstimulating.

These experiences and descriptions closely resonated with aspects of the new urban experience in Europe (or the United States)—namely, "the intensification of emotional life due to the swift and continuous shift of external and internal stimuli" that German sociologist Georg Simmel describes in his 1903 essay "The Metropolis and Mental Life."[17] Evoking Simmel's account of European urban modernization, many Latin American publications described urban living as an intensified sensorial experience at once menacing and alluring. A Buenos Aires film trade journal saw urban stimuli as an imminent threat: "We live

FIGURE 1. "Bill Posting Prohibited," *Caras y Caretas* (Buenos Aires), 22 March 1919. Courtesy of BNE.

in continuous shock[;] the nerves vibrate, shake, and burst into a true hysteric crisis."[18] Other journals celebrated urban stimuli, albeit recognizing their caustic effects on the psyche. A *porteño* (from Buenos Aires) column on strategies of visual solicitation read, "The modern city has become a great exhibit.... Each poster aims to be noticed and injures the public's imagination in an instant.... We are the juries of this gigantic exhibit.... The art of the poster [lies] in experimental psychology."[19] Bogotá periodicals were no different. The film magazine *Películas* trumpeted, "The vertiginous advance of the centuries has brought us new concerns, new dangers, new forms of expression."[20] Another large-print publication proclaimed, "Cosmopolitanism, imposed by transportation speed, modified sensibility and therefore the forms of expression."[21] In Mexico City, illustrations functioned as "a major site" for diffusing a sense of the modern "dependent on the circulation of a global visual culture."[22] Hence the exceedingly elaborate depictions of cities such as New York, the "Babylon of Steel," by correspondent illustrators taken by the "great traffic," "automatic cafés," and "motorist flappers" (see figure 2).[23] Across the continent, periodicals thrilled to a ubiquitous preoccupation, the sensorial intensity of city life, (re)producing its image on page after page.

If the early twentieth-century press in Latin America suggests an ambivalent understanding of modernity and modernization—a cause of both angst and frisson—Latin American scholarship on the topic, for the most part, has been equally ambivalent. The latter's inconsistency, however, resides in conjoining the notions of modernity and modernization. Consequently, academic treatment has reproduced what Nicola Miller labels the "metanarrative of the deficient," whereby Latin American modernity "is continually found to be lacking or tardy or otherwise inadequate" compared to an allegedly felicitous model in Europe or the United States.[24] To counter this tenacious perspective, we must first reconsider the very idea of modernity and divest it of its immediate association with time. Instead, to borrow from philosopher Peter Osborne, it is crucial to understand modernity as "a qualitative, not a chronological, category."[25] The precedence of experience over temporality evinces the freighted assumptions feeding the narrative of the deficient. The sense of inadequacy, tardiness, or lack inherent to Latin American modernity arises from what I term "adjectival modernity"—that is, from the nominalizations that Latin American scholars, over time, have coined to describe its unique character. Beatriz Sarlo's "peripheral modernity,"[26] Julio Ramos' "uneven modernity,"[27] Jesús Martín-Barbero

FIGURE 2. "Babylon of Steel," *Revista de Revistas* (Mexico City), May 1928. Courtesy of BLT.

and Herman Herlinghaus's "anachronistic" modernity,[28] and—more recently—Roberto Schwarz's "out-of-place" modernity,[29] and even the rather abstruse-sounding "multi-temporal heterogeneity" Néstor García Canclini proposes,[30] all assume nonadjectival modernity to happen elsewhere, a modernity to which Latin American modernity can only problematically aspire.

As a corrective, recent early modern studies reframe how then-new ways of being and circuits—of commodities, raw materials, and bodies—came about as a result of colonial enterprises. With colonialism, Europe entered into contact with Asia and Latin America. On a global scale, Latin America therefore comprised a fundamental vector of modernity, not an actor tardily trying to catch up with modern change, particularly evident during the nineteenth and early twentieth centuries.[31] Enrique Dussel contends, "Modernity is the fruit of these events, not its cause."[32] One may recall, as Adam Sharman repeatedly does, that in Europe "not everything in the modern age is modern."[33] What Latin American scholars of modernity have taken as a homogenous process of European modernization was in fact an utterly uneven one; indeed, very few leading urban centers epitomized the qualities of modern change.[34] Such irregularity, Osborne affirms, developed in Europe the idea that certain European urban centers in fact spearheaded "progress" and "civilization." This notion established the basis for colonial discourse, which yielded comparisons between "different European countries themselves, and thereafter ... globally, in an expanding dialectic of differentiation and homogenization."[35] Perhaps unwillingly, Latin American scholarship has propelled a similar discourse, premised on simultaneity, geographical difference, and a centrifugal conception of modern progress, with Europe at its center.[36] For my purposes, I attend to some of the issues these dominant currents conjure about how transnational film historiography reproduces such discursive centers and peripheries to this day: in general terms when it understands "cinema as a *consequence* of modernity" (read: the product of Euro-American technological achievements as well as urban hyperstimulus), and in particular when it relates the development of early cinema to a Latin American "modernity [that] was, above all, still a fantasy and a profound desire."[37] The first chapter revises this perspective in the context of film markets before and during the Great War.

The fraught idea of Latin American modernity as a tardy or incomplete project originates from overlapping the *experience* of modernity with other, historically specific social and economic processes that first occurred in (parts of) Europe. Bound together in the term *modernization*, these processes include the emergence of capitalist relations of production, industrialization, urbanization, state bureaucratization, secularization,[38] the privileging of empirical sciences and technology as the primary source of knowledge, the promotion of individualism, and the separation of public and private spheres. The obsession of Latin American scholars with pinpointing *the moment* modernity arrived in the region further reproduces this sense of modernity as an achievable—yet always deferred—state. Sharman notes how "nuances apart, all the work on Latin American modernity by Sarlo, García Canclini, Jesús Martín-Barbero, Carlos Monsiváis, [José Joaquín] Brunner, and Julio Ramos binds the region's modernity to the Second Industrial Revolution."[39] Leaving aside Sharman's own Eurocentric chronology, he keenly notices how Latin American scholars concur in locating Latin American modernity as a historical period centered on the region's most rapid modernization processes, which took place roughly between 1880 and 1930. During this period some countries, particularly Argentina, "underwent one of the fastest processes of modernization in the world."[40] In 1900, Buenos Aires had a larger population than many paradigmatic European cities (one million inhabitants). By 1914, 30 percent of inhabitants in Argentina were born elsewhere—a higher percentage "than was ever reached in the United States."[41] Other cities throughout the continent underwent modernization processes that did not yield such awe-inspiring statistics propelled by transnational migration. Even so, their processes were no less radical. Each region and city in Latin America experienced modernization in different ways and degrees, which in turn yielded different forms of melodrama to register and make sense of such change, as the following chapters explore.

By challenging adjectival modernity, this book does not suggest that we break with the seminal work scholars have produced on Latin American modernity. Rather, it builds on their work and, supported by the archive, trains its lens on the multiple unfolding processes taking place during the fastest period of modernization in the region. Applying alternating focus between modernity and modernization, here the former points to the (aesthetic) experience of a historically specific, socioeconomic reality in flux.[42] Modernity is a felt experience, a reaction to rapid change situated on a critical threshold between present and past. As we shall see, the role of affect proves crucial to melodrama in documenting, representing, and responding to these changes. Recalling Sharman's mantra—not everything in modernity is modern—this book is therefore not "about 'creative destruction,'"⁴³ nor does it consider the tense coexistence of new forms with forms of tradition and with the past as an alternative exemplar of modernity.⁴⁴ On the contrary, it proposes that this double bind (between rupture and continuation) epitomizes the experiences of modernity—importantly, made visible in the *uses* of melodrama by diverse social actors in text and moving images to both register and process modern change. Thus, adopting a "multiple modernities perspective,"⁴⁵ this book traces how different—and at times contrasting—processes of modernization resulted in equally different experiences of modernity, recorded in and circulated through melodramatic narratives. There is, however, one discursive constant traversing these different experiences. For Miller, quoting Alfonso Reyes, these experiences "dream of a modernity that [is] 'fully and totally human.' Their visions . . . founded on the faith in fellow human beings that had been a feature of many Enlightenment works."⁴⁶ As I explore in the following section, the seed-germ of liberal philosophy is at the core of both Latin American modernities and melodramas.

Different experiences of modern change challenge teleological approaches to Latin American modernity. They demand analyzing Latin American *modernities*—in plural—in their own right. How are we to study modernization processes that led to the "sacralization" of certain societies,⁴⁷ for instance, processes that yielded a very different conception of modernity—materially progressive yet socially conservative—and that consequently question the very conditions of possibility for melodrama, when understood as a "post-Sacred" narrative form?⁴⁸ Rather than considering Latin American modernity as always deferred, this study elucidates the diverse visualizations and experiences of modern change, using Latin American silent films and silent film cultures as its primary material. Attentive to the archival traces left by producers and consumers of melodramatic narratives, this study proposes a comparative framework centered on the urban to explore connections between, and contrasts across, diverse melodramatic cultures.

Why give precedence to melodrama to study the varying experiences of modernity? This book builds on a shared premise among Euro-American and Latin American melodrama scholars: "recognizing" melodrama as "a central fact of modern sensibility."⁴⁹ In early twentieth-century Latin America, melodrama shaped—and was shaped by—modern changes. It made visible and intelligible multiple experiences of modernity, as it provided a contested site of representation in service of diverse social actors.

MEANINGS OF MELODRAMA

Writing for the newspaper *El Universal*, published out of Mexico City, the film critic Carlos Noriega Hope shared with his South American counterparts an ambivalent take on melodrama. Under the pen name Silvestre Bonnard, in 1922 he wrote a column on "His majesty the *culebrón*."[50] The very title betrays the ambivalence Latin American film critics felt regarding the form—melodrama being majestic in its popularity and yet rife with sinuous twists and turns.[51] Accompanied by pictures of "the eternal Valentino," the Fairbanks twins, and Wallace Reid, the column focuses on *Way Down East* (dir. D. W. Griffith, 1920). Though acknowledging its transnational success, Noriega Hope concludes that the film is "not a *chef d'oeuvre*," but rather a "mediocre, and even, bad work." He particularly dislikes the "repetitive" plot of the film, "the eternal story of the maiden seduced by a vulgar womanizer, [a story] as old as the world." He praises the skill of Lillian Gish before the camera but determines that trite conventions ultimately overshadow her performance with "basic elements of vulgar cinematography: the villain, the hero, the heroine, the wedding at the end." After summarizing such "vulgarity" in film, Noriega Hope seems to nevertheless incorporate twists and turns in his very assessment—as if the *culebrón* begins to command his own text. With a turn of phrase, Noriega Hope grudgingly recognizes how "we end up admiring the art of renovation," despite the "commercial influence [that] continuously spoils 'that little art we love so much.'"[52]

From the specific "flaws" of *Way Down East* to broader claims on narrative film—"ese pequeño arte que tanto amamos," as contributors of *El Universal* would fondly call the cinema—Noriega Hope identifies key features of melodrama: narrative conventions, popular appeal, and constant renovation. Some eighty years later, Linda Williams would also turn to Griffith's masterpiece, in her view a "typical melodrama,"[53] to define the melodramatic mode. With its massive appeal and its narrative formulae, Williams concludes, akin to Noriega Hope, that melodrama is "a perpetually modernizing form," always "reformulating itself."[54] But unlike the Mexican critic, her assessment does not reflect cultural anxieties often associated with analyzing a "vulgar" narrative medium. Williams's and Noriega Hope's understandings of melodrama—as popular, conventional, and yet always self-renovating—point to the functions and uses of melodrama that this study explores.

Without delving into the predicament of Anna Moore (Lillian Gish), a poor country girl tricked into a fake wedding and later abandoned when she becomes pregnant, *Way Down East* contends with social opprobrium and Anna's ensuing struggle for recognition—as a wronged individual, loving mother, and ultimately a member of society with equal rights and responsibilities. Importantly, this struggle takes shape by *making visible* Anna's plight and—through this attitude of revelation—by harnessing a vicarious experience of pathos.[55] The films, or fragments of films, discussed in this book tend to be narratives akin to that of Anna, stories similarly negotiating (in)visibilities and affective links within and beyond film. Through narratives of the "fall" of demure seamstresses in porteño *cinedramas*; star-crossed lovers vying to subvert patriarchal mores through cross-class marriages in Bogotá and Medellín productions; the masked identities of action-packed railroad melodrama in Orizaban (Mexico) films; and even "cameos" of Theodore Roosevelt and Uncle Sam in the loss of the Panama Isthmus, melodrama expounds upon struggles for recognition premised on revealing *or concealing* social injustice. More specifically, and as we shall see, melodrama operates by revealing or concealing the unfulfilled promises of liberal philosophy: liberty, equality, and solidarity. I contend that these three promises and their (in)visibility animate melodrama's core.

Latin American and Euro-American scholars concur in locating the origins of melodrama in the aftermath of the French Revolution.[56] Following Peter Brooks's seminal work *The Melodramatic Imagination: Balzac, Henry James, Melodrama, and the Mode of Excess* (1976), scholars accept the axiom that melodrama constitutes a "central fact of modern sensibility."[57] For Brooks, this sensibility stems from an experience of loss, initially felt at the end of the eighteenth century. He proposes that *mélodrame*—the play combining gestural language and music to punctuate dramatic tension[58]—proffered moral bearings to a post-revolutionary world divested of its structuring principles (the king, church, and aristocracy). Melodrama's function therefore consisted in revealing such bearings, which had become "occulted" and were made evident in clashes between Manichean characters representing cosmic forces: the perennial battle between Good and Evil.[59] But this Manichean structure waned, "if still present, by the 1860s."[60] Melodrama's revelatory capacity led Brooks to describe it as a particular form of struggle: "the drama of recognition."[61] From Brooks on, this expression became a catchphrase among several melodrama scholars, slowly leading to a broader understanding of melodrama, one beyond its "excessive" nature—a common vilification that, perhaps unintentionally, Brooks also propagated.

Today, scholars highlight the sense of justice suffusing melodrama.[62] This does not mean that melodrama, then or now, appeals to universal or atemporal ethical values. Rather, melodrama offers contrasts "between how things are and how they could be, or should be,"[63] in different historical moments.[64] Such contrasts contour to historically specific, sociocultural contexts as well as to individual and group agendas. From the outset, nevertheless, melodramatic conventions reverberated with the origins of liberalism in France. Theatrical mélodrame produced narratives in which individuals stood up to socially oppressive forces. Melodrama unmasked class privilege and the injustices of absolute power by means of melodramatic conventions—virtuous (female) victims and leering (male) villains—as in Guilbert de Pixérecourt's *Cœlina ou l'enfant du mystère* (1800).[65] Thus, melodrama aimed at making sense of the complexities of the Revolution and the reconfiguration of society—politically, economically, and socially. And most important, by making visible—that is, by conferring visibility on different forms of inequity—melodrama denounced the fact that the three promises were yet to be fulfilled.[66]

Considering that the sense of justice at play in melodrama is not always objectively just, this study goes one step further in considering the mode a "drama of recognition." For Brooks, the type of recognition melodrama entails is clear: through a character's virtue, melodrama manifests hidden moral bearings. But moral recognition eschews other forms of recognition, therefore limiting melodrama's concerns and uses to pedagogy or ethics. Contra Brooks, I argue that melodrama comprises multiple forms of recognition, inside and outside of narrative. Indeed, Latin American scholars have expanded melodrama's received conception as a "drama of recognition." Studying melodrama's contemporary uses by individuals and social groups, they foreground its mediating role in making sense of everyday life and fomenting forms of association.[67] This expanded understanding of melodrama—as mediation in the service of recognition and representation—allows for considering its capacity for community building and debate in the public arena. Through melodrama, as Martín-Barbero contends, "not only individual subjects, but collective subjects, be it social classes or political actors, make and remake themselves in the symbolic weave of interpellations and recognitions."[68] Explicating everyday life at individual and group levels, melodrama functions as a heuristics, a language, a form of translation—from things or situations (narrative or real-life experiences) into the body and the sensibility of bodies (individual and collective) encountering those situations.

Likewise, as a visibilizing and interpretive enterprise, melodrama carries a political dimension. Here, "political" is understood in a broad sense, akin to Jacques Rancière's relational conception of politics. For Rancière, the essence of politics consists in interrupting an established visual regime, "by supplementing it with those who have no part in the perceptual coordinates in the community, thereby modifying the very aesthetic-political field of possibility."[69] As such, melodrama's political potential lies in its ability to distribute and apportion what is visible and invisible and to interrogate who has access to representation. In Latin America, because of modern change this process was stronger than ever between 1880 and 1930, when serialized melodrama in print facilitated "an unprecedented democratization of literature" and "equalized the reading public."[70] As the first, truly popular narrative form, the feuilleton hosted the emergence of the professional writer and attested to the birth of the first "cross-class" reading public.[71] Brooks aptly puts it in a broader context: with the emergence of the professional writer preoccupied with representing his own social reality, "melodrama becomes a chosen vehicle for the attempt to change the world."[72] In the press, and later in film, melodrama consisted of the historical, narrative platform on which multiple social actors shaped and enacted diverse configurations of the social order. But this is not to say that melodrama always strove for—or yielded—socially inclusive happy endings.

During the silent period, film critics were well aware of the political weight proper to filmic melodrama. "Today the cinematograph has a greater power over public opinion than the press," a critic for *Heraldo de México* stated. With a Manichean bent, he further contended, "The cinematograph is a weapon that can be harnessed for good things, but used for wicked propaganda it can have disastrous consequences."[73] The critic thus limns that filmic melodrama can fail to provide felicitous encounters between individuals or social groups in community building. The critic finds threatening melodrama's cross-class reach and ability to question social arrangements. This small example reveals how melodrama shapes—and is shaped by—individual and group agendas. Therefore, and to return to melodrama's historical origins, melodrama does not revolve around finding lost moral bearings in a postsacred world or new bearings in the wake of liberalism. Instead, it exposes *or conceals* the unfulfilled promises of the French Revolution in service of diverse social actors. By exposing, melodrama draws attention to the unfulfilled promises. By concealing, it offers palliatives for social injustice; without truly addressing structural inequities, it reproduces uneven social orders.

The promises of liberty, equality, and fraternity appear to be somewhat at odds with the state of Latin American societies during the silent period. But their hopes and ideals resonated with the contemporary reading publics—lest we forget, reading publics from the nations that not too long before were republicanism and democracy's "vanguard of the Atlantic world."[74] "The Spanish-speaking America[,] from the banks of the Rio Grande to the tip of Argentina, celebrates freedom," *La Prensa* of San Antonio, Texas, extols in a full-page article highlighting the three promises quoted in fifteen national anthems of Latin American nations.[75] Likewise, a column commemorating the French Revolution in *Heraldo de Mexico* reads: "The French Revolution signaled the incomparable path of redemption; it opened the path for other revolutions emanating from the sacred desires of Humanity, marching united under the benevolent protection of Liberty, Equality, and Fraternity."[76] The column celebrates the Revolution's influence across the continent, as it "especially influenced the revolutionary movements that have been developed in America."[77] But this celebratory tenor clashed with the social realities melodrama made visible, realities that departed from the three promises. Myriad factors—uneven social conditions, the emergence of new groups in representation, and the expansion of the public sphere as these groups gained access to representation through print media and moving images—highlighted the gap, fueling melodrama's relevance, as modern individuals found themselves struggling for recognition at multiple levels, demanding a just social order and seeking to improve individual and collective conditions.

As the Frankfurt school's current director Axel Honneth suggests, the problem of inequality lies in an "internal contradiction" within the principles of the French Revolution—namely, its liberal understanding of freedom.[78] The advent of the nation-state and the new forms of association it fostered provided the conditions of possibility for hampering the realization of the three promises. The nation-state, combined with the market economy, produced what economic historian Karl Polanyi called the "Market Society," a novel form of association and exchange that "altered human consciousness, from one based on reciprocity and redistribution to one based on utility and self-interest."[79] The French Revolution—"the 'bourgeois' revolution par excellence," Thomas Piketty reminds us—sought to create a political and social order based entirely on equality of rights and opportunities. But as Piketty shows, comparing the concentration of wealth in Britain and in France after the latter's Revolution, "equality of rights in the marketplace cannot ensure equality of rights *tout court*."[80] The three promises commit to economic, social, and political rights. In the Latin American context, or in any context, suggesting that postrevolutionary markets altered the human psyche may be farfetched. There is no question, however, that the Spanish American revolutions—in which criollo elites led the struggle—provided a new order that guaranteed the utility and self-interest of criollo oligarchs over the lower classes and racialized citizens who constituted the majority of the population. The "myth of the revolution" ascribed to Latin America—even if premised on "rupturist rhetoric"[81]—reaped colonial-postcolonial nations that "went on being the old colonies; social conditions remained unchanged[,] now reality . . . hidden under layers of liberal and democratic rhetoric."[82] As Mary Louise Pratt eloquently puts it, in the South American revolutions, "not everyone was to be liberated, equalized, and fraternized . . . any more than they were by those in France or the United States."[83]

In Latin America, as elsewhere, the liberal understanding of freedom yielded to the individual pursuit of private interest, the license to accumulate private wealth—and, correlatively, the right to take advantage of others, within legal limits.[84] Naturally, interpretation prevented fulfillment of the other two principles: equality and fraternity, or in Honneth's terms, "mutual responsibility in solidarity."[85] In this sense, individualistic freedom implies a particular form of recognition, but one—to return to the topic at hand—at odds with dominant readings of melodrama. This form of recognition is not the sympathetic recognition of the individual. Instead, it is a subjugating "recognition" of the other: seeing individuals as a means of utility or gain. The "irony, not lost in melodrama"—Christine Gledhill observes—"is that the newly forming, discrete individual becomes as mired and imprisoned as under previous hierarchies in the by now abstracted economic and political forces that justify inequalities and inequities in the name of personal freedoms."[86] Highlighting this aporia, Honneth considers that the three promises can only be reconciled as long as liberty is understood less in an individualistic manner and more in an intersubjective one, as a form of freedom in which individuals supplement each other, a form that would ideally satisfy the demands for equality and solidarity.[87] It is here—in the realm of intersubjectivity—that I find a powerful engine for melodrama. For if melodrama indeed consists of a "drama of recognitions," it consists of reciprocal forms of recognition deployed through shifting regimes of visibility. These in turn yield intersubjective affective experiences. In melodrama, the (in)felicitous realization of liberty, equality, and solidarity—for individuals and groups alike—entirely depends on intersubjective relationships of recognition.

The types of recognition that melodrama elicits, however, require further specification—for melodramatic recognition operates at individual and collective levels within and beyond narrative. Honneth highlights three primary dimensions in claims to intersubjective relations of recognition: love, rights, and esteem.[88] The felicitous acquisition of these three dimensions, in Honneth's view, would yield autonomous, fully realized, and socially capable individuals invested with correlative "self-confidence, self-respect, and self-esteem."[89] Not coincidentally, melodrama navigates similar claims of recognition at equally interlocking levels, from personal-emotional recognition, to legal recognition, to social esteem. As in *Way Down East* or any other story, melodrama narrativizes struggles for recognition by disclosing various forms of *mis*recognition.[90] It deals with the violation of the body (emotionally, physically), the denial of rights within a given community, and the disparagement of individuals or social groups. Here lies melodrama's critical capacity: when it reveals the unredeemed promises of liberty, equality, and solidarity, when it makes injustice visible. Visualizing social, political, and economic struggles, melodrama "move[s] people to act, join movements, and participate in projects of social, political, and economic transformation."[91]

But melodrama can serve other purposes, as this book also explores. Not by disclosing but by *concealing*, melodrama can reproduce social inequality and uneven power relations—what Matthew Bush describes as "the underside of melodrama."[92] In this sense, melodrama comprises a contested site of representation. It is the platform through which different social actors deploy their own visualizations of society and, in so doing, aim to impose (that is, to dominate with) their particular visual regimes. In either case, within a given public sphere,[93] melodrama traffics in forms of recognition that represent various identities and communities, big and small. And through these communities, it articulates (or critiques) social bodies and orders. It can forward senses of social justice by expanding access to representation. But it can also deliver palliatives for social injustice—uncritically or willfully replicating inequality—thereby curtailing the access to representation. Melodrama can be a vehicle through which individuals or groups seek to be recognized and therefore included in felicitous forms of reciprocal recognition, or it can push forms of consent that yield vertically exclusionary understandings of community. With this formulation, I suggest a nuanced reading of melodrama as a contested site of representation. It is neither an offspring of mass consumer culture, manipulating mass society into passivity, as Adorno and Horkheimer would have it in *Dialectic of Enlightenment* (1944),[94] nor is it a felicitous locus for oppositional readings and resistance, per Martín-Barbero. Assuming a broad range of positions between these two poles, melodrama—put to uses that give contour to historical and sociopolitical contexts— evinces more elaborate interconnections between storytelling, access to representation, current events, everyday life, and subject and group formations. Such is the case in Latin America and elsewhere—during the silent period, before, and after.[95]

STRUGGLES FOR RECOGNITION

This book presents a new history of Latin American silent cinema that traces in multiple urban centers the ways in which melodrama procured sites of intelligibility to both register and make sense of modern change. To be sure, it by no means aims at a totalizing picture. Based on archival research in five countries—Argentina, Colombia, Mexico, Italy, and the United States—this study reframes the notion of national cinema. Even if the film cultures discussed in this book spring up in—and some extend across—different nations, national referents in press materials and films discussed here do not necessarily respond to "imagined communities" comfortably overlapping national borders.[96] Instead, with a comparative approach, this study thinks in productive ways about multidirectional transnational connections within and beyond national contexts. As the case studies in this book, chosen from the largest film production centers in the subcontinent, show, film cultures operated within—and interacted with—more specific communities associated with urban centers and their areas of influence. Some of these competed for national cultural hegemony, as was the case between Bogotá and Medellín, in Colombia, or entered into dialogue across national borders. The struggle for dominance between urban centers and their film cultures does not confirm the presence of national cultures. On the contrary, it authorizes the status of the latter as discursive aspirations in the process of realization. Not for nothing did film critics throughout the period emphasize that "regarding the cinema, the word nation turns out to be narrow."[97] Taking film culture as a key critical category, this study traces transnational—as well as transcultural—relations in periodicals, narrative cinema, the question of representation, and the film trade (between the cases under study, Europe, and the United States).

Struggles for Recognition scaffolds its analysis through close readings of surviving film footage, reconstructions of lost films from press accounts, and other archival resources. It examines illustrated magazines, weekly novels, feuilletons, popular theater, tango, and the reception of both domestic and foreign films in the burgeoning film trade journals and fan magazines of the time, as well as in consular documents. With this abundance of fresh material, the book explores overlapping contexts—social, cultural, and political—that shed light on the way melodrama visualized and shaped the social arena of urban modernity in Buenos Aires, Bogotá, Medellín, Mexico City, Orizaba (Veracruz), and Los Angeles (California). The book's original research builds on various approaches—from film studies, Latin American cultural studies, and melodrama theories—to draw critical connections between recent and canonical scholarship on the relations between melodrama and modernity—namely, academic products from Latin America and Euro-America that have seldom been put into dialogue. Instead of positing a dearth—or recent development—of scholarship on Latin American silent cinema produced in Latin America, this book builds on the rich Latin American corpus to fill gaps in American scholarship on the topic.[98] Tracing transnational connections—both archival and scholarly—this study proposes an approach to film cultures as simultaneously intermedial, locally inflected, and global.

Situating silent film production of multiple Latin American cities in a broader context, chapter 1 charts the global circulation of moving images and the popularization of filmic melodrama across Latin America before and during World War I. The Great War rearranged the cinematic world market and turned Latin America into coveted territory. Grounded in local perspectives found in the press, the chapter emphasizes how local distributors and exhibitors across the continent appropriated the cinemas of major film-exporting nations (particularly Italy, France, and the United States). Local distributors and exhibitors either embraced the global circulation of moving images or, in some regions, engaged in protectionist practices to deter American advance in favor of European fare. Unearthing local preferences for specific global imports, chapter 1 also explores how the predominance of particular foreign cinemas in specific local markets shaped filmic melodrama and film cultures in Buenos Aires, Bogotá, and Mexico City. As such, this chapter analyzes the emergence of local melodramatic conventions and culture proper to different Latin American urban centers. Contextualizing the films and film cultures studied in the following chapters, these conventions distinguish the form and content of melodrama and its relation to varying experiences of modernity.

Recent scholarship on Argentine silent cinema has focused on the popular gaucho genre: films about Argentine cowboys pitted against the forces of modernization. By stressing the genre's nationalistic importance, this scholarship has overlooked another, equally popular genre: *cinedrama porteño*. Chapter 2 tends to this urban-specific genre and the overstimulating urban experience it depicts. Porteño cinedrama, to anglicize the term, competed with—and eventually ousted—gaucho films during the 1920s. It consisted of melodramas revolving around urban outcasts, white slavery, and other forms of (sexual) exploitation. Unlike the nationalist gaucho films—bent on elevating the gaucho as a national identity symbol—porteño cinedrama depicted an unstable social fabric. Set in the late 1910s and 1920s, cinedrama critically visualized a bleak Buenos Aires in constant transformation: massive immigration, industrialization, and an accelerated everyday life. Drawing on surviving film fragments, film trade journals, and fan magazines, chapter 2 argues that porteño cinedrama showcased Buenos Aires as a contested space in which varying degrees of sociocultural separation and proximity embodied cultural anxieties of urbanization and social mobility. Through narratives of "fallen women" and well-dressed wastrels, porteño cinedrama foregrounded social instability by confronting emergent and established social actors in specific urban spaces: city streets, cabarets, department stores, garçonnières, and overcrowded boardinghouses. Harnessing new cinematic techniques and special effects, these films visually constructed fast-paced worlds assailed by modern city life. With special attention to the films of José A. Ferreyra and Edmo Comminetti, I examine how porteño cinedrama rendered complex forms of circulation and displacement of bodies and goods—and bodies as goods—in early twentieth-century Buenos Aires. Reflecting (upon) transformations of the time, these films explore segregating practices that regulated social interactions and, at the same time, tantalized spectators with encounters between the gendered underclasses and the elite.

Chapter 3 looks at Bogotá and Medellín films, contrasting examples to porteño cinedrama. Canonical studies of melodrama (Brooks, Singer) and of Latin American modernity (García Canclini) take secularization as the primary condition of both melodrama and modernity, but archival material and extant film footage betray this assumption in certain Latin American modernities—where "being modern" did not, in fact, pit rupture against continuation. This evident theoretical impasse challenges melodrama's function as a "drama of morality fitted to a post-Sacred age," a question recent scholarship has raised.[99] It demonstrates melodrama's uses in shaping social bodies by means of revealing *and* occluding specific visual regimes, even when the struggle for visibility is posited in moralist terms. In the first decades of the twentieth century, Colombia underwent a steady process of conservative modernization, a "sacralization of society," as Colombian historians concur.[100] At its peak, and based on strict Catholic morals, sacralization regulated almost every aspect of Colombians' everyday lives—from domestic mores to work ethics and leisurely practices in public space, including film going and filmmaking. Chapter 3 analyzes the reach of sacralization at the levels of film reception and film production. Based on press materials and surviving film footage, I argue that during the 1920s narrative films from the two fastest-growing cities produced (and were the product of) a hegemonic visual regime supported by both state and church, aimed at morally controlling social subjects and legitimizing traditional social hierarchies while extolling material progress. Premised on fervent Catholicism, this visual regime had a simple but suggestive name: *la moral*. This regime was not without its critics, however. Chapter 3 also traces dissident voices in film and in the illustrated press that, even if rare, eloquently questioned la moral's predominance. Instead of reproducing its disciplinary discourses, these voices condemned and made visible the double standards of early twentieth-century Bogotá and Medellín societies. They depicted both societies as driven by the strictest moral values while smitten with a highly eroticized social body.

Chapter 4 engages with contemporary issues of preservation and filmic reconstruction, while examining the (in)visibilities melodrama makes possible through film. I study two surviving Mexican feature-length films produced in the city of Orizaba, Veracruz. Both *El tren fantasma* (*The Phantom Train*; dir. Gabriel García Moreno, 1926) and *Puño de hierro* (*Iron Fist*; dir. Gabriel García Moreno, 1927) epitomize melodramatic filmmaking produced outside of Mexico City and, respectively, melodrama's ability to conceal or reveal social inequities. Appropriating the conventions of action-packed American cinema, both films, as shown in surviving footage, make visible the achievements— and the by-products—of urbanization and transportation technologies in urban centers other than the capital city. While exhibiting Orizaba's modern, fashionable society—incarnated by the *pelona*, a female figure akin to the American flapper—*El tren* exploits thrilling narratives of banditry in railway networks reminiscent of American serials, sidelining contemporary social strife in its textile industry and railroad system. Rather critical of "prophylaxis campaigns" and biopolitical discourses of the period, *Puño* sheds light on the issue of drug abuse while indicting state-sponsored hygiene officials for promoting and capitalizing on opiates. This chapter pays close attention to the material history of both films. Restored and "reconstructed" multiple times, both *El tren* and *Puño* raise important questions about film preservation and appropriation. Tracing the particulars of the third and latest restoration process, this chapter analyzes both films under the framework of *compilation films*: contemporary films premised on repurposing silent film footage. As compilation films, both *El tren* and *Puño* question constructs of authority and the historical accuracy of restored films. Through close readings of key sequences supported by intellectual property archival documents, I enter a current debate among Mexican film scholars: Is the latest restoration the "definitive version" of both films—as current copies available on DVD and streaming claim—or is it an attempt to "modernize" the remnants of forever-lost films, as the prominent film historian Aurelio de los Reyes maintains? Without offering a definitive answer, the discussion allows me to consider the ways in which preservationists and educated spectators project their (present-day) melodramatic horizons of expectation onto the melodramas of the past.

Bracketing the preceding three chapters, the final chapter echoes chapter 1's transnational outlook. Centered on the transnational celebrity culture proper to the late 1920s, chapter 5 examines different border crossings between Hollywood and local film cultures by tracing the "personalization of the social" that star personas make possible. To borrow from Christine Gledhill, the two case studies in this chapter map the ways in which the star "combines recognition of individuality and a socioethical emblematic function characteristic of melodrama."[101] Echoing the complex circulation of moving images discussed in chapter 1, chapter 5 questions "one-way" historical accounts of American dominance over Latin American film and film cultures, by contrast presenting "two-way" film production and reception processes as reciprocally shaping films and film cultures in Buenos Aires, Santiago de Cali (Colombia), and multiple cities in the Hispanic Caribbean and the United States. The first case study looks at certain impasses that melodramatic (in)visibilities make possible. It tackles the unique production and reception conditions of *Una nueva y gloriosa nación* (*The Charge of the Gauchos*; dir. Albert H. Kelly, 1928). Believed to be lost, but recently restored at the Cineteca del Friuli, Italy, *The Charge of the Gauchos* epitomizes the fantasy of many silent-era Latin American filmmakers: to make movies in Hollywood.[102] A prominent film distributor from Buenos Aires, Julián de Ajuria, wrote the script and funded the film, an epic romance of Argentina's independence centered on the historical *libertador* Manuel Belgrano. Harnessing American star power, the film received both praise and criticism in Argentina and the United States. In Argentina, the film was well received, but Ajuria's all-American payroll cast doubts on the film's nationalistic sentiment. In the United States, reviews show differing opinions but concur in being unable to categorize the film (romance, western?). Interestingly, the reviews blame the difficulty on the scriptwriter. Press materials therefore suggest the ambivalent nature of Ajuria's film. Intended for both American and Argentine audiences, *Charge of the Gauchos* problematically followed melodramatic conventions not entirely familiar to either Argentine or American spectators, thus casting doubts on the "universal" transferability of the melodramatic mode. The second case looks at *Garras de Oro* (Talons of gold; dir. P. P. Jambrina, 1926) and melodrama's ability to upend visual regimes and geopolitical hierarchies. The film focuses on the polemic separation of Panama from Colombia and overtly critiques Teddy Roosevelt's "Big Stick" diplomacy through a narrative revolving around Roosevelt's libel suit scandal against Joseph Pulitzer's *New York World*. To date, the origin of the film is uncertain. Some scholars hypothesize that Cali Film outsourced production to an Italian studio. What is known is that consular documents at the United States National Archives reveal the move by American consular agents to suppress the film in Latin American countries. Through close readings supported by these and other archival documents, I analyze the ways in which this elusive film deployed anti-US discourses that, even if briefly, cast aspersions on US foreign policy and disrupted the predominantly US-based, southbound current of moving images.

The reader may have already deduced this study's concern with relations between present and past, as it expounds the alliances between melodrama and modernity through northbound travel. It is inevitable—and perhaps impossible—to fully depart from concerns of the present even when sifting through the archives of the past. For Siegfried Kracauer, it would be "foolish" to deny "the historian is moved by present interest.... The fact that we live only once involves a moral obligation toward the living."[103] This is not to say that only present interest motivates historical inquiry. Inspired by Kracauer, this study aims at "a better understanding of the issues" surrounding discrete struggles for recognition via melodrama in early twentieth-century Latin America. Aware that "the knowledge of what has happened then does not tell us anything about our own prospects," but hopeful—particularly regarding the three promises—"it will at least enable us to look at the contemporary scene from a distance."[104]

CHAPTER 1

"Filmdom" before and during the Great War

The absence of speech imbues the cinematograph with a
limitless capacity for cosmopolitanism. All films—be them
Yankee, Russian, Danish, or Italian—circulate the globe
and are understood everywhere.
—Alfonso Reyes

IMPORTING ENTERTAINMENT

In 1916 Léon Gaumont—a pioneer of the motion picture industry in France, or as an American film critic put it, "one of the most dynamic and useful forces in filmdom"—bemoaned the effects of the Great War on European film markets. "This war was made for America," he decried in an interview.[1] Two years later, referring to a broader territory, Italian producers lamented that they were "losing America" as their market presence across Latin America waned.[2] Indeed, World War I changed the course of film history. It rearranged the circulation of moving images on a global scale, reshuffling the dominance of particular national cinemas in regions beyond their national borders. As film historian Kristin Thompson suggests in her seminal work *Exporting Entertainment*, the "long term [global] dominance" of Hollywood cinema came about during and after World War I "by eroding" the markets of the European film industries outside of Europe.[3] While most Europeans lamented the new postwar order, a smaller group—although reluctant to accept the North American advance—lauded how the horizons of "filmdom" were broadening in such an extraordinary manner during that period. Writing in 1919, the French film critic Louis Delluc acknowledged that "cinema goes everywhere" and celebrated the fact that "in every country, film theaters are built by the thousands. Films are shot around the entire globe. Merchants, by sale or trade, make this expressive industry more intense." A staunch devotee of the cinema, he claimed that the film industry would "reach the simultaneous perfection of art and traffic."[4] As cinema brought distant lands and epochs onto the screen, for Delluc it also prompted new perceptions.

This novel understanding of a networked world heralded the cinematic colonization of the planet. Filmmakers, film critics, and local impresarios recognized this new world borne out of shifting markets and warfare. Immediately after the war, they vied to conquer it. The filmic sense of a networked world—ripe for the taking, but not necessarily Americanized—impacted the Americas, in plural. For local and foreign distributors and exhibitors, Latin American markets became a territory to be acquired. In fact, Latin American markets were a determining factor in consolidating the filmic world order that, in many ways, still operates today.[5] Before 1916, American entertainment was not dominant in the region. A critic in Santiago de Chile recalled in 1918 that "when Pathé presented *Les misérables* and Cines *Quo Vadis* [1913], Yankee cinematography was still in diapers."[6] Even in markets close to the United States a similar impression persisted. "[Hollywood film] was perfectly unpopular, to the level it had to be removed from the programs," a prominent Mexican film critic reminisced in 1928.[7] Indeed, in Mexico City between 1914 and 1917, Italian cinema held "the largest share of the exhibition market . . . peaking at 54 percent of all features shown in 1916."[8] However, this state of affairs radically changed after the war. Weakened by the conflict, European producers could not satisfy the Latin American demand. American studios quickly marketed to the opening niche and, in so doing, consolidated Hollywood's dominance. According to Thompson, "Fox's avenue of entry into large-scale exploration was South America."[9] During the same period, Goldwyn and Universal also established global market dominance through incursions into the Latin American region.[10]

Importantly, this process was not one of mere commercial and cultural imperialism. Latin American exhibitors strategically adapted to the Great War's effects on local markets. Acknowledging shifting market conditions, Valente Cervantes, a prominent impresario of Puebla, Mexico, recognized the Americanization of local venues: "During the First World War French material was gone. . . . We [exhibitors] entered a crisis. . . . American films, series [and] episodes, flooded the market. They saved us."[11] From a seemingly passive standpoint, Cervantes saw American films as the new savior from the unkind tides of postwar film markets. Though Cervantes's observations may come across as acquiescent, many Latin American distributors and exhibitors played an active role in establishing the global circuits of foreign films.[12] "Tell me which cinema you frequent, and I'll tell you who you are," stated a popular Santiago de Chile newspaper, hinting at the diverse publics and programs available to patrons in Santiago by the war's end.[13] As distributors and exhibitors eventually turned to production, their role as mediators shaped locally inflected film melodrama across the region.

Attending to such nuances at the local level, the first section of this chapter explores how Latin American impresarios engaged in "negotiated readings"[14] to shape local film markets and, consequently, local film cultures prior to and during the Great War. These readings, in turn, yielded calculated appropriations of film styles, progressively consolidating melodramatic storytelling throughout the region. As different cases across Latin America show, this active role amplified the pluralistic character of Latin American film circuits rather than reducing them to passive recipients of foreign imports. Ultimately, as local distributors turned to production, their choices—commercial, ideological, and aesthetic—sparked the emergence of distinct, melodramatic film cultures, a subject I expound upon in the second section. In the third section I explicate local film pioneers' aesthetic choices and their attempt to elevate cinema's cultural status as they turned to the Latin American nineteenth-century (melodramatic) literary canon.[15] Thus, in three stages this chapter lays the groundwork for the specific case studies in the following chapters: it describes the film fronts proper to importing entertainment and melodrama's advance on, and eventual takeover of, narrative film in Latin America in the 1910s. These developments did not occur in a clear-cut, chronological, or spatial progression across the region.

FILM FRONTS

In the late 1910s and throughout the 1920s, distributor advertisements across the Americas signaled a bellicose thrust to seize new Latin American markets. "Imperial metaphors" in local periodicals evoked the North American industry's "self-declared 'invasion' of South American markets," initially deployed through *Moving Picture World* and *Cine-Mundial*, its Spanish-language version.[16] Echoing the causes of the Great War, local ads visually rendered the expansion of Latin American markets in terms of a territorial dispute. Here, space—a "visual and textual construction"—"put into practice symbolic ... and material conquests," as Georgina Torello keenly observes in the case of Uruguay.[17]

Indeed, across the continent many ads from local and foreign distributors consisted of illustrated maps indicating economic power and hierarchical territories, as if trying to overpower competitors by means of cartography.[18] The Di Domenico brothers—two Italian immigrants who built a distribution and exhibition empire headquartered in Bogotá, Colombia, that spanned the north of South America, Central America, and the Lesser Antilles—posted ads in *Cine-Mundial* depicting their company's breadth of influence. In high angle, with a sun-like company logo shining over its transnational market domains, the Latin American Industrial Cinematographic Society (or SICLA, its Spanish-language acronym) flaunted its reach from South America to the Caribbean.[19]

Southern Cone companies evinced similar aspirations. Aiming to conquer South America, the Corporación Argentina Americana de Films circulated ads animated by cartographic northward advances. Evoking war maps in its ads, the Corporación depicted the region traversed by vectors radiating from Buenos Aires and extending to every corner of the subcontinent.[20] In local periodicals, American companies also showed their expansive ambitions. A 1920 Fox Film ad in *Cine Universal*, published out of Buenos Aires, depicted a multi-eyed globe representing the "human eyes" that saw "the best cinematographic production in the universe."[21] With the planet presented from a high angle, the ad offered a somewhat ominous and potentially overweening image of the studio's reach. Reminiscent of a mythical deity, the Fox globe displayed a thoroughly conquered planet: the Americas and a rather shapeless Eurasia fully covered in Fox-film-watching eyes (see figure 3). These ads, however, did not accurately represent the contested Latin American markets. Instead, as Ben Singer points out regarding American film trade journals, these maps are valuable as historical evidence "less for their ostensible content than for the wishful thinking and underlying discursive agendas they betray."[22]

Filmic cartographies in film trade journals are archives of ruthless competition, attesting to the aims of local and foreign competitors to dominate local film markets. In territory they imagined as hostile, exhibitors and distributors tried to gain higher ground through various means, particularly by deploying obsequious rhetoric in the press. The first issue of *Cine-Mundial* (1916–1946), dedicated to "the genius of the Latin American race," foregrounded in an amicable editorial the "very important enterprise of bringing closer together the two continents of the New World."[23] Yet despite the fraternal appeal, the editorial betrayed *Cine-Mundial*'s agenda: to promote American over European

FIGURE 3. Fox Film advertisement, *Cine Universal* (Buenos Aires), 3 April 1920. Courtesy of BNA.

films in local markets. And it did so by appealing to the former's emergent global preeminence, while tendentiously soliciting local collaboration: "It is a fact that American cinematography has gained innumerable allies and supporters in the Latin countries of the Old Europe.... [T]his foretells an analogous triumph in the progressive communities of Latin America."[24] *Cine-Mundial*'s original title, *Pan-América Cinematográfica*, further stresses the journal's goal of regional outreach under the aegis of Pan-Americanism (read: American dominance).[25] In correspondence to American consular offices inquiring about local market conditions in the port city of Barranquilla, Colombia, "PAN-AMERICA CINEMATOGRAFICA, the Spanish version of *Moving Picture World*," acknowledges its effort to be "the first American trade journal of its kind to take up this Spanish work systematically."[26] Perhaps attentive to local sensibilities, *Cine-Mundial* may have reconsidered its original title, as it could have evoked local anxieties vis-à-vis the "New Monroe Doctrine" that was gathering momentum in the United States.[27]

Despite *Cine-Mundial*'s aims, during the Great War local distributors and exhibitors did import European productions, fostering negotiated readings vectored in multiple directions. In the Southern Cone, European films, mostly French, entered the continent through Buenos Aires, where two companies, Max Glücksmann and the Sociedad General Cinematográfica, had cornered the market.[28] These near-monopolies imported films through London, the global distribution center until new customs duties and submarine warfare (1915–1917) shifted regional distribution to New York City.[29] In the north of South America, Thompson affirms, quoting an "American official," exhibition consisted of "waste basket" films, that is "the [American] plays the American public refus[ed] to see."[30] This official's remarks suggest that before and during the Great War locals exhibited whatever material was available—regardless of its quality—reproducing uneven center-periphery relations vis-à-vis American imports. Local exhibitors appear to have had very little to no agency in navigating the ebb and flow of global markets affected by the conflict. But as film historian Fernando Purcell affirms in tracing Hollywood's impact in the region during World War I, "It would be a mistake to think that [Hollywood] imposed its cinematic tastes without attending to the sensibilities and reactions of audiences."[31] Indeed, American consular officials in Colombia recognized that local film patrons were "very exacting" regarding film quality.[32] They insisted, "the people here are just as critical as the American public."[33] In fact, negotiated readings—as well as the market potential of

Latin America—inverted the trajectories of power relations between North and South, highlighting the active role of the latter in shaping the cinema consumer's tastes. In 1922, for instance, the foreign and export editor of *New York Commercial*, William Edmund Aughinbaugh, called for the "immediate reappraisal of business methods" in order to tap into Latin American markets: markets "with potential resources and purchasing power so colossal that the commercial eyes of the entire world are centered on the republics of Central and South America." Lest American businessmen "fai[l] completely" in their pursuits, Aughinbaugh encouraged American businesses to better study Latin American markets, "because those in charge of . . . advertising and selling campaigns proceed blithely on the assumption that what appeals to an American will appeal to a Brazilian, an Argentinian, or a Chilean."[34]

Pace Thompson, Colombian exhibitors did not project scratched American films. To local consular agents' concern, "the chief competitors at present are the [French and] Italian films."[35] Preceding and throughout the Great War, Colombian venues exhibited European films (mostly Italian) and, importantly, *current* films: *Quo Vadis?* (dir. Enrico Guazzoni, 1913), *Cabiria* (dir. Giovanni Pastrone, 1914), Italian diva films, and the films of Maciste as well as other Italian strongmen, such as Luciano Albertini in *Sansono contro i filistei* (Samson against the Philistines; dir. Domenico Gaido, 1918).[36] This is no surprise given the influence and reach the Di Domenicos had in the region.[37] American powerhouses, including Goldwyn Distribution Co., saw their incursion efforts stymied by these Italian immigrants.[38] In addition, and not incongruously, Colombian exhibitors—including the Di Domenicos—screened current American productions, particularly serial melodramas and the super productions of D. W. Griffith and Cecil B. DeMille, as film programs in local film trade journals publicized.

The coexistence of contemporary European and American fare in local film markets casts doubts on the centers and peripheries that film historiography has imposed on Latin American film markets, a position recent scholarship has tackled.[39] The prominence of contemporary European and American productions points to the active, calculated role of distribution and exhibition practices, in which local companies engaged in the face of shifting world markets. Clearly factors other than "waste basket films"[40] shaped the circulation of global images in Latin America.[41] In certain instances, capitalist concerns motivated Latin American exhibitors to prefer cheaper European productions to American imports, as Thompson suggests.[42] Likewise, commercial, aesthetic, and identity factors—which cannot be reduced to nationalism—shaped local markets before local film production began. For instance, in response to Pan-Americanist anxieties, the Di Domenicos did not show films featuring the American flag, for fear of negative responses from local patrons.[43] Similarly, their only competitor in the Colombian Caribbean, Belisario Díaz, "eliminate[d] the American Flag in all that they exhibit[ed] because of strong public opinion," a consular document reports.[44] These interventions in foreign imports do not reflect a nationalist concern but rather point to ideological and commercial imperatives that informed the circulation and consumption of those very imports at transnational levels.[45]

In this context, early Latin American film trade journals attested to the negotiated circulation of moving images. Likewise, local periodicals shaped the (trans)national film cultures emerging in the region. In their pages, journalists and film critics recorded the different trends in local markets. Nevertheless, we cannot take the ads and articles in local trade journals and film magazines at face value. Much like *Cine-Mundial*, its Latin American counterparts yearned to shape minds and markets. But it is worth noting that local film trade journals—and through them, local exhibitors—aimed at manipulating local demand favoring both American *and* European cinema, depending on the impresarios' trade networks and cultural allegiances.

The complex partis pris of local distributors and exhibitors yielded, in print, multiple film cultures across the region. Analogous to the visibilities and invisibilities apropos of the cinematic medium, film trade journals and film magazines strategically showcased—and occulted—the impact of film in everyday lives. Despite leanings toward American or European films, which I delve into later, most periodicals expressed the cinematic appropriation of the everyday. Buenos Aires, for instance, was entirely suffused with cinema, according to the press. As an ever-growing number of movie theaters and other venues exhibited foreign and local productions,[46] and as spectators across the social spectrum avidly consumed moving images, local trade journals underscored how individuals quickly incorporated film culture into their lives. An article in the trade journal *La Película* (1919–1950) claimed that by the end of the 1910s, "cinematograph-mania" had invaded the city. The enthusiastic column recounts:

> Cinematographic obsession has gone to the limit. Luxury candy shops display in their pompous shop windows artistic candy boxes whose silky covers present the most brilliant cinema stars. Bookstores and postcard sellers display photographs of actors and popular actresses of the screen.... In

convenience stores and dairy stores, the so-called *cinema caramels* are sold with portraits of Margarita Clarck [sic], Theda Bara, the [Mary] Pickford, the [Dorothy] Dalton, etc[.], in their wrappings. There are tangos with themes dedicated to William S. Hart, Douglas Fairbanks, and other aces of the screen. The streets are filled with announcers carrying lively posters of the mute scene. Cinemas display ever-bigger posters with allegories of the most renowned films. Households use cinematographic stamps for wallpaper. Illustrated magazines occupy space with reviews and prints of the actuality of film. Religion, politics, commerce, industry and schools, they all tap into cinema to propagate their ideals and products. We are in full cinematographic frenzy! It is the civilizing wave that invades the universe![47]

The title of the column, Cinematografomanía, epitomizes cinema's exacerbation of the already-frantic circulation of images and audiovisual stimuli proper to Buenos Aires, discussed in the introduction. Well beyond the lights and shadows projected on screen, the column suggests, porteño audiences openly adopted film culture, incorporating it into nearly every aspect of their lives. Nevertheless, and again, the column's celebratory cinephilia should not be taken at face value. The references in the column reveal how the trade journal *La Película* favored American productions and stars over European ones. By obliterating the latter, the column suggests European films and stars did not partake in local film culture. One of the most influential journals of the period, *La Película* betrayed "a clear 'orientational' intention" to steer the cinematic market toward its main sponsors: Paramount Pictures, Warner Brothers, Fox Film, National Pictures, and Vitagraph.[48] Such an orientation captivated Buenos Aires throughout the decade.[49]

If Buenos Aires's large-print publications favored mostly American fare, Colombian film trade journals, most notably *Películas*, published out of Bogotá, defended European productions. Remarkably, *Películas* promoted a Colombian-cum-Italian nationalistic discourse that championed European cinema (mostly Italian but also French) as an art form essential to Colombian modernization.[50] Many columns praise European "cinematographic tendencies," highlighting their elevated conception of cinematic art. According to *Películas*, the artistic nature of European film—evident in its "realist" film style—"educates and refines," whereas American productions "exploit *feuilleton*-esque motifs woven from unrealities."[51] Interestingly, and despite the demeaning reference to the serialized novel, the films *Películas* defended were melodramas in their own right, but melodramas of a different tenor than American imports. In a heated debate between film critics for *Películas* and *Cine-Mundial*—which took place between March and August 1919 and proves how film periodicals dialogically read each other *across* the Americas—the critics of *Películas* claimed, "You cannot compare Ruth Roland or Pearl White with [Lyda] Borelli or [Francesca] Bertini."[52] In a passionate defense of the Italian divas over American serial queens, the magazine fired back against the criticism of Rafael Bermúdez Zataraín. The Mexican critic and regular contributor to *Cine-Mundial* had disparaged the artistic virtues of Lyda Borelli, Francesca Bertini, and Pina Menichelli in the American publication. Bermúdez Zataraín retorted by exposing *Películas*'s covert agenda: "[*Películas*] is a Di Domenico organ. [What] thrills them [the Di Domenicos] is not artistic effects . . . but simply box-office effects."[53] Bermúdez Zataraín's riposte denounced *Películas*'s aesthetic claim for what it truly was: a marketing strategy on the part of the Di Domenico brothers. The Di Domenicos owned *Películas*, yet throughout its pages proclaimed the journal's independence from SICLA and other Di Domenico-owned companies.[54] In the same article, *Películas* pushes an identity argument in favor of Italian films. The correspondent claims the "Colombian people"—a highly unstable category at the time—"by race . . . are Italophiles [italianófilos]" and relates this purported racial identity to cinematic taste: "Artistic orientations vary by race."[55]

The polemic between the two journals betrays the hidden designs of both *Películas* and *Cine-Mundial*. Although *Películas* was a Di Domenico marketing platform, the Di Domenicos praised Italian films and film culture on paper while exhibiting American serials in their theaters—as indicated in film programs and ads in *Películas*.[56] This discrepancy sheds light on the different types of negotiations in which local distributors and exhibitors engaged. As this case exemplifies, at times these negotiations were motivated by factors other than profit. The Italian-owned *Películas* defended Italian films in Di Domenico circuits and even suggested Italian films were an integral part of local identity (a claim systematically deployed in editorials, film reviews, and other articles). In this sense, the Di Domenicos' investment was ideological—echoing the transnational senses of belonging they aligned with—as well as aesthetic. Thus, their exhibition practices show how stakeholders in local film markets negotiated with both American *and* European films. In this fashion, local exhibitors and distributors appropriated—and shaped—the import of their messages and, through the press, crafted local filmic tastes.[57] In a similar vein, *Cine-Mundial* promoted American cinema across Latin America in celebratory guise—echoing the Americanized, porteño "cinematograph-mania" quoted previously—through the voice of the renowned Bermúdez Zataraín and other Hispanic and

Anglo voices. For instance, multiple articles in *Cine-Mundial* chronicled the pervasive *estrellitis*—or American "film star-itis"—that was taking over the continent. One article even suggests that American film culture is becoming Latin America's new object of veneration, as it exchanges "the Immaculate [Virgin Mary] and Saint Louis" for "Theda Bara, the sensual vamp, on the headboards of Latin American homes."[58]

Before and during the Great War, global film culture did permeate everyday life in Latin America, but as the polemic between *Películas* and *Cine-Mundial* suggests, starstruck audiences nurtured their local film cultures with both American and European influences. In Mexico City, film periodicals also revealed an obsession with Italian divas. Not without reservations, they documented *menichellismo*, a trend among young women who had a penchant for imitating Pina Menichelli's histrionics and attire. Even if local publications condemned the practice,[59] menichellismo indicates an equally pervasive, European-fused cinephilia, compared to the porteño "cinematograph-mania."[60] Likewise, Mexico City periodicals revealed a cultural obsession with Asta Nielsen, the "eminent tragedian from Denmark,"[61] expanding the constellations local film cultures traced when consuming global stars.

Mexico's geographical and (fraught) cultural proximity to Hollywood further complicates the ways in which Mexicans imported entertainment. How so-called greaser films—racist American productions that capitalized on vilifying Mexicans—elicited boycotts at local film theaters in Mexico while stirring Mexican American animosity in several American states bordering Mexico has been thoroughly examined.[62] It is no surprise, then, that *Cine-Mundial*, in its efforts to push American productions into Mexico and other Latin American nations, would ultimately condemn racist depictions of Mexicans in American films. An editorial from as early as 1917 reads:

> Some [American] production houses, luckily very few, still offer ... films whose plot represent the only case that can be argued in favor of censorship. We saw one the other day: Each pseudo-Mexican appearing on the screen was a bandit and, obviously, a "desperado." And the handsome protagonist, when he was not enamoring the daughter of the governor or rescuing fashionably dressed Yankee ladies in the Chihuahua desert, took leisure by fist-fighting with the entire army of a neighboring republic. The Latin public should not judge North American productions on the basis of such nonsense.[63]

The racist image of the mustachioed, sombrero-clad *bandido* circulated widely in American films of the period.[64] Editorials such as the one quoted—published in an American film trade journal devoted to bolstering American sales in Latin America—implicitly draw attention to the active role of Latin American distributors and exhibitors in directing their local markets and cultivating local tastes for international cinemas. Laura Serna questions academic readings of American cinema in terms of cultural imperialism, proposing, on the contrary, that Mexican audiences—on either side of the border—critically appropriated American films and film culture through a process of negotiated reading that generated "meanings beyond those imagined by either American filmmakers or film companies."[65] Part of this critical reading, Serna highlights, was an awareness of the racial hierarchies inherent in American silent cinema. In a similar vein, the polemic between the Di Domenico-run *Películas* and *Cine-Mundial* quoted previously exemplifies other forms of negotiated readings in Latin America, premised on ideological, commercial, and identity factors. These forms of negotiated reading, I add, went hand in hand with the development of discrete forms of melodramatic storytelling across the region.

NACIONALISMOS: MELODRAMA ADVANCES

France seems to be an inescapable reference in the early days of Latin American filmmaking. According to Latin American film historiography, another Frenchman, the Lumière cameraman Gabriel Veyre, seems to have sparked Latin American film production. Historians of different countries tend to build their histories upon Veyre's southbound travels, from Mexico, to Cuba, to Colombia (which then included what is now Panama), and finally to Venezuela. For Héctor García Mesa, Veyre not only exhibited Lumière films on his travels but "also produced the first Latin American moving images between July 1896 and October 1897."[66] Veyre is best known for his presence in Mexico City, where he shadowed the dictator Porfirio Díaz in his daily activities and his magnificent processions.[67] With the help of another Lumière agent, Fernand Bon Bernard, Veyre recorded the "first [films] shot in Mexico City" and exhibited the "first views of Díaz" outside the nation's capital, writes John Fullerton.[68] Likewise, courting Mexico's highest social circles, Veyre produced the first Mexican topicals—of socialites riding their elegant carriages on the French-inspired Paseo de la Reforma—thus recording "for the first time" the boulevard that epitomized Mexico City's modernity, stresses Aurelio de los Reyes.[69] With a zeal for historical accuracy, historian Emmanuel Vincenot records that on February 7, 1897, Veyre shot "the first film in the history of Cuban cinema."[70] Ana

López concurs.[71] In Colombia, a country divided by contested regional identities, film historians point out the "curiosity" of Veyre's "first films" being first shot in the Caribbean (a backwater region in some local film histories), only later arriving in the more industrious Andean regions and Bogotá, the capital city.[72] This recurring claim in nation-specific film histories—of Veyre's "first [demonym] film"—points to the transnational nature of moving images in Latin America during the silent period, despite the fact that the idea of "nation" structures most of these historians' writings.[73] In this sense, Latin American film historians, perhaps inadvertently, have always already questioned the nationalist frameworks deployed to study local film production.[74] Clinging to these frameworks, they have conceived local productions as global assemblages of distribution, exhibition, production, and reception.

Reframing the notion of national cinemas, in this section I look at how local distributors and exhibitors ventured into filmmaking and how they made their first films within such global assemblages. I argue that if their films had a nationalistic bent, it was not necessarily a result of nationalistic fervor. Instead, the first filmmakers engaged in negotiated readings—of local discourses and (trans)national markets—in service of their incipient industries. They aligned their films to dominant local discourses, as the Di Domenicos did by equating Italian films with conservative identity discourses in Colombia.[75] Such practices reveal how fluid national visual regimes could be at the time and, for the purposes of this study, how melodrama proved ideal to support such dynamism.

In the 1910s, Latin American distributors, exhibitors, and even film critics embarked upon filmmaking efforts. Most of these pioneers were immigrants, still tied in various ways to the countries from which they imported films to their host countries.[76] Further complicating the relations between foreign and local, Latin American pioneers negotiated their status as foreign immigrants and the status of their productions as local—the latter a means to legitimize the former.[77] If the distribution of moving images intersected with local exhibition practices and film cultures in globally complex, sense-producing ways, as discussed in the previous section, at first glance local film production seems to have taken shape, univocally, in the guise of nationalism. By looking closer at these films, however, this section foregrounds how homegrown pioneers strategically shaped their early productions by negotiating local nationalist discourses and appropriating global film styles. These developments yielded context-specific forms of melodramatic storytelling.

The first narrative films capitalized on the effervescence inherent to the Centenarios, the centennial celebrations of independence in several Latin American countries. In this context, tapping into nationalist themes allowed filmmakers to seamlessly introduce their work into the dominant visual regimes of the time, thereby effectively competing in emerging film markets. This strategy allowed melodrama to progressively take over local narrative cinema. To tap into local markets, film pioneers first turned to cinematic *tableaux* and later to the (originally French) genre of *film d'art*, discussed in the following section. Thus, they further strengthened their positions in local markets while elevating cinema's cultural status. This process was contemporaneous to the advances of narrative cinema elsewhere. Argentine silent film production peaked between 1914 and 1918, when the ravages of the Great War considerably reduced European film imports.[78] But porteño film production was well underway by the beginning of the war. Italian immigrant Mario Gallo shot a first series of one-act films around 1909 whose historical themes resonated with the independence celebrations of the Argentine Centenario. The general public initially received his first narrative films—centered on Argentine history and celebrating criollo culture—as "instruments of patriotic education."[79] At the same time, his films introduced melodrama into porteño narrative cinema.

La revolución de mayo (The May Revolution; dir. Mario Gallo, 1909), for instance, now considered the first Argentine fiction film, lacked a self-contained narration and yet told the story of the birth of a nation. The film relied heavily on contemporary nationalist narratives and discourses appearing across different media—through monuments, the press, and the many lectures delivered by the porteño intelligentsia. Drawing upon the multiple exchanges taking place around the Centenario, *La revolución* illustrates different episodes of the 1810 May Revolution that sparked Argentina's struggle for independence, such as the people united in front of the Cabildo (the town hall) and the revolutionaries Domingo French and Antonio Luis Beruti handing out ribbons. *La revolución* presents these and other episodes in *tableaux vivants*, didactically exhibiting the historical episodes while foregoing concern for realism in their compositions: buildings and interiors in scenery flats are considerably smaller than the actors, the discrepancies in scale providing actors with narrative prominence.

In the apotheosis, General José San Martín, wrapped in the Argentine flag and in full dress uniform, hovers above the Cabildo, as the crowd below fervently points and waves at the Libertador. With this composition, *La revolución* re-presented the foundational moment and elevated, literally, General San Martín to the figure of *prócer* (founding father). Importantly, by means of tableaux the film taps into the conventions of melodrama. To borrow from Peter Brooks, by employing tableaux the film harnesses "the plastic figurability of emotion."[80] As in stage melodrama, the apotheosis comprises an impressive visual summary of the affective situation—in this case, the triumph of independence at the hands of brave revolutionaries. Relying on extra-diegetic narrative and historical reenactments, *La revolución de mayo* inaugurated the harnessing of emotion through moving images in Buenos Aires; through affect, it brought the public closer to a nationalistic project.[81]

The Italian immigrants Francesco and Vincenzo Di Domenico produced the first fiction films in Bogotá around 1915. An advertisement from their company shows the brothers embarked early on the production of fiction films and actualities.[82] In November of that same year, the Di Domenicos exhibited *El drama del 15 de octubre* (The October 15th Drama), of which until very recently only one frame was known.[83] The film reconstructs the assassination of General Rafael Uribe Uribe, a prominent military and political leader.[84] Surviving footage mostly consists of actuality-like shots of crowds in downtown Bogotá and of Uribe Uribe's funeral at the Central Cemetery. Tapping into the particulars of the crime and its emotional effects, as we shall see, *El drama* paved the way for melodrama's entry into local film production.

Film historians concur that the film produced great moral commotion among the national public. The national press at the time condemned *El drama* and its producers, particularly because the Di Domenicos hired the real assassins to reconstruct the crime. In a provoking response, many periodicals engaged in a sabotage campaign to deter their readers from going to theaters and watching the film.[85] Even the governmental authorities of Cundinamarca (at the time Bogotá was under its jurisdiction) banned the film from local theaters.[86] Scholars have analyzed this phenomenon as a proof of active spectatorship—namely, of a spectator who candidly demanded positive representations of national identities and could not digest critiques of national figures in moving images.[87] Archival documents further problematize such claims; spectators of the time critically responded to the film through debate in the public arena. An article in the liberal newspaper *Mundo al día* celebrated the film, maintaining that this "documentary film" [*película documentaria*] was "a complete box-office success all over the country."[88] Despite the film's "imperfect and primitive" photography, the article nevertheless acknowledges that *El drama* "helped to transmit around the country the pain that Bogotá felt with the October crime."

This second perspective further illuminates the film's reception and melodrama's local uses. Conservative Party newspapers condemned the film.[89] Its loyal partisans mustered the sabotage campaign to impose their ideology through moralistic arguments in an attempt to shape local film culture. This is no surprise. After all, *El drama* was a panegyric to Uribe Uribe, a leader of the political opposition, the Liberal Party. It is also worth speculating about whether the disruptive efforts had the contrary effect, stimulating the public's curiosity. Most important, however, and as the article previously quoted suggests, if the film served as a medium for the transmission of pain—if it brokered the "distribution of the visibility of suffering"—*El drama* should be considered the first local attempt at storytelling premised on pathos.[90] As such, *El drama* constitutes Colombian film's proto-melodrama. Located on the "weak ontological frontier" proper to early cinema[91]—between crime reenactment, documentary, and drama and between registering current events and (melodramatically) narrativizing those events—*El drama* dispensed with distinctions between fact and fiction in favor of pathos.[92] In the long term, this subtle shift in visual regimes would shape later productions. Blurring the lines between fact and fiction in the service of pathos was stretched to new limits in Colombia's dearest narrative, *María*, which I discuss in the following section. The polemic surrounding *El drama del 15 de octubre* reveals that nationalist visual regimes were not only quite contested at the time but also quite fluid.

Such mercurial variability is being revised in current film histories and complicates current understandings of melodrama and its relation to modernity. If the reception of *El drama* reveals political instability, a Mexican film shows the persistence of the "traditional Sacred" in Latin American film cultures, an important element in need of revision.[93] The Mexican film *Tepeyac: Adaptación cinematográfica de una tradición mexicana* (*Tepeyac: Cinematographic Adaptation of a Mexican Tradition*, 1917) best portrays the protean nature of nationalist discourses permeating Latin American early filmmaking. Directed by Carlos E. Gonzáles, José Manuel Ramos, and Fernando Sáyago, *Tepeyac* combines Mexican history with religious and nationalist fervor, presenting religious tradition as a refuge from modern uncertainties in an increasingly transnational world.[94] Revolving around the legend of the Virgin of Guadalupe and her miraculous appearance before Juan Diego, the film combines multiple identity discourses, ranging from the nation's indigenous origins and its Catholic substratum, to clashes between tradition and modernity, to Mexico's place in a world engulfed by the Great War.

The plot is simple enough to allow for complex narrative structure. The film begins with state official Carlos Fernández (Roberto Arroyo Carrillo) embarking on a trip to France "with a delicate task," as expository titles read, while his fiancée, Guadalupe Flores (Pilar Cota), waits for his return in Mexico City. She reads in newspapers that a German U-boat has sunk the French ship in which Carlos was traveling. Fearing he is dead and yet desperately awaiting her lover's return, Guadalupe finds solace in reading about the apparition of the Virgin of Guadalupe. Her absorption introduces a framed narrative about Mexico's colonial past and locates modern Mexico's origins on the hill of Tepeyac, where it is said the Virgin appeared before Juan Diego in 1531.

From the very beginning, *Tepeyac* reproduces national discourses at odds with a secular understanding of the modern state. As mentioned, in the film nationalism is imbued with religious fervor. Drawing on the authority of the Nahua intellectual Ignacio Manuel Altamirano, a prominent journalist and political figure in late nineteenth-century Mexico, the film depicts the Lady of Guadalupe as the Mexican national symbol par excellence. Quoting Altamirano in the opening expository titles, the film maintains: "The day that the Virgin of Tepeyac is no longer worshiped on this land, certainly Mexican nationality and even the memory of contemporary Mexicans will have disappeared." A second title further explains that different sectors of Mexican society, regardless of their religious inclinations, consider the Virgin of Guadalupe "an essentially Mexican SYMBOL": Catholics "because of their religion," "liberals . . . because of the 1810 flag,"[95] and "Indians" because she is "their sole deity."

Tepeyac not only reproduces Altamirano's discourse in moving images but also closely aligns with dominant visual regimes of national cohesion in postrevolutionary Mexico. During the period, periodicals followed the massive yearly pilgrimages to the Basilica of Our Lady of Guadalupe in Tepeyac. Not surprisingly, they echo almost verbatim the words quoted in the film, linking nationalism with religious zeal: "Every year, with exalted and more intense piety, our country venerates its dear and loving Mother. . . . She is a symbol in the heart of every Mexican Christian and her image accompanied our Liberators in the greatest battles of Independence. She lives in the simple heart of our Indians, the only loving idea that comforts them. Their piety and belief is such, that they unite the idea of the Fatherland [*Patria*] with their true love for the Virgin of Guadalupe."⁹⁶ Referring to the "Mother of the Mexicans,"⁹⁷ a phrase ubiquitous in multiple media and Mexicans' everyday life, the film *Tepeyac* elevates the cinematic medium by appealing to the dominant visual regime of Mexico in the late 1910s: nationalism. But in the case of Mexico, nationalism was merged with religious practice.

Like *La revolución de mayo* and *El drama del 15 de octubre*, *Tepeyac* pioneered cinematic narrative and appropriated nationalist discourses in melodramatic key, framing Mexico's foundational narrative in a contemporary story of star-crossed lovers (Guadalupe and Carlos) that harkens to Mexico's colonial past. Despite recent historiographical developments that recognize how the religious is mobilized to support national projects in this film, concurrent approaches are dismissive of *Tepeyac*, considering it part of a group of "religious films" and therefore of no "great consequence in terms of the evolution of cinematic form in Latin America."⁹⁸ As such, they disparage the film as "a sort of primitive scene of Mexican cinema,"⁹⁹ particularly because "without contradiction [it juxtaposes] the knickknacks of modernity with the perpetuation of tradition."¹⁰⁰ These contentions about this particular film point to broader theoretical issues in Latin American film historiography. Such observations spring from an examination of modernity as a purportedly univocal experience premised on rupture and therefore unfulfilled in certain Latin American nations and problematically reflected in local film productions.¹⁰¹ As this book argues, following a "multiple modernities" perspective,¹⁰² different social and historical conditions yielded different experiences of modernity, including the strengthened bonds between the Catholic Church, religious practice, and the state, the very pillars of *Tepeyac*'s twentieth-century nationalism. Thus, *Tepeyac* epitomizes another form of negotiation proper to Mexican modernity, one that anticlerical revolutionary leaders were willing to engage in the face of a predominantly Catholic population¹⁰³ and one for which the "traditional Sacred" coexisted with an emerging, secularizing nation-state.¹⁰⁴ This is not to say *Tepeyac* was particularly inclusive. As Mónica García-Blizzard contends, the film reproduces "raced asymmetrical power relations ... shaped by colonialism" that have been "reconfigured" in this representation of modern Mexico.¹⁰⁵ But it is to say that *Tepeyac*—through melodrama—presents, and makes sense of, a discrete experience of modernity, among other experiences of modernity. The film appropriates melodramatic conventions in service of nationalism in a transnational context, conjoining Mexico's colonial past—Juan

Diego's quest for the Virgin's recognition—and Mexico's modern present: Mexico's recognition on the World War I world stage (suggested through Carlos's international assignment and uncertain fate as he travels across the Atlantic).[106]

Tepeyac—as well as earlier films such as *El drama del 15 de octubre* and *La revolución de mayo*—evinces how the development of narrative cinema in Latin America corresponds to the remediation of melodrama in the cinematic medium. Latin American pioneers first developed the form by tapping into the larger themes of nationalism and identity discourse. Like the Frenchman Gabriel Veyre, most of these pioneers were European immigrants, but unlike Veyre, they established themselves in their host countries. In discrete attempts to expand their business into film production, they carefully balanced the affective powers of nationalism with commercial interests, which does not necessarily mean that their cinematic endeavors were motivated by nation-building imperatives. Through negotiated readings and appropriations, they built niches for their productions within established transnational distribution circuits, in local urban settings. The elaboration of melodramatic storytelling in cinematic form further supports a more nuanced reading, questioning the national framework, as local pioneers looked at the (transnational) Latin American literary canon to further elevate the cultural status of their productions.

FILM D'ART: MELODRAMA TAKES OVER

So far, I have traced how before and during the Great War the transnational circulation of moving images in Latin America consisted of negotiated readings and critical appropriations in the spheres of film distribution, exhibition, and production across different urban centers. In the first two spheres, foreign and local distributors vied to dominate Latin American markets with American and European films (mostly French and Italian, but press materials also register Danish, German, and Russian productions). In the sphere of production, film pioneers—many of them immigrants—also engaged in negotiated readings of sociocultural contexts and film styles. By strategically appropriating local nation-building discourses while combining them with melodramatic conventions, they secured positions for their productions in local film circuits. In seeking a niche in such contested markets, local film producers first tapped into nationalist visual regimes that resonated with the Centennial celebrations fitting to each Latin American nation. However, appealing to nationalism—itself a contested discourse at the time—did not necessarily warrant the cultural respectability of narrative cinema. In order to culturally elevate narrative film for local audiences, local filmmakers resorted to appropriating and repurposing Latin America's most cherished cultural patrimony, the nineteenth-century novel, particularly the works of literary founding fathers (and mothers), the *letrados*, which most academics have studied under the rubric "foundational fictions." The appeal of these novels, most of which were initially published as *folletines*, was premised on their transnational resonance, not their "amalgamating" powers.[107] As early as the mid-nineteenth century, Domingo Faustino Sarmiento recognized that the emerging literature of the continent was "American, rather than national; in every part of our civilization it is more or less one [literature]: the language, the manners, the ideas, and even the historical memories, have not been traced with precise limits."[108] With a distinctive form of remediation—by appropriating foundational fictions into a distinct form of *foundational film d'art*—film pioneers consolidated the dominance of melodrama in the region.[109]

Before discussing this process, however, highlighting the moral and cultural ambivalence narrative cinema first elicited in Latin America is in order. In the 1910s, local publics were weary of imported narrative cinema, press materials suggest. For instance, as film historian Rielle Navitski has thoroughly studied, crime serials produced "ambiguous reality effects" across the region. She particularly stresses the ways in which the press claimed that the cinema, in a twisted logic, provoked increasingly elaborate—and therefore more and more modern—forms of crime in large urban centers, such as Mexico City with its grey automobile gang.[110] "Decisive," a journalist labeled the sway of cinema on the "knaves of Mexico [City]," in an article whose title encapsulates the new source of anxiety: "The Influence of the Cinematograph in the Modern Ways of Dispossessing Fellow Men from What Legitimately Belongs to Them."[111] Similarly, the Catholic press in Buenos Aires condemned cinema's threat to Catholic morals as it purportedly imported foreign forms of vice.[112] As early as 1915, the Catholic newspaper *La Cruzada Católica* of Bogotá condemned the serial *Fantômas* (dir. Louis Feuillade, 1913) on the grounds that it "teaches young men how to steal" and "does not evoke good emotions."[113]

In response to a pervasive angst—and as film historians have amply documented—Latin American filmmakers resorted to film d'art in order to mitigate the qualms of local audiences while elevating cinema's cultural status.[114] In France between 1908 and 1911, film d'art accrued cultural capital by adapting prestigious literary works and bringing prominent actors of La Comédie-Française onto the screen.[115] In a similar vein, Latin American filmmakers turned to (transnationally) renowned nineteenth-century Latin American novels and hired known stage actors to culturally elevate their first feature-length films.[116] The porteño distribution and exhibition tycoon Max Glücksman produced *Amalia* (1914), an adaptation of José Mármol's eponymous romantic novel (1844). Not only did the film promote cinema's cultural status by adapting Mármol's narrative (which at the time was considered one of "Argentina's guiding fictions"[117]), but Glücksman cast the propertied elite of Buenos Aires to perform—a patrician group "by bonds of blood *linked* to the important characters of the historical novel," asserted a review published in Montevideo.[118] *Amalia* premiered in the prestigious Teatro Colón, the "temple" of the porteño bourgeoisie.[119] Shot with—and shown to—the highest social circles, *Amalia* was a product by and for the crème de la crème of the city, with ripple effects across the River Plate. In a similar yet perhaps more critical way, Mexican journalist Luis G. Peredo adapted Federico Gamboa's popular novel *Santa* (1903) in 1918. The novel—more aligned with naturalism than with social romanticism—tells the tale of a disgraced country girl who migrates to Mexico City, where she becomes the most coveted courtesan. Despite the opportunities to quit prostitution her affluent suitors offer, Santa dies poor and alone of uterine cancer. Literary scholars consider the novel an allegory of turn-of-the-century Mexico that decries the moral corruption during Porfirio Díaz's rule and consequently demands the (moral) rebirth of Mexico through society's breakdown.[120] *Santa*'s relevance for Mexican culture and melodrama has been amply discussed[121] and is evident in its four adaptations for the screen during and after our period of study.[122]

The cross-media narrative that best epitomizes cinema's cultural elevation through nineteenth-century fiction is Jorge Isaacs's *María* (1867), the story of star-crossed lovers set in the sugarcane plantations of the Cauca Valley, Colombia. This Latin American paragon of foundational fiction played a key role in the development of local filmmaking beyond Colombian borders. The Mexican film critic Rafael Bermúdez Zataraín produced the first adaptation. Starting in the silent period, Jorge Isaacs's novel has been cinematized multiple times in Colombia and other Latin American nations[123]—not surprisingly, given that *María* is "the most widely read nineteenth-century Spanish American novel and the one about which most has been written," as Antonio Benítez-Rojo contends.[124] *María*'s cultural relevance—before, during, and beyond the silent period—complicates Latin American (film) historiography's national frameworks.[125] Across national borders and historical periods, *María* has served as a cultural touchstone for many Latin American readers and spectators for over two centuries.

Particularly in Colombia, where the novel was first published, it maintains an enduring presence in everyday life. On the 50,000 peso banknote, *María*-inspired imagery and excerpts from the novel effectively turn melodrama into the everyday currency of Colombians. A unique example of the "cash nexus"—a nineteenth-century literary trope in which "representation is up for grabs"[126]—the banknote demonstrates melodrama's ubiquitous presence and versatility to monopolize the collective imagination. For comparison's sake, a theoretical American equivalent would be a $100 bill on which little Eva and Uncle Tom, along with Harriet Beecher Stowe, appear on one side, while a rendering of the song "My Old Kentucky Home" appears on the other. Instead of founding fathers, the Colombian banknote makes visible—and circulates—*María*'s nostalgia for the patriarchal hacienda (and the plantation, its correlative space) as the origin of the nation. Thus, in the bill, just as in film adaptations and adaptions to other media, the iteration of *María* epitomizes the "sense of duration" media scholar Jesús Martín-Barbero identifies as distinctive of melodrama. For Martín-Barbero, iteration and repetition constitute melodrama's means to "blend" itself "with [everyday] life."[127] With its ubiquitous presence, *María* does precisely that.

To return to the silent period, *María*—the cross-media narrative, that is—circulated within Colombia and well beyond its borders. In September 1922, the Blanca Podestá Company (a theater troupe affiliated with the Podestá family, the founders of Argentine and Uruguayan theater) adapted the novel to the porteño stage.[128] Two years later, and across the Atlantic, an opera version premiered in Barcelona, written by the Spanish composer Guillermo Serra Roxlo.[129] Interestingly, the first film adaptation of *María* was not made in Colombia but in Mexico, further attesting to the narrative's transnational appeal. The 1918 version directed by Rafael Bermúdez Zataraín, the contributor to *Cine-Mundial*, has unfortunately been lost. But again, its very production casts doubt on the relevance of the "national" as the defining framework through which to study Latin American silent film and silent film cultures (and further questions the national specificity of "foundational fictions," which since their inception have been circulating across the region without being limited to specific countries). By tapping into the *María* narrative, Bermúdez Zataraín's film undermines the arbitrary boundaries scholars have tried to impose on identity discourses and visual regimes of early twentieth-century Latin America. It demonstrates how melodramatic narratives circulated through different discourses and media regardless of national borders.

In Bogotá, remediating *María* to film had been in the mind of the Di Domenico brothers for some time. They saw the novel as a way of energizing local film production while elevating cinema's cultural status. It was their means of harnessing the European "success" of film d'art, as Francesco Di Domenico declared.[130] In an interview, Di Domenico describes his pioneering filmmaking project and seems to ignore the Mexican version, which had premiered the previous year. Given the interconnections between Latin American markets—and the polemic Bermúdez Zataraín engaged in with *Películas* through *Cine-Mundial* (as discussed previously)—it is likely that the Di Domenicos were aware of Bermúdez Zataraín's cinematic achievement. In fact, an article in *Películas* mentions the Mexican film. It does not mention its formal qualities, but rather stresses the narrative's cultural relevance at a transnational level: "*María*'s [cinematic] form makes evident, once again, the old and always growing sympathy that everywhere, not only in Colombia, the glory of Isaacs [i.e., the novel] awakens."[131] Adapting *María* to film was particularly important in Colombia, a society that, at the time of its Centennial celebration, zealously clung to its colonial social structures while incorporating the technological advances ushered in by modernization.[132] Despite their initial intent, the Di Domenicos were not the ones to capitalize on *María*'s adaptation. Another immigrant, the Spanish-born Máximo de Calvo—who at the time was shooting newsreels for Fox News in Panama—brought the novel to the screen in 1922.

Of de Calvo's *María*, only twenty-five seconds' worth of footage remains.[133] Comprised of long shots and extreme long shots of two characters riding into or across scenic landscapes, extant footage offers very little information on Colombia's first feature-length film. The film likely contained a considerable amount of landscape and scenic sequences, given the relevance of landscape in the novel.[134] The scant footage has led to fraught teleological readings that, echoing criticism of *Tepeyac*, deem *María* an example of "backward state [cinema] with regards to form and content."[135] Archival press materials do not offer much insight to challenge this assumption. For the most part, columns published around the time of the film's premiere refrain from describing its formal qualities. Most praise the film as *the* endeavor to bring Isaacs's novel to the screen, revitalizing the novel's nostalgic eulogy to the plantation and its traditional ways.[136] However, an album in the archives of the Fundación Patrimonio Fílmico Colombiano (the Colombian Film Heritage Foundation), until now unacknowledged in scholarship on the film, sheds light on the cinematic complexity and reception of this lost film. Printed around 1930, it consists of thirty production stills—mostly interior shots—tracking the book's narrative. With quotations from the novel serving as captions, the album suggests that the film invested in closely reproducing Isaacs's work in a new medium.[137]

Like the film (according to some reviews), the album assumes a reader proficient in the *María* narrative.[138] On the facing page of each still, brief titles allude to climactic moments of the narrative but never refer to them explicitly, thereby requiring the reader to actively link title, production still, and narrative episode. Some titles are quite straightforward. "The first goodbye," for instance, refers to the protagonist's initial departure at the beginning of the novel. Others are rather obscure. "The tempest takes down the oak tree," introduces a full shot of a group surrounding an old man in his sickbed (see figure 4). The accompanying quotation from the novel does not clarify who the characters are, only referring to the "doctor" by title.[139] The example can only make sense for a reader/spectator familiar with the novel, one who can consequently recognize in the image the bedridden patriarch, his children, and the family doctor. Reference to the "oak tree," much like the novel's patriarchal world, metaphorically gives meaning to the entire composition by articulating the characters around the axial fatherly figure. With the father at the center of the composition—in an exceptional moment of weakness—text, image, and reading proficiency render legible the entire group, united by the centripetal pull of the patriarch. With the sickbed positioned at an unusually steep angle to maximize the father's exposure, the composition suggests that the film privileged tableau-like, fixed camera shooting. However, other stills depart from the frontal shot, casting doubt on any teleological claim of primitivism in the film's style.[140]

As an iteration of *María*, the "album" restates Isaacs's narrative as *the* national melodrama. But it does so while questioning the national limits of the narrative's influence, as it highlights *María*'s relevance in a transnational context. With an epigraph, the album compares Jorge Isaacs to Simon Bolívar, the founding father of Colombia, Venezuela, and Ecuador.[141] Likewise, it appeals to nationalism through melodrama

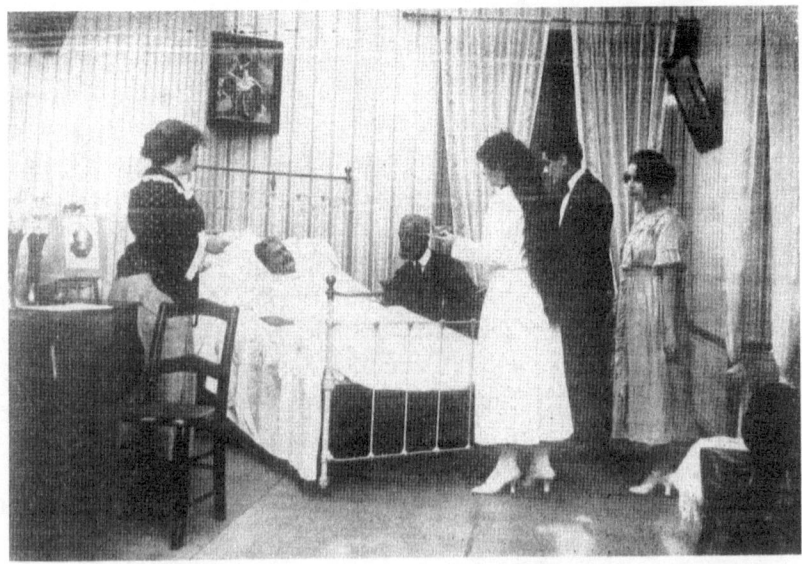

FIGURE 4. "The tempest takes down the oak tree." Production still with quotation from Jorge Isaacs's novel, *María* album (ca. 1930). Courtesy of FPFC.

by blurring the lines between historical fact and melodramatic fiction, echoing the ways in which *El drama del 15 de octubre* first introduced melodrama to local film production. The first still offers an establishing shot of the actual hacienda El Paraíso, near the city of Cali, which was owned by the Isaacs family between 1854 and 1858. Combining image and text, this initial still suggests that María's story actually took place. Unlike the rest of the album, this caption does not consist of a quotation from the novel. Instead, a line with no explicit source reads, "In this place a hundred years ago . . . ," thus introducing a degree of ontological uncertainty to the entire text. In the still, the photographed facade sets up an actual origin, in space and time, for this foundational melodrama. This establishing shot fashions an "existential bond" between the photochemical image, melodramatic narrative, and precinematic event[142]—in this case, on-location shooting at the hacienda El Paraíso, which by the early 1920s was already a profoundly nostalgic nationalist symbol, as expressed in the press.[143]

The album—which a letter suggests was a gift from de Calvo to film historian Hernando Salcedo Silva in 1930[144]—evinces the elevated cultural capital *María* harnessed during and after its release. Nevertheless, rather than elucidating the film's cultural status, a heated debate among Colombian film scholars obscures an analysis of the reception of the film. Based on accounts of de Calvo's family and acquaintances in Luis Ospina's documentary *En busca de María* (In Search of María, 1985),[145] film scholars have deemed *María* either a cinematic failure or an example of cinematic primitivism, as noted. These accounts, which question the film's historical relevance for its very producers and de Calvo's heirs, have led Colombian film historians to consider *María* a historically important film only "under patriotic pressure," as Hernando Salcedo Silva stated in an interview with Ospina for the documentary. The film, however, may have been cinematically relevant and commercially successful. Unlike any other local production, an extraordinary number of copies of the film were made—twelve in total—to be distributed at home and abroad.[146] There are no national or foreign sales records to confirm whether the film had a boom or bust. But as film historian Diego Rojas astutely suggested on one of my trips to Bogotá, de Calvo's mansion in Cali—located in the Granada neighborhood, one of the most affluent neighborhoods in the city in the first half of the twentieth-century—attests to the film's financial success. Since he had invested all of his capital in the film, de Calvo's mansion proves that the revenue he received must have been considerable. That he continued making films, newsreels, and the first narrative sound films in Colombia also suggests the cinematic importance of *María* in his career. De Calvo not only contributed to early filmmaking in Colombia but also pioneered local film production for decades to come.

Latin American film d'art did not consist merely of adapting literary classics or filming plays in order to advance cinema's status, as in France, but also of a very particular form of remediation, in which transnationally renowned nineteenth-century fictions (re)gained prominence among a broader readership/spectatorship while at the same time elevating the cultural capital of locally produced films. The fact that film pioneers chose to adapt foundational fictions evinces particular forms of negotiated readings and appropriations—readings and appropriations quite distant from the "mimetic attitude" vis-à-vis French film d'art some film histories have maintained.[147] The foundational film d'art evinces an expanded melodramatic corpus circulating around the region and beyond national borders. Over the novels of Latin American writers José Mármol, Federico Gamboa, and Jorge Isaacs discussed in this chapter, local pioneers tapped into the works of nineteenth-century letrados from multiple Latin American countries—even from the Iberian Peninsula. Film pioneers adapted works from the Brazilian José de

Alencar—*O Guaraní* (The Guarani; dir. Vittorio Capellaro, 1916 and 1926), *Iracema* (dir. Capellaro, 1917)—the Mexican Amado Nervo—*Amnesia* (dir. Ernesto Vollrath, 1921)—and the Colombian José María Vargas Vila—*Aura o las violetas* (Aura or the Violets; dir. Pedro Moreno Garzón and Vicente Di Domenico, 1924). They also drew on the works of nineteenth-century peninsular authors. In Havana, Enrique Díaz Quesada adapted Joaquín Dicenta's *Juan José* (1910). In Buenos Aires, Mario Gallo followed suit with Ángela Guimerá's *Tierra baja* (Lowland, 1912). In Brazil, Camilo Castelo Branco's novel *Amor de perdição* (Doomed Love) yielded two adaptations, a first attempt in Rio Grande do Sul directed by Francisco Santos (1913) and a second version in Rio de Janeiro by José Vianna (1917). In Mexico City, the Spanish-born Manuel Noriega adapted his fellow countryman Carlos Arniches's *El pobre Valbuena* (Poor Valbuena, 1916).[148]

The multiple iterations of some of these productions visibilize the "sense of duration" melodrama already possessed in print culture throughout the region, now transposed into cinematic form. Among these films *María* warrants particular attention, for it embodies the emergent transnational networks shaping Latin American film melodrama. As Paulo Antonio Paranaguá asserts, *María* "turns out to be emblematic because of the confluence of efforts [in its production:] between a Franciscan priest, Antonio José Posada, producer of the film; a Spanish cameraman settled in the Cauca Valley; and another peninsular, the actor Alfredo del Diestro, then on tour in the region along with his wife Emma Roldán (both of whom will become known figures of Mexican cinema)."[149] In the four key components of film circuits—production, distribution, exhibition, and reception—*María* epitomizes the transnational character of filmic melodrama across Latin America.

CONCLUSION

Until a copy of de Calvo's *María* is discovered—along with press materials from other countries—the full scope of the film's transnational relevance will remain obscure. If several copies did circulate in other countries, one may still survive elsewhere. The success of the film must have been considerable, if periodicals in cities as distant as Buenos Aires are any indication of the film's regional appeal. The newspaper *Última Hora* celebrated the adaptation of Isaacs's work, "one of the most popular romantic novels," and anticipated that the film would reach porteño theaters in the following "winter season."[150] For the time being, the *María* narrative, cinematically repurposed in Mexico City and in Cali, sheds light on other cinematic circuits that demand further attention from film scholars—the "South-to-South exchanges" through which local exhibitors and distributors circulated Latin American films within Latin America.[151] Records show that other Latin American films made their way across the Americas, Eduardo Martínez de la Pera and Ernesto Gunche's *Nobleza Gaucha* (Gaucho Nobility, 1915) being a case in point. Without lingering on the film's reception, in a brief note the Di Domenicos' *Películas* deemed the porteño film a "success" in local theaters.[152] The relevance of *Nobleza Gaucha* in Argentine film history has been amply discussed; it was reportedly seen by fifty thousand spectators in 1915 in Buenos Aires alone and was continually exhibited into the late 1910s.[153] Still, its relevance outside of Argentina remains understudied.[154] In a similar vein, Latin American endeavors geared toward sales in the United States and Europe also demand further scrutiny. Missing to date, *México ante los ojos del mundo* (Mexico Before the Eyes of the World, ca. 1925), directed by the Chilean journalist Miguel Chejade B., comprises a travelogue that Chejade intended for exhibition across the Americas and Europe, with the hopes of showing "everything valuable and beautiful that *our* country envelops."[155] Considering Mexico his own country, the Chilean director incorporated shots of Mexico's archaeology, architecture, industry, and "unexplored forests," among other "valuables." Even if it belongs to a different genre, Chejade's visual imperative was shaped by uneven representational practices in melodramatic films circulating transnationally. He was particularly engaged in contesting Hollywood "denigrating films"—that is, narrative greaser films—that misrepresented Mexicans; he aimed at "counteracting the discrediting campaign that some [American] production companies have embarked in to present us abroad as an uncultured people."[156]

These examples complicate the ways in which Latin American distributors imported—and later produced—entertainment before and during the Great War. Far from passively enduring processes of cultural imperialism and oppressive market forces, Latin American exhibitors, distributors, and producers negotiated American and European fare to partake in the burgeoning Latin American market. With commercial, ideological, and aesthetic motives, they favored different cinematic styles—American and European—to shape local cinematic tastes and cater to local audiences. They deployed these preferences through film programs and local film trade journals. In the meantime, and despite the economic and technological disadvantages of competing against established foreign film industries, many local distributors ventured into filmmaking themselves. To open a niche in local markets, they resorted first to nationalist fervor and later to adapting the Latin American melodramatic literary canon. In the process, these filmic narratives ushered in melodrama's advance in the 1910s and the eventual takeover of narrative film in the 1920s, thereby turning melodrama into the dominant visual regime for recording and making sense of Latin America's multiple modernities. Centered on urban enclaves and not limited by national borders, the melodramatic cultures and correlative modernities of Latin America varied from region to region, and even from city to city, as the following chapters explore.

CHAPTER 2

Buenos Aires Shadows

Urban Space, Fallen Women, and Destitute Men

Just as you turned fourteen you gave yourself to carousing,
[to] the delights of *gotán* [tango].
—Flor de Fango

In 1922, L. Torres and J. Bernat composed a script that assembled a myriad of Buenos Aires "types": abandoned girls, physicians, underworld ruffians, and—curiously enough—one Mary Pickford, a housemaid with dreams of becoming a movie star. Their script won the Buenos Aires Film screenwriting contest, a competition devised to bolster sales of local films in local theaters.[1] Publicized in the popular newspaper *Crítica*, the studio's campaign proved to be a success. In fact, this triumph was the result of a dedicated and increasingly complex investment in fostering interest in local film production among the ever-growing spectatorship (and investors as well). This focus on local production invited mass participation and presented local filmmaking as an economically viable enterprise. Appealing to cinema lovers across the social spectrum, for years *Crítica* had fostered active participation with its contests. "Can there be a greater proof of cinematic calling? We don't think so," *Crítica* rhetorically inquired.[2] Starting in 1919, *Crítica* began fostering spectators' personal investment in local film production with annual "Grand Cinematographic Contest[s]." The contests culminated in the fourth and fifth iterations: access to "the *Crítica* Free Academy" of acting and shooting the winning film script, respectively.[3] The fifth contest's resulting film, *Sombras de Buenos Aires* (Buenos Aires Shadows; dir. Julio Irigoyen, 1923), gathered more than two thousand spectators at its private pre-premiere. The press attributed the film's success to Buenos Aires Film's production strategy and to the "felicitous selection of episodes and situations" the film showed.[4] *Sombras* participated in what press accounts recognized as a "trend in [local] cinematographic production." In the 1920s, urban themes—and urban outcasts—began to populate local productions.[5] Films about Buenos Aires presented adaptations of tango songs, *sainete* (a popular genre of one-act plays), and original scripts inspired by the city's underworld. Press accounts singled out these films among local productions, describing them as "always successful" in the box office, for they purportedly resonated with the very fibers of being of local spectators, particularly those in marginal neighborhoods.[6]

Through the press and an expanded degree of public participation, Buenos Aires subsumed Argentine silent cinema during the 1920s. Unlike gaucho films of the 1910s—which participated in the nation-building projects that made both gaucho and pampas the repositories of national identity[7]—films about Buenos Aires offered a cynical take on big city life. In an effort to pin down their spatial and emotional tenor, film trade journals coined many trade names for the growing number of urban-set films, the precursors of early sound tango films.[8] *Drama de arrabal* and *folletín de arrabal* explicitly pointed to the melodramatic substratum of these films.[9] Perhaps the term *cinedrama porteño* best captured the essence of these films, for it encompassed the broader urban space they explored.[10] Moreover, the label underlines an important aspect of the genre: it not only focused on life in the *arrabal* (the slums and marginal neighborhoods), but it also mapped the socioeconomic breadth of Buenos Aires while elucidating its urban fabric. *Porteño cinedrama* showcased big-city life, at once attractive and provocative, dangerous and forbidding. Trafficking in consumerist titillation, cinedrama drew from multiple narrative sources in popular culture, most notably tango, weekly novels, and sainete. The genre portrayed a bleak Buenos Aires of mass-scale immigration and accelerated urbanization, a city in which opulence was reserved for the few and poverty was ubiquitous, particularly in immigrant barrios. Thus, within the ideological flexibility melodrama facilitates with its maneuvers to reveal and conceal, porteño cinedrama made visible the ways in which economic—and gendered—disparities took on spatial dimensions in the city.[11]

Porteño cinedramas were mainly viewed as cautionary tales about the perils of social climbing. Mostly focused on barrio women who ventured into the world of the rich—the intoxicating atmosphere of cafés and cabarets—these films perpetuated the "fallen woman" trope

FIGURE 5. "Sinner." Cover of tango sheet music (1927). Courtesy of AGNM.

that dominated weekly novels, tango, and sainete. The popularity of the trope resounded across the continent, extending all the way to Mexico, particularly through tango (see figure 5). However, this chapter focuses on films produced at the epicenter, Buenos Aires, where a cross-media narrative, "imbued with a spirit of fatalistic resignation," dominated.[12]

The fallen woman narrative, centered on vertical mobility and arousal, directly appealed to the emergent masses. Porteño cinedrama registered urban space, foregrounding its many threats and thus generating an archive of a morally questionable present while offering tantalizing urban typologies, such as the demure seamstress turned *bataclana*, or cabaret dancer (see figure 6). Some porteño cinedrama filmmakers appealed to the emerging mass public through diverse circuits of exchange. Going to great lengths, some filmmakers even reached out to potential audiences in order to include them in the creative process—as was the case with the now-lost *Sombras de Buenos Aires*. Between admonition and provocation, porteño cinedrama also disseminated subversive messages through its play of light and shadow, revelation and concealment. As this chapter proposes, by blurring the boundaries between conservatism and subversion proper to the liminal spaces of Buenos Aires, porteño cinedrama delivered an implicit critique of gender and social inequality in film.

A synopsis of *La costurerita que dio aquel mal paso* (The Little Seamstress Who Stumbled; dir. José A. Ferreyra, 1926) epitomizes porteño cinedrama's narrative conventions, fully established by the mid-1920s, as film trade journals recognized: "It is a pretty production full of sentimentalism and barrio emotion [emoción arrabalera]. Ferreyra knows how to treat these themes. . . . The story is about a working girl who stumbles through the quagmires until she finds true love, which only looks upon the spiritual and immaculate side of her soul. The plot, as is well known, is inspired by the popular verses of [Evaristo] Carriego. The public loved this new film and applauded at the end. It will be a success in barrio cinemas."[13] Porteño cinedrama invested in an appeal to sentiment, status anxiety, and moral self-consciousness. Importantly, the synopsis also assumes a strong reading proficiency on the part of the spectator. Brevity in plot description and reference to Carriego's poetry point to the viewer's considerable knowledge of genre conventions. Further, reference to Carriego alludes to the narrative's conspicuous cross-media sources.[14] As the synopsis suggests, the proliferation of "fallen woman" stories catered to a mass cultural demand on diverse media and went hand in hand with the development of an acute understanding of the genre among spectators, readers, and tango listeners, while exploring the urban spaces of Buenos Aires.[15]

Argentina's early twentieth-century melodramatic mass culture—of which cinedrama was a part—disseminated an image of a "rigidly

FIGURE 6. Picture of a cabaret dancer on cover of *Fray Mocho* (Buenos Aires), 23 June 1925. Courtesy of BNA.

stratified Argentina,"[16] in stark contrast to the complex class structures shaping daily experience in porteño barrios. Even though mass culture represented a polarized city in periodicals, theater plays, and the cinema, historian Adrián Gorelik suggests that a "homogeneous heterogeneity" defined the city.[17] Indeed, Buenos Aires barrios were incredibly diverse. Comprising heterogeneous groups of residents from a variety of class backgrounds and representing many languages and nationalities, barrio communities forged neighborhood associations that gathered residents together to advance their collective interests. As a result, a strong sense of localism developed, and barrio identity took precedence over any sense of belonging associated with the metropolitan area as a whole. In Gorelik's view, the barrios shaped Buenos Aires into a "mosaic of spatial fragments" that displayed varying degrees of infrastructural development, ethnic diversity, and integration.

To popular culture historian Mathew Karush, this complex mosaic was nevertheless the subject of numerous formulaic descriptions of an ossified, stratified urban pattern that prevailed in mass culture.[18] Regarding silent cinema, however, I argue that porteño cinedramas presented urban space as a contested space. Paying particular attention to location, I trace the social landscapes and identitary strategies shaping the genre. More specifically, I argue that porteño cinedramas visually constructed sociocultural barriers in specific locations, through what I call *intimate distances*, a term that evokes a visual regime in which opposing social drives construct the films' urban spaces. Two particular forces are at play: an erotics of space, pulling emergent and established social actors together, and its correlative centripetal force, partitioning urban space in multiple ways. Both forces dialectically forge spatial, social, and emotional distances. Drawing from Adriana Bergero's analysis of cultural geographies in Buenos Aires, I use the notion of intimate distances to point to an unstable regime of sociocultural separation and proximity that shapes and is shaped by urban space.[19] As we shall see, following individuals through different urban locations, porteño cinedramas erected *and disrupted* sociocultural and gendered barriers in film. Catering to what Giuliana Bruno describes as "modernity's desire for site-seeing," porteño cinedramas included a wide array of urban locations, "turn[ing] sites into sights."[20] By way of example, I focus on three recurrent settings: tenement housing, department stores, and cabarets and garçonnières (bachelor apartments).

TENEMENT HOUSING: OVERCROWDING AND (MORAL) DISEASE

In the 1910s and 1920s, depictions of tenement housing circulated widely in porteño mass culture. Replete with newly arrived immigrants—anarchists and socialists, racial minorities, dockworkers, workingwomen, prostitutes, and pimps—tenement housing proliferated as the setting for narratives across multiple media. Two views predominated. Some stories emphasized dangerously porous boundaries between humble barrios, affluent neighborhoods, and the bustling city center. Other stories, epitomized by the films of José Agustín Ferreyra, depicted the *conventillo*[21] and the barrio more broadly as the surviving loci of working-class solidarity in urban space. In a Manichean world in which the haves (usually male) manipulate the have-nots (usually female), returning to the humble conventillo offered the sole respite in the hectic city. Stories of the first kind resonated with top-down anxieties regarding social mobility, while the second kind seemed to undermine this perspective by both provoking readerly and spectatorial sympathy for the downtrodden and reflecting a certain degree of social awareness.

The first narrative category exploited biopolitical discourses of the period. As early as the turn of the twentieth century, purportedly unsanitary tenement homes were depicted as menacing sources of endemic illness. In political discourse—particularly in the late 1910s and early 1920s—tenement homes were considered spaces of moral decay, eyesores in the urban landscape.[22] Building upon these discourses, some films proposed preventive distances. One case in point was *La mosca y sus peligros* (The Fly and Its Dangers; dir. Eduardo Martínez de la Pera and Ernesto Gunche 1920). The thirty-five-minute "scientific-divulgation" film, as described in the local press,[23] inextricably linked pathogenic bacteria and immigrant conventillos in Buenos Aires. The local scientific community praised the film for its "microcinematograpic" technical achievements and pedagogical imperative.[24] Nevertheless, the film fused scientific and xenophobic discourses and mapped them out in urban space—connecting shots of bacteria under the microscope with extreme close-ups of carrier flies and conjoining them with conventillos through editing.

De la Pera and Gunche tapped into pseudoscientific and cinematic languages to partition urban space in favor of the elites. It is no surprise that the directors known for *Nobleza Gaucha* (Gaucho Nobility, 1915), one of the most renowned films of the Argentine silent period, forwarded a visual regime premised on partitioning urban space. As members of the prestigious Argentine Photographic Society of Enthusiasts, the directors brought the society's agenda to the medium, visually extolling conservative, material progress.[25] In *Nobleza Gaucha*, the directors' aim is most clearly evidenced. In their first feature-length film, De la Pera and Gunche enlist the progress generated by criollos (nonimmigrant Argentines), fusing rural and urban aspects of Argentine identity to exalt and monumentalize national achievements.[26] In contrast, *La mosca* trained the microscope on a different but equally stratified take on the social fabric while banishing the immigrant Other to the city's margins. In a series of striking sequences harnessing microscopy technologies and an educational narrative of urban disease, *La mosca* establishes links between pathogenic bacteria and immigrant boardinghouses in Buenos Aires.[27]

In a similar vein, narrative films portraying quotidian life in the boardinghouse linked *moral* decadence to overcrowding, including de la Pera and Gunche's second feature-length film, *Hasta después de muerta* (Even after Death, 1916). The film centers on two medical students and boardinghouse residents who, while aligned with the dominant ideals of public health by their choice of career, have circumvented the social barriers demanded by "hygiene." Retreating entirely from the monumental outdoors of *Nobleza Gaucha*, surviving footage of the film mostly consists of interior scenes. The focus on confined, private spaces imbues the boardinghouse with a claustrophobic quality. Evoking medical and xenophobic discourses of public hygiene, the film highlights the dangers of overcrowding and, most important, pits institutional power against unethical medical practices and class solidarity against gender exploitation.

Intersecting medical discourse and everyday life in a boardinghouse, the film tackles two of the key themes in porteño cinedramas under discussion: gender exploitation and the desire for upward mobility. *Hasta después de muerta* revolves around Elvira (Silvia Parodi), a young woman who moves from a small town to Buenos Aires to work as a cashier. Her dreams of independence vanish, however, as she finds herself enmeshed in a web of competing interests that lead to her untimely death. Living in a "respectable" boardinghouse, an intertitle suggests, Elvira falls for the medical student Luis. Her regular visits to the room shared by Luis (Argentino Gómez) and his classmate (Florencio Parravacini) risk damaging her reputation. Shared cross-class notions of female honor keep sexual danger at bay until Luis's own desires for upward mobility lead to dire consequences: he becomes a regular at his professor's residence and starts courting the professor's daughter, while continuing to lead Elvira on solely to take advantage of her.

Hasta después de muerta describes overcrowding in terms of a dog-eat-dog world in which gullible female tenants are constantly at risk.[28] In fact, it is precisely Elvira's innocence that enables her "fall." Luis first pushes her to steal money from the store's safe, with which, unbeknownst to Elvira, he buys expensive gifts for the doctor's daughter. Eventually, Elvira loses her job when she is caught, and then becomes ill. Helpless, she asks Luis to treat her; he prescribes an "excessive amount of narcotic," intertitles explain. Only after Elvira dies giving birth to a fatherless child does the spectator understand why Luis prescribed the elevated dose: off-screen, he had sexually assaulted her while she was unconscious.[29]

Elvira's predicament epitomizes top-down anxieties surrounding the close proximity between men and women in boardinghouses. These close quarters gave rise to what a 1916 study on female labor termed "the most atrocious promiscuity imaginable."[30] The film alludes to aggressive sexual violation and licentiousness, glossing over pressing concerns about sexual abuse in tenement housing and ultimately exempting Luis from social censure. The film invests in female abjection to such a degree that at the end, Elvira donates her lifeless body for Luis's research. Even though her unconditional love temporarily drives Luis mad and ultimately reforms him, it minimizes the consequences of rape in boardinghouses—which in the film is ultimately pardoned "even after death," as the film's title suggests.

These examples point to the ways in which pedagogical films and certain porteño cinedramas passed moral judgment on tenement housing and its dwellers, particularly female dwellers. They depicted overcrowded residences as sites of danger and sexual violence, and as teeming with disease. As such, they visually and narratively partitioned urban space in ways that contained socioeconomically and culturally stigmatized ethnic groups in unsanitary housing.

However, in porteño cinedramas, the conventillo had a different function than boardinghouses, as we shall see in the following section. The conventillo figured the melodramatic "space of innocence," a real or imagined retreat where "virtue takes pleasure in itself."[31] Some cinedramas coded the conventillo as a place in which dreams of upward mobility for the disenfranchised could still manifest. The conventillo was a bastion of working-class identity that stood in opposition to the affluent sectors of the city's downtown. Particularly in the films of Agustín

Ferreyra, barrio shots (mostly focused on children at play) depicted the innocent life associated with the conventillo. In worlds divided between the barrio and downtown, the conflict at the heart of porteño cinedrama consisted of the impossibility of fully regaining the space of innocence once it is lost. This unresolvable problem leads to what scholars have highlighted as the genre's fatalistic outlook.[32] Even though surviving shots of the barrio repeatedly present children at play, the happiness on display is immediately undercut by depictions of human interactions in the adult world. Thus, in department store cinedramas, shots of children playing circle games foreshadow the circulation of human bodies as commercial goods.

THE DEPARTMENT STORE: WORKING WOMEN AND CONSUMER CULTURE

Films about barrio women working in department stores most clearly explored an erotics of urban space. Dividing the city between barrios and an exploitative city center, these films appropriated a feature that was "nearly omnipresent by the 1920s" in Buenos Aires's mass culture:[33] the sexually inflected trope of the "girl who stumbled." It was the tale of the young, innocent woman who leaves her simple life in the humble conventillo for the promises of upward mobility through work in the downtown, where inexorable ruin awaits her. Like the American serial-queen melodrama, popularized throughout Latin America during the 1910s,[34] porteño cinedramas of workingwomen reflected upon "the expansion of female mobility and circulation in the heterosocial public arena of urban modernity."[35] But unlike the serial queens who, modeled on the figure of the New Woman, displayed vigorous and assertive representations of womanhood (see figure 7), the fallen women of porteño cinedramas embodied new forms of gender subordination in urban space. Harnessing urban modernity's desire for "site-seeing," to recall Bruno's observation, dramas of workingwomen highlighted social issues, taking a critical perspective on new forms of circulation and generating pathos centered on female protagonists.

Before delving into these films, a brief contextualization is in order. The percentage of lower- and middle-class women in the workforce reached critical mass in Argentina by 1909, when the household all but ceased to be a self-sufficient sphere of production in an expanding urban consumer society. Workingwomen earned less than half the wages men received and consequently were suspected of supplementing

FIGURE 7. Serial-queen melodrama advertisement, *The Moving Picture World* (New York), 17 April 1920. Courtesy of MHDL.

their earnings through sexual favors.[36] The discussion of the "problem" of workingwomen in Argentina can be traced back to as early as 1880,[37] but it only fully emerged as a conspicuous issue within mass culture in the 1910s. The press, textbooks, tango, sainete, and films indulged in narratives of despoiled women forced into prostitution as a result of inhumane working conditions. These narratives framed women's transition into the workforce "as a threat to both the family and social order."[38] The historical realities of misogynistic, erotically charged workplaces gave weight to this perspective. Lacking any changing rooms, female factory workers were made to undress in public, exposing themselves to sexual advances from male coworkers.[39] Similar conditions prevailed in department stores. These new, lavish bastions of capitalism also lacked changing rooms and facilitated advances from male superiors.[40]

Particularly relevant for my analysis is a 1916 study of female labor by Carolina Muzilli, an activist for women.[41] Her indictment of labor conditions defended department store saleswomen, even while questioning their morals. With a strong critical tone, Muzilli indicts the role of saleswomen in the blooming visual and sensual cultures in department stores. Just as in early twentieth-century department stores in large American cities, porteño department stores consisted of "palace[s] of consumption," to borrow from Lucy Fisher, that "not only sold goods but appealed to women's desire for luxury and elegance."[42] When Harrods opened in Buenos Aires in 1914, the distinguished magazine *Caras y Caretas* described the "magnificent building" on Florida Street, between Córdoba and Paraguay, as a "Palace of Elegance," in which great social solemnities "resounded with the murmur of conversation and the *froufrou* of elegant, feminine *toilettes*."[43] Department store shop windows in stores on Florida Street—from la Ciudad de Londres to Gath & Chaves, to the luxurious Casa Peyrú—were described as "paradises of desire."[44] Indeed, department stores were a feast for the senses. Sounds, perfumes, textures, and sights overwhelmed customers who wandered through their sumptuous spaces (see figure 8). Resonating with department stores' sensual appeal, Muzilli explains, saleswomen in downtown Buenos Aires were also on display in these vast palaces, "dressed in classic, black ensembles with elegant hairstyles, resembl[ing] small works of art." She further posits that "luxury and vanity turn [saleswomen] into mannequins controlled by the boss."[45] In her description, reified women hint at illicit sexual practices proper to the department store and the novel economies of consumption, in a space that Muzilli labels "a school that degrades and corrupts" innocent, disenfranchised women.

Muzilli contends that the emergent mass culture contributed to the "problem" of women in the workforce. Avid readers of *folletines* (serialized novels) and regulars at matinees "frequented by questionable [male] individuals," saleswomen were immersed in popular culture and therefore, in Muzilli's view, had little opportunity to "contribute to their

FIGURE 8. Grand lobby of Gath & Chavez department store (1908), corner of Florida and Piedad Streets, Buenos Aires. Courtesy of BNA.

own moral elevation."[46] Muzilli's study reveals that workingwomen participated considerably in mass consumer culture, even though their integration in social spaces such as film theaters was still viewed with suspicion. Her account points to the emergence of new forms of public participation reminiscent of the "alternative public sphere" that Miriam Hansen traces in the American nickelodeon.[47] Indeed, film trade journals suggest that porteño cinedramas courted the growing patronage of women,[48] confirming that Argentine publications and films established the conditions for the emergence of novel "spheres of participation."[49]

Muzilli's account of department store saleswomen flocking to the cinema recalls Siegfried Kracauer's series of articles, collectively titled

"The Little Shop Girls Go to the Movies," which address similar concerns about female consumerism and the practice of female moviegoing in the Weimar Republic.[50] For Kracauer, the infantilized figure of the shop girl embodies the uncritical masses and points to the potential dangers of spectacle—the film industry recasting "oppression into more appealing forms of adventure, romance, and comedy."[51] Blatantly condescending, Kracauer argues that young saleswomen epitomize lower-class spectators, who consume "even more bourgeois [films] than those aimed at the finer audiences, precisely because they hint at subversive points of view without exploring them."[52] He suggests that "little shop girls" console themselves with "*daydreams of society*" (bourgeois films) that uncritically present disparities of class and gender.[53] With Kracauer's assessment of Weimar film culture and consumer culture in mind, it is worth considering whether porteño cinedramas provided ideological consolation for social injustices or whether the genre—inspired by and catering to porteño dreams of social mobility—established a platform to denounce society's ills. After all, in his essay Kracauer seems to hint at the (in)visibilities melodrama makes possible, when he recognizes that through the "daydreams of society" cinema offers "actual reality comes to the fore."[54]

Porteño cinedrama begs the question of the uses and usefulness of melodrama in Buenos Aires film and film culture in the 1920s. Recent scholarship, building upon Jorge Miguel Couselo's seminal study on director José Agustín Ferreyra,[55] has opted for reading porteño cinedrama as ideological consolation. Particularly focusing on Ferreyra's work, such academic views label the genre in terms of "lighthearted productions" that "pacified anxieties surrounding Buenos Aires marginalized sectors while integrating them into the sphere of mass culture."[56] Based on surviving film fragments, I propose a more nuanced reading. I look at the ways in which porteño cinedramas offered both palliative and denunciatory fare as they turned sites into sights, conferring visibility on emergent social actors.

In cinedramas featuring department store saleswomen, social criticism came to the fore. By entering the luxurious spaces and economies of the department store, saleswomen engaged in multiple displacements (spatial, social, identity based) in a tantalizing chain of desire. In these films, saleswomen engage in extra-economic arrangements in order to fulfill their wants. Unable to purchase the products they put on display—but enticed by the magazines that echoed affluent lifestyles[57]—saleswomen became easy prey to sexual exploitation.

Most of these films condemned female characters' desires for upward mobility by portraying them as misguided and consequently star crossed. Some films, such as *Perdón, viejita* (Forgive Me Dear Mother; dir. José A. Ferreyra, 1927), did absolve "fallen" women, celebrating their happy return to the conventillo family life. Film synopses suggest that in many films, "fallen" women can only find solace after returning to the barrio and marrying blue-collar workers, who see beyond women's dubious pasts and rescue them by reinstalling them in a traditional gender role.[58] Other films, however, presented morally complex situations that did not fit a clear divide between the good woman—who returns home and marries—and the bad woman—who ventures out on her own and is consequently punished by fate. Ferreyra's *La chica de la calle Florida* (The Girl of Florida Street, 1922) best portrays such situations as they unfold within an unstable social milieu. In the film, characters give expression to complex urban realities in which working-women strive for economic independence against the challenges of an eroticized urban space. The film tackles how some women—as underpaid consumers—resort to bestowing sexual favors in order to obtain otherwise unattainable products, and how other women—as (abused) workers—endure sexual subordination to sustain impoverished families in the barrio.

La chica focuses on department store saleswomen on busy Florida Street, an important commercial artery that by the 1900s hosted several department stores. A stunning sequence—rife with high-angle shots, tracking shots, and point-of-view shots, complemented by fast cutting and dissolves—captures Florida Street's spectacular mobility and social complexity. Images of shimmering shop windows and elegant stores depict a world of superficial beauty. However, the sequence presents this enthralling world as a backdrop for concealed abuses. An intertitle punctuating the sequence reads, "a mark, a scar betrays [saleswomen]," tarnishing the veneer of Florida Street city life. Stressing the idea of surface-level beauty, the intertitle continues, "[T]he blue illusions of these small birds, dreamt the night before in the little house in the sad barrio, die in the great golden cages of silks, sparkles, and colors." Comparing department stores to opulent birdcages, and saleswomen to small birds, the intertitle highlights how department stores entrap saleswomen. Confined, they serve as paid workers and eroticized showpieces. Advertising refined products with their own bodies, saleswomen expose themselves to sexualized peril in the heterosocial spaces of Buenos Aires.

In the film, the department store establishes a gendered social order mapped onto the divide between haves and have-nots. Like other surviving fragments of porteño cinedramas, *La chica de la calle Florida* rarely presents bodily use and abuse explicitly. Rather, expository titles and dialogue intertitles refer to these practices, while different sequences hint at saleswomen's ordeals through costuming and body language. Reminiscent of American "white slavery" films of the mid-1910s, porteño cinedramas present female debasement through spatial displacement:[59] "fallen" women aimlessly roam the streets, slouched and wearing darker colors.

Covering a broad span of the social spectrum, *La chica* revolves around multiple exchanges—shaped by social stratification and desire—between female department store workers and male managers and owners. The film focuses on Alcira (Lidia Liss), a demure saleswoman who has a secret relationship with the owner's son, Jorge (Jorge Lafuente). A naive law student, Jorge is unaware that the store manager, Lamberti, is harassing the young saleswomen and demanding sexual favors in exchange for job security. Yet female employees are also complicit in the abuse. Juana (Elena Guido), the manager's typist, colludes with the manager; her departures from the management office quickly become an indication that abuse is taking place in the film. Alcira, the protagonist, is the only woman who does not succumb to the manager's advances. But her moral tenacity comes with a price: she loses her job, while her boyfriend loses his place in society after the manager reveals the young lovers' secret relationship. As the plot unfolds, loss allows for the two lovers to exhibit their moral superiority through manual labor. In sequences recalling educational films, Alcira works as a seamstress while Jorge toils as a blue-collar worker. A factory accident, however, forces Alcira to reach out to Lamberti with the hope of contacting Jorge's father.

This unfortunate twist motivates a narrative situation rarely shown in cinedrama porteño. By the end of the surviving footage, Alcira visits Lamberty in his private quarters. After hearing Alcira's plight, the manager sees the opportunity to finally take advantage of her. In a striking, swiftly paced montage of medium shots and close-ups, Lamberti violently forces himself on Alcira. In the meantime, Juana (the manager's accomplice) watches the struggle through the window. Fueled by resentment (she has also been fired), Juana shoots Lamberti and saves Alcira in the nick of time. Editing and sharp contrasts between light and shadow stress the sequence's Manichean struggle between good and evil. The chiaroscuro lighting and the shadow play of Juana's gun projected on the window drapes evoke Cecil B. DeMille's dramatic low-key lighting epitomized in the concluding struggle in *The Cheat* (Lasky production company, 1915),[60] in which a socialite (Fannie Ward) shoots a wealthy admirer (Sessue Hayakawa) when he tries to subdue her after she rejects his advances. Indeed, *La chica*'s sequence could very well exemplify DeMille's "Rembrandt lighting," as he himself described his lighting effects.[61] There is no evidence that *The Cheat* directly influenced Ferreyra's lighting choices in this film; however, articles penned by DeMille on lighting and filmmaking in general—which compared the filmmaker's work to the "painter['s with his] canvas"—circulated in *Cine-Mundial* as early as 1917 and may suggest an indirect influence not only on Ferreyra, but also on other porteño directors.[62]

The battle between good and evil in the sequence is problematized once the manager's murderer is revealed—Juana, his former assistant. Surviving footage concludes with intertitles in which Juana justifies her actions. She states, "It was I! That man forever destroyed my life. He made me his passing fancy and his toy. That is why I killed him. For me. For all women. For her [Alcira]. He also wanted to drag her to the abyss, as he did with me." As suggested in this sequence, the female body in porteño cinedrama serves two functions: as a sexualized object of exchange and an embodiment of the gendered injustice of urban space through pathos. In these films, women are constantly exposed to psychological and bodily harm. Strikingly, it is Juana's experience of shame that morally pushes her to solidary action. Injured and indignant, Juana opts for a sacrifice of sorts—to kill and, consequently, to kill herself as a civic subject—to protect a fellow female victim. With her action, Juana puts into practice the struggle for recognition at the core of melodrama. And importantly, she challenges, not on her behalf but on behalf of Alcira, the three interlocking forms of misrecognition that structure the melodramatic mode: the violation of the body, the denial of rights within a society, and the denigration of individuals or social groups (see the introduction to this volume). Nevertheless, the moral economies of cinedrama are complicated by the awareness of some female figures who, within this context, realize their bodies have value as objects of exchange and can consequently be used in the quest for upward mobility.

The relation between female desires for upward mobility, sexual favors, and sexual abuse springs from the circulation of bodies and goods—and bodies as goods—in urban space. Films like *La chica de la calle Florida* vacillate between entertainment and indictment. Insistence on the dangers of female social mobility represent class mobility as a moral threat but at the same time highlight the intersection between gender and class conflict in terms of sexual exploitation and rape, as well as in terms of class competition and gendered class solidarity. Juana and Alcira show how women's agency is constantly under pressure when pitted against sexualized subordination in the public sphere. Their experiences of downward and fleetingly upward mobility point to the dynamics of urban traffic determined by the circulation of classed and gendered bodies. Their movements to and from downtown visualize a social fabric of displaced social actors. They also highlight the discrepancies of class and gender that shape the tantalizing chain of desire instituted by an emerging consumer culture.

CABARETS AND GARÇONNIÈRES: SEXUAL ECONOMIES AND MALE DISPLACEMENTS

Another prominent location in porteño cinedramas was Buenos Aires cabarets and garçonnières, or bachelor apartments. On the threshold of private and public spheres, these spaces further blurred the boundaries between "public" women (prostitutes) and workingwomen. Epitomizing consumerist titillation in film, images of cabarets and garçonnières constituted the most lavish narrative excesses, the locus in which conventillo dreams inevitably turn into sexualized nightmares. As I have suggested in the previous sections, prostitution in porteño cinedramas encompasses multiple forms of social interaction mediated by bodily exchanges. These complex forms of exchange complicate gender relations in urban spaces and, consequently, complicate the notion of female victimhood. A cursory reading of cabaret-centered films could support the argument that early Buenos Aires mass media culture reinforced traditional ideologies of gender through narratives of female punishment.[63] However, porteño cinedramas show how elite and lower classes mixed via sexual economies in cabarets and garçonnières. These films visualize complex, extra-economic exchanges in which women are actively engaged—that is to say, women could be victims, but they could also be perpetrators.

In a study of early twentieth-century porteño prostitution, historian Andrés Carretero classifies seven different types of prostitutes, categorized by their modus operandi and location.[64] Two types, the *cocotte* (i.e., coquette) and the *cabaretera*, flirted with the highest social circles in cafés and cabarets. Both types—celebrated and denigrated in tango, sainete, and film—pointed to forms of exchange in which women capitalized on the consumer culture that reified them. In so doing, they flouted conventional mores. As both objects and subjects of exchange, women also exerted influence on male wastrels, impelling them into spatial and identity displacements of their own. To examine these male displacements, in this section I turn to male-centered cabaret films.

Cabaret culture was at its height in Buenos Aires between 1910 and 1930. As tango crossed social boundaries both locally and internationally, cabarets became forbidden sites inhabited by porteño elites, to which the upwardly mobile classes also sought entry. According to historian Sirena Pellarolo, cabarets performed two functions: they were "subsidiar[ies] of the growing prostitution industry [and] recruitment centers for tango talent."[65] As I have suggested, the social dynamics of these spaces complicated the figure of the prostitute. The cabaret encouraged unabashed consumption of stimulants and reified female bodies. Tango lyrics hinged upon dancers who sat with male customers, encouraging them to drink. The famous tango "Melenita de Oro" (Samuel Linning, 1922) best captures the cabaretera's protean identity, mediated by spatial relationships. Concealing her true identity—"they call me Little Mane of Golden Hair" (the phrase that gives the tango its title)—the parasitic cabaretera seeks to profit from the cabaret's intimate distances, premised on varying degrees of class-based separation and sexual proximity. In the conventional voice of the suffering male singer, "Melenita de Oro" laments the cabaretera's active sexuality and power over men. The singer's lament revolves around his emasculation, which itself results from having his fantasy of being her sole possessor continually be frustrated: "Your lipstick stains me / Your lips are still warm from a previous date / I don't want to see you ever again / Come back tomorrow!" As the tango suggests, the cabaret engages women and men in constant negotiation.

Tango left its impression on film in multiple ways. Film theater orchestras played tangos during film screenings, while audiences responded enthusiastically to tango interpretations. At certain premieres, the star of the film performed a tango written exclusively for that particular cinedrama.[66] Most important, tango provided an inventory of urban character types and their social practices. Sergio Piñero, a regular collaborator in the letrado magazine *Martín Fierro*, satirized tango's formulaic structure. Not without flippancy, the porteño intellectual affirmed: "Tango constitutes binoculars for viewing certain social phenomena. [It] involves harmony of opposite passions [and] accentuates women's subordinated condition. . . . For these very women, there is the jealous seducer who does not respect prejudices, conditions, virginities or modesties. [Women] are attracted by his deceitful voluptuousness." Like other *Martín Fierro* collaborators, Piñero described tango and popular culture with disdain.[67] Unwillingly, however, the author summarized tango's legacy in film. The fallen women and the questionable suitors he mentions—the *compadrito* (urban ruffian) and the *niño bien* (rich kid)—are but a few examples of familiar figures populating both tango *and* film. *La costurerita que dio aquel mal paso* (the little seamstress who stumbled), the organ grinder, the blind man, the drunken husband, the unconditionally loving mother, and others peopled the porteño cinedrama cityscape (see figure 9). Interestingly, the city types expanded to hyperbole in Piñero's column nonetheless reflected "social phenomena," according to the author.

In this sense, tango types attested to the processes of change. Thus, both tango and porteño cinedrama shared the compulsion to archive a (morally dubious) experience of the present. A column announcing the premiere of the lost film *El organito de la tarde* (*Evening Little Barrel Organ*, 1925), also directed by Ferreyra, could well summarize porteño cinedrama's moral concern with present times: "[*El organito*] is a facet of life in the suburbs, with its ambitions and egotisms, its desires for intense life, its illusions of grandeur. Downtown city lights attract butterflies from the conventillo and burn their wings."[68] As the synopsis of the film suggests, the moral concern in *El organito* is explicitly gendered: "Virtue [*honra*] is exchanged for a suit and a tango in the cabaret. There is a moral to the story, like a calling: the return to the conventillo from which she left in search of luxury and pleasure."[69] Like many tangos, porteño cinedramas equate women in the public sphere with "public women" (prostitutes). As mentioned previously, the return to the humble conventillo life—a volitional act of repentance on the part of the fallen woman—most generally figured as the sole atonement for "fallen" women.

According to Carlos Monsiváis, appropriating tango reinforced fiction film's "melodramatic efficiency."[70] The cultural critic keenly suggests that the popular music facilitated powerful ways for the public to sympathize with the situations portrayed in film. Actively embodying narrative pathos while singing, "the listener (the singer)" says Monsiváis, "appropriates the role of the rejected, the enamored, the sufferer, and develops it in two or three minutes. . . . To find himself turned into the characters of the songs, who rejects such a role?"[71] As Monsiváis duly suggests, tango's mass popular appeal was pervasive and provided

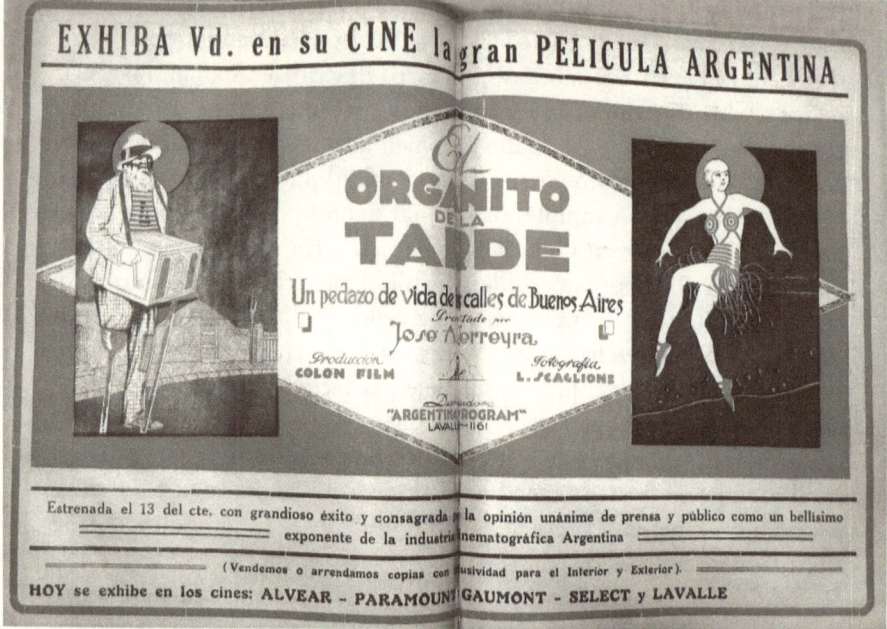

FIGURE 9. Organ grinder and "fallen" woman in advertisement for *El organito de la tarde*. The ad reads, "A piece of the life on the streets of Buenos Aires" (center). Courtesy of ENERC.

a new way of experiencing pathos on the most intimate level. Simply put, tango was *entrañable*—embodied *and* embodying. Thus, tango performance and aesthetics implanted bodily modes of perception, affect, and interpretation in the heart—or I should say gut, the *entrañas*—of melodrama.[72]

Let us return to the locus of tango (the cabaret) in film. To date, Ferreyra's two-reel *La vuelta al bulín* (1926), restored and digitized in 2009, presents the clearest surviving images of the Buenos Aires cabaret. Featuring the prominent stage comedian Álvaro Escobar, *La vuelta* was originally shot for Escobar's variety show. A minor work in Ferreyra's career, the film lingers on shots of a small café and a conventillo room. In stark contrast to these humble locations, the film presents a lavishly produced cabaret sequence that has led film historians to hypothesize another source for the sequence: Ferreyra's lost film *Melenita de oro* (1923).[73] Filled with countless extras and sumptuous furnishings, the sequence offers the spectator a seductive view of porteño nightlife: tuxedoed men and flappers, pomp and tango. The short film revolves around the misfortunes of Mucha Espuma (Escobar), a spineless good-for-nothing depicted sympathetically, whose wife abandons him for the cabaret highlife. Briefly venturing into the exclusive cabaret, *La vuelta* sets in motion tensions between haves and have-nots and unveils the porous boundaries of urban space.

Mixed-class, sexualized interactions at the cabaret further harness modernity's "desire for site-seeing," as mentioned previously. Turning sites into (erotic) sights, cabaret films visualize elaborate dynamics of consumption—of stimulants, fashion, and bodies. For instance, the opening sequence of Edmo Cominetti's *La borrachera del tango* (*Tango Inebriation*, 1928) evocatively depicts the intoxicating and alluring effects of the cabaret. Through dissolves and superimpositions, the sequence is framed from the point of view of a niño bien after an overindulgent soirée. Beginning with a close-up of the young man sleeping in bed, which serves as a background for a series of superimposed images, metonymies of cabaret dissipation progressively occupy the frame: close-ups of a clown inflating a balloon, a saxophone player, the tapping legs of a flapper, a twirling spiral, a drummer, a tighter close-up on the flapper's inviting face, an assenting automaton. A final dissolve on a spiral followed by an image of superimposed streamers concludes the sequence. Here, editing conveys the enticing yet threatening appeal of Buenos Aires nightlife. Spectacle, music, the fragmented female body, and, most evidently, the nodding automaton juxtaposed with the woman's inviting face engulf the spectator in porteño temptations.

Directed by Cominetti and photographed by Alberto Biasotti, *La borrachera del tango* brought Elías Alippi and Carlos Schaeffer Gallo's eponymous sainete (1921) to the screen. Both the sainete and the film, the latter advertised as a "super-production,"[74] follow a narrative structure of upward and downward mobility similar to that of *La chica de la calle Florida*. Instead of featuring two workingwomen, however, *La borrachera* focuses on two brothers, first-generation Argentines born to an affluent immigrant family. Luis (Felipe Farah), an engineer who embodies material progress, follows the upward path of moral rectitude, while his younger brother, Fernando (Eduardo Morera), descends deeper and deeper into the porteño nightlife. Their opposing economic and moral trajectories thrust them into radically disparate settings. The engineer is positioned within a locus of progress outside the city, a hydroelectric dam under construction in the "Sierra," which he temporarily abandons when his brother threatens the family's unity. Their trajectories converge, however, on one young woman, Lucía (Nedda

Francy). Practically a member of the family, Lucía has lived in the household since her childhood. Considering her a younger sister, Luis has always sought to protect her. Fernando, on the contrary, woos her with promises of marriage but later abandons her and their unborn child to an uncertain fate. To avoid a scandal, Luis and his parents take Lucía to the Sierra, where she gives birth and pretends to be Luis's wife while Fernando wastes away in Buenos Aires.

Interestingly, the sainete *La borrachera* revolves around the cabaret, while the eponymous film eschews the cabaret altogether to focus on the garçonnière. The variation highlights different social practices in each space. In the sainete, the cabaret—premised on gendered and classed hierarchies—allows for violent spectacle. Dramatic tension culminates as Fernando flaunts his male bravado by battering two cocottes. Unapologetic, and driven to dominate women, his character recalls Lamberti of *La chica de la calle Florida*. Following the bleak conventions of sainete, the play offers a lurid depiction of male abuse that almost condones Fernando's actions—in fact, the prose seems to celebrate his violent masculinity. On the contrary—and as we shall see—by focusing on the garçonnière, the film ultimately portrays Fernando as an emasculated man. Paradoxically, the bachelor's apartment—the site of excess and lewd abuses perpetrated by affluent men against insolvent women—foregrounds male identity displacements.

Unlike the public space of cabarets, regulated to some degree by public visibility, the private space of garçonnières gave free rein to the economic and sexual exploitation of female bodies. The relations garçonnières enabled, however, were premised on the gendered access to capital (which the film ultimately portrays as detrimental to both women *and* men, as we shall see). In the film, Fernando frequents a friend's garçonnière where cocottes compete, as courtesans, for the men's wealth. Luis's search for Fernando in the Buenos Aires nightlife strikingly depicts these practices. When Fernando's friends see Luis down the street approaching the garçonnière, they hurry to give him a "welcome worthy of this house," an intertitle announces. As the door opens, Luis is confronted with a striking tableau: a nude woman, framed in full shot from his point of view, her slender figure accentuated by the dark cape of a vampiric-looking man behind her. A cut brings the man's face into close-up as he places his index finger on his lips. Mockingly, the vampire prompts Luis to keep the sexual secrets of the garçonnière. The sequence further stresses the space as sexual and deviant—with close-ups of a woman in drag insolently smoking and, in a brief flurry of stop-motion animation, medium shots of a wide-eyed man in profile whose cigarette lengthens in a clearly phallic montage. Zealously protecting its sexual territories through sexual extravagance, the garçonnière shocks Luis. The sequence concludes with the sculptural woman clinging to Luis's neck, prompting him to remove her hands in disgust.

The sexual economies on display throughout the sequence complicate gender relations in the garçonnière—and by extension in cinedrama porteño. Women do not merely act as sexual servants; they collude with the men to defend the sexualized territories in dispute. Like the vampire who feeds upon the cocottes' bodies, women also engage in parasitic relationships to safeguard their privileged access to wealth.[75] Fernando's last visit to the garçonnière, however, highlights the gendered subtleties shaping urban space. Without his father's monetary allowance and abandoned by his family, Fernando is forced into spatial and identitary displacements of his own. In a sequence echoing Luis's previous visit, Fernando unsuccessfully tries to reenter the garçonnière. Helpless and friendless, he looks for his latest infatuation. Like his brother, Fernando hesitates to ring the bell. Through intercutting—between full shots of an impoverished Fernando on the street looking up and full shots of the party inside the garçonnière—the sequence spatializes class boundaries. Indoor shots display a cabaretera spectacle. A lone woman in skimpy clothes and a top hat performs a sultry number against a backdrop of wealthy men and cocottes. Building up the courage to enter, Fernando rings the bell but is not allowed inside. A maid stops him at the door and, carrying his message, announces him to a cocotte. In a medium shot, the cocotte shakes her head and with histrionic gestures quiets everyone down. Intercutting between shots of Fernando in the doorway listening and other shots of men playing jokes on the cocottes and breaking the silence, the film language spatializes Fernando's displacement. Rejected and embarrassed, Fernando takes to the street.

As mentioned previously, the garçonnière grants gendered forms of access to its sexualized territories mediated by capital. Courtesans and sexual servants come in "freely" and engage in parasitic exchanges: women consume male wealth, while men consume female bodies. *La borrachera* reifies the latter in a vampiric tableau. The vampire seen in Luis's visit suggests a degree of passivity on the women's part. Fernando's visit, however, shows that women are not necessarily victims in the garçonnière; they can actively engage in parasitic exchanges as well, to the detriment of men. Penniless, Fernando is expelled by the object of his desire. She determines that Fernando can no longer penetrate the garçonnière. Once he has squandered his wealth, not only the cocotte but also his fellow bon vivants question Fernando's virility. His identity shattered—a niño bien turned everyman—Fernando finds himself lost in the metropolis and turns to his family in the Sierra.

Following Fernando's transformation from subject of desire to object of scorn, the film takes the audience on a visual tour of big-city nightlife, but it does not only indulge the spectators' voyeurism. Exploring the places where the urban elite and the underworld meet, *La borrachera* offers a broader spatial experience than meets the eye: it brokers affective and sensual experiences of urban space, sympathizing with the displaced while arousing the senses. Fernando's individual predicament points, more generally, to the ways in which porteño cinedramas prompted spectators to vicariously share the pathos of the downtrodden and, at the same time, enticed them through an erotics of urban space.

CONCLUSION

Harnessing visual spectacle, porteño cinedramas affectively engaged spectators, negotiating degrees of sociocultural separation or proximity through their senses. By focusing on key locations that figured prominently in porteño cinedramas—tenement housing, department stores, and the cabaret-garçonnière—the genre traced sociocultural cartographies and identitary strategies in contested sites of 1920s Buenos Aires. Through melodramas of "fallen women" and sometimes of dispossessed men, the genre rendered visible varying degrees of sociocultural proximity and separation, apportioning urban space in terms of gender and class. Taking location shooting as a film practice that could destabilize the early film spectator's experience of lived space,[76] and considering the erotics relating the latter to the cinematic,[77] cinedrama porteño transformed urban spaces into meaningful, tangible sights.

Triggered by arousing explorations of urban space, cinedrama porteño spectators accessed intimate spaces from the safe distance of their seats, experiencing the films' sites not only through sight but also through the totality of their senses. The lived spaces visualized in these films were familiar to their historical audience. While the spectator could not literally touch the cape of the vampire looming over a nude woman or sympathetically share the masculine ban from the garçonnière, porteño cinedramas made the world they depicted palpable, moving their audiences with urban pathos and thrills. Trafficking in bodies as goods, the genre also negotiated between entertainment and social critique. At a time of unprecedented urban transformations, porteño cinedramas foregrounded modernity's underdogs, oscillating between conservatism and subversion.

The bleakest description of Buenos Aires can be found in the tango "Yira yira" (*lunfardo* for Turns and turns), first interpreted by Carlos Gardel in 1930. Enrique Santos Discépolo composed the song when optical sound technology was taking over porteño theaters, and films such as *¡Tango!* (dir. Luis Moglia Barth, 1933) were bringing the "fallen woman" to sound film. Centered on the cynical apathy of the (urban) world, "Yira yira" describes Buenos Aires and its effects on the individual:

> When you don't even have faith,
> Nor yesterday's *mate* leaves drying under the sun . . .
> the indifference of the world,
> which is deaf and mute,
> you will feel . . .
> You will see that everything is a lie,
> You will see that nothing is love,
> that the world does not care about a thing.
> [It] turns and turns.

As in the singer's plight, the men and women of tango and porteño cinedrama find themselves unsettled in the face of urbanization. To borrow from Ben Singer in his study of Euro-American early film melodrama, they find themselves "helpless and unfriended in a postsacred . . . world of moral ambiguity and material vulnerability."[78] In a way, tango and cinedrama porteño propose a visual regime that smoothly dovetails with accounts of melodrama and modernity such as Singer's or Brooks's, where the loss of the "traditional Sacred" conditions the possibility of melodrama.[79] In other Latin American regions, however, modernization and the experience of modernity embraced the religious, yielding filmic melodramas that revolved around faith, religion, and their presence in modern everyday life. The next chapter explores such a case.

CHAPTER 3

Bogotá and Medellín

*A Tale of Two Cities
and Conservative Progress*

Censorship committees will not pass representations
containing . . . acts or expressions contrary to morals
and good manners, or to the dogmas of the [Catholic]
religion, or to the practices of the faith.

—*Código de policía del Departamento de Caldas*

"Profound optimism invades our spirit," celebrated an editorial in *Cine Colombia*.[1] "Today's ceremony," the column continued, "full of patriotic significance, gives us an intimate delight. A patriotic deed His Grace [Archbishop] Perdomo has done blessing our new industry. A patriotic deed Mr. President and his Secretaries have done supporting his blessing. Under the auspices of such great dignities, the Church and Civil Power, *Cinematográfica Colombia* will be a source of artistic wealth." The editorial was referring to the company's inauguration ceremony (see figure 10). The archbishop of Bogotá, in the presence of President Pedro Nel Ospina and the secretaries of industry and public works, blessed the studio, also known as Colombia Film, which would soon produce an overtly religious film titled *La tragedia del silencio* (*The Tragedy of Silence*, 1924). Combining patriotism, institutionalized power brokers, and industrial art, the ceremony highlights the influential forces at play in Bogotá's modernization. Not only the state and the church, but also religious practice, were at the core of material progress in the city. As the event and its press account suggest, from the start, Bogotan narrative filmmaking turned out to be an officially progressive—and holy—endeavor.

The triangle among religious, civil, and industrial powers also operated in the most industrialized city in the country. Through film, the city of Medellín aimed at showcasing its industrial achievements; interestingly, it did so with melodramas rife with Catholic imagery. At the peak

FIGURE 10. Blessing of Colombia Film studios. Courtesy of BNC.

of dramatic tension, *Bajo el cielo antioqueño* (*Under the Antioquia Sky*, 1925), set in court, likens the male protagonist, who has been wrongfully accused of murder, to a suffering Christ. Through iris in/outs transposing both characters, the film equates Álvaro (Juan B. Naranjo), sitting on the bench of the accused, with the bust of a bleeding Jesus Christ, wearing a crown of thorns (see figure 11). Conjoining civic authority and the moral cipher implied in religious piety—still to be recognized at this turning point in the story—*Bajo el cielo* hints at the perceptual coordinates informing the body politic of the film. The production conditions of *La tragedia*, as well as editing in *Bajo el cielo*—a narrative film produced to exhibit Medellín's industrial achievements—suggests the cultural significance attributed to Catholicism in local melodrama and modernity. Not only *La tragedia* and *Bajo el cielo*, but all of the surviving feature-length films preserved by the Fundación Patrimonio Fílmico Colombiano (Colombian Film Heritage Foundation), use narrative arcs of guilt, punishment, and atonement to forward a culturally conservative yet materially progressivist agenda. In so doing, these films challenge the tenets underpinning current studies of melodrama, at the same time questioning the secularizing frameworks that have dominated the study of Latin American modernity.

This chapter explores how the growing involvement of the Catholic Church and religious practice, in both private and public spheres, operated during one of the fastest modernization periods in Colombian history, and how it shaped film melodrama in both Bogotá and Medellín. I argue that, during the 1920s, narrative films in the two fastest-growing urban centers in the country reproduced—and were the product of—a hegemonic visual regime supported by both state and church. Aimed at legitimizing traditional social hierarchies while extolling material progress by morally controlling social subjects via fervent Catholicism,[2] this visual regime had a simple yet suggestive name: *la moral* (morality).[3] If Buenos Aires urban films revealed urbanization's underdogs and thus appeal to spectators' sympathy through their visibility,[4] Bogotá and Medellín narratives concealed society's ills under the discourse of la moral. In so doing, these melodramas extolled conservative progressivism during the process of urbanization.

Since melodrama's inception in pantomime, Catholic imagery and pious gestures have been part of its repertoire of signs and gesticulation, which later carried over to theatrical forms and media, particularly through the *tableau vivant*, as Peter Brooks has noted.[5] However, in his

FIGURE 11. Iris in/outs equate the suffering male lead with a bleeding Christ. Stills from *Bajo el cielo antioqueño* (1925). Courtesy of FPFC.

seminal work on melodrama, Brooks proposes a definition of melodrama and its relation to modernity at odds with depictions of religion and its practice in certain Latin American silent films. For Brooks, melodrama constitutes a "central fact of modern sensibility," characterizing the modern period as a postsacred era in which moral and spiritual values have been "masked," or become inoperative.[6] Therefore, in the absence of the traditional Sacred, melodrama yearns to make those lost moral valences visible, but does not necessarily succeed. Locating the origins of modernity in the French Revolution, Brooks describes the dissolution of an organic and hierarchically cohesive society, along with its representative institutions (king, church, and the aristocracy), as ushering in the age of melodrama.[7] Several melodrama scholars have followed suit, as mentioned in the previous chapter. Only very recently have a few scholars begun to consider more nuanced positions for melodrama and the Sacred in the modern world.[8]

Latin American scholars concur that the loss of the traditional Sacred is at the heart of Latin American state formation and modernity. In his seminal study *Hybrid Cultures*, Néstor García Canclini highlights how multiple factors—secularization, growing individualism, rationalization, technical innovation, expanding capitalism, education, and specialized knowledge—were entrusted with "realizing rational and moral evolution" in the separation of state and church.[9] Somewhat uncritically, Latin American film scholars have taken this reading of the modern experience at face value. Consequently, they regard "religious films" as rife with contradictions,[10] having "primitive" mise-en-scène and editing, and being premised on narrative "simplicity" of "no great consequence" to the development of "the cinematic form in Latin America," as I discussed in chapter 1.[11] With these assessments in mind, the role Brooks attributes to melodrama does not require further revision. However, in Latin America the experience of modernity and modernization varied from country to country and from region to region. In Colombian urban centers, the modernization processes described here did not result in secular societies. Instead, they yielded what historian Miguel Ángel Urrego has aptly termed a "sacralization of society,"[12] or the growing involvement of the church—alongside the practice of Catholicism and Catholic mores—in private and public affairs: a modernization process premised not on rupture but on continuation.

To intertwine the processes of sacralization and material progress challenges the certainty that modernization equates with secularization. The Bogotá and Medellín cases warrant a broader understanding of the latter term. Secularization, for Jürgen Habermas, functions less "as a filter separating out the contents of traditions" than "as a transformer which redirects the flow of traditions."[13] Echoing Habermas, recent academic debates on secularization have challenged what secularization entails. Scholars, recognizing the social importance of religion vis-à-vis modern change, have questioned the secularization debate, to the point of stressing that "today almost nobody speaks of the imminent 'extinction' of religions or of the religious any longer."[14] Rather than forwarding a teleological narrative of demise or proposing a return to a defunct practice, scholars are showing a renewed interest in religion as a constitutive element of modern and contemporary times.[15] This paradigm shift reconsiders the social role of religion by acknowledging how religions persist in modern societies.[16] In fact, for the philosopher Charles Taylor, our current secular societies indicate that (non)believers reflect on their position in pluralist societies—societies in which believers and nonbelievers can, and do, coexist. Consequently, as Habermas has suggested, religion should not be excluded from public discourse[17] (or scholarly inquiry, for that matter).

Rereading the secular, that is, the active social, role of religion in early twentieth-century Bogotá and Medellín narrative films, this chapter proposes a "pluralist" approach to understanding Latin American modernity and its contested visual regimes. Instead of a monolithic process, the Latin American experience of modernity is better framed in terms of *modernities*, in the plural: as the product of multiple processes that yielded different experiences of—and takes on—the modern. As a case in point, the films discussed in this chapter locate religion and the religious at the heart of modernization processes. Likewise, being products of their time, these films appropriated religious practices and imagery to reflect and shape local filmic melodrama.

THE VIRTUE OF MARRIAGE TRIUMPHS

From the start, the relation between state and church influenced the production conditions of *La tragedia del silencio*. During the 1920s, seventeen local productions premiered in Colombia,[18] all but four between 1924 and 1926. Most likely, *La tragedia* first embedded Catholic imagery in Colombian narrative cinema. According to film historian Pilar Duque, *La tragedia*'s Catholic overtones guaranteed its success, not only among Colombian audiences but also in countries such as Venezuela and Panama.[19] Directed by the influential Bogotan Arturo Acevedo, the film received popular acclaim because of its Catholic themes and portrayals thought to defend "la moral y las buenas costumbres";[20] recall that "morals and good manners" was the nineteenth-century Latin American urbanity mantra, deeply rooted in Catholic morals.[21] *La tragedia* showcases Bogotá's highest social circles and material progress, at the same time pointing to issues of public health, particularly leprosy.[22] Catering to local audiences, the film connected old traditions to modern change under the aegis of Catholic values, most evident in public events presided over by Catholic priests—such as blessing a steel bridge at its inauguration ceremony. Apparently, upon its premiere the film touched the right notes in its (elite) audience: President Ospina officially endorsed the film, and consequently the film was also promoted through official channels.[23]

La tragedia del silencio, with its stately and ecclesiastical endorsement, points to a modernizing force premised not on rupture but on continuation. In her magisterial essay "Early Cinema and Modernity in Latin America," Ana López stresses that, in Latin America as elsewhere, early cinema capitalized on "the panoply of modern technologies, including urban development, media, and new amusements."[24] López recognizes how local traditional experiences and practices inflected local films, yielding "an ambiguous symbiosis"[25] of the modern and the traditional. Nevertheless, by highlighting material change and technological rupture, her article pays less attention to lingering traditional experiences and practices that also shaped Latin American films of the period. One of these factors, paramount in the Colombian context, was Catholic doctrine and imagery.

The peak of ecclesiastical and religious influence on Colombian modernization took place during the period known as the Hegemonía Conservadora (Conservative Hegemony). It was an époque, between 1886 and 1930, in which the Conservative Party monopolized national politics and imposed disciplinary models to motivate material progress while regulating the everyday life of its citizens through religious practices and mores. During the Hegemonía, the Conservative Party not only systematically excluded the oppositional Liberal Party from national politics but also deployed la moral to reproduce its hegemonic power and control the population. At its core lay a strictly Catholic moral code, incorporated into the Constitution of 1886 and supported by a series of concordats with the church in subsequent years. Of particular importance is that in 1888 the government signed an agreement with the church giving the latter full powers to organize and manage public education, including curriculum and textbook reform on a national scale (the polar opposite of Canclini's liberal education model, mentioned previously).[26] The church's control over education further supported the Hegemonía's regime by ushering in new platforms to deploy its moral order across civil society: mandatory spiritual retreats at schools, mushrooming laic-Catholic associations,[27] charities, the establishment and practice of official religious celebrations, censorship committees, confiscating and burning improper books,[28] and the morality police. Working in unison, these platforms enforced corporeal as well as spiritual discipline across the social landscape. They focused on disciplining the body—that is, controlling "the passions"—and making the church and religion the sole sources of authority and social order.[29] Thus, during the fastest period of modernization in Colombian history, society underwent, and reproduced, a state of permanent inspection and vigilance aimed at regulating public order, public health, and moral comportment. In this context, it is no surprise that President Pedro Nel Ospina publicly endorsed a film such as *La tragedia del silencio*—a film attuned to la moral—which celebrated conservative progress by making visible the various associations and religious-cum-laic institutions that reproduced such order.

La tragedia del silencio renders visible la moral at a structural level, in a narrative arc of guilt, self-inflicted punishment, and atonement. In the film, tragedy falls on the house of Alberto López (Alberto López Isaza). Due to mishandled samples in a medical laboratory, the affluent engineer and philanthropist is mistakenly diagnosed with leprosy— a disease depicted as hereditary and highly contagious in the film. In guilty anguish, Alberto decides to isolate himself from his loving wife and child. Rejected, his wife resorts to prayer in her private quarters and asks God to bring the family together again. Her retreat from social life allows for a flurry of pious compositions that amount to "a moral symbolic system"; prayer shots, shots of crucifixes, and shots of other religious imagery align her—and by extension her affluent family—with the moral bearings the film proposes.[30] At social events, however, her loneliness catches the eye of a younger but less affluent socialite, who tries to woo her. She never gives in to his solicitations. At one gathering at the Lopez household, Alberto catches a glimpse of the suitor and questions the fidelity of his wife. In despair, he resolves to commit suicide in his private studio. Fortunately, as he is about to pull the trigger, his son rushes in. Clinging to Alberto's leg, the toddler makes his father miss the shot. Hearing the detonation, a reaction shot suggests that Alberto's wife rushes in, too. Conveniently, the doctor calls at that precise moment to correct the diagnosis. With a full shot of the family reunited, an intertitle reads, "The virtue of marriage triumphs," highlighting the moral valence of the film. Surviving footage concludes with the morally questionable characters leaving the López household: the younger suitor and Isabela, Alberto's female suitor in lost footage, as suggested in a novelization of the film (see later in the chapter). The film conveys a clear message about a social problem while celebrating the status quo: the Catholic family overcomes debauchery and vice, thereby perpetuating the rigid echelons of Bogotá society. Leprosy, therefore, ultimately consists of another Catholic-inflected trope in service of visualizing (classed) moral fortitude.

Press materials suggest that the film was framed with an overtly religious prologue, as Duque indicates. The illustrated journal *Cine Colombia* (1924), the Acevedo family's venture into the film trade print business, corroborates the strategy. The first number, dated May 1924, includes the first installment of *La tragedia*'s novelization, penned by Acevedo's son-in-law and physician, Heliodoro González Coutin. In the only surviving installment found to date, the plot structure varies considerably from that in the surviving film footage. Apparently a dialogue in a wheat field between Christ and his Apostles brackets or introduces the Lopezes' story. Loosely inspired by the parable of the grain of wheat (John 12:24–26), the prologue of the illustrated *novela cinematográfica* foreshadows the film's core obstacle to family union (leprosy) and with it introduces the film's religious interpretative key. In the prologue, after walking across the wheat field, Peter the apostle sits on a rock on which, according to Jesus, Lazarus had sat before. Terrified, Peter throws himself at Jesus's feet and asks if he will be saved from Lazarus's illness. Jesus asks Peter to trust him and, addressing the entire group, declares: "Have faith, and you shall see miracles."[31] Three asterisks abruptly conclude the prologue, and a description of the Bogotá plateau introduces the main plot.[32] Interspersed with photograms of the film, the first installment of the novela cinematográfica does not include any images related to the prologue, other than an illustration of Christ. However, another popular magazine corroborates the hypothesis that lost footage may have introduced or bracketed the main plot with the parable. In a brief advertisement for the film, a photogram depicts Jesus and three other men in a wheat field. The caption reads: "'The wheat kernel miracle,' scene from the national film *La tragedia del silencio* that will soon premier at the Faenza Theater."[33] Based on the loose connections the prologue establishes with the main plot, it is clear that references to the New Testament aimed at catering to an audience with religious inclinations. Likewise, the promise of miracles on the condition of unquestionable faith present in the novela builds anticipation for the "trials and miracles" audiences would delight in in the film.

The institution of marriage, pious gestures, and close-ups on crucifixes and other religious imagery are but obvious examples of Catholic imagery in *La tragedia del silencio*. The film further visualizes la moral in subtler ways, particularly by depicting sacred everyday practices of mid-1920s Bogotá. Following Alberto's engineering projects and charitable deeds, the spectator participates in several urban development celebrations, including the inauguration of a railway steel bridge and a leprosy hospital. Both projects epitomize modernization processes regarding transportation and public health, respectively. Reminiscent of the topicals Acevedo had filmed for his newsreels—mostly religious and official processions in surviving film footage—the spectator sees in these modern venues how church officials played a central role in urban development. As in other countries in Latin America, blessing new infrastructural projects was an important aspect of inauguration events (and a prominent episode in the film's novela cinematográfica as well).[34] Thus, infrastructural progress and communal development were associated with the religious during the 1920s. The link among the three—infrastructure, community, and religion—was even described with an ethical bent. Hospitals, for instance, were labeled paradigms of "moral and material progress" in the popular press.[35] Likewise, in the film, feats of engineering and religious practice present material and moral progress as one and the same. Following the protagonists' projects and philanthropic practices, *La tragedia* showcases urban progress. Through religious-cum-modern events, the film conjoins material progress with Christian morality and mores. In the surviving film footage, the priest stands for the omnipresence of the church in state and civil affairs. With a considerable screen time, a contemporary spectator could infer that the priest is one of the main characters of the film; however, the novela cinematográfica suggests that Alberto's and his family's strife with (moral) disease articulates the plot. The focus on family drama, rather than on the social role of the church, consequently deploys a visual repertoire that, on the grounds of Catholic moral comportment, celebrates a progressive yet highly stratified, traditionalist society.

INDUSTRY AND MORAL FORTITUDE

La tragedia del silencio's success at the box office caught the attention of Gonzalo Mejía, the land and air transportation tycoon of Medellín. Following Acevedo's steps, Mejía founded the Compañía Filmadora de Medellín, or Medellín Filmmaking Company, in 1924, with the sole purpose of producing *Bajo el cielo antioqueño* (1925). Even if the company envisaged producing films with "national themes," regionalism and local advertising motivated its sole production.[36] Medellín high society comprised the entire cast—the only "foreigners," that is, Bogotans, were Arturo Acevedo and his son, hired as director and cameraman, respectively. Medellín's mushrooming industries also featured prominently in the film, betraying the promotional imperatives that motivated most narrative film production in the fastest-growing cities in Colombia. The currently lost *Nido de Cóndores* (*Nest of Condors*, 1926) is a case in point. Press material suggests that the film, produced by the Society for Civic Improvement of the city of Pereira,[37] revolved around a love story between a prominent industrialist's daughter and a German investor. Its true focus, however, was city progress—Pereira's "civility and energy," an article stressed.[38] *Bajo el cielo antioqueño* was no different. In a 1924 article, Acevedo himself disclosed the production's true yet concealed imperatives; the film would show the "modern aspects of the city ... within the plot [Acevedo] devised, so that the commercial tenor [*exposición comercial*] of the film is less obvious."[39] In the film, the love story between an industrialist's daughter and a well-dressed wastrel frames the display of Medellín's industrial prowess.

If promoting the city's industrial and economic progress motivated the production of the film, it is not immediately obvious why *Bajo el cielo* infuses its narrative with Catholic imagery and religion in everyday practices. Not only does Catholic imagery appear at several climactic episodes in the film, such as when the female protagonist clings to the imposing, six-foot-long cross standing over her mother's tomb at the San Pedro cemetery or, through iris in/outs, likens the male protagonist to Jesus Christ. The film also elevates the main characters by relating them to Catholic institutions—the female protagonist studies at a Catholic boarding school, for instance—and highlighting their Catholic moral fortitude. Combining concentrated capital, material progress, and the religious, *Bajo el cielo antioqueño* deploys la moral in the guise of a local industrial model that combines fervent Catholicism with capitalist factory production to legitimatize local industrialists' expanding power.[40] Here, la moral binds both factory owners and workers, the latter's productivity and comportment linked to religious values and the former having a moral responsibility rooted in Catholic values to "protect" their workers. For historian Ann Farnsworth-Alvear, this model came to fruition in Medellín during the 1930s and 1940s.[41] Nevertheless, *Bajo el cielo antioqueño*—as well as *La tragedia*—reveals in moving images how the notion of conservative progress operated a decade earlier. As we shall see, the film constructs a world in which moral comportment and productivity laid the foundations of a paternalistic domain with Catholic values at its core.[42]

By the 1920s, Medellín had experienced one of the fastest processes of industrialization in Colombia. The coffee boom and merchant fortunes of local importers supported capital investment in industry as early as the turn of the century.[43] Fast-paced industrialization also spelled accelerated urbanization. By 1900, Medellín possessed a university, an electric plant, streetlights, and a slaughterhouse. Construction of a citywide sewage system began in 1913, and in 1919, a network of trolley cars accelerated circulation across the Aberrá Valley. Medellín also boasted a Grand Cathedral that, by its completion in 1931, epitomized the city's idea of conservative progress. An impressive feat of engineering, the temple was at the time one of the largest brick buildings in the world.[44] As in Pereira, the affluent members of Medellín's Sociedad de Mejoras Públicas (Civic Improvement Association) brokered the city's embellishment and modernization. Protectionist tariffs and import substitution fueled city growth and, with it, rural-to-urban migration. In the face of a quickly growing working class, the association participated in the design and development of worker neighborhoods. In the process, early industrialists began to see themselves as both local tycoons and social engineers. Thus, Medellín's material progress conjoined family-owned firms, protectionism, and a paternalistic order, binding factory owners and workers in economic and extra-economic relationships. Proud of their achievements, and with their oligopoly being threatened by industrialists from other regions, Medellín tycoons strove to exhibit Medellín's material and moral progress. Such exhibitionistic imperatives shaped the city's first feature-length film.

Preserved almost in its entirety, *Bajo el cielo antioqueño* tapped into societal narcissistic pleasure, casting Medellín's crème de la crème and showcasing the region's burgeoning industries—coffee plantations, livestock, tobacco processing, mining, the soda industry, and modern transportation—beyond regional and national borders.[45] *Bajo el cielo* draws upon explicit Catholic imagery to highlight melodramatic tension, much like *La tragedia del silencio*. In a similar vein, the film connects the elite to religious institutions and practices. In this film, however, rather than supporting class difference, Christ-like victimization and love are at the service of Medellín's local notion of industrial progress, imbued with la moral.

In *Bajo el cielo*, the daughter of a steadfast industrialist, Lina (Alicia Arango de Mejía), falls in love with Álvaro (Juan B. Naranjo), a profligate heir to a fortune. Her father, Don Bernardo (Gonzalo Mejía), disapproves of their romance and does everything in his power to keep them apart. Going against her father's wishes, Lina decides to elope. At the magnificent Ferrocarril de Antioquia train station, however, Lina and Álvaro run into a sickly woman who, by telling her own star-crossed love story, discourages them from leaving the city. The woman beggar (Rosa Jaramillo) warns Lina against running away from home. Repentant, the beggar tells Lina her own tale of moral debasement. She left home for a man "who became [her] executioner," the intertitles read. Metaphorically, the "fallen" woman equates breaking la moral's ways with (social) death. Her story pushes Lina to reconsider her elopement plans, and in gratitude, she gives the beggar her jewelry. Álvaro, in his turn, bandages the woman's injured arm with his handkerchief, a fine piece decorated with Álvaro's embroidered monogram. Unbeknownst to them, two thieves are spying on the scene. Immediately after the affluent couple leaves, the thieves pounce on the beggar, kill her, and run away with the jewels. The police find her dead body and, in an unfortunate turn of events, the embroidered monogram in Álvaro's handkerchief incriminates the Medellín socialite, who is eventually charged.

During the heated trial that follows, Lina's father takes her away to their luscious coffee plantation on the outskirts of Medellín. There, Don Bernardo prevents her from reading the newspapers—rife with sensationalistic accounts of the young socialite's trial in the city—and seeks to adapt her to the patriarchal ways of the hacienda. After accidentally reading an account of Álvaro's trial while on a luxurious steamboat, Lina rushes back to Medellín. At court, and putting her honor at risk, she reveals their aborted elopement plans and restores Álvaro's honor with an eloquent defense. Conveniently, at that precise moment the killers are captured and brought into the courthouse with Lina's jewels.[46] Even though Álvaro regains his honor, Lina's father still disapproves of him. In an unexpected twist, Lina marries an Englishman (Harold Maynham) whom she meets at a country club costume party. By the end of the film, the spectators realize that the marriage was part of a second elopement plan, this time without Lina losing her virtue in the face of Medellín society. By then, Álvaro has already squandered his fortune, but fortunately he finds gold deposits in the bucolic land, away from the city, where he and Lina will spend the rest of their lives.

The plot betrays Medellín society's contradictory understanding of morals and social status. Don Bernardo's reservations point to Medellín society's (idealized) work ethic. Early in the film, Álvaro asks Don Bernardo for his daughter's hand, to which he replies, "For your position and incomparable family, of course. But I will only give my daughter's hand to a man who knows how to live from the fruit of his labor." His reply conveys the sense that work, rather than lineage, reproduces Medellín's highest social circles. And yet Don Bernardo plays the role of uncontested patriarch, object of admiration and fealty, throughout the film (interestingly, the producer Gonzalo Mejía plays the part himself). At the same time, *Bajo el cielo* ultimately condones Álvaro's prodigal behavior by granting him, with a lucky strike, a fortune that he can claim as his own. The serendipitous gold deposits he finds metonymically connect Álvaro with regionalism and Antioquia identity discourses (in the nineteenth century, gold mining galvanized trailblazers into colonizing the region). Hinting at Antioquia's origins, the film endorses a pioneer pedigree of sorts that bails out its improvident members. Furthermore, and in a similar vein, the film shows a fraught celebration of women's agency that betrays the double standards of la moral regarding gender and class, a point I return to later.

Bajo el cielo's presentational imperative is clear. As film scholar Juana Suárez has also noted, love in *Bajo el cielo* is contaminated by the flow of capital and commercial exchange.[47] For Suárez, the film proposes an urban/rural divide that reproduces the opposition between civilization and barbarism (indeed, an important trope in Latin American narratives and film, particularly in the Southern Cone). Her reading, however, fails to address the complexities of commercial and industrial exchange depicted in the film. Through Lina and Álvaro's story, *Bajo el cielo* documents the urban *and* rural industrial progress of the Aberrá Valley (with Medellín as its economic and industrial powerhouse). Even if some rural sequences resort to bucolic themes, the city and its rural periphery are inextricably connected. Stunning arrests of narrative flow best portray these connections. For instance, at her father's hacienda, Lina's story stops for a sip of coffee. A close-up on Lina, taking pleasure in the drink, brings the narrative to a halt and through iris in/outs presents the entire coffee production process. Importantly, editing connects traditional and industrial aspects of the process: from manually sowing seeds, to drying coffee beans, to unloading coffee sacks from gasoline-powered trucks in a city warehouse. The sequence comes full circle at the hacienda, when Lina puts down her coffee cup in close-up and the story resumes. The presentational imperative is entirely motivated and yet interrupts narration in favor of exhibiting rural-cum-urban industrialism. By regulating what can be seen and told throughout the sequence, the film pictures the capitalist production that supports the progressive yet conservative ways of Antioquia society. In other sequences, Lina's stay at the hacienda exhibits, and exalts, paternalistic practices. Her father acts as the paterfamilias both at home and at the plantation. Throughout the film, Don Bernardo enforces colonial fealty across an extended familial structure in both urban and rural settings, revealing extra-economic control over the workforce. Lina also participates in such conservative social structures: at the coffee plantation and on cattle pastures, workers bow and pay homage to her—as if she were highborn.

With *Bajo el cielo*, Medellín had recourse to moving image technology and melodrama to affirm the city's economic and cultural superiority on regional and national levels. Gonzalo Mejía himself published an article that described the film's aspirations: "Of deep moral and social background, including details of our customs, racial types, landscapes of our fields and, especially, the culture of Antioquia feminism [*la cultura del feminismo antioqueño*] [this] film, which will make us known elsewhere, will parade our most beautiful buildings, streets, parks, as well as the main architectural oeuvres we possess. All of this will contribute to the prestige of Medellín."[48]

Mejía's claim to feminism demands special attention. By the mid-1920s, Colombian periodicals targeted at female readers were engaged in lively discussions about feminism. Particularly in the Antioquia region, press materials suggest that feminism championed the liberation of women through two avenues: joining the workforce while at the same time fulfilling their roles as mothers. A 1926 article eloquently describes this interpretation of feminism in terms of female economic independence at the service of the family household: "To practice feminism is not necessary to fight off motherhood[; it is] to help the husband a little bit in the fight for life and, further, base one's pride and spend one's energy in possessing something more useful than facial beauty."[49] The article also stresses women's unique responsibility to "create honest citizens" out of their children. This notion is crucial to understanding female agency in the film.

Through Lina and Álvaro's love story, the film aims at displaying the allegedly liberal ways of Medellín society, particularly regarding female agency. However, the survival of colonial practices and mores complicates Mejía's progressive claim of Antioquia feminist culture. *Bajo el cielo* champions female agency but does so in the service of a conservative agenda. Struck by the beggar's tale, Lina confesses her aborted elopement plans to her father. Consequently, Don Bernardo takes her to the coffee hacienda and on a luxurious steamboat voyage, in the meantime preventing her from reading the newspaper, whose headlines sensationally follow Álvaro's murder case. In other words, Don Bernardo isolates his daughter from the rest of the world while providing spectators with views of rural progress.

Limiting the female lead's mobility and awareness of current events, *Bajo el cielo* puts into practice Mejía's feminist claim through other means. Lina's liveliness, competence, and moral fortitude closely align her with serial-queen melodrama heroines.[50] She presents, like the serial queens, "culturally positive behavioral traits" that "destabiliz[e]" traditional ideologies of gender.[51] Destabilization may be too strong a term for a film that supports the societal status quo. But it must be noted that by having recourse to serial-queen melodrama traits, the film constructs a vision of local transformative processes while celebrating Medellín's conservative ways. Episodes such as rescuing her beau at the courthouse demonstrate Lina's moral fortitude. Other episodes also emulate the serial queens' impetus: diving into the waters in one scene, Lina prevents a fellow señorita (high-society lady) from drowning in a river, for instance; likewise, to quickly return to her beloved and save him, Lina flies in a hydroplane, showcasing thrilling views of the economically productive yet naturally beautiful Aberrá Valley. Harnessing thrills rather than pathos, *Bajo el cielo* builds a world that is both very traditional and very progressive. Instead of being a counterweight to capitalist growth, tradition in this film constitutes an essential condition for progress.

Recourse to serial-queen melodrama comes as no surprise in Colombian family melodramas, considering Colombian popular mass culture during the 1920s. Advertisements in magazines and other press materials show how American serials circulated—and were avidly consumed—early on, yet were tightly controlled by local impresarios who favored European fare.[52] Also, spectators enthusiastically consumed press material on serial queens such as Ruth Roland and Pearl White. Given the prevalence of serial queens in local silent film culture, we must not think that Antioquia producers had cultural or cinematic innovation in mind when recurring to female bouts and bounds. A promotional enterprise, after all, *Bajo el cielo* exploited what was in popular demand in Medellín: modernity, regionalism, serial queens, fashion, and popular fiction. Thus, the film unproblematically juxtaposes Christ-like figures and female impetus as a paean to the modern yet traditional Antioquia society. Álvaro and Lina's love story takes the spectator on a tour of rural landscapes and cityscapes that reflect the film's social and bodily terms, whereby everything is in circulation—horizontally; indeed, the film contemplates no such thing as upward social mobility. The beggar's brief appearance casts doubt on the film's purported female liberalism, however. It points to the uneven standards la moral imposed on its subjects, particularly when the film condemns the "amoral" beggar to an untimely death but ultimately spares the affluent señorita from opprobrium. Barely hinted at in Medellín's first feature-length film, the question of (a)moral discipline and justice for the downtrodden takes center stage in a subsequent Bogotá film, *Alma provinciana* (*Soul of the Province*, 1926).

DOUBLE STANDARDS AND LA MORAL

The movements between rural and urban, and the relations between progress and tradition, are also at the center of the only film the National Film Heritage Foundation has preserved in its entirety. Unlike *Bajo el cielo antioqueño*, *Alma provinciana* (dir. Félix J. Rodríguez, 1926) was not a promotional venture. It was the product of a late *modernista* of sorts, a young law student and poet who had traveled across the United States, where he eventually landed a series of side jobs in Hollywood.[53] Unlike the landed gentry and tycoons who intended to showcase their regions' material progress, Rodríguez's film eschews productive sites and instead zooms in on the lives of rural students in Bogotá and the everyday life of the pauper. Further, unlike in Acevedo's or Mejía's films, Rodríguez did not resort to explicit Catholic imagery in *Alma* to push his take on the social fabric. Nevertheless, la moral structures the film under a veneer of apparent social critique.

Film historians Rito Torres and Jorge Durán stress *Alma*'s commitment to realism, epitomized in the director's insistence on hiring non-professional actors.[54] The film explores the everyday lives of the poor, described in intertitles by the female lead as "victims of misery,"⁵⁵ a common trope in local sensationalist weekly novels. But unlike the urban *miseria* suffusing popular periodicals such as *Los misterios del crimen* (1924–1926), *Alma* tackles social concerns, both rural and urban. The film initially seems to demonstrate how class differences can be resolved through love. The ten-reel film tells the tale of two siblings, children of landed gentry, who are studying in Bogotá. Gerardo (Alí Bonel) leads a spendthrift's life until he meets and falls in love with Rosa (Maga Dalla), a demure factory worker. His sister María, in her turn, goes to the hacienda on vacation, where she falls in love with the foreman, Juan Antonio. Gerardo and María's father zealously objects to both unions and forbids his children to marry below their class. However, several twists and turns will reveal to Don Julián how genuine and virtuous his potential daughter-in-law and son-in-law are. The film ends with two weddings and a felicitous return to home: the rural hacienda.

The film symmetrically balances both plots. The first act focuses on María's "Life in the province," while the second recounts Gerardo's "Life and miracle" in Bogotá, title cards explain. Though the film's structure separates urban from rural space, the film also shows how rural mores operate in urban settings (problematically, to contemporary eyes). The film lingers on practices proper to both countryside and city in topical-like sequences, such as bullfighting honoring the family patriarch's birthday and the Student Carnival of 1925 in Bogotá. The two-part structure allowed Rodríguez to focus on folklore in the countryside and on material progress in the city: shots of Bolívar Square, Independence Park, and even Congress's nighttime illuminations converted these progressive sites into cinematic sights.

Despite the rural-urban divide, *Alma* exhibits, and to a certain degree condemns, conflicting rural practices *within* urban everyday life, especially in the second act.⁵⁶ The film particularly takes issue with gender relations in public space, whether at the factory or on the street. At a textile mill, *Alma* offers a counternarrative to *Bajo el cielo antioqueño*'s celebration of female agency. In a sequence of frontal medium and full shots, the factory owner's son tries to seduce Rosa. Ordering her to carry a crate of virgin wool, he lures her into the factory warehouse to secretly make his advances. Inflamed by Rosa's rejections, the man attempts to force himself on her, but Rosa fiercely defends her "honor," intertitles explain. At the peak of the struggle—a battle between vice and virtue—the man's father comes in and, in the nick of time, prevents the rape from taking place. However, he does not rebuke his son; he fires Rosa instead. Disregarding Rosa's supplications, his decision eventually buries Rosa and her sickly family deeper in urban miseria (see figure 12). Instead of celebrating Rosa's choice, the productive forces invoked in the film punish Rosa for exercising her agency.

Reminiscent of porteño cinedrama, the sequence casts aspersions on women's unequal entry into the workforce and questions the gendered moral codes at play in early twentieth-century work environments. But unlike cinedrama, this sequence portrays the reproduction of rural labor relations inflected by colonial vassalage in the modern city factory. According to Miguel Ángel Urrego, during the period "backward" means of sociability imposed in the city "extra-economic controls over the workforce and subjugate[d] the female body."[57] Peasant women who migrated to the cities saw certain "rights"—such as the droit du seigneur depicted in this sequence (the feudal right to have sexual intercourse with a vassal)—transferred to new figures of authority: the factory owner, the barrio shopkeeper, or the bourgeois paterfamilias. As the sequence described shows, in early twentieth-century Colombia the urban did not imply opposition to the rural. However, to label these practices as backward, à la Urrego, implies that they consisted of anachronistic phenomena, a deviation from a "normal" modernization process. On the contrary, the practices depicted in these films, in Rosa's sequence and even in Lina's heady sequences, suggest otherwise. They point to the fraught coexistence of modern and traditional practices as a distinctive trait of local modernities. Rosa's father further stresses the ambivalence of these practices. After Rosa loses her job at the factory, and despite having raised his daughter with a strong sense of virtue, he rebukes her for rejecting Alberto's advances, "We the poor have no right to be virtuous [honrados]," he says in intertitles. As David Wood has noted, the father's reproach highlights "the poor's obligation to prostitute their bodies, their labor, and their ideals."[58] But this is not to say that the film uncritically reproduces such practices.

At the time the film was being shown in theaters, a small number of publications were questioning la moral's double standards and critiquing some of its agents. Particularly satirical magazines such as *Sal y pimienta* (Salt and Pepper, 1926), published out of Bogotá, condemned the city's highest social circles, government officials, and other authority figures, issuing criticism through explicit cartoons. For instance, "In the hands of the vulture" depicts a manager making advances on a female employee. From his desk—and with the company safe and a picture of

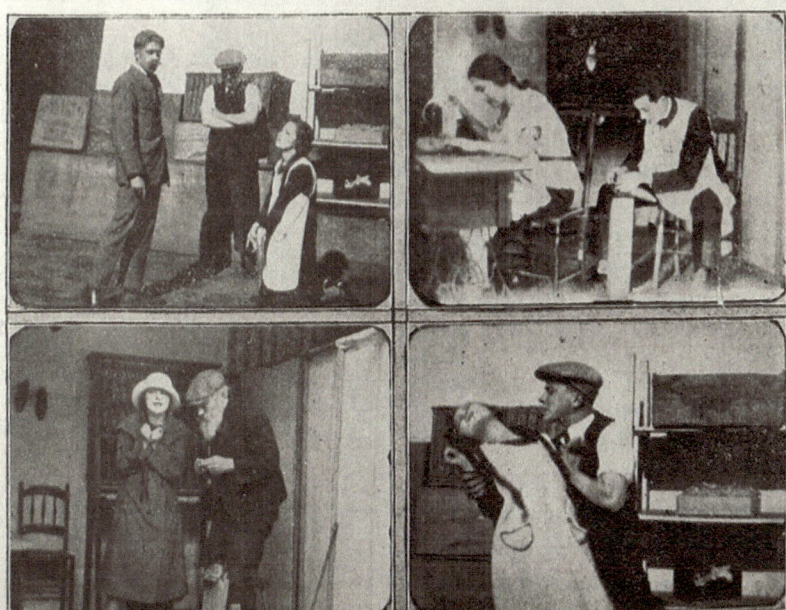

FIGURE 12. Scenes from *Alma provinciana* featuring Rosa's plight (bottom half). From *El Gráfico* (Bogotá), 20 February 1926. Courtesy of BNC.

the Sacred Heart of Jesus in the background—the manager reaches for the woman's hand. The woman, ashamed, reaches for her forehead with her free hand. Below the image, dialogue calls further attention to the woman's predicament. The manager says, "Either you warm up to me, or I will be forced to immediately fix your account" (see figure 13).[59] Aligning the manager with wealth and, with a religious icon, suggesting his disregard for Catholic values, the magazine overtly critiqued the double standards of la moral. *Sal y pimienta* specifically rebuked the figure of "the censor." As mentioned previously, during the Hegemonía Conservadora several censorship figures mushroomed and regulated most aspects of everyday life, but they did not limit themselves to spectacles and leisurely venues. With its zany humor, *Sal y pimienta* condemned the censor as a figure who participated in the practices he demonized, as suggested by a cover on which, amid a crowd in front of the Catedral Primada, Bogotá's main cathedral, a tall-hatted, coat-clad censor ogles a "modern" woman's legs (see figure 14). The magazine also criticized the censor as a figure who, hypocritically, reproduced immoral behavior by zealously defending la moral.

For instance, a noteworthy article lists the reach of censorship in the city, from the regulated height of women's skirts, to ogling in public spaces, to regulations on "skin" exposure in mannequins. Not without sarcasm, the author, "Don Fulano" (Mr. John Doe), mockingly highlights how the exertions of censorship impinged on the desires of the average passerby. On the policy of mannequin attire, he declares, "I don't think any man or woman has considered wasting a naughty thought on three or four centimeters of varnished wood.... [W]ithout a doubt, while staring [at those centimeters] one would run across a screw or hinge and there the whole fantasy would die."[60] After targeting the Sociedad de Damas Católicas (Society of Catholic Ladies)—inviting them to promote a similar policy for dressing up *calungo* dogs, a hairless breed—he lectures readers on the relativity of morals while rebuking the censor. "Regarding la moral, everything depends on your point of view. One of these censors is capable of stalking a young woman all day in order to prove the evil influence [*malévola sugestión*] of women's garters, and confirm she is indeed wearing them—even if she ties her socks with laces." Even if not as explicit, but certainly critical of the ambivalences of the time, *Alma provinciana* makes visible the double standards underpinning la moral.

In her study on female labor in textile mills, Farnsworth-Alvear stresses how then-current melodramatic narratives of sexual danger and rescue not only described workingwomen as abject figures but also

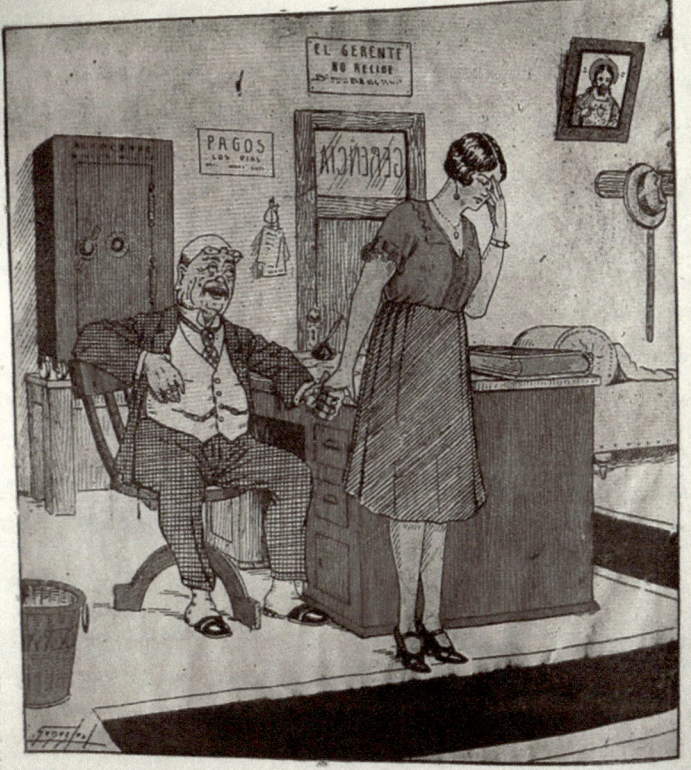

FIGURE 13. "In the hands of the vulture," *Sal y pimienta*, 22 March 1922. Courtesy of BNC.

FIGURE 14. A "censorship committee member" in a top hat ogles a woman's legs. From *Sal y pimienta*, 13 March 1926. Courtesy of BNC.

pushed certain factory owners to assume a "protective" role over their employees.[61] Not surprisingly, this top-down approach shaped la moral's disciplinary model—to the detriment of female workers. For instance, several textile mills constructed *patronatos*, boardinghouses for female employees in which workingwomen found food, board, and moral education. Managed by priests and affluent señoritas, patronatos took workingwomen to be ignorant and sexually vulnerable and therefore in need of protection and monitoring through lectures, spiritual retreats, and leisure activities—including watching films preapproved by the church on the workers' sole unsupervised day, Sunday.[62] Importantly, la moral's disciplinary model focused on sexual chastity to distinguish "good girls" from "bad girls," to the point that, for female workers, protecting their virginity equated to job security. The emphasis on moral comportment, or the "woman question" as defined at the time, did not demand the same level of rigor of male workers. One can only imagine the leniency toward the sons of factory owners la moral granted, which unlike other Colombian films of the period *Alma provinciana* made clear.

Apparently, genteel activities in patronatos—such as dancing with society señoritas to the pianola's beat, or watching proper films—were of little avail in keeping young female employees, usually rural immigrants, from taking to the streets in search of entertainment and socializing. *Alma* also registers the problematic relations between women and men when a fraught model of moral comportment ensues in public spaces. In the film Gerardo, the male lead, and Rosa the factory girl first meet on the street. In this encounter, Gerardo crassly approaches her. Prompted by her lower-class attire and emboldened by the late hour, Gerardo initially sees her as a sexual object unquestioningly available to him. Interestingly, her "virtuous" refusal, according to intertitles, is what captivates him and pushes Gerardo to yearn for a sentimental relationship with Rosa that will eventually result in their marriage. According to this scene, virtue constitutes a precondition to recognizing the other as equal, in the highly stratified and gendered world of the film. But the film does not necessarily question male characters when they seek to bend the rules of la moral, as in this case in which an affluent young man initially pursues a fleeting encounter with a woman below his class.

In this film, virtue—coded as demureness—carries Catholic *and* titillating connotations. Rosa, intertitles indicate, will strive to remain "immaculate," that is, a virgin free of sin, throughout the film, therefore standing out as an object of desire. Unlike *La tragedia del silencio* or *Bajo el cielo antioqueño*, *Alma provinciana* does not draw upon explicit

Catholic imagery to accentuate paroxysms of pain, but rather allocates a place for religion in its world in terms of everyday practices and morals. The zeal with which Rosa defends her virtue taps into the cult of feminine spiritual superiority known as *marianismo*. Political scientist Evelyn P. Stevens coined the term—not to be confused with the cult of the iconic maternal figure originally based on the Virgin Mary—to denote "a secular edifice of beliefs and practices related to the position of women in society" in Colombia in particular and Latin America in general.[63] Departing from the iconic figure, marianismo professed women's moral superiority and spiritual strength compared to men. Colombian silent films also traded in this practice. In *Alma provinciana*, Rosa's actions—guarding her body from sexual intercourse—signal her moral fortitude to other characters (and entice men to pursue her). Importantly, by means of example, Rosa reforms degenerate men, particularly Gerardo; she discourages him from indulging in urban debauchery and, in the end, makes him walk the line in holy wedlock. Thus, the cultural practice of marianismo constitutes the coin of virtue in the film.[64] (Such is also the case in *Bajo el cielo antioqueño*, in which Lina's moral superiority and valor recuperate her beau legally and morally; because of Lina, Álvaro ultimately mends his unproductive ways.) Marianismo distinguishes Rosa and Lina from other stock literary female figures, such as the "Angel in the House," which portrays female characters selflessly attending to the demands of the domestic circle and subordinate female labor enabling male activity.[65] Rosa and Lina devotedly fashion their own female identities and consequently affect their milieu by spreading moral fortitude. This attitude does not conflict with Christian deference; on the contrary, it denounces secular social problems while upholding Catholic morals.

As such, female deference determines female agency in these films. Marketing strategies in periodicals further point to the ways in which these films deployed a combination of demureness and dynamism to attract filmgoers. For instance, an advertisement for *Bajo el cielo antioqueño* promised that "the film will be the finest sprout where gentleness, softness, tears, sighs, the omnipotent weaknesses of the feminine soul [*las omnipotentes flaquezas del alma femenina*], will open up new pathways [*harán surgir caminos nuevos*], will reveal deep secrets."[66] The oxymoronic quality of marianismo—female omnipotent weakness—posits solutions to social issues by means of example. In this respect, and to return to Rosa's story, *Alma provinciana* operates as a film *à these*, a social problem film. Just like the didactic novel, the film indicates through one of its characters the source of social problems: class difference and miseria. In intertitles, Rosa explains: "[Social] inequality is not God's deed. It is the result of human disposition. Man always wants to stand out. And in order to do so, he needs the prostration of others." Rosa's moral fortitude stems from her impetus to undermine worldly sociability on behalf of an egalitarian divine order. Epitomizing marianismo, she ultimately defines herself and redefines her world when she is at her weakest.

The sequences above shed light on *Alma provinciana*'s visual regime. The film visualizes vertical interactions between rural and urban, pauper and rich, proper women and (menacingly) improper men. Both high and low sectors of society gain narrative saliency, and yet, in the final analysis, the film reproduces a petrified social order through what is visible and what is not.[67] As I have suggested with the three films analyzed in this chapter, Bogotá and Medellín film melodramas conjoin material change with societal conservatism. Despite Rosa's indictments, *Alma provinciana*'s visual regime ultimately favors social stratification, evident in the outcomes of Rosa and Juan Antonio, the hacienda foreman. In Rosa's case, neither respectability nor chastity guarantees her social elevation. After her virtue has been confirmed in the face of adversity, her social background remains an obstacle to wedlock. Only the late discovery of kinship between the families allows Gerardo to marry Rosa (Don Julián eventually finds out that Rosa's mother is a distant cousin). Consequently—and from the very beginning—Rosa was destined to be part of the upper class. In a similar vein, the film elevates foreman Juan Antonio through heightened personal qualities only to grant him, at the end, social ascension through other means. He is a self-taught man, an avid reader with a "romantic spirit," expository titles explain. However sensible and refined Juan Antonio may be, he can only marry María after he finds a fortune in gold deposits. As in *Bajo el cielo*, flows of capital shape love in *Alma provinciana*. In both films, spending power and kinship ultimately justify the lovers' union: Rosa's bloodline justifies vertical social mobility, while Juan Antonio's fortuitous discovery allows for the sole chance to actually climb the social ladder in the film. The double happy ending does not promote "utopian longings" that could potentially induce longing for social change, a pattern Michael Denning attributes to certain nineteenth-century American serial fictions.[68] Instead, the ending echoes then-current Latin American serial literature, which Beatriz Sarlo describes as "happiness literature": stories of social inequality that ultimately do not promote social change but offer palliatives for lower-class readers.[69]

La tragedia del silencio, *Bajo el cielo antioqueño*, and *Alma provinciana* propose a conservative yet material progressivist view of local modernities. This is not to say that traditionalist family melodramas eschewed the advent of new social actors in the public sphere. Tensions between old and new fitting to modern experiences not only brought rural practices to the urban and vice versa, they also conferred visibility on new figures in urban space. *Alma* does so with short, comic vignettes that interrupt narrative flow. The film draws upon an emergent typology that was developing in humor magazines such as *Sal y pimienta* (1926) and *Fantoches* (1926–1932).[70] In *Alma provinciana* these types include the student who migrates to the capital, the pension owner and the elusive renter, and the cop-and-housemaid street corner flirts, to name a few.

Perhaps the most interesting type is the *filipichín*, a "likeable Tenorio"[71] who seeks social ascent by courting high society ladies. Unlike Tirso de Molina's Don Juan Tenorio in *El burlador de Sevilla* (*The Trickster of Seville*, 1616), this Don Juan is destined not to trick but to be tricked. Product of an ever-changing urban milieu, the filipichín tries to access higher social circles by emulating their ways and attire, but he lacks the reading proficiency to successfully imitate the visual codes and manners of refined Bogotans. Even though he invests in signifiers of elegance (boots, gloves, cane, handkerchief), society women brand him a "fool," "insipid," "sticky and enamored."[72] *Alma* grants narrative salience to this urban type. In society, he passes as a regular friend of Gerardo, Julio. But in private, Julio reveals the essence of the filipichín: penniless, he cannot buy ostentatious clothes. Instead, he resorts to a complicated system of suspenders and string in order to feign elegance (see figure 15). In a brief sequence in which Julio prepares for a "date," intertitles explain, we see how, under his blazer, he does not wear a shirt or waistcoat. With his intricate system, only collar, cuffs, and other pieces of cloth compose his dandy demeanor. Entirely based on pretense, the filipichín is a direct product of Bogotá's early twentieth-century urban transformative processes. He foregrounds a visual regime centered primarily on surface impressions. Julio emulates that which is immediately perceivable through sight: the fashionable images circulating in illustrated magazines and in the cinema (incidentally the filipichín's favorite place for making his advances, popular magazines explain). Hence his name; in the 1920s, "filipichín" literally referred to a patterned wool cloth.[73] Lacking an obverse, the filipichín's ontological status resides in surface-level appearances. With his looks, he navigates a milieu of ever-changing semblance. But as illustrated magazines suggest, the elaborate

FIGURE 15. The filipichín gets ready for a date. Still from *Alma provinciana* (1926). Courtesy of FPFC.

codes of Bogotá society turn the filipichín into a fool while stressing the former's impermeability.

CONCLUSION

Recurrent topoi reveal how family melodrama is beholden to the ubiquitous influence of Catholic everyday practices and imagery in Bogotá and Medellín silent film. The three films discussed use narrative arcs of guilt, punishment, and atonement to foster a conservative yet materially progressivist visual regime. Centered on the patriarchal family and the institution of marriage, the three films uphold modern social stratification through traditional values and mores. Protagonists, champions of Catholic morals, demonstrate their virtue through self-sacrifice rather than personal gain (but this does not mean that as members of the upper echelons of society, they are not favored by fortune). In some instances, montage sequences harnessing pathos compare female and male leads to suffering Christian imagery. Nevertheless, neither pathos nor virtuous deeds ultimately determine an individual's social rise. On the contrary, access to the flow of capital and heredity give the *impression* of crossing social boundaries that are in fact impenetrable. Thus, in the three films love and Catholic morals regulate a social order in which gender roles and class concerns are constantly at issue but ultimately placated. Particularly referring to the oxymoronic, omnipotent weakness of female protagonists, *La tragedia del silencio*, *Bajo el cielo antioqueño*, and even *Alma provinciana* sustain economic and sociocultural conservative change.

At the same time, the three films show that la moral, even if pervasive, was a subject of debate during the late 1920s. Favoring rigidly stratified societies, yet making visible their fraught contradictions, these films invite us to continuously reread the ways in which melodrama made visible, and processed, the changes proper to Latin American modernities. More specifically, they push us to reconsider our own spectatorial positions and horizons of expectation when looking back at the beginnings of film melodrama across Latin America. As I have discussed, in both Bogotá and Medellín, family melodramas recorded and reproduced regulatory discourses and practices proper to conservative change. But they did so in a milieu in which—unlike dominant historical accounts of the Hegemonía Conservadora—the regulatory powers of la moral were, to a certain extent, under scrutiny. This begs the question: To what extent do our contemporary readings and curatorial practices imbue surviving film footage and cross-media narratives with an anachronistic sense of the melodramatic? If surviving films question dominant historical narratives, it may be possible that our "archive fever" sheds light on the historical discourses traversing surviving films.[74] Conversely, it is also true that archival research produces such discourses by creating novel constellations of film footage, press materials, and photographs. When it comes to analyzing surviving film footage, also at stake is reconsidering how we "restore" extant footage and how we repurpose it, how we give it new meanings as we make it available for more spectators through digitization, DVD collections, and streaming platforms. Looking at the social issues made visible in films produced around 1927 in Orizaba, a textile city equidistant from Mexico City and the port city of Veracruz, the next chapter tackles the question: What happens when we look at yesterday's melodrama today?

CHAPTER 4

Orizaba, Veracruz

Yesterday's Melodrama Today

Product of extensive research, we can now watch this film
owing to its rescue and reconstruction.
—*Cine en línea*, Filmoteca UNAM

"After working with these films for so long, you *feel* where the intertitles should go," asserts film preservationist Esperanza Vázquez in an interview.[1] Her answer—to my question about where she inserted missing intertitles in two restored silent films—resonates with the pillars of this study on silent film melodrama. It reveals how in her restorative work—or as she would say, "reconstructive" work—feelings and bodily sensations, as well as visibilities and invisibilities, shape the cinematic. Inadvertently, her answer also points to the role of the senses and sensation in fashioning melodramatic conventions and intelligibility. If melodrama, as Linda Williams formulates, "always offers the contrast between how things are and how they could be, or should be,"[2] Vázquez's work, rather than a restoration, constitutes a melodramatic rereading of extant film footage. The surviving footage of *El tren fantasma* and *El puño de hierro*—for years hidden by a zealous teenager who later became Mexico's most prominent film historian—lacked certain sequences and intertitles. To reconstruct the missing titles, Vázquez adapted excerpts from the films' synopses, which she found at the Archivo General de la Nación (AGNM). She incorporated her titles in the latest and, as the DVD booklet states, "definitive" version of both films (a problematic claim that also appears in expository titles in the versions currently available for streaming at the Filmoteca UNAM website). Borrowing from studies on the Mexican Revolution documentary film, I propose that rather than being restorations, Vázquez's reconstructions partake in the broader practice of "compilation films": films premised on repurposing found footage, "updating and interrogating" it.³ Unlike purportedly definitive versions, compilation films put into crisis the notion of author and play with the spectators' horizons of expectation. In the case of Mexican cinema, from the silent period to the present, compilation films have kept local and foreign silent cinema alive, constantly repurposing previous footage.⁴

As compilation films, *El tren* and *El puño* present a rather ambivalent case, for both have been exhibited and advertised as restorations of Gabriel García Moreno's original 1927 films, yet their multiple (re)editors have considered their work not in terms of restoration but in terms of reconstruction: vacillation between recuperating a former condition and acknowledging a present-day intervention. On the cusp between past and present, the current versions of both films invoke Walter Benjamin's dialectical images. For Benjamin, in dialectical images "what is past" (here, the surviving film footage) does not "cast its light on what is present, or what is present its light on what is past." Rather, the dialectical image "is that wherein what has been comes together in a flash with the now to form a constellation."⁵ In this chapter I examine the shapes these constellations take—and the effects they produce—when *El tren* and *El puño* offer fleeting images synthesizing present and past. I consider the ways in which preservationists project their (present-day) melodramatic horizons of expectation on surviving film footage. At the same time, I look at two dominant discourses in both films that I alluded to in the two previous chapters—fashion and biopolitics—to delve deeper into the revelations and concealments melodrama offers of 1920s Orizaba.⁶ Racking the focus between present and past, I touch on a current debate among Mexican film scholars: Is the latest restoration the "definitive version" of both films—as current copies available on DVD and through streaming claim—or is it an attempt to "modernize" the remnants of forever-lost films, as the prominent film historian Aurelio de los Reyes criticizes?⁷ As historic artifacts, films are always unstable, prone to scratches, fragmentation, decay, and other interventions throughout their existence. In this sense, no film discussed in this study can be considered a definitive version.⁸ Nevertheless, tapping into the debate allows me to examine how, despite the complications associated with the restored (reconstructed) nature of both films, they are still able to relate—that is, connect and narrate—the melodrama and modernity of 1920s Orizaba, while at the same time shedding light on the (archival) visibilities and invisibilities implied in reconstructing silent film melodrama today.

A TALE OF TWO MOVIES

El tren fantasma and *El puño de hierro* not only constitute the only two surviving Mexican feature-length films kept almost in their entirety but also epitomize a short-lived boom in local film production in the late 1920s in urban centers outside of Mexico City that did not survive the advent of American synchronized sound imports.[9] The story of both films available today, however, begins in the second half of the twentieth century. At fifteen years old, when he was working as an office boy in Mexico City Aurelio de los Reyes—arguably the father of film studies in Mexico—discovered the negatives of both *El tren* and *El puño* at the hardware store Casa William Mayer. The story that de los Reyes and other scholars circulate revolves around the boy's sensibility to what would become his lifelong passion: recuperating the history of Mexican cinema. Most accounts converge on the same episode.[10] One day, as the young Aurelio was learning various tasks at the office, the man in charge of the mail—a man less inclined to film preservation—taught him how to make powerful glue for sealing paper envelopes. The man said, "'Look,'" de los Reyes reminisces, "'I'm going to show you how to make a good glue: you take these bits of film (the intertitles, which were in a different film can separated from the negatives) and you put them in a little container with acetone, so that they dissolve. You let it sit for a couple of days. Once dissolved, you get the glue.'"[11] Even at his young age, de los Reyes found the practice "monstrous," and he ignored the man's instructions. Instead, he hid the rest of the cans. Two years later, as the company grew and Aurelio was given more responsibility, he hid the cans in a safer location in a new wing of the building. The cans remained there until the office moved from its downtown location on Dolores Street to Iguarán Street in the Bondojito neighborhood. In a series of responses to potential risks to the film cans, de los Reyes hid them in increasingly secluded places at the office. By his early twenties, and after reading about the very titles he had seen written on the cans, he realized the historical importance of both films. In 1969, already a historian, he reached out to the company manager—the son of the founder, William Mayer, who had cofinanced both films—and requested that the films be donated to the newly founded Filmoteca of the National Autonomous University of Mexico. Mayer agreed, the film cans were sent to the Filmoteca UNAM, and the negatives were copied without properly registering the sequential numbers written on each can. Then the worst happened: a fire burned the original rolls to a crisp—the film footage that, in de los Reyes's view, constituted the masters of both films. The copies survived, but the correct order of the films was forever lost; from then on, a series of restoration and reediting projects took place that resulted in the current versions available on DVD and through streaming at the Filmoteca website.

This narrative by de los Reyes limns the fraught history of both films. If William Mayer's cans held separate types of film—sequences and intertitles—then they could not have contained the masters from which the original films were copied—that is, the films spectators saw in 1927. Paying close attention to the material history of both films, and having interviewed the editors and researchers who worked on the multiple versions, David M. J. Wood reached the conclusion that the Mayer cans contained not masters but "rushes," unedited footage developed during the production of both films.[12] Indeed, the extant material seems too fragmented to consist of masters. After the Filmoteca fire, the films' fragmented nature motivated four restoration attempts, or as the restorers have more precisely called their work, "reedition[s]," "testimonies of surviving footage,"[13] and even "editorial reconstructions."[14] De los Reyes considers Esperanza Vázquez's first of two restorations to be the "best" one, despite lacking intertitles. In his opinion, the second one, the one available today to the general public on DVD and through streaming, is "an attempt to make a 'modern,' 'agile' film" in opposition to the first restoration, which in his view "keeps some defective scenes" and thus "conveys the difficulties in integrating" the surviving footage.[15]

This chapter focuses on the second attempt: what Vázquez, in her own terms, describes as reconstructions, therefore acknowledging the intervention on extant footage that her project implies. Understood as an intervention, Vázquez's work situates itself on the cusp of reassembly and creation. It consists of both a reconstruction of a now lost—because fragmented—original and a new film, based on archival footage and other archival documents. The synthesis, nevertheless, sheds light on one factor operating in both the present and the past: how action-based melodrama structures *El tren* and *El puño*, and how, consequently, both films—harnessing melodramatic conventions premised on thrills, speed, and dynamism—register and make legible Orizaba's modernization processes.

A brief comment on the first restoration attempt is in order, however, to distinguish between the restoration processes. As noted, the first restoration of *El tren* lacked intertitles. Further, and importantly, in the first restoration of both *El tren* and *El puño* (2002), the agents of the reconstruction process are immediately evident. After describing the "restoration" process, which I discuss later, an expository title lists Esperanza Vázquez and her team.[16] The current version available on DVD omits such a title. Just as the shift from the realist to the naturalist novel in nineteenth-century fiction implies incrementally eliminating the narrator, so the shift from the first to the second restoration phases out the author. By omitting this key expository title, the current versions convey a stronger sense of originality, while masking the interventions and aesthetic choices Vázquez and her team made when reconstructing both films.

Nevertheless, when considering the process through which Vázquez produced the films available today, both reconstructions straightaway relate present and past. After discovering two "synopses" of both films at the AGNM, Vázquez compared the surviving footage stored at the Filmoteca UNAM to the archival documents, then composed new film scripts for both films, based on which the new versions were edited.[17] Three to four pages long, the original synopses consist of plot summaries that Gabriel García Moreno submitted to register his films as his intellectual property in 1927. Comparing the AGNM documents and extant footage, Vázquez realized that almost at the very end of *El tren*, one sequence and all of its intertitles were missing. *El puño*, on the contrary, was complete except for the initial intertitles.[18] Based on her own scripts, Vázquez reedited both films with film editor Manuel Rodríguez. Because of the missing film footage, *El tren*'s reconstruction—at first glance—constitutes a greater intervention on surviving footage. Even if *El puño*'s footage survived in its entirety, according to Vázquez, it also presents noteworthy variations in its current version compared to its synopsis. On both films, missing intertitles were replaced by new intertitles based on the AGNM synopses. Following the conventions of *El puño*, intertitles appear both in Spanish and English (bilingual titles point to García Moreno's ambition to distribute his films in the United States).[19] Not surprisingly, expository titles in *El tren* prevail over dialogue intertitles.[20] *El puño*, on the contrary, contains a more balanced distribution between original expository titles and original dialogue intertitles. It must be noted, nonetheless, that Vázquez added extra titles to the film to better guide the spectator. In both cases, titles appear in a strikingly small number compared to contemporary films studied in previous chapters.

El tren's lost sequence betrays an attempt to create an "agile" reconstruction, to recall de los Reyes's indictment. Vázquez and Rodríguez opted for reconstructing the missing sequence with still frames taken from surviving footage and production stills found at the AGNM. The sequence is properly introduced to separate it from the rest of the film.[21] However, after careful observation of the archival documents, one notes that an occulted intervention comes to light. Vázquez and Rodríguez cropped the AGNM stills to produce tighter frames on the actors. Some photos were even taken out of context. For instance, according to the synopsis, the bandits "kidnap" the female lead's "uncle," without adding much information on how this subplot connects to the main narrative. Here, Vázquez departed considerably from the original synopsis,[22] and used a production still of the bandits surrounding a man too young to be the female lead's uncle. In the grain of certain still frames, particularly a close-up on the villain, it appears that Vázquez and Rodríguez also enlarged the latter. Indeed, Vázquez revealed her aim to (re)construct a thrilling effect when she explained how she selected the still frames for this particular sequence. "At this point [of the process] you know the film as well as don Gabriel [García Moreno] did [laughs]. . . . I would say, 'oh I need a face like this, a face of angst, a face of expectancy,' and then I would request the still frame [from the Filmoteca UNAM]."[23] Echoing the opening comment of this chapter, Vázquez drew from her own horizon of expectations and her own understanding of how a late 1920s film could be, or should be—a film premised on affect, thrills, fast cutting, and tighter frames.

As mentioned, *El puño de hierro* seems to have survived in its entirety, according to Vázquez's observations. When it comes to editing, however, the current version offers one of the most compelling alterations of both reconstructions. Vázquez has stressed how she struggled trying to make sense of the film. She was further disconcerted when looking at the previous restoration, edited by Jaime Ponce and available in the Brazilian VHS series *Tesouros do Cinema Latino-Americano* (1998).[24] Ponce's version—which lacks the synopsis-based expository titles Vázquez added throughout the film—consists of a series of juxtaposed linear sequences. Overall, in Ponce's version the plot is not easy to follow, particularly regarding two sequences: one in which the villain tricks the female lead into a morphine den and another in which two young characters watch the villain taking the female lead somewhere (the den) and later try to find its secret entrance (see plot details later). According to Vázquez, Manuel Rodríguez "discovered" that both sequences—rather than being separate, linear sequences—were in fact one single sequence in parallel editing. In our interview, Vázquez did not linger on the basis for Rodríguez's discovery.[25] But Rodríguez's assumptions about film narrative shape the current version problematically, for they foreground the film's ambivalent status as a reconstructed yet "definitive" version.

Vázquez's and Rodríguez's aesthetic choices bring to mind the "controversy" over two versions of Edwin S. Porter's *Life of an American Fireman* (1902).[26] Lost until the 1940s, when two contradictory versions were discovered, Porter's film sparked a debate that challenged the "evolution" of early cinema. The first version was recovered at the Museum of Modern Art in New York. The second consisted of the paper print archived at the Library of Congress. The MoMA print used parallel editing and matching action in the fire rescue sequence—a technique Porter would not use in his following film, *The Great Train Robbery* (1903)—while the LoC paper print used linear, repetitive sequences to depict the action, first inside and then outside of the burning building. Evidence indicates that the LoC paper print is the original version.[27] However, the debate raised (patriarchal) questions about the pioneering "discovery" of parallel editing: Who was the actual "father" of parallel editing, Porter or Griffith?[28] Importantly, the debate led scholars to consider the intercut sequence in the MoMA version a deliberate, anachronistic attempt to "modernize" the film.[29] De los Reyes, as quoted previously, produced a similar indictment vis-à-vis Vázquez's reconstructions, questioning her work as a veiled—and therefore questionable—anachronism. Without stoking controversy, but rereading Vázquez's work in terms of a melodramatic "repurposing of found footage,"[30] the following sections delve deeper into the ways in which her films, even if reconstructed, record and make legible the modernization processes of 1920s Orizaba. Likewise, and in parallel, the following sections explore how both films reconstruct yesterday's melodrama today.

EL TREN FANTASMA: FAST-ACTION MELODRAMA

The best way to grasp the intended tenor of the original films—to understand if they, indeed, catered to audiences with an "agile" sense of the "modern"—is to look at advertisements and columns found in newspapers and illustrated periodicals, along with other paracinematic materials. These archival documents shed light on the visual regimes shaping filmic melodrama and everyday life, for example, showing that *El tren* exploited thrills and emotions to attract spectators. The lobby cards that Vázquez cropped for her reconstruction consist of still frames and copy advertising the film. Highlighting dramatic moments—such as the male lead saving an elderly stationmaster from a rushing locomotive or railroad bandits drinking and playing at a tavern—the cards read "Exciting Mexican Production" and "A plot of intense emotion, love, and intrigue," respectively.[31] Advertisements in newspapers echoed the thrilling nature of the film. Announcing the premier in the city of Veracruz, *El Dictamen* describes the plot as "rife with great emotions."[32] The following day, the copy varied somewhat, promoting the film as "the most grandiose national film to date, with a plot replete with sensationalism."[33] The film's emotional tenor even crossed the US-Mexico border. Contemporary advertisements for *El tren* in Angelino newspapers describe it as "a film filled with emotions."[34]

The film emulated the filmic conventions of American adventure serials,[35] at the same time that it closely resonated with contemporary news about train assaults committed by local *bandoleros* and train assaults connected to the Cristero war (1926–1929),[36] a vicious conflict between Catholic extremists and the secularist Mexican government. Newspapers registered these assaults in sensationalist rhetoric and illustrations. *El tren* tapped into such sensationalism, which closed the gap between reality and fiction in the broader mass culture of film and periodicals. Particularly between 1926 and 1927, the press paid close attention to crime on railway tracks and to a machinists' strike, which steadily picked up steam and eventually exploded close to the film's premiere in February 1927.[37]

The illustrations accompanying these accounts appropriated imagery proper to action melodrama serials. Locomotives crashing into each other and thieves clinging onto the sides of rushing train cars populated the press.[38] Using sensationalist prose, newspaper headlines capitalized on the thrilling effects of crime and accidents on the tracks.[39] Cartoons in newspapers also exploited the rush of railway crimes. The article titled "A Wretched Passerby Was Tied to the Tracks So That the Train Would Crush Him" epitomizes the overlap between sensational melodrama and current events (see figure 16). Near the town of Mazatlán, Sinaloa, four bandits robbed Enrique Galaviz and then tied him to the tracks "to quench their bloodthirstiness [*sanguinarismo*],"[40] the cartoon's accompanying article reads. Mr. Galaviz did not die that day, despite the heart-wrenching prose of the article. Instead, he was "piously

FIGURE 16. "A Wretched Passerby," *El Demócrata* (Mexico City), 24 April 1926. Courtesy of BLT.

picked up by the crew of the *Ferrocarril Pacífico-Sud* train." From the text, one gathers that the machinists had enough distance and time to see Mr. Galaviz tied to the tracks, stop the train, and save him from his predicament. Notwithstanding the happy yet anticlimactic ending of the article—an article that wholeheartedly invests in the reader's taste for tabloids—the cartoon plays on themes of voyeuristic pleasure and the thrill of criminality. In the foreground, the cartoon depicts the wretched passerby. Tied to the tracks, his horrified expression suggests he can hear the locomotive's inevitable approach. Between the man and the looming train in the background, two stereotypical bandits in the middle ground—booted, kerchief- and sombrero-wearing bad hombres—leer at the man in anticipation of the accident.[41]

Appealing to readers' taste for sensationalism, "A Wretched Passerby" locates readers in a position akin to the bandits' in the cartoon. The composition locates the reader slightly to the right of the tracks, immediately in front of the wretched man and aligned with the expectant bandits in the middle ground. Like the bandits, the reader awaits the puffing locomotive and the dire accident to come. The setting suggests that the event occurs in a rather unpopulated environment. But the criminals, the locomotive, and the overall melodramatic composition recall the modern milieu in which the situation takes place. As Rielle Navitski has thoroughly studied, this cartoon is part of a broader popular imaginary of criminality that "[recast] violence as a threatening yet thrilling sign of local modernity" in early twentieth-century Mexico.[42] Even if "A Wretched Passerby" or the other articles mentioned are published far from Mexico's larger urban centers, they participate in a sense of the present moment shaped by modern transportation technologies and infested with modernity's criminal by-products.

El tren fantasma partook in such imaginary. Briefly, *El tren* focuses on Adolfo Mariel (Carlos Villatoro), a railroad engineer who is sent to Orizaba to investigate "irregularities" taking place in the railway company's local office, as the intertitles explain. Spectators discover that Adolfo's investigation reveals that the company has been infiltrated by a criminal gang. Its leader, El Rubí, or the Ruby, leads a double life as Paco Mendoza, an Orizaban socialite (Manuel de los Ríos). Unbeknownst to Adolfo, he is engaging in a twofold competition with Mendoza, as he tries to dismantle the criminal gang and competes for the love of the stationmaster's daughter, Elena (Clara Ibáñez). The love triangle allows views of Orizaba's modernization, particularly in transportation technologies and, through the character of Elena, Orizaban fashion—an important theme I return to later. For production, the National Railroad operators cooperated with director García Moreno, playing different roles and operating the steam and electric engines in the film. Steam and electric engines play no small role in *El tren*. As de los Reyes notes, the symbol of the Mexican Revolution's mobility—the locomotive—from steampower to electricity shifts to a symbol of local modernization in the film.[43]

Harnessing the speed of steam and electric engines, García Moreno strove to produce a dynamic film. The fight sequence on a locomotive attests to the director's efforts. In a twisted attempt to impress Elena, Mendoza has his bandits kidnap the young woman so that he can later "rescue" her. Adolfo, a few meters away, sees the bandits abducting Elena and making their escape on a steam engine. He runs to intercept the locomotive and manages to climb onto the rail guards. Once Adolfo is on the engine, a fierce fight ensues. Depicted through an arrangement of full shots and medium shots, a bandit sneaks up behind Adolfo and tries to push him off the speeding train. Both Adolfo and the bandit throw punches and kick each other, but the bandit quickly gains the upper hand. He drops Adolfo to the engine floor and steps on his hand to throw him off. Exhibiting a masterful sense of focal length and choreography, dramatic tension reaches its peak in a sustained medium shot—free of tampering by Vázquez's editing. This shot is key. After the turbulent series of long shots and medium shots just described, interspersed with long shots of the Veracruzan landscape sweeping by as the train advances, the bandit overpowers Adolfo. He pummels the hero to the point of Adolfo's losing his footing. A quick cutaway shows another engine, puffing toward the spectator. The sequence then cuts back to Adolfo, who, in medium shot and barely conscious, clings to the side railings. In the nick of time—and in the same shot—he lifts himself up, saving himself from certain death (see figure 17).

The sequence plays on dynamism at multiple levels. The fight takes place on the archetype of modern transportation technologies—the train engine—while fast cutting further accentuates the action-packed sequence. When interviewed, Vázquez underlined how the sequence harnesses special effects, observing that in this sequence García Moreno filmed the action at differing speeds to heighten dramatic tension. This sequence presents the landscape passing by and the fight taking place at a slightly accelerated pace. However, without archival accounts describing the sequence or similar effects in the film, and lacking any records on the projection speed at which the film was actually run at local theaters, it is impossible to confirm if this effect was notably reproduced in screenings of the time or how it affected the spectators' experience. Nevertheless, fast-paced editing and the mechanical systems García Moreno developed to shoot railroad sequences attest to his intention to produce a dynamic, thrilling film.[44] Vázquez confirmed that, unlike the crosscut sequence in *El puño*, her team did not intervene in the parallel editing of this fight sequence. Overall, and particularly with

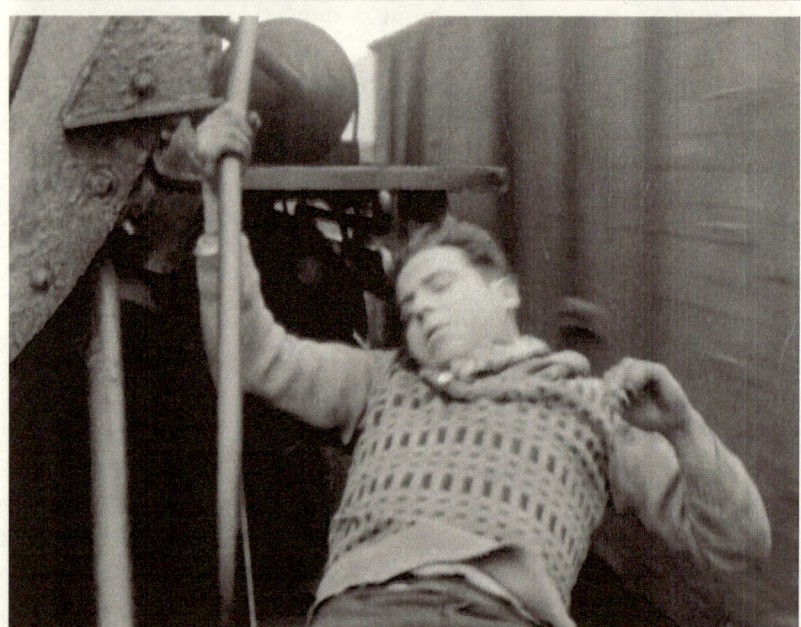

FIGURE 17. Adolfo gets up in the nick of time. Still from *El tren fantasma* (1926). Courtesy of Filmoteca UNAM.

the sustained—that is, uncut and not reconstructed—medium shot previously mentioned, the sequence demonstrates a clear aim to harness thrills and appeal to the heightened senses of spectators.

Noteworthy discrepancies between the surviving film footage and the synopsis of the film at the AGNM further complicate the nature of the current film available on DVD and through streaming. In the case of this particular film sequence, the synopsis reads that Adolfo falls from the engine when the bandit hits him in the head with the butt of his pistol. Extant footage shows a far more dramatic conclusion to the fight. The bandit hits Adolfo with the pistol but keeps pummeling him and even tries to choke him. Adolfo falls into a semiconscious state, hanging onto the engine's side railings, in medium shot. The bandit then climbs over Adolfo and tramples on his hand. An extreme close-up irises into the bandit's foot crushing Adolfo's fingers. In medium shot, Adolfo loses his grip, and the bandit pushes him off the engine. The discrepancy reveals that the synopsis is not a faithful record of the original film (or suggests that the surviving rushes do not necessarily match the purportedly lost original film, which might have followed the synopsis more closely). Further scrutiny of the synopsis's accuracy indicates that certain sequences are absent in the intellectual property document kept at the AGNM—more specifically, a sequence in which Carmela (Angelita Ibáñez), El Rubí's jealous girlfriend, is killed by one of the bandits, and El Rubí, dressed as Mendoza, kisses her before she dies. The divergences do not necessarily undermine the "agile" or "modernized" elements in the film, which de los Reyes attributes to Vázquez's reconstruction, but they do cast doubts on the current version's paratextual claim to be the "definitive" version of *El tren fantasma*.

Fast-paced action was not the only way *El tren* brokered in melodrama and modernity. Fashion, particularly female fashion, also attests to Orizaba's modernization in the film. Modern fashion satisfies "the desire for change and contrast," to quote Georg Simmel's 1904 essay.[45] Importantly for Simmel, fashion offers two forms of contrast: it differentiates individuals between social classes and distinguishes current fashion from previous and future fashions. Fashion therefore deals with a socially structuring sense of the present moment even as it is imbued with a diachronic sense of rupture with the past and the future. The diachronic dimension of fashion affects all individuals, objects, and mores—from leisurely practices to market demands, to film styles, to social conduct, to clothing. In what follows, I pay particular attention to the latter. Playing an important role in the film, fashionable clothes partook in the ways in which local visual culture recorded and shaped social and individual subject formations in Orizaba.[46] Embodied in the character of Elena—the stationmaster's daughter for whom Adolfo and Mendoza compete—fashion in *El tren* champions Orizaba's modern capacity to be "up to date;" an obsession among Latin American communities since the nineteenth century, borne from shifting dynamics between centers and peripheries.[47] Produced by affluent members of the Orizaba Rotary Club, *El tren* showcases Orizaba's economic and industrial achievements, as well as its social accomplishments.[48] If steam and electric engines epitomize the former in the film, Elena's style incarnates the latter.

With her bobbed hair—and short, straight, loose dresses—Elena embodies the pelona (i.e., without hair) in the film. Though her skimpy style is akin to the American flapper's, the figure of the pelona cannot be reduced to a Spanish-speaking version of the popular character. Despite the fact that the "North American" flapper—"à la bob," "feline," and "vampiric"[49]—appeared in the local press, the pelona was the product of (and responded to) local market and cultural conditions. As Joanne Hershfield argues, the proliferation of American and European commodities during the 1920s imbued the *chica moderna* (modern girl) with a sense of the foreign.[50] Nevertheless, this chica did not just emulate the models she saw in illustrated periodicals and magazines. The chica moderna consisted of a "hybrid creature."[51] She embodied an amalgam of nationalist discourses and private market interests, making her both and at once postrevolutionary and transnational. Hershfield's study focuses on the *flapperista*, the *china poblana*, and the *india*, arguably three dominant types in Mexican fashion. These types, however, do not perfectly fit the figure of the pelona, as they depict a modern woman "domesticated" by advertisements and other market forces.[52] Notwithstanding, they are a productive starting point to consider how changes in economic sectors produce gendered cultural transformations. The pelona is similar to these types. But, as a pelona, Elena is never seen in a domestic tableau or performing household chores; on the contrary, her locus is the public arena of Orizaba.

Simmel associated fashion with a lack of individual freedom, particularly for the middle class.[53] Simmel's assertion holds true if we consider his claim that fashion allows the individual to join the community by imitating as best as possible the community's dominant fashion, but it demands further scrutiny when we assess a third element of contrast in fashion: the organization of sexual difference. Instead of curtailing freedom, in the contested sites of urban modernity fashion served empowering functions. Local press accounts in 1920s Veracruz suggest that fashion conveyed a (threatening) degree of female agency, an emergent power that women, as civic subjects, were accruing over their bodies and selves. The pelona best portrayed this cultural transformation. Some articles celebrated the pelona's choice to shorten her hair in terms of a felicitously modern-cum-utilitarian choice. "Of course," an article reads, "hygiene, comfort, and the tyrannical goddess named Fashion, proclaim the triumph of women who cut their hair."[54] In the same vein, cartoons depicted the pelona's power over men in a new market of gendered social encounters. "Love of Today" by Cabral, whose cartoons depicted modern urban types in a few elegant strokes, portrays a Valentino-like suitor kneeling before a blasé pelona. The caption reads, "—What words should I say for you to love me?" "—Two million pesos!" the pelona replies.[55]

The growing visibility of fashionable women yielded imagery of female empowerment over emasculated men. The cover of a poetry collection titled *Nettles and Violets*—two metaphors for the women who inspired the poems therein—depicts a bent, tuxedoed man wearing a regal crown and rings on his ten fingers (see figure 18).[56] He also dons a very fine bridle—for his crowned queen to ride him. The queen, in a close-fitting negligee, has no need for a riding crop, however. Instead, she controls her "good husband," a caption reads, by waving in front of him an exquisite heart-shaped pendant. The image recalls "The Bourgeois King" (1888), the short story written by the *moderista* poet Ruben Darío. As in the story, here delicate riches surround the bourgeois king. But unlike Darío's king, who amasses all kinds of finery—and with his economic power can even subdue the refined spirit of the Poet—this king's very access to capital subjects him to his queen's whims. From the early period of accelerated Latin American modernization (1880s) to its end (late 1920s), the male capitalist's power was undermined by the growing presence of the feminine in the public arena. In the illustration, the queen's power emanates from at least two sources: her fashionable outlook, exerting economic pressure on the husband, and her "heart," an open-ended metaphor that by its very vagueness is all empowering. That this poetry collection was produced by the women's magazine *El Hogar* suggests that empowering images of women as well as the novel victimhood of men catered to a feminine demand for such imagery.[57]

FIGURE 18. Cover of *Nettles and Violets* (1920). Courtesy of AGNM.

Elena, the pelona of *El tren fantasma*, shares with the pelonas of illustrated magazines a distinctive insouciance vis-à-vis her suitors. Like the pelonas of the broader visual culture, she is the center of attention in her milieu. Also like her illustrated counterparts, she manifests "the deco body": short hair; long, thin limbs and torso; and a vigorous yet graceful physicality.[58] Recalling American serial queens, Elena runs, gets kidnapped onto trains, and jumps off of trains, all in the most luxurious fashion. But unlike the most-celebrated serial queen melodramas, *El tren* does not offer a "sustained fantasy of female power" premised on both feminine glamour and feminine heroism in a male environment.[59] On the contrary, the film revolves around Elena's repeatedly being in need of rescue, from real or staged danger. Not a Helen Holmes in *The Hazards of Helen* (1914–1927), but rather closer to a Pearl White in *The Perils of Pauline* (1914), Elena's agency is considerably curtailed in the film. In the coarse environments of the railroad or the refined gardens where Adolfo and Mendoza vie for her love, Elena serves as a charming yet imperiled object of admiration rather than an intrepid heroine.

Elena's modernizing function is best understood at the end of the film. In an unexpected turn of events, Adolfo finds himself in El Rubí's lair when Mendoza arrives in his elegant attire, therefore revealing his double identity. Holding Adolfo at gunpoint, Mendoza goes through his belongings and finds the documents on the "irregularities" at the train station that Adolfo had collected. Leaving Adolfo tied down and helpless and having taken the evidence, Mendoza heads to Elena's home and urges her to elope with him. Wavering, Elena gets on an electric engine with Mendoza. In the meantime, at the lair, Mendoza's jealous girlfriend—another bob-haired belle—strikes provocative poses to distract one of the bandits while her little brother frees Adolfo. Cut to the tracks, where Mendoza has lost control of the engine and now urges Elena to jump off the train. Mendoza leaps, unlike the hesitant Elena. Fortunately Adolfo reaches the engine on horseback and saves her from certain death, right before a spectacular explosion masterfully rendered with miniatures. Enter the missing sequence, in which a listless Mendoza—struck by the purported death of his beloved—loses leadership of the gang when in an act of benevolence he returns the belongings of an old man the gang had kidnapped. This man happens to be Elena's uncle, who was going to his niece's wedding. According to the synopsis, at this point Mendoza realizes that Elena did not die in the explosion. The other vengeful bandits, however, after hearing the news, head to the tracks to blow away the train carrying the "newlyweds." Surviving footage shows a bandit burying sticks of dynamite under the tracks and later, in parallel editing, shows Mendoza fighting the bandit and then running to pull the fuse as the train approaches. Mendoza saves the day but is run over in doing so. Once the train stops, Adolfo alights, recognizes his competitor, and heads back to his car. He withholds information from

Elena, lying blatantly, "A poor man, maybe he was out of his mind," he says in intertitles. The train resumes its course, while Elena wonders, looking at the fleeting tracks from the caboose, "perhaps his girlfriend awaits him."[60] The sequence ends with a kiss—of the neat beau and the beautiful Elena, in a cloche hat with a delicate appliqué of embroidered flowers.

This final sequence brings economic and gendered order to the film's world. Riding the symbol of technological modernity, the engineer and his stylish wife unify the modern forces that confer on the city of Orizaba economic and cultural legitimacy: technical development and up-to-date sophistication. Away from danger, Elena impersonates the "modern woman" born of consumer culture, whose "main concern is to look pretty, elegant, and chic."[61] Her iconic, passive role serves underlying economic purposes, however. Midway between Mexico City and Veracruz (Mexico City's port and gateway to world markets), Orizaba in the late 1920s finds itself with a waning economy, one that, akin to Mendoza, is in desperate need of recognition, while dealing with social unrest.[62] Not unlike the films discussed in the previous chapter, *El tren fantasma*, understood as an economic enterprise by local businessmen to showcase the city, taps into the attractive figure of Elena not to visualize gender trouble in a dominantly male environment but rather to enlist her fashionable figure to exhibit contrast and change vis-à-vis other productive urban centers.[63] Orizaban women—metonymically represented in Elena and her deco body—don the latest garments of international consumer culture and inhabit an outstandingly modernized milieu—epitomized in the electric engine.[64] Thus, by means of a passive pelona, *El tren* harnesses the active powers of fashion. In Mexico, liberating and active powers had been attributed to fashion since roughly the mid-nineteenth century. The journalist Francisco Zarco, for instance, celebrated fashion as a community-building economic engine, fed by foreign imports. "In our époque of civilization and progress," he exclaimed, "[fashion is] a high priestess of sorts whose grandiose mission consists of preserving and expanding the links that bind together the human species."[65] Without amassing the reach of Zarco's priestess, Elena passively binds together Orizaba's higher circles and—as a product of an expanded consumer culture—showcases a modern, burgeoning Orizaba through moving images. Her looks—unproblematically more important than her individuality—render her the standard-bearer of Orizaba's modernized, economic potential.

EL PUÑO DE HIERRO: DRUGS, THUGS, AND PUBLIC HEALTH

If *El tren fantasma* conjoins technical development and fashion to showcase a modern Orizaba, *El puño* tackles the by-products of modernization within a biopolitical framework—particularly looking at government-sponsored "social prophylaxis" campaigns.[66] Unlike *El tren*, which was shown in multiple cities and even exhibited in California, *El puño* never reached a broader audience outside Orizaba (most likely due to its disparaging take on national public health policies). Again, even though *El puño* kept most of its intertitles, Vázquez and her team substantially intervened in the film to grant the story more narrative legibility, through editing and by adding a second set of expository titles based on the film's synopsis found at the AGNM.[67] Because *El puño*'s narrative also revolves around the melodramatic trope of masked identities, earlier reconstructions were quite demanding of the spectator. Aurelio de los Reyes has further hypothesized that both films, *El puño* and *El tren*, were first conceived as serials, hence the repetitive and "uneven narrative" present in surviving footage.[68] Despite the active role *El puño* requires of the spectator, extant sequences visualize moralistic discourses that preach against the bodily and moral degeneration of drug users, attuned to the nationwide prophylactic or "sanitary campaigns"[69] organized by the Department of Public Health (DPH) and the Secretaries of Education and Agriculture during the 1920s. For de los Reyes, *El puño* thus "follows closely" the official discourse on drug abuse and hygiene campaigns of the time, supported—in his view—by the documentary footage the film uses of the Orizaba public hospital:[70] scenes of deformed children and adults, suggesting that drug abuse entails not only addiction but also effects on abusers' bodies and their progeny, who are burdened by bodily malformations.

Pace de los Reyes, *El puño* lends itself to a rereading of "prophylaxis" campaigns. Film historians other than de los Reyes have questioned the film's allegiance to then-current biopolitical discourses. Ricardo Pérez Monfortt points out the film's "ambivalence, from the medical point of view" between use and abuse of opiates. In a similar vein, Federico Dávalos sees the hospital sequence as "artificial and dishonest" when it shows maladies not necessarily associated with drug abuse.[71] In this section, paying attention to press accounts of local drug campaigns and the mistrust among local journalists of such campaigns, I argue that rather than aligning itself with official national discourses, *El puño de hierro* evinces a critical appropriation of biopolitical and disciplinary discourses of the period. It sheds light on local issues of drug abuse while indicting state-sponsored hygiene officials for promoting and capitalizing on opiates. Reframing official discourse and its uses, this section considers the critical capacity of melodrama when—playing with visibilities and invisibilities—it echoes the alarms the press has raised in local processes of modernization.

Mexico in the 1920s—during the presidencies of Álvaro Obregón and Plutarco Elías Calles—saw an extraordinary shift in national policy. Building on the nationalistic identity discourses in the aftermath of the Revolution, particularly during the second half of the decade, Mexico experienced the construction of a new state in its material infrastructure and in its institutional and legal apparatuses.[72] Cinema played no small role in this process.[73] The Secretaries of Education and Agriculture, as well as the DPH, produced a plethora of educational films.[74] These films were not only screened in public spaces; they backed public health conferences—on topics as diverse as tuberculosis, sexually transmitted diseases, alcoholism, and drug abuse—with documentary fact. Between 7 and 13 March 1927, for instance, the DPH launched the "Antinarcotic Week," a series of conferences in Mexico City. Aimed at "build[ing] a strong and respectable nation," the conferences promised "TO FIGHT AGAINST THE VICE OF HEROIC DRUGS [opiates]."[75] To do so, they were accompanied by "prophylaxis campaigns" in multiple institutions, including schools, barracks, prisons, "correctional educational establishments," and hospitals. The campaigns brought "distinguished members of the capital's Medical Body [physicians]" to such institutions, the article boasts, and "were illustrated by cinematographic films." As I return to later, *El puño* critically binds together the institutionalized figure of the physician and the cinematic.

To better understand how biopolitics operates in the film, Dávalos's claim about the "artificial and dishonest" tenor of *El puño* requires historical revision. As noted, Dávalos labels the film tendentious because of the ways it exploits documentary footage of patients in Orizaba's public hospital. Campaigns such as the Antinarcotic Week in Mexico City were not foreign to the Veracruzan city.[76] Similar campaigns took place in Orizaba and exhibited educational films as well.[77] Therefore, it is safe to say that *El puño* makes use of the discourses and film styles germane to these campaigns. Based on press accounts of Antinarcotic Week and local campaigns in the state of Veracruz, bodily malformations in the progeny of drug abusers seem to have been taken as a given at the time (or at least were axiomatic in official discourse). During the Antinarcotic Week, both physicians and films "la[id] bare the damage narcotics produce on the organism and the propagation of the species," press materials explain.[78] One year before an article about a national crackdown on irregular sales in pharmacies had denounced the abusive sale of morphine and "heroic drugs" as a "crime against the *patria* [fatherland] and humanity." It warned against the bodily "degeneration of the race," associating the spread of scrofula among children of drug abusers with their parents' addiction. Purportedly, drug abuse "marks with an infamous stigma the aching neck of the children of tomorrow."[79] It is therefore not surprising that *El puño* purveys a similarly pseudoscientific yet discursively positivistic claim, according to which drug addiction in parents leads to bodily degeneration in children. Therefore, the film's critical take on such discourses lies elsewhere—in its melodramatic backbone.

The "reconstructed" film consists of at least four intertwined plotlines revolving around morphine addiction and drug dealing.[80] The film begins when Carlos (Octavio Valencia), an Orizaban *fifí*, or boater-sporting socialite, out of curiosity injects himself with morphine at the den of two dealers, El Buitre and El Tieso (the Vulture and the Stiff One) (Ignacio Ojeda and Manuel de los Ríos, respectively). Even though the initial sequence blatantly shows in close-up Carlos's punctured arm—with the Vulture's hand pumping the syringe into Carlos's body—the film initially depicts drug abuse not without humor; the following shot, outdoors, shows Carlos courting a donkey he calls Laura. Then, when his girlfriend Laura (Hortensia Valencia) arrives, a point-of-view medium shot shows her multiplied in superimposed images, to which Carlos cries out, "Away, spirits!" Upset, his girlfriend asks him if her love is not enough for him to stop his "depravity" of drug abuse, the intertitles read. An abrupt cut swiftly changes the tenor of the film. At the city's main square, Carlos and Laura attend Dr. Anselmo Ortiz's (Manuel de los Ríos) comparative lecture on the capacities of morphine, "applied in hospitals by trained hands," and the dire effects of drug abuse. The sequence intercuts footage of the surgical ward, where morphine acts as an anesthetic, with the material mentioned previously: "deformities in the children of drug addicts," expository titles explain, and shots of the psychiatric ward populated by both adults and children. The public lecture sequence asserts a patently pedagogical stance on drug use and abuse, laying the groundwork for the unexpected reversal that turns the film from comical to didactic to melodramatically critical of then-current biopolitical discourses.[81]

El puño best dialogues with 1920s biopolitics and its correlative discourses at the morphine den. A hidden basement accessible only through a secret passage, the den contains multiple orientalist references. Reminiscent of an opium den, in it quilts and cushions comfort listless addicts on the floor. Two Persian rugs adorn the room; the second one, on the wall, depicts the prayer hall of a mosque with circular-framed Arabic inscriptions, evoking the inside of Hagia Sophia in Istanbul.[82] By the entrance, a life-size drawing of a Chinese man—wearing only a loincloth and holding an ax and knife, surrounded by ideogram-looking scribbles—reinforces the orientalist atmosphere.

Orientalism not only served an exoticizing function in the film; it also appropriated contemporary discourses in mass culture and public policy. These discourses, as in the film, superimposed Middle and Far Eastern tropes to warn against an infectious, exoticized Other within the Mexican social body. Periodicals across the nation fused foreign immigration with the opiate crisis. In Monterrey, *El Porvenir* blamed post–World War I immigrants, "a legion of foreign parasites," for introducing cocaine and morphine to the populace. Before the "threatening" arrival of the immigrants, locals—purportedly—had "barely heard" of such drugs.[83] Other newspapers highlighted the role of Chinese immigrants in the spread of opiate sales and, consequently, of addiction. *El Demócrata* of Mexico City covered how officials raided Chinese restaurants in search of drugs in Chihuahua.[84] Closer to Orizaba, *El Dictamen* of Veracruz covered a campaign to "banish [. . .] opium smoking dens" run by Chinese immigrants from the state of Veracruz.[85] If the orientalist threat was Chinese, other articles and illustrations suggest that Middle Eastern currents granted allure to consuming—and pushing—"artificial paradises." For instance, the short story "The Hashish Pipe" drew upon the dangers of and power fantasies associated with drugs. It focused on a hashish-smoking black "wizard" who intoxicates a beautiful woman and makes her dance for him. Then, threatened by her husband, the wizard intoxicates the man and orders him to kill his own wife (see figure 19).[86] Bringing together Chinese and Middle Eastern exoticism in the Palacio del Alambique—the "Still Palace," as the den is called in the film—*El puño de hierro*, as if by distillation, accentuates the seduction and frisson of drugs, luring characters and spectators alike into a beguiling and imperiling Orizaban underbelly.

El Buitre and El Tieso, the dealers who run the Still Palace, by their very names present themselves as foreign Others. With a self-explanatory name, "The Vulture" serves as a bird of prey, feeding off the carrion of

FIGURE 19. Orientalist depiction of drug use in *El Demócrata* (Mexico City), 6 May 1923. Courtesy of BLT.

addicts. "The Stiff One," on the contrary, impersonates an exotic Other within but in fact points to an even more threatening, because veiled, figure: the institutionalized Same. The parallel editing sequence that editor Manuel Rodríguez "discovered" (see previous discussion) highlights an important melodramatic trope in *El puño* that García Moreno had already employed in his previous film. Just as in *El tren fantasma*, in *El puño* members of society mask their identities to pursue criminal deeds. The film progressively involves Dr. Ortiz with the Vulture's illegal activities. In the parallel sequence, when the doctor takes Laura to the den ostensibly to look for Carlos (but in fact looking to take advantage of her), the doctor's double identity is revealed. During a brawl that ensues at the den, the doctor escapes through a secret trap door, and moments later The Stiff One comes in. With a limp and a stiff arm, El Tieso enters the fight, but his wooden prosthetics do not hamper his ability to fight, which leads Antonio—the leader of a gang of black-hooded bandits—to question the pusher's identity. Moments later, in an outdoor shot, the young boy who followed the doctor in the parallel sequence stabs El Tieso in his supposedly wooden leg. In shock from the pain, El Tieso loses control of the situation. Antonio rips off El Tieso's beard and reveals his true identity: he is Dr. Ortiz in disguise.

By fusing the physician with the dealer, two polar opposites in official discourses,[87] *El puño* tarnishes the virtuous veneer of government-sponsored social prophylactic campaigns. The film suggests that not an Other within, but the very government officials sent to educate the people, are the ones instigating and capitalizing on the opiate crisis. In this regard, *El puño* was not alone in suggesting mistrust vis-à-vis government officials and members of the medical community. On the contrary, it echoed growing suspicions expressed by the local press. Official discourse defended the authority of doctors handling addictive substances. An official bulletin, reminiscent of Dr. Ortiz's speech, contends that "in the hands of the doctor, cocaine can be a docile and submissive slave, always ready to breach the unbreachable barriers of pain." It also contrasted the virtuous deeds of the doctor with drug abuse, the "macabre film parading the victims of artificial paradises."[88] Local, unofficial press columns were wary, instead. They covered illegal heroine sales in pharmacies.[89] They raised the alarm about doctors prescribing too much morphine, which in their view opened a gateway to "heroic drug" addiction.[90] The fact that prophylaxis campaigns relied on "traveling doctors," hardly accountable after they moved on, further raised concerns.[91] The alarm about medical malpractice reached such levels of anxiety in Veracruz that it even allowed for bouts of dark humor; film advertisements appropriated medical tropes of impending danger to promote local screenings. With a layout and prose mimicking a scientific article, an ad recounted the uproar a "new pest" was producing among the community—a "microbe christened... leptos pira keaton," discovered by "Dr. Buster Keaton." Inverting the roles of medical practice, in the article Dr. Keaton invites patrons to the theater not to immunize them against the illness, but on the contrary "to make them feel the symptoms of the terrible disease [of] laugh-o-mania [*risalomanía*]."[92]

To return to *El puño*, the revelatory brawls at the den take place with an intoxicated Carlos in the background, the curious *fifí* at the beginning of the film. His narrative arc—until the end of the film apparently minor—gains crucial importance. After Dr. Ortiz has been exposed, only Carlos, the Vulture, and a woman remain in the den. The Vulture tries to force himself on the woman, while the lethargic Carlos tries to stop him. At that moment—the woman disappears in a dissolve—Carlos wakes up from a morphine "dream," Vázquez's intertitle explains. With only Carlos and the Vulture present, the scene suggests that the film consisted of the dream induced by the very first injection of the opening sequence. Carlos exits the Still Palace "and encounters almost all of the characters that took part in this dream, safe and sound," an original intertitle reads (I return later to the ambivalence this "almost all" suggests). The final sequence takes place at a mansion's porch. Carlos meets Laura, who is sitting on a set of stairs leading to the porch. The final title of the film, based on the synopsis, reads: "[Carlos] swears to Laura that he will fight this vile addiction [opiates]." The last shot consists of Carlos and Laura sitting pleasantly on the stairs, while a knife-wielding member of the black-hooded "Bat Gang"—and therefore part of the dream—threateningly approaches, unbeknownst to them. A final expository title, which does not specify if it is based on the synopsis or not, problematically concludes: "The film ends here. The remainder of the scene is lost. Probably Juanito, disguised as a hooded [bandit], was playing a prank on the couple."

Despite Vázquez's final title, the final shot casts doubt on the return to order in the film. With her final title, a title effacing her intervention, Vázquez imposes a conventional happy ending on the film. Akin to the "happiness literature" Beatriz Sarlo finds in Argentine weekly novels—for Sarlo, an "acritical" fulfilling of fantasies of social climbing[93]—Vázquez's title turns the wrongdoings of Dr. Ortiz into a mere pretext for thrilling action combined with harmless, urban spelunking. If *El puño* indeed consisted of a framed narrative, bracketed by a morphine dream as the synopsis suggests, the hooded assassin at the end brings the film closer to the fantastic genre.[94] In fact, several fantastic elements structure the film, such as the doppelgänger (the double) and the ambivalently accountable presence of "almost all" of the characters close to the film's end. The most important one, at the end of the film, produces an uncanny effect: the suggestion that the fantastic (the dream) may inhabit the realm of the real.[95]

The ending appropriates the hallmark of the fantastic: the unstable "movement between two similar, but not identical equilibria" that confers on the spectator an active role.[96] He or she must choose if the dream was indeed a dream or if the dream may, inexplicably, exist in reality. In the latter case, the ambivalence of the uncanny elicits a harrowing yet critical stance, for it opens up a dimension of uncertainty vis-à-vis the future, premised on an ambiguous present.[97] Thus, surviving footage offers an open-ended ambivalence inviting further interpretation. And importantly, this interpretation need not impose clarity on extant footage, for "clarity and certainty are qualities the fantastic is doing everything in its power to obfuscate."[98] Considering then-current press accounts in local newspapers that wearily followed the social prophylaxis campaigns in Veracruz, it is worth pondering the critical capacity of *El puño*. Without a definitive ending, but with an open-ended opportunity, *El puño* lends itself to reflection on then-current biopolitical and alterity discourses. More specifically, one can reflect on how—concealed through those discourses yet made visible in film—double agents playing the Other and the Same indeed partook in an opiate crisis of national proportions, a historical incident that, even if concealed in national official discourse, at the local level this film and the press brought to light.

CONCLUSION

It is worth noting that the synopsis of *El puño de hierro* makes no mention of Juanito—the boy-detective—playing a prank on the couple at the end. It makes no mention of the hooded bandit present in the final scene, either. These discrepancies bring back the uncertainties with which Esperanza Vázquez had to cope when making aesthetic choices in her reconstructions—for instance, how and where to add the aforementioned death scene of Mendoza's jealous girlfriend in *El tren*, another scene absent in the synopses. She opted to feel her way through the reconstruction, adding a melodramatic substratum to her practice; she felt how the film could be, or should be. As noted, to locate these unaccountable scenes in a meaningful way draws upon the horizons of expectations of editors, who project and reconstruct surviving footage based on their understanding of melodramatic conventions in 1920s narrative cinema: thrilling action, fast cutting, and tight frames. In *El tren*, Vázquez added dynamism to the reconstructed scene based on production stills and still frames. In *El puño*, she merged two separate sequences through parallel editing and added some explanatory titles.

These interventions do not imply that the current versions consist of "modernized" films that arbitrarily appropriate surviving footage, as de los Reyes suggests. They do cater to a contemporary audience, making surviving footage more legible based on (still-current) melodramatic conventions and by adding intertitles. Nevertheless, surviving footage—supported by archival documents—shows in its content stylistic and narrative choices premised on an intrinsic sense of fast-paced melodrama. Therefore the modern, dynamic elements in both films seem to have been present in the original films, albeit films that—based on Wood's rushes hypothesis—may have differed considerably from extant footage.

As compilation films, films that repurpose and interrogate surviving footage, *El tren* and *El puño* raise important questions about film preservation and appropriation. Vázquez's reconstructions play a vital role in preserving Mexico's moving image patrimony. In the case of *El tren*, reconstruction manipulates archival materials to make sense of surviving footage and, premised on melodrama conventions, rebuild as seamlessly as possible a lost film. In the case of *El puño*, however, reconstruction curtails the open-ended interpretative potential of the footage. As I provocatively suggested, in the latest reconstruction of *El puño* surviving footage recalls elements proper to the fantastic, when the ending of the film calls into question its own diegetic laws establishing real and dream worlds.[99] In so doing, it proposes an ambivalence that yields a fecund ambiguity, in turn demanding further interpretation and debate—ultimately demanding a methodological revolution and a rewriting of cinema history premised on "a cinema of uncertainty."[100] With its intrinsic play between worlds and temporalities, *El puño* highlights the play between present and past embedded in Vázquez's latest reconstructions. They cannot be reduced to "definitive versions," as advertised by the Filmoteca UNAM. On the contrary, as always-unstable film texts, they offer a broad platform for the analysis of film preservation in the present and of melodrama and modernity in the past, particularly regarding 1920s Orizaba.

Looking at fashion, drug abuse, and biopolitical discourses, I analyzed how both *El tren* and *El puño* visualize and conceal different processes of modernization. This play between visibilities and invisibilities betrays underlying, and even contrasting, agendas on both films. *El tren* harnesses action melodrama conventions and fashion to showcase Orizaba's economic and technical potential, in the guise of transportation technologies and the fashionable pelona. In this film, criminality serves as a thrilling backdrop to a return-to-order narrative. With train engines and fashionable characters, the film advertises the city and, at the same time, conceals the social unrest consuming several local industries—a visual regime that the happy ending confirms. *El puño*, on the contrary, proposes a more critical stance. It draws on late 1920s prophylaxis campaigns focused on drug abuse and on then-current biopolitical discourses to echo local press indictments of medical malpractice and unaccountability—despite Vázquez's forced, and consequently reductive, happy ending.

El puño—the original film, that is—was itself an exercise in repurposed footage. García Moreno incorporated scenes from *El buitre* (The Vulture, 1926), shot in Mexico City, to bolster his narrative of drug dealers and users. Drawing on the hypotheses of scholars quoted previously in this chapter, Navitski wonders whether, because "of its imperfect integration of repurposed and new footage or its potentially subversive approach to modernizing initiatives," the original *El puño* was "poorly received" and never exhibited in the capital city, "bringing García Moreno's career in Mexican cinema to a close"[101] and pushing him to migrate to Hollywood. The question demands further attention and, until a decisive archival document is unearthed, will remain unanswered. My analysis suggests the latter factor may have been influential. This chapter aimed at stressing the ways in which melodrama brokers with exposing and concealing modernization processes and experiences of modernity and how it can serve diverse underlying agendas. Likewise, raising the melodramatic analysis to the level of archival studies, this chapter looked at the (in)visibilities implied by curatorial work on silent melodrama. The ambivalence thus foregrounds an ethics proper to melodrama. As dialectical images, *El tren* and *El puño*—both lost originals and reconstructions—uphold the influence of what should be against what is. On the cusp between present and past, they exert a pressing claim on our canons of melodramatic conventions and of interpreting (past) narratives and events. As demonstrated by both films, the ethics of melodrama, with its visibilities and invisibilities, with its different loci of enunciation, is never objectively just but fulfills a sense-making enterprise, yesterday and today. Following García Moreno's northbound trajectory, the final chapter looks at two dimensions of melodrama yet to be covered in this study: transnational celebrity culture and certain Latin American melodramas' fraught relation with Hollywood and the United States more broadly.

CHAPTER 5

South to North

Latin American Modernities

Mary Pickford, Charles Chaplin, Douglas Fairbanks and
D. W. Griffith . . . are all the rage now throughout the South
American states.
—"Latin Americans Wideawake [sic]," *Moving Picture World*

Julián de Ajuria "realized the golden dream of *every* exhibitor and cinematographer from Spain to Spanish America," trade journals celebrated.[1] That dream was "to shoot in Hollywood a film that is ours, with a patrician [*castizo*] topic, and with a typical North American veneer that embellishes whatever it touches."[2] The super-production *Una nueva y gloriosa nación* (dir. Albert H. Kelly, 1928)—written and produced by the Spanish-born Buenos Aires impresario Julián de Ajuria—indeed epitomized the northbound fantasies of many silent-era Latin American filmmakers. For critics, the film held the promise of consolidation, bringing together film cultures across the continent. The enthusiasm of Hispanic critics who saw in the film the advent of a "new tendency" of Hispanic American coproductions was short lived, however.[3] *Charge of the Gauchos*, as it was titled in English, was a unique case in Argentine and Latin American silent-film production.[4] Shot at Fox Film Corporation studios yet fully produced by the "South American theatre magnate" Ajuria,[5] *Charge* is an epic romance set against the backdrop of the 1810 Mayo Revolution. As we shall see, this film would test the very limits of Hollywood film style. Despite the enthusiasm it first evoked, *Charge* signals the insurmountable impasses Hollywood star power could produce between and across melodramatic film cultures in the Americas—particularly when, through the maneuvers of melodrama, two contested visual regimes collide.

137

In contrast, an elusive film company in the city of Cali, Colombia, commissioned an Italian studio, probably in Milan, to produce a film aimed at crossing national boundaries and indicting US foreign policy. Framed through the anti-American sentiment revolving around the figure of Theodore Roosevelt, *Garras de Oro* (Talons of gold; dir. P. P. Jambrina, 1926) stoked regional sentiments of emotional legitimacy. This chapter, by delving into two cases revolving around star power and transnational celebrity culture in the latter years of the decade, explores the ways that different forms of border crossing question what I term "one-way" historical accounts of American dominance over Latin American film and film cultures: the persistent "silences" in film studies "imposed by a market and distribution system that privileges North-to-South consumption at the expense of South-to-North and South-to-South exchanges."[6] In contrast, the chapter traces "two-way," or rather, multivectored, instances of melodrama that motivated overlapping and at times contrasting readings of its narrative limits, instances that questioned who had access—and the right—to produce such narratives and, harnessing the power of transnational celebrities, even propelled "reality-effects" of geopolitical consequence across borders.[7] In the case of *Garras*, these effects had diplomatic and political import, as they reverberated among several Colombian cities, cities in the Hispanic Caribbean, and Washington, DC.

This final chapter reaches an endpoint—across the border—in the northbound route this book has traced so far, which critically harkens back to the Latin American film cultures previously discussed. With this double movement, the chapter aims to shed light on the complex networks Latin American film cultures established *across* the Americas, networks premised on turning Hollywood's global dominance to local advantage while, in these two cases, having influence in US film circuits and even on US foreign policy. The following case studies thus focus on transferable elements between the fixed places we have studied so far, in order to highlight the mobile spaces shaping film and film cultures from Buenos Aires to Los Angeles.[8] The previous chapters, looking at contested urban environments, traced how melodrama processed and made site-specific contexts—discursive, cultural, and political—visible in struggles for representation. What follows explores international connections between film cultures in the Americas and the representational possibilities and limitations melodrama makes possible in the dimensions of production, distribution, and exhibition (or the attempts to curtail the latter). In so doing, the chapter looks at understudied margins of continental market and distribution systems. Privileging

South-to-North and South-to-South exchanges, different forms of border crossing emerge.

PORTEÑO LOS ANGELES: THE LIMITS OF MELODRAMA

Ajuria's film produced mixed receptions at home and abroad. The travails of the libertador Manuel Belgrano (Francis X. Bushman) point to the limits of star power and to the stalemates melodramatic conventions faced across film cultures in the late 1920s. *Charge* was screened in several Latin American and European countries as well as in the United States, mostly in the Midwest.[9] For the purposes of this study, however, this section limits its focus to "two-way" vectors between film cultures in Argentina and the United States. To complement the analysis, the section draws on the Italian *reduzione*—the extant "reduction" of the film—housed at the Cineteca del Friuli.[10] Blurring the lines of the national in its very production conditions, *Charge* upended the expectations of both Argentine and American audiences. Shot with an entirely Angeleno cast and crew,[11] it received praise and disparagement in both countries. In Argentina, press materials and other documents suggest the film was well received, but Ajuria's all-American payroll cast doubts on the film's nationalistic sentiment in the service of spectacle. In the United States, reviews in local trade journals showed differing readings of the film but concurred in not being able to categorize it under a particular genre. Archival sources therefore hint at the protean nature of Ajuria's film and shed light on the limits of melodrama. Intended for both American and Argentine audiences, *Charge of the Gauchos* problematically deployed melodramatic conventions not entirely familiar to either Argentine or American spectators at the time. In so doing, the film limned "two-way" dynamics that complicate melodrama's transferability between film cultures.

One of the immigrant pioneers who first developed melodramatic storytelling in Argentina,[12] Ajuria tapped into the appeal of nationalism and the gaucho (then the repository of an *argentinidad* in the making) in his earliest productions.[13] By 1928, however, appealing to nationalism was not Ajuria's way to strategically position his film in local film markets while assimilating to his host country (see chapter 1). With *Charge*, Ajuria catered to both local and foreign markets under the guise of Argentine nationalism. In his memoirs, published eighteen years after the film's release, Ajuria confirms his transnational ambitions, claiming to have made the film, "in order to glorify the Argentine image [*el concepto argentino*] before all the nations of the Earth . . . and at the same time exhort the government [to support] national productions in our film theaters."[14] His most ambitious production was not merely a way to "win over" Argentine patrons by appropriating their values;[15] it was his vehicle to *hacer la América*—in Argentina and beyond.[16] Over nationalistic fervor, or a patriotic commitment to local markets, Ajuria saw in the cinema an aesthetically amalgamating—and monetarily expanding—medium. "All the arts, converging in the cinematograph[, are] held to a commercial calculation so that their revenue may feed its living forces, shaping the cinematograph and expanding it," he declared.[17] *Charge* was his most ambitious transnational investment and most cherished aesthetic enterprise (see figure 20).

The transnational circulation of moving images takes a nationalistic tone in Ajuria's film, complicating the persistent silences in Latin American film studies mentioned previously. In his memoirs, Ajuria stresses his dream of producing a film on "the historical events" of Argentina's independence as a form of "gratitude" toward his host country: "for its hospitality and the years of prosperity and happiness it has provided [him]."[18] Even so, his ambition was to produce an Argentine film of the magnitude of Hollywood films. He courted American producers, unsuccessfully and for several years, to take on the project in Hollywood. Tired of being rejected, he opted for producing the film himself.[19] Press materials indicate that Ajuria invested through his distribution company a capital of a million dollars,[20] an amount on a par with other contemporary Hollywood productions.[21] Ajuria's account—hinting at South-to-North and South-to-South cultural, economic, and affective exchanges—traces vectors in multiple directions, as he turned his Hollywood dream into cinematic reality. Not only did cinephilia incline Ajuria toward Hollywood cinema or its American producers; Ajuria himself was an instrument of Hollywood's expansion through the Southern Cone in the wake of the Great War.[22] In 1914, he became the largest shareholder of Sociedad General Cinematográfica (founded in 1912), which distributed Paramount and other American fare. Centered in Buenos Aires, by the 1920s the Sociedad had branches in the largest Argentine cities.[23] The reach of its distribution network is important in order to consider the expansion and hegemonic imposition of discrete urban film cultures within national borders that *Charge of the Gauchos* implies.

To return to Ajuria's purportedly nationalistic motivations: at first glance, the production conditions of *Charge* burst with patriotic enthusiasm, but a closer look reveals transnational finances shaping the film.

FIGURE 20. Ajuria (l) and Francis X. Bushman (r) on the set of *Una nueva y gloriosa nación*. From *El cinematógrafo como espejo del mundo*.

"Born from a feeling of generous sympathy," Ajuria declares, "I made this film in order to make the characters of Argentine History known across the globe."[24] He claims to have drawn upon the Argentine founding fathers as a source of inspiration in writing the script, particularly the words of General Bartolomé Mitre in defense of the immigrant; the latter, for Mitre, is a means to "save the race," "improve the social condition [*estado social*]," and "strengthen nationality."[25] Ajuria maintains that Mitre's words shaped his cinematic enterprise. His patriotic tenor nevertheless reveals economic and aesthetic interests in the service of expanding his relevance in cinematic circuits at home and abroad. Ajuria's sustained praise of the immigrant sheds light on his cast and crew selection as well as on the "two-way" market relations they imply. By 1926, the American Secretary of Commerce ranked Argentina the third buyer of Hollywood films worldwide.[26] The quality and star power of Hollywood films had triumphed over local and European productions in Buenos Aires.[27] In such a context, making a Hollywood-style film with a "patrician" topic guaranteed sales in local markets. Consequently, "importing" foreign talent mined local market demand but also allowed Ajuria to offer his film to a broader, non-Argentine audience. To formulate this dual address, Ajuria capitalized by casting renowned Hollywood stars and hiring a prominent crew. Francis X. Bushman—the athletic Messala of *Ben-Hur* (dir. Fred Niblo, 1925)—played the role of the historical Manuel Belgrano. Jacqueline Logan—Mary Magdalene in *The King of Kings* (dir. Cecil B. De Mille, 1927)—played the fictional character Monica Salazar, Belgrano's closest ally and object of affection in the film.[28] The casting of Bushman, based on his transnational star power, was further supported by a local survey in Buenos Aires periodicals in which Ajuria's company asked readers to choose the male lead.[29] Ajuria entrusted the photography to Nicholas Musuraca and Georges Benoît, the latter a French cinematographer who worked mostly in Hollywood but had shot the porteño film *Juan sin Ropa* (dir. José Quiroga, 1919) a decade before.[30]

Briefly, in the film Belgrano plots against the Spanish viceroy and commands an army of gauchos in the struggle for independence. He would not be able to achieve his goal without the help of his beloved Monica Salazar, daughter of a Spanish loyalist, who gathers intelligence for the rebels. Belgrano's convoluted plans progressively impress Salazar, thus shifting the film's focus from historical account to fictional romance. The spectacular charge of the gauchos (hence the film's title) displays hundreds of extras and awe-inspiring explosions,[31] but the plot truly revolves around the indoor schemes of—and secret relationship between—Belgrano and Salazar. After the Spaniards lose their hold on the populace halfway through the film, *Charge* zooms in on the pursuit of "the beautiful spy."[32] After a few close calls, Salazar is discovered by her loyalist suitor, who takes her to court and has her condemned to the gallows. Defying the laws of verisimilitude (evident to a porteño spectator), Belgrano receives in Salta news of her impending execution, gallops to Buenos Aires, and saves her in the nick of time.[33] The film ends with a reference to marriage: Belgrano and Salazar, in medium shot, yearningly look at each other in a palatial interior, followed by a jump cut to a church facade, with bells tolling. The plot confirms the opening expository title summarizing the film: "The most palpitating love episode with a background of the struggle for freedom in Argentina." Rather than foundational fiction, *Una nueva y gloriosa nación* comprises a spectacularly thrilling, romantic-epic melodrama—a mannerist mix that proved difficult to pitch.

Blurring the lines between history and fiction, *Charge* faces its first impasse in catering to audiences—with distinct reading proficiencies—at home and abroad. Vast distances are collapsed in the service of action, evident in Salazar's rescue. The lovers and other rebels meet on precipitous hills overseeing Buenos Aires, misrepresenting the "prairie," as intertitles read, characteristic of Argentina: the endless pampa. In addition to its geographical inaccuracies, as Andrea Cuarterolo highlights in a meticulous study, the film betrays many historical discrepancies. Establishing shots of Buenos Aires based on the work of Italian painter Giulio Ferrario (1767–1847)—"divorced from the geographical and architectonic reality of the River Plate"—as well as Napoleonic interiors and costume design—unlike the "austere [porteño] society" of the time—offer a "rather spectacular" and "international image of the country that, despite its loose historical footing" provides, for Cuarterolo, a "more effective" reception.[34] These discrepancies demand that spectators enter a fictional pact, premised more on melodramatic conventions—thrills, star-crossed lovers, and the race against time—than on historical or geographical accuracy. To be sure, these conventions proved to be both effective and ineffective, depending on their reception by respective film cultures in Argentina and the United States.

If the film, as Cuarterolo suggests, eschews *costumbrista* (nineteenth-century aesthetics focused on local customs and manners) elements in favor of a "Europeanizing transmutation"—or a "universal nationalism"[35] catering to nonnational audiences, a point she belabors—by foregrounding the gaucho, *Charge* addresses the discrete porteño film culture that Ajuria's exhibition network pushed across Argentina. Belgrano commands a gaucho army, in its turn led by the gaucho Juan Lopez (Paul Ellis), a supporting character who interpellates local audiences more strongly than the protagonist. Although some attempts were made to relate Bushman's personality to Belgrano's—the former "respectable and physically similar to our founding father," an article reads[36]—the libertador instead resonates with the film's nonnational mode of address. Film and press materials compare him to George Washington, the latter figuring as a universal standard-bearer for freedom.[37] Even though Lopez—like Salazar—is a fictional character, his recurring appearance in the film evokes his true function. Appearing at decisive peaks of dramatic tension that dovetail with key historical episodes (such as the birth of the Argentine flag), Lopez repudiates historical accuracy. Nevertheless, intertitles state that "in [Lopez] resides a memory that does not die."

Early twentieth-century nationalist discourse in Buenos Aires transformed the gaucho into the repository of argentinidad, even though this figure betrays the imposition of local identity politics on a national level. In the realm of film culture, the gaucho reproduces an equally imposing disposition. In the 1910s, the porteño intelligentsia imbued in the gaucho the symbolic charge to represent their cultural heritage and the physical feat of "conquering the desert" (the pampa). Leopoldo Lugones, for instance, describes in *El Payador* (1916) an epic gaucho whose poetry "invented a new language" that, in its turn, shaped "the soul of the race in formation" while "establish[ing] the foundation of the fatherland."[38] Narrative cinema quickly repurposed the gaucho's inherent poesy—and prowess as a horseman—fashioning one of the two dominant porteño film genres of the time: *ambiente campero* film.[39] In struggles between tradition and material progress,[40] campero films deploy criollo values of porteño supremacy over rural subordinates, while unproblematically showcasing gaucho skill.[41] Campero films were remarkably successful in local theaters.[42] Ten years after its release, the paradigmatic *Nobleza Gaucha* (Gaucho Nobility; dir. Ernesto Martínez de la Pera and Ernesto Gunche, 1915) was considered the porteño "film that has given the most profits." "Despite running for so many years, it makes publics respond with the same efficacy," a trade journal maintained.[43] However, even if pushed as national imagery, the gaucho in campero films consists of *argentino* imagery—that is, of the River Plate and the city of Buenos Aires—that eventually expanded to encompass what was later considered "a national self."[44] Consequently, even if framed as nationalist discourse, a "two-way" dialect undergirds *Charge of the Gauchos*. In the veneer of Hollywood film style, *Charge* stimulates a dialogue between Hollywood film culture and a discretely porteño (film) culture in expansion at the time.

The porteño elite immediately revered the film. In a personal missive to Ajuria, President Marcelo Torcuato de Alvear expresses his "highly satisfactory impression [of the film]" and celebrates *Charge*'s "efficient patriotic teachings."[45] The director of the Museum of National History, Antonio Dellepiane, conveyed to Ajuria the "patriotic emotion" the film produced. In his view, *Charge* exhibited "on screen the continental expansion of the Argentine Revolution, freer of peoples and founder of nations."[46] Likewise, Ricardo Rojas—author of the first encyclopedic *History of Argentine Literature* (1917–1922) and adamant detractor of melodramatic storytelling[47]—praised both director and film. "Sober in its novelistic intrigue and serious in its patriotic episodes," *Charge*, for Rojas, did not "corrupt the moral sensibility and aesthetics of the people," unlike narrative films in general. Rojas thus encouraged Ajuria to produce similar films and professed with *Charge* the origin of a new cinematic "species."[48]

Criollos such as Alvear, Dellepiane, and Rojas identified in the film a "noble cinematographic effort" in the service of their nationalist agenda, but the film was not without its critics. Rojas "abstain[ed him]self" from expressing his "qualms over certain details of historical [accuracy]" on the grounds of the film's "merit."[49] The press followed suit. *La Prensa* criticized the recurring presence of the gaucho Juan Lopez "in historical days of the Revolution"; yet, reproducing the narrative conventions of campero films, *La Prensa* extols Lopez as "truly convincing" when horse riding among his fellow gauchos.[50] Unlike the criollo elite, which was rather interested in harvesting the "patriotic education" *Charge* made possible,[51] the press condones historical inaccuracy in favor of melodramatic spectacle, as celebrating Lopez on his mount suggests. To elaborate on this point, the article recognizes that *Charge* "does not aspire to copy faithfully the facts, except situations clearly defined as historical. [Therefore] the romance of Belgrano and Monica [Salazar] befits a measured and respectful fantasy."[52]

In a similar vein, Ajuria deployed an unprecedented promotional campaign more inclined to showcasing cinematic spectacle than historical fidelity.[53] For the specific case of *Charge*, the Sociedad General Cinematográfica emulated the marketing strategies of Hollywood advertisers, "the masters of the North," in aggressively promoting the film.⁵⁴ Full-page and two-page color ads in the broadsheet-sized *Revista del Exhibidor*, which Ajuria partially owned, boast of the film's American cast and lob elevated numbers at the reader.⁵⁵ In conjunction with these ads, articles ascribe the success of the film across Latin America to its melodramatic conventions rather than to its nationalist tenor. After the film's successful run in Montevideo and Santiago de Chile, an article predicted "the romancesque [*romancesco*] theme of 'A New and Glorious Nation' will allow all of the spectators of the Earth to follow, with interest, the development of the film; the historical events that appear in it causing no difficulty in understanding the film's plot . . . in the case of our brotherly nations of the continent, [the film's appeal] demonstrates that the work don Julian Ajuria has done in Hollywood enjoys such popularity that theaters have seen full houses until now." Without fully eschewing the effects that a patrician topic could produce in privileged circles outside of Buenos Aires—thus elevating the film's cultural status at home and abroad—the article stresses that, in both Montevideo and Santiago, *Charge* "attracted a select audience, among which men of outstanding public and literary service stood out."⁵⁶ Ajuria's campaign aimed at foregrounding the "Hollywood veneer" of his film, accentuated by the patina an elite patronage could muster, while sidelining historical accuracy.

Despite Ajuria's efforts, the ambivalent reception of the film—on the cusp of historical (in)accuracy and melodramatic fiction—describes *Charge* as a fraught dialectic between porteño and Hollywood film cultures. Although the porteño press generally extolled the film's plot as well as its nationalist tenor and star power, its production conditions led critics to vilify *Charge*. Even before production began, critics were deeply skeptical of Ajuria's Hollywood production: "We already know that the Yankees don't fool around with the business of recreating period settings. And, above all, if its action should take place in Buenos Aires, capital of the Republic of Rio de Janeiro, you can imagine if there is room enough for the whims of a director's fantasy."⁵⁷ The film's production conditions also raised suspicions regarding Ajuria's nationalist commitment. Not without sarcasm, a column in *Cine-Mundial*—which had ample readership in Buenos Aires—praised the "attitude of Fox and United Artist" for hiring Latin and Spanish-speaking actors "in stark contrast to [the attitude of] the Hispano-American Ajuria Productions Company who dispenses with such actors in all work related to producing its Argentine film in Hollywood."⁵⁸ Drawing on the Hollywood

"Latin craze," *Cine-Mundial*'s critic undermined Ajuria's business acumen in casting American actors while depriving the production of its nationalistic veneer.

In a similar way, *Charge* suffered from comparably wavering reception in the United States. Even if the film draws on late 1920s Hollywood representations of Argentina, "a charming and exotic setting best suited for melodramas of romantic love and fierce independence,"[59] it comprises a mannerist mix that proved difficult to pitch: a spectacularly thrilling, romantic-epic melodrama. Evidently, "historical" could be added to the list. These descriptors accurately depict many episodes in surviving film footage. At the same time, they point to the problematically protean nature of Ajuria's "melodrama of the Argentine."[60] Distributed by F.B.O. across the United States,[61] *Charge* provoked a motley reception. Film trade journals suggest this was primarily due to the film's atypical narrative conventions, which proved unclassifiable to local exhibitors. Before and after the film's release, *Charge*'s nature was unclear in the United States. In 1927, the *Film Daily* described *Charge* as an "Argentine production, being filmed [in Hollywood] under the direction of Albert Kelley."[62] In 1929, the *Film Daily Yearbook* included the film under "1928 Feature Imports" to the United States.[63] Neither Angeleno nor porteña, *Charge* vacillated between film cultures and cinematic conventions. Brief synopses in trade journals—meant to guide local exhibitors through film programs—present the film inconsistently. Some read "romance" between the protagonists among a "band of freedom-loving people" (the gauchos).[64] Others highlight the epic tenor of "a lavish screen spectacle [of the] strenuous story of the Argentine."[65] Others advertise the film "for those who like their screen fare peppery," as if it were sprinkled here and there with thrilling spice.[66]

If synopses were inconsistent, most reviews seem to convey the frustration of exhibitors unable to fulfill their expectations of genre conventions. *Exhibitors Herald and Moving Picture World*—a regional trade journal for exhibitors in the Midwest, which by the end of the silent period became one of the most important papers in the film industry—best articulates local exhibitors' vexation. The journal's section "What the Picture Did for Me: Verdicts on Films in Language of the Exhibitor" records local exhibitors' comments on the boom or bust of specific films. Overall, the section maintains that *Charge* "failed to please" in the Midwest, further highlighting the genre trouble *Charge* faced at local theaters. R. C. Metzger, an exhibitor from Wagner, South Dakota, celebrates the film's cast but stresses that it "failed to register up to a regular Western."[67] Even though a few reviews endorsed the film—"Special cast. Had more good reports on this one than I have on any one picture," claims an exhibitor from Milan, Michigan[68]—most "verdicts" echo Metzger's judgment. The "Box Office Record"—an "authoritative compilation" of exhibitor's reports "published during the last six months in . . . 'What the Picture Did for Me'"—assembles a string of disappointments. In Greenville, Michigan, the film came across as "slow and tiresome until last reel, then some action." Arma, Kansas, followed suit: "Action drags all the way." Kansas City, Missouri, had entirely different expectations: "Only one or two laughs throughout the picture." Beyond the Midwest, in Moore Haven, Florida, *Charge* was not epic enough: "The miserably thin ranks of the army at the battle of Salta and the little handful of gauchos audaciously charging killed a brilliant idea. Only fair entertainment."[69] Exhibitors across the United States were unable to grasp *Charge*'s cinematic conventions. Checking the film against Hollywood genres—western, action, and even comedy—local exhibitors found themselves puzzled by *Una nueva y gloriosa nación*.

The film's reception in the United States even devolved into vitriol, progressively visibilizing the emergent nativist culture brewing in the North. Innocuous commentary—"They call it a special but it even failed to please the kids"—led to disparaging the cast—"Bushman too old for a lover"[70]—and to attacking the plot and Ajuria himself, in terms reminiscent of "denigrating films" disparaging Mexicans. Building on the ridicule of "old-timer" Bushman, a review in *Variety* concludes that the producer was to blame for the film's poor performance. After narrativizing Ajuria's "landing in Hollywood with a bankroll," the column asserts: "The producer wrote the story, which may . . . have been the cause for this mess [the film]. It gets to the screen in the most hokey form." Reminiscent of representational practices associated with denigrating films, the column continues: "The whole thing impresses like Mexican rookies lined up with West Point seniors."[71] The review shows blatant hostility toward the protean film—in this case, not a matter of film style but of the film's unique production conditions. Elaborating on the Salta battle scene—in which *chiripá*- and sombrero-wearing gauchos charge Spanish soldiers in Napoleonic uniform—the review manages to turn the technical feats of the film, and Ajuria's storytelling, into the stuff of disheveled Hispanics.

A small number of encouraging reviews further complicate the conditions of *Charge*'s reception as well as the dialectic between film cultures that this unique production embodies. In some American theaters, the film was well received. Both disparaging and favorable reports indicate that patrons saw different versions of the film. The *Variety* review quoted previously describes a running time of "about 65 minutes" at Loew's State Theatre in New York City.[72] Avoiding the inaccuracies applicable to projection speeds, *Exhibitors Herald* records screenings by number of reels. Reports on *Charge* range from six-, to seven-, to eight-reel screenings.[73] More reels, however, do not yield a more favorable reception, negating any assumption that the film's poor appeal was based on patrons' inability to follow a fragmented plot (or the exhibitor's disingenuous ability to squeeze film programs). A six-reeler in Weeks, Louisiana, was deemed "a very good action picture,"[74] while eight reels delivered a "very pleasing picture" in Curtis, Nebraska.[75] The film's general failure in US circuits therefore lies in factors other than length;[76] it rests in fraught melodramatic conventions and unfulfilled expectations of spectators proficient in melodramatic film style.

Not long ago rediscovered—as Andrea Cuarterolo combed the archives at the Cineteca del Friuli in Italy—surviving footage of the film runs for an hour and thirty-seven seconds, at twenty frames per second.[77] Also distributed by F.B.O. across Europe, the film, in Italian theaters, went by a verbatim translation of its English title (with a hint of nation building): *La carica dei gauchos: Episodio dell' independenza argentina*. At the beginning, an expository title echoes the film's unstandardized exhibition in the United States: "Produzione F.B.O. Riduzione italiana di Vittorio Malpasutti." The footage's self-prescribed status as an "Italian reduction," authored by a renowned writer,[78] leads Cuarterolo to conclude that at least two versions of the film were made. She posits that F.B.O. distributed in Argentina "a longer [version] directed at the Argentine public and another, abbreviated version, striped of more localist scenes and catering to foreign markets."[79] *Variety*'s running time and *La carica*'s matching duration support her proposal, but exhibitor reports in *Exhibitors Herald* suggest a more complex scenario. Reports indicate multiple theaters across the United States projected longer versions as well. Extant footage, compared to Ajuria's synopsis in his memoirs,[80] suggests these versions include—to varying degrees—the "localist" scenes meaningful to a porteño public but perhaps unintelligible to localized American audiences. Scenes evoking historical milestones in the Argentine struggle—such as Domingo French and Antonio Luis Beruti handing out ribbons in front of the Cabildo—may have been unable to "command" in American audiences what Benedict Anderson calls "profound emotional legitimacy."[81] Argentines or porteños may have felt an affective effect, being more given to the nationalist hegemony proper to their discrete "imagined community." While Americans described the film as an unclassifiable "drag," Argentines may have seen in the film a stylistically refined foundational melodrama, despite the film's geographic and historical license.

The warp and weave of *Charge*'s distribution recalls Miriam Hansen's dictum that, transnationally, Hollywood-style films meant different things to different people and publics.[82] It further suggests that by the end of the 1920s, the purported global dominance of Hollywood films still yielded problematic star vehicles that did not fully conform, and therefore did not equally appeal, to specific local film cultures.[83] The case of *Charge* goes one step further. On the margins of transnational film circuits, while being the product of unique transnational production conditions, *Charge* points to the miscommunications melodrama can also make possible. A pervasive, sensemaking "narrative medium,"[84] melodrama signals particular forms of "merging aesthetic practices," as Christine Gledhill suggests.[85] But these practices, I believe, these dynamic sets of narrative conventions and horizons of expectations, need not be universally intelligible or immediately transferable between differentiated melodramatic (film) cultures. Ajuria's film epitomizes just such an impasse.

Una nueva y gloriosa nación premiered in Buenos Aires on 10 March 1928, at the elite Cervantes Theater. An orchestra of fifty musicians and a choir of thirty voices performed a score specially composed to aggrandize the event.[86] In Argentina, "*Una nueva y gloriosa nación* was the most successful silent film of all," states film historian Jorge Finkielman,[87] despite certain voices of skepticism in the press. In the United States, on the contrary, *Charge of the Gauchos* appeared, for the most part, in small venues across the Midwest, where its mix of Hollywood-style and porteño nation building did not spell grandiosity but rather a grandiose misconception. When it comes to reception, Ajuria's film may have disproved that "the North American veneer embellishes whatever it touches," as Hispanic film critics initially extolled *Charge*'s promise of a "patrician" topic in Hollywood film style.[88] Thus, *Charge* sheds light on "two-way" vectors informing the expansion of cinematic melodrama. Unable to cater to differentiated reading proficiencies while amalgamating melodramatic conventions, *Charge* complicates our understanding of melodrama and the ways in which a purportedly "universal" narrative language could be, and in fact was, (mis)apprehended in specific film cultures across borders.

TALONS OF GOLD: ANTI-US SENTIMENT AT HOME AND ABROAD

In 1911, on a visit to the University of California, Berkeley, President Theodore Roosevelt delivered a speech whose impact rippled across the Americas. At the Greek Theatre, after celebrating achievements in the sciences and the arts as well as the westward course of "civilization," Roosevelt boasted before a roaring crowd, "I took the Isthmus [of Panama]," without congressional approval.[89] Had he not overstepped his authority, Roosevelt asserted, the link between the oceans—"the greatest feat" attempted by "civilized mankind"—would have taken decades to complete. True to his blasé personality, he concluded, "I left Congress not to debate the canal, but debate me." The American press highlighted the crowd's enthusiastic support.[90] Conversely, Latin American newspapers saw a recent wound being torn open—their "patriotic emotion," to recall Benedict Anderson, being threatened by an overweening nation. In Buenos Aires, periodicals stressed the need for the American Congress to investigate Roosevelt's claim[91] and recalled the sensationalist libel suit that had pitted Roosevelt against Joseph Pulitzer's *New York World* in 1904 and 1908[92]—the case that "arose out of a melodramatic series of events" connected with the purchase of the Panama Canal zone.[93] In Mexico City, some periodicals questioned the boast's popular appeal in Berkeley as a sign of rising jingoism north of the border,[94] while others raised the alarm against "the Colossus of the North" (that is, the United States), devourer of southern nations, confirmed by "Mr. Roosevelt brutally and unjustly depriving Colombia of its territory."[95] Not surprisingly, the boast hit home in Colombia, the country directly affected by the loss of the Isthmus. Questioning the democratic leadership of the United States, local periodicals appealed to the Latin American press to divulge "on both Continents [South and North America], how Panama was stolen by the cynical hunter of peoples[,] the insatiable Roosevelt."[96] Such "saturation coverage" echoed the emerging celebrity culture associated with stars. Lest we forget, Roosevelt was the first US president to embody the "interweaving" of political leadership and film stardom in the emerging "celebrity-centered media economy."[97] Like the (mis)deeds of other celebrities, Roosevelt's boast reverberated across Spanish America, thereby yielding "reality-effects" with geopolitical resonance.[98] Upending the poles of civilization and barbarism, the Latin American press transmuted Roosevelt from the leader of Progress to the brutish chieftain of Big Stick diplomacy.[99]

By the 1920s, the regional anti-US sentiment epitomized in feelings against Roosevelt raised the alarm among American consular officials, who feared "campaigns of rapprochement," deployed through the press, between Latin American nations and "elements in Colombia disaffected towards the United States."[100] In 1926, the sentiment produced a film, *Garras de Oro* (Talons of gold; dir. P. P. Jambrina), that would briefly disrupt the dominant direction of transnational film circuits: the predominantly southbound, "one-way" directionality of film markets and power relations in the Americas. The film proposes a problematic reversal in representational practices that would spark among American diplomats an international huddle to prevent it from being exhibited across nations, while hinting at melodrama's countercultural potential in shifting visual regimes. There are no records of the film being exhibited beyond Colombian borders, but its potentially disruptive influence reached the cities of the Hispanic Caribbean, the Colombian interior, and Washington, DC.[101]

The affective dimension of nationalism—which Benedict Anderson explores but scholars often overlook[102]—carries a melodramatic substratum. For Anderson, nations become "emotionally plausible and politically viable [through] narratives" that forge identities on the grounds of "emotional change" and the remembrance of such change.[103] In a similar vein, current scholarship on melodrama reads the mode as a rhetorical strategy that, premised on affective exchanges, legitimizes violent state power at home and abroad, "hail[ing] a particular type of citizen."[104] Even if illuminating, such Althusserian understandings of community building through affective narrative demand a finer approach. For, as this book proposes, melodrama's ideological flexibility as well as the (in)visibilities it produces have been mobilized for both liberal and illiberal ends. Revolving around Roosevelt's persona, and evident in the effects it produced among American diplomats, *Garras* reveals the ways that melodrama can push consent, advocate for dissent, or articulate more nuanced political positions at the service of different social actors. As a recent study on the film's anti-American sentiment suggests, and evoking this study's concern with melodramatic visibility, *Garras* deploys a "moral judgement regarding situations of historical disdain, injustice, and lack of recognition . . . that persist in the national memory or that take place in different environments of everyday life."[105] These positions, mobilized through melodramatic narratives, can affect modern imageries of social interaction in transnational contexts—in this case, US foreign policy in the region.

Based on real events but surrendering to melodramatic plotting, *Garras* recalls Roosevelt's libel suit against Pulitzer to compose an adventure film rife with anti-US sentiment. In the film James Moore, a fictional editor at the *New York World*, sends Paterson, a former "government detective," to Colombia to secure proof of Roosevelt's transnational misdeeds and therefore to protect the *World* from the libel suit. Paterson—who had a change of heart on US foreign policy thanks to his Colombian girlfriend—infiltrates the "Legation of Yankeeland" in Colombia with his accomplice Smith and eventually extracts the incriminating documents from Secretary Careless.[106] The film concludes with Moore being absolved, Paterson married (and with Colombian American children), and Roosevelt tarnished; "Thus fell the republican emperor of modern times," intertitles read.

In a clash between government secrecy and freedom of the press—embodied in the "detectives of *The World*" and the "spies of Yankeeland"—the film deploys, by turns indirectly and blatantly, its anti-American sentiment. When the *World*'s editorial breaks in New York City—in the film considered "the moral capital of Yankeeland," intertitles read—a group of tuxedoed American men at the "Battery Club" comment on the column: "Justice finally arrives. This imperialist regime cannot continue. This policy of absorption, moved by the *dollar*, will bring us one day, not so far away, all the hate and rancor of the peoples of the Earth."[107] Likewise, to convince Paterson, his girlfriend's father describes (in intertitles) how the Colombian flag "wavering on the Isthmus [was] ripped ... by the golden talon." He continues, "If you the Yankeelanders knew the history of Panama, I am certain you would join us [in our claim to sovereignty over the isthmus]." If such commentary sprinkled throughout surviving footage was insufficient, two attraction-like sequences bracketing the main narrative confirm the film's denunciation of US policy. Rather flagrantly, at the beginning of the film a monstrous Uncle Sam walks toward a map of the north of South America, looks at the spectator, and rips Panama off Colombian territory. A close-up on his hands—talons, in fact—shows a minuscule map of the isthmus, the word "Panama" written across it. In closing, a similar sequence with the same map serving as a backdrop shows Uncle Sam and Lady Justice, the latter holding on one of her scales the isthmus Uncle Sam had ripped at the beginning of the film. Uncle Sam grudgingly places three sacks of money on the opposite scale, one after the other. To his mounting exasperation, the scales refuse to budge in his favor. A final close-up on the sacks—which, juxtaposed, spell

FIGURE 21. Monstrous Uncle Sam and Lady Justice. Still from *Garras de oro* (1927). Courtesy of FPFC.

"$25.000.000"—derides the compensation the United States negotiated with Colombia for the loss of the Panama Isthmus in 1922 (see figure 21).[108]

To bolster its narration, *Garras* draws upon monstration to visualize cartographies of transnational political intervention: the gruesome Uncle Sam and Lady Justice.[109] Reminiscent of the cinema of attractions, framing and mise-en-scène in both sequences demand from spectators a "topographic reading"—that is, a scanning of the entire frame in search of meaningful signs: Uncle Sam, broken borders, (in)justice.[110]

The message: American compensation did not absolve the Colossus of the North from regional shame. For Thomas Elsaesser, monstration allows for linking narration, diegetic spaces, and enunciation.[111] In *Garras*, these two sequences define a clear locus of enunciation, which the film aligns with an anti-US sentiment that harkens to the late nineteenth century. With this turn-of-the-century connection, we see that monsters and monstration are not that far apart.

As early as the 1880s, Latin American intellectuals such as the continental luminary José Martí cautioned Latin American powerbrokers about North American imperial interests. Martí's essay "Nuestra América" (Our America), initially published in Mexico City in 1891, offers the first explicit metaphors depicting a monstrous United States: "the giant with seven league-boots," "the Colossus of the North."[112] His chronicles, published across the Americas, range from sincere awe to acute analyses of bitter (North) American realities, such as labor exploitation and racial discrimination. Foreshadowing continental anxieties in the decades to come, Martí's chronicles maintain that the US fixation with "manifest destiny" would not be satisfied until its possessions extend "to the Isthmus of Panama and its dictates, to the Straits of Magellan."[113]

Martí's writings also circulated in Colombia. His renowned chronicle "Coney Island" (first published in Bogotá in 1881) reports on American modernity, oscillating between earnest wonder and incisive critique, "Nothing in the history of mankind has ever equaled the marvelous prosperity of the United States. Time will tell ... whether the ties of sacrifice and common sorrow that bind some people together are stronger than those of common interests [or] whether this colossal nation carries in its entrails ferocious or tremendous elements."[114] For Martí, material progress in the United States exuded a "profound emotional legitimacy," to borrow again from Anderson, in the service of the North American nation.[115] Nevertheless, the *letrado* also perceives a degree of entrapment inherent to American prosperity, which hints at the monstrous potentiality of the United States:

> All is heavenly [at Coney Island]: the orchestras, the dances, the clamor, the rumble of the waves, the noise of men, the ringing of laughter, the air's caresses, the loud calls, the rapid trains, the stately carriages, until the time comes to return home. Then, as a monster emptying its entrails into the hungry gullet of another monster, the colossal, crushed, compact crowds rush to catch the trains, which, bursting under their weight, seem to pant in their ride through solitude, until they deliver their motley load onto gigantic ships.

These latter, livened by harps and violins, take the exhausted tourists to the piers of New York and distribute them in the thousand cars and along the thousand tracks that like veins of steel traverse the sleeping city.[116]

Martí's account of Coney Island is an uncanny one. Although it does not exactly demonize the United States, the chronicle nevertheless alludes to its monstrous palpitations. Familiar pleasures make readers shudder, as leisure deviously disguises the productive-yet-appalling social body lurking beyond New York Harbor. Like Martí, after collectively accepting the loss of Panama in 1904, Colombian letrados examined the national and international consequences as well as the import of economical liaisons with the Colossus of the North. At the time, Colombian writer José María Vargas Vila rebuked US foreign policy and fostered anti-imperialist feelings by stating that the United States was the "brutal and rough North that despises us."[117]

Again, monsters and monstration are not that far apart. From the Latin *monstrum*—monster or portent—one can easily extrapolate connections between discursive anxieties vis-à-vis America's expansive potential and *Garras*'s monstrous Uncle Sam. Dropping the connotation of warning or admonition (*monere*), *monstrare*—to show—is also part of the monster's etymological origins.[118] Like the cinema of attractions, a monster harnesses visibility in order to draw attention to itself and implies an "arrest in narrative and life flows."[119] Thus it attains its elusive ontological status, that of a wicked yet imaginary creature. In *Garras*, the monstrous Uncle Sam commands our attention with a documentary yet fictional spectacle, which Colombian political cartoonists had turned into a recurrent trope at the time.[120] Indeed, not unlike political cartoons, both sequences provoke a topographic reading of the frame and present a fragmented topography for the spectator to read, its torn elements punctuated by an affective response to the transnational affront. By harnessing a historical, transnational locus of enunciation, the film proposes, to loosely borrow from Assia Djebar, *une réalité monstre*: a monstrous reality, allegorically and indexically presented to the spectator.[121]

Uncle Sam therefore serves a key disruptive function. As a "cultural *dispositif* oriented towards productively *interrupting* dominant discourses," he turns the familiar into the uncanny, thus "connect[ing] the fields of ethics [and] politics."[122] By linking monstration to narration—that is, Uncle Sam and the Roosevelt-inspired plot—*Garras* triggered a series of reactions on the part of American diplomats across national borders. Archival documents indicate that the film's potential to stir up animosity was deemed threatening to American interests in the region.[123] Indeed, the reactions of American diplomats attest to melodrama's potential for dissent in transnational circuits. Initially discovered by historian Orlando Melo, a series of consular missives and telegrams housed at the National Archives at College Park, Maryland, trace the circulation of *Garras* and urge consular offices in Bogotá, Barranquilla (Colombia), Colón (Panama), and Panama City to prevent the film's screening, on the grounds that it was "derogatory to President Roosevelt."[124]

Echoing the film's plot, the drama behind the communiqués spells an interurban crisis involving Colombian and Panamanian cities in which government secrecy takes the lead role. Thus, the turmoil *Garras* produced was not limited to "two-way" exchanges; it traced dynamics in multiple directions across an expanded region defined by, but not limited to, national borders. Reference to the film in official correspondence evinces such dynamics. A telegram from Panama City reports that *Garras* was screened in the coastal city of Buenaventura (Colombia). Describing the film as "a sort of history of the Panama Canal [and] most objectionable against the United States and Panama," the American Legation in Panama "invokes the [State] Department's good offices in arranging informally for the suppression of [the] film"[125]—to which the Department of State replied first with a request for investigation,[126] later recommending cautionary measures: "Should the film be shown again, the Legation [in Panama] will be informed and may under certain circumstances take informal action against it."[127] Favoring secrecy, the telegram concludes, "For the present, the matter will not be brought to the attention of the Colombian Government by the Legation." For its part, and with a keen understanding of local anti-US sentiment, the American Legation in Bogotá was wary of suppressing the film. The head of the legation, Samuel H. Piles, recommended, "Better let matter rest for the present as action on our part, which would undoubtedly get publicity through unfriendly press, might under present circumstances create demand for film and unfavorable comment."[128] Despite Piles's warnings, through its consular agents the Department of State eventually managed to steer the Colombian secretary of government to telegraph "every Governor of every Department in the Republic to order the film suppressed with instructions that if the operators did not cease operating they were to be arrested and jailed."[129]

Samuel H. Piles quickly verified his prognosis. The local press described the order as an "unprecedented outrage" and a "proof of

Yankee imperialism."[130] The press further stoked animosity by underlining the double standards in Hollywood cinematic representation. To defend *Garras* while disparaging American (film) culture, an editorial in *El Tiempo*—the largest newspaper in the country—recalled the representational practices of denigrating films: "The low film, filled with wickedness, destined to ridicule not a certain class of individuals or certain governments but entire peoples, is a Yankee invention. In every city ... of the United States, films in which the Mexican is always the bandit and the South American the savage have been seen for years ... without a doubt the film shot in Cali [Colombia] will pale by comparison to the ones shot in the very city of Los Angeles."[131] Confirming Roosevelt's boast in the Colombian imagination—seventeen years since his remarks at UC Berkeley—the column concludes, "The film may be destroyed[,] but as long as a phrase such as '*I took Panama*' lives on, history will be more despicable than a film." The ban on the film was quickly revoked, and there is no record that copies of the film were deliberately destroyed. As Piles anticipated, however, the ban drew crowds to the theaters even in smaller cities: "The premier of *Garras de oro* [in the city of Ibagué is] awaited with great curiosity, especially because its exhibition was prohibited in certain cities due to the influences of the American Legation in Bogotá," a local column reads.[132]

The communiqués between Washington and its legations in the Caribbean and Bogotá trace the film's passage and point to its reception among local audiences. No records suggest a single operator was incarcerated for exhibiting the film. The correspondence registers, instead, screenings in the Colombian port cities of Buenaventura, Barranquilla, Puerto Berrío, and Honda—a path similar to the one Paterson follows on a steamboat to extract the documents incriminating Roosevelt up the Magdalena River to the Caribbean—and the Andean cities of Cali, Manizales, and Medellín.[133] Regarding the film's reception, records contradict each other. The Department of State claims the film "attracted little attention" in Buenaventura,[134] while the American Legation in Bogotá maintains that the film was shown twice in the coastal city: once in a theater before five hundred patrons, and a second time "'gratis' on the public square." Piles reports, "Some parts [of the film] evoked [among the public] a display of patriotic enthusiasm," and describes the film as "somewhat anti-American and in parts provocative."[135]

Piles's missives to the secretary of state bring us back to the formal qualities of *Garras* and hint at its elusive production conditions. In his letters, Piles moderates the posture of the film—as "somewhat" anti-American—but specifies in which parts it is "provocative." In a letter reporting exhibitions in Cartago (Colombia), Piles transcribes a telegram he received from José Vicente Navia, a Colombian who claims to be the sole owner of the rights to the film's "argument."[136] The telegram stresses how, through "the force of the legends" (intertitles), *Garras* "has for its only end the creation of an unpleasant atmosphere and keep[s] alive hatreds against the American nation."[137] In effect, other than the monstration sequences, only the intertitles present the film's anti-US sentiment. But the bulk of surviving footage—Paterson's adventures, his star-crossed love story with the Colombian girlfriend, and even an incomplete subplot about an antagonist female spy—does not necessarily reveal nationalistic animosity. It is the juxtaposition of titles and sequences that, through a sort of Kuleshov effect, produces an anti-American film.[138]

Puzzled by the discrepancies between sequences and titles and by the ethnicity of most of the actors, Colombian film historians hypothesize about the obscure origins of the film. Building on Hernando Martínez Pardo and other historians who consider the fixed shot the trademark of mid-1920s local filmmaking,[139] Juan G. Buenaventura first challenged the film's supposed Colombian origin.[140] Highlighting its unique continuity sequences compared to Colombian films of the period, he proposed that the bulk of extant footage consists of European footage spliced with local footage: the intertitles, the monstration sequences, and newsreels. Looking at outdoor shots, Suárez and Arbeláez conjectured that some sequences were shot in Europe and others in the city of Cali, Colombia.[141] Film director Luis Ospina, recalling a "vietato fumare" (no smoking) sign in footage of the steamboat, pointed to the Italian origins of the film. The revelatory footage did not survive digitization, however.[142] Ultimately, Arbeláez asserted that *Garras* was shot in Italy, based on press materials in his possession written by "friends" of writer and film critic Alfonso Martínez Velasco, the purported director of the film.[143] These documents, Arbeláez claims, affirm that *Garras* was shot in Milan.[144]

Indeed, the film is visually unique among Colombian productions of the period, in both editing and mise-en-scène. And most important, its obscure, transnational production conditions point to "two-way" exchanges at multiple levels. Echoing the production conditions of *Charge of the Gauchos*, *Garras*'s production suggests a negotiated appropriation of transnational film circuits—of production and consumption— in the service of a transnational ideological agenda. Surviving footage, particularly the intertitles, indicates that Cali Film commissioned *Garras* to be shot in Italy. Two sets of intertitles operate in the film: one set rife with inverted diacritics, proper to Italian spelling but nonexistent in Spanish, and a second set with exemplary spelling and copious prose.[145] Both sets contain "provocative" copy, to recall Piles's observations, and therefore both sets undermine Buenaventura's hypothesis that the film consists of repurposed foreign sequences and locally inserted footage— titles, tableau-like sequences, and newsreel footage—that would amount to a Colombian example of "compilation film," such as the films discussed in the previous chapter. On the contrary, the titles suggest that the film was imported to Colombia already containing misspelled Spanish intertitles, some of which very closely echo the film's plot recorded in Navia's telegram to Piles.[146] The second set as well as some short sequences may have been added in Colombia, however. These epitomize another example of the Kuleshov effect at work in the film, appealing to emotional legitimacy through editing. For instance, a tinted Colombian flag—being lowered and framed in an iris mask—cuts to newsreel footage of American battle cruisers and immediately afterward to an iris on the American flag on one of the ships. Through editing, the sequence turns the latter into an invading armada.[147] Despite Buenaventura's contentions, the allegorical monstration sequences do not partake in these examples of Colombian intervention on the Italian footage. Rather, they are of Italian execution; the woman who impersonates Lady Justice is the same actress who plays the role of Paterson's girlfriend, most likely an actress by the name of Lucia Zanussi.[148]

If Ajuria traveled to Hollywood to realize his super-production and capitalize on nationalism in the service of spectacle, Cali Film's shareholders contracted Italian filmmakers to harness production value in the support of nationalist vitriol. That Colombian impresarios resorted to the Italian film industry is of no surprise. In chapter 1, I trace the intersection of Colombian and Italian nationalisms and film cultures in Colombian exhibition practices in the 1910s.[149] From the earliest years of silent film exhibition in Colombia, the Italian-born Di Domenico brothers forged a "protectionist" distribution and exhibition circuit headquartered in Bogotá and favoring Italian and French films over American imports. At its peak, their distribution and exhibition empire extended across the north of South America, Central America, and the Minor Antilles. That Hollywood studios were unable to establish exchanges or subsidiaries in Colombian cities during the silent period attests to the Di Domenicos' dominance in local markets.[150] During the

1920s, the Di Domenicos and other local filmmakers first tapped into Italian films to model their own productions, and even hired Italian actors, directors, and cameramen to make their films. Such was the case for Colombia Film—the company from which Cali Film would spring—which "imported" Italian actors to produce "national films," as described in press accounts.[151] According to film historian Hernando Salcedo Silva, Colombia Film commissioned Martínez Velasco to travel to Italy and hire the troupe, supporting the hypothesis that Martínez Velasco established networks making it possible for Cali Film to commission *Garras* in Milan.[152] Notary documents confirm Cali Film's investment in hiring Italian personnel and importing Italian equipment for the purposes of filmmaking.[153]

Restored by the Colombian Film Heritage Foundation in partnership with the New York Museum of Modern Art film department, and complemented by a second restoration by the Goethe Institut in Mexico, *Garras de oro* remains shrouded in mystery. Until further archival documents are found, knowledge of the film's production and distribution networks will remain elusive. The film nevertheless is part of a series of "orphan" films that played a role in "recording, representing, constructing, and imagining the state," as the symposium where it was first exhibited for contemporary audiences proposes.[154] True to its orphan nature—"a motion picture abandoned by its owner or caretaker"[155]—*Garras* departs from a specific national rooting to propose, instead, a rhizomatic origin, shaped by modern transnational networks of markets and ideologies.[156] Extant footage reveals "two-way"—or better yet, multivectored—exchanges in film production, distribution, and consumption fitting for the late 1920s north of South America, all built upon a scathing construction of Theodore Roosevelt. Even if American films and serials were taking over exhibition circuits in the region, Colombian filmmakers—influenced by "protectionist" local circuits favoring European fare—sought to contest American cinematic dominance by harnessing other film industries. At the same time, particularly in the case of Cali Film, they audaciously spectacularized "patriotic enthusiasm," to recall Samuel H. Piles, as a gesture against the United States in order to produce a film that would stir nation-bound emotional legitimacy targeted at audiences beyond national borders.

These exchanges evince melodrama's affective power to upend market dynamics and visual regimes. As the documents housed at the National Archives indicate, American diplomats in Panama, Colombia, and Washington traced the film's circulation in multiple Colombian cities, particularly in the Caribbean, fearing its broader accessibility could hamper American interests in the region. The motivation for the film's production—an emotionally charged national affront of historical consequence—as well as the American countermeasures that ensued, attest to melodrama's ability to mobilize social actors under uneven social arrangements. Through struggles of recognition, visualized in narration and monstration sequences, *Garras* reveals a political stance against the power relations shaping both geopolitical hierarchies and asymmetrical forms of representation.

CONCLUSION

Evidenced in these case studies, "two-way" exchanges shaped late 1920s melodramatic film cultures across the Americas. Ajuria's Hollywood-patrician production and the elusive *Garras de oro* point to connections melodrama facilitated across transnational film circuits and (film) cultures. Each case evinces discrete ways of grappling with modernities' changes on transnational levels through the heuristic function proper to star personas (or the celebrity-like "media saturation" Roosevelt elicited). Thus, different forms of border crossing emerge, visibilizing the margins of continental market and distribution systems: South-to-North and South-to-South exchanges. They suggest rapport among film cultures directed toward—or against—the United States, rather than among or between Latin American film cultures. Certain films, such as *Charge of the Gauchos*, did circulate among or between Latin American nations. But the scant references to this and other films in periodicals during the period depict instead a triangular movement of discrete film cultures and commercial networks between Latin America and the United States, and between Latin America and Europe (particularly Italy, in the case of *Garras* and other Colombian films).[157]

During the period under study, not many Latin American films crossed between Latin American countries, let alone the urban film cultures studied in this book. Argentine and Mexican films were screened throughout Latin America in the 1930s through 1950s, influencing film cultures across the continent,[158] but to read a similar phenomenon from the limited references in periodicals during the 1910s and 1920s would be anachronistic.[159] The "two-way" exchanges this chapter explores show, instead, instances in which aesthetic, economic, and ideological factors concurrently shaped films and film cultures under disparate economic and geopolitical frameworks marked by American influence over the region. They also show how Hollywood's film style and star system, its transnational market dominance, and American (self-) interest of different kinds had to negotiate—and even face disruptive resistance at—local levels.

Capitalizing on Hollywood star power, Julián de Ajuria's superproduction, *Una nueva y gloriosa nación*, represents a unique form of border crossing. Premised on a problematic amalgam of Hollywood melodramatic conventions and porteño film culture, his film epitomizes the communicational impasses melodrama can suffer between and across (film) cultures. Ajuria's combination of Hollywood film style and a "patrician" topic did not usher in a new age of spectacular Hispanic American coproductions, as film critics initially foresaw, nor did it fully satisfy the nationalistic expectations of porteño spectators. On the contrary, evincing the limits of melodrama's combinatorial powers, it epitomized the unhappy merger of aesthetic practices in which the melodramatic mode also partakes. Nevertheless, Ajuria's film constitutes a unique instance of South-to-North exchanges directly engaged against the headwinds of Hollywood's southbound advance across the Americas.

If aesthetic and commercial reasons drew Ajuria to Hollywood, ideological motives pushed Cali Film away from Hollywood and closer to Italy to produce *Garras de oro*. Gaps in the archive still shroud the film in mystery but point to complex "two-way" exchanges mediated by melodramatic narrative, particularly its effects in transnational relations. *Garras* proposes alternative South-to-North and South-to-South vectors shaped by—and shaping—alternative film circuits as well as regional sentiments of emotional legitimacy, framed through the anti-American sentiment revolving around the figure of Theodore Roosevelt. These vectors, in turn, yielded "two-way" discursive exchanges across borders between American legations and local officials in Panamanian and Colombian cities as well as in Washington, DC. Unlike Ajuria's film, which was exhibited across multiple borders, *Garras* was curtailed in its distribution. Even so, in diplomatic documents and the popular press, it gained political import as a potentially subversive film, thus highlighting melodrama's ability to upend visual regimes and social arrangements across borders and geopolitical hierarchies.

Conclusion

Struggles for Recognition

Tell me which cinema you frequent, and I will tell you who you are.
—*Las Últimas Noticias*, 3 March 1919

Adopting a multiple modernities perspective, this book has traced how melodrama consistently served a heuristic function in recording and making sense of modern change during the silent period across Latin America. In multiple urban enclaves—from Buenos Aires to Los Angeles—melodrama procured sites of intelligibility that, in turn, affected the dynamics of public participation. As such, melodrama intervened in representation as well as the perceptual coordinates of specific communities by revealing or concealing uneven socioeconomic conditions. As it relates to social injustice, the play between visibilities and invisibilities inherent to melodrama exposes the mode's structuring principle, (in)visibilizing the unfulfilled promises of liberal philosophy: liberty, equality, and solidarity. Filmic melodrama made visible, in Buenos Aires, the abuses "fallen women" were subject to when entering the department store workforce. Conversely, Bogotá and Medellín films concealed social inequities under the veil of *la moral* under President Pedro Nel Ospina's conservative modernization. In Orizaba, melodrama served the functions of both revealing—the opiate crisis biopolitical initiatives produced during Plutarco Elías Calles's presidency—and concealing—social unrest in industrial mills—while branding the city as modern through fashion and action-packed narrative. Looking at the fraught relations with Hollywood film culture and the United States in general, the last chapter tackled the impasses melodrama faced to convey a universalist visual regime in transnational contexts, as well as its disruptive potential as a vehicle of dissent from geopolitical subjection in transnational film circuits.

As this study shows, melodrama's cries for justice were not objectively just across film cultures. On the contrary, they served the agendas of diverse social actors in struggles for recognition conjured by early twentieth-century modernization. Modifying the "aesthetic-political field of possibility," diverse social actors reconfigured what was visible and what was invisible and vied for access to representation through melodrama.[1] In short, they articulated—or critiqued—social bodies and orders. These struggles varied from region to region, even from city to city, yielding distinct types of melodramatic genres and conventions in cinematic form. These contested sites of representation—revolving around 1920s filmic melodrama—drew upon broader, and earlier, melodramatic cultures across the Americas. Chapter 1 traced the processes through which melodramatic conventions pierced into, and later took over, narrative film across the region before and during the Great War. These processes, which did not follow a clear-cut chronological or spatial development, first tapped into nationalist discourses and narratives to later appropriate the nineteenth-century melodramatic literary canon of the subcontinent. The development of local melodramatic conventions was the product of negotiated readings in which film pioneers engaged as they exhibited and appropriated European and American fare, despite the expansive "Yankee invasion" taking over local markets during the period.

To be sure, more research is needed in archives of urban enclaves across the continent, the cities, and respective areas of influence that also registered and made sense of local modernities through melodrama during the silent period. In the four pillars of film circuits—production, distribution, exhibition, and reception—melodrama engaged in social, ideological, and economic struggles on local and transnational scales across the continent. In an extensive study, Jorge Iturriaga tells a "conflicted ... history of popular empowerment" in Chilean film cultures.[2] For Iturriaga, local exhibitors, distributors, and critics built a popular culture from below. But surviving footage hints at film cultures akin to the ones of Bogotá and Medellín, which deny melodrama's socially empowering function and question the mode's "post-Sacred world" condition of possibility.[3] Shot in Concepción, *Canta y no llores, corazón* (Sing and do not cry; dir. Juan Pérez Berrocal, 1925) revolves around a foreman who divests his master of his fortune and, in a final coup, tries to marry his son to the deceased master's daughter. *Incendio* (Fire; dir.

Carlos del Mudo, 1926), shot in Valparaíso and intended as an homage to local firefighters, rewards a fireman's bravery by marrying him to an affluent flapper, who was also courted by a vicious social climber. In both films the nouveau riche and social climbers are the villains; in *Canta*, moneyed victims foresee that eventually "God will punish [the arrivistes]" and indeed, in *Incendio* the social climber dies in a fire—a sign of "Divine Justice," intertitles read.[4] Likewise, Georgina Torello's recent study foregrounds the role of women's charitable associations in shaping Uruguayan cinema and, through it, in reproducing the elite. Most interestingly, she looks at "intermedial continuities and ruptures" throughout the period, wherein the magic lantern becomes a powerful medium to create alternative, patrician platforms in theaters exhibiting foreign films.[5]

In a similar, exclusionary vein, Bolivia's only surviving narrative film, *Wara Wara* (dir. José María Velasco Maidana, 1930), ponders the place of indigenous populations in the modern nation. Revolving around the story of star-crossed lovers, an Inca princess and a conquistador, the film draws on local strands of *indigenismo* to propose an ideal body politic premised on miscegenation. Recalling the disputed appropriations of American and European aesthetics that film producers engaged in, *Wara Wara* reveals a penchant for the latter, as it borrows the film style of early Italian epics despite the undisputed success of the "Yankee invasion" by the late 1920s.[6] The film was screened to full houses in La Paz thirty-two times but was shown no more than twice in Cochabamba, Oruro, and Sucre—all cities with large indigenous populations.[7] As this and other cases suggest, during the silent period multiple forces and actors shaped the relations between melodrama and modernity across the continent as well as the (in)visibilities these relations made possible. Melodrama distributes and apportions what is visible and what is invisible and challenges (or interrogates) who has access to representation. It therefore comprises a contested site of representation, in which multiple social actors shape, perform, and enact diverse configurations of the social order.

This book invites scholars to revisit the relation between melodrama and representational transformations associated with forces of urbanization and economic development in later periods, as well as the ways that Latin American film cultures draw meaningful connections within and across national borders. The advent of sound reshuffled the visual regimes filmic melodrama made possible. Canonical as well as recent studies of the Golden Age of Latin American cinemas examine Argentine and Mexican films' continental circulation in the 1930s through 1950s, influencing (film) cultures across the continent.[8] Akin to American cinema, these national cinemas pushed thematic and stylistic conventions beyond their national borders while developing nationalistic imagery. If, early on, Argentine films enjoyed greater quality and diversity of genres while Mexico stumbled upon—and stuck to—the successful formulae of the *comedia ranchera* (ranch comedies) and *cabaretera* (cabaret dancer) films, in the heyday of the Golden Age Mexico would dominate Latin American filmic melodrama. Argentina would see its industry wane after the United States banned exports of raw film in response to Argentina's adopting neutrality in World War II.[9]

The global redistribution of power, in World War II and the Great War, directly affected the flows of capital and raw materials shaping local film industries. It also defined the ideological underpinnings and commercial ambitions of local film industries, which slowly but surely accrued a national character while adopting the conventions of Hollywood film style. Negotiated readings led to adaptations of Hollywood studio cinema, as national film industries harnessed popular musical genres to distinguish their productions as national. *Ranchera*, tango, and bolero—as well as samba in Brazil—defined cinematic melodrama from the 1930s through the 1950s. As Carlos Monsiváis persuasively argues, resorting to popular music at this historical juncture "does not derive from Hollywood guidelines," but instead points to the transnational connections other media—particularly radio—facilitated in the production of continental senses of belonging premised on pathos. "Popular music," for Monsiváis, "is the mainstay of Latin American cinema [because] of the effectively central role music has in the melodramatic imaginary of its subscribers (almost all [Latin Americans])."[10] More recently, and in a similar vein, Ana López sees in this moment of "profound intermediality" the emergence of "strategies of appropriation, accommodation, and, ultimately, layers of differentiation" across the continent.[11]

In the later years of the Golden Age, Latin American studios produced patriotic narratives, usually framed in romantic conflicts, with high production values that were "hailed ... as a sign of national progress."[12] In Buenos Aires, sound cinema first followed the "formulae" of tango lyrics.[13] However, the porteño urban films that inaugurated sound cinema—new iterations of cinedrama porteño—experienced institutional pushback, as multiple state agents questioned the "decorum" of the national images they conveyed.[14] In response, and as a result of negotiated "agreements, resistances, and subjugations" between studios and the state, the criollo representation of rural space—the vast pampa and the gaucho as the repositories of argentinidad, or national identity—"eventually becomes the default."[15] These films were no less melodramatic than their urban counterparts.[16] Even if urban melodramas persisted during the industrial period, the "peaceful and harmonious mythology of the gaucho," along with an "ideologized vision of landscape," became the state's chosen vehicle to push renderings of a prosperous national space and state-driven modernization.[17] In Brazil, the third prominent producer at the time, Vera Cruz Studio produced historical epics while continuing to draw on popular genres—such as musical comedies, or *chanchadas*—out of São Paulo.[18] In Mexico City, director Emilio "el indio" Fernández's films and Gabriel Figueroa's virtuoso compositions ushered in a nationalist aesthetic that, supported by the state, would impose a harmonious sense of *mexicanidad*. Recent studies have questioned the supposed overlap of national cohesion and the "low angle shots [and] fluffy Figueroan skies" these films propose.[19] They have reread the "myth" of 1940s Mexican cinema delving into its instabilities, raced incoherencies, and transnational influences inherent to the cultural nationalism of mexicanidad.[20]

While studio cinema—and later cinemas, such as New Latin American Cinema and "New, New" Latin American cinemas[21]—have been productively read through national frameworks, recent studies have challenged the national in favor of transnational approaches. Instead of using national cinemas as a way to organize the historiography of Latin American cinema,[22] recent scholarship on early sound has proposed a "cosmopolitan nationalist" aesthetic in Southern Cone films that recognizes the allusion to international films and the incorporation of local popular traditions, arguing in favor of a transnational stylistics.[23] Looking at South-to-South exchanges, the articles in *Pantallas Transnacionales* collectively trace the commercial, stylistic, and technical exchanges between Argentine and Mexican cinemas, from the silent period to the 1950s.[24] Peredo Castro's provocative study locates Mexican Golden Age cinema at the center of ideological debacles during World War II, in which Allied forces—particularly the United States and the United Kingdom—weaponized Mexican cinema's "Mexican nationalism to promote sentiments of Latin American cohesion and strengthen Pan Americanism" against the looming fascist threat in the region.[25] South-to-North exchanges have also redefined the production conditions of Golden Age film. Rereading the origins of comedia ranchera in the *género chico* (short plays with music) and the *revista* (multi-act popular entertainment with music, dance, and sketches)—a given in Mexican film histories[26]—as a Mexico City-Angeleno process, while examining the mass market of Spanish-language films in Greater Mexico, recent studies propose that both the comedia ranchera and cabaretera cinema, as well as Spanish-language Hollywood films, are the products of hybridization between film cultures and industries in Mexico City and Los Angeles.[27]

Cine hispano—Hollywood's attempt at Spanish-language filmmaking—stresses the aporia and the challenges of writing the history of Latin American cinema in relation to forces of change. Faced with mounting competition from cinema produced in Mexico, Argentina, and—until the beginning of its Civil War—Spain, the term came into use to distinguish Hollywood productions from the Hispanic productions of its competitors. Of this short-lived genre, only Carlos Gardel's films were popular throughout Latin America. For Paul Schroeder-Rodríguez, this is "because they were by and large Argentinean."[28] Unlike Ajuria's Hollywood super-production, Paramount's *El día que me quieras* (*The Day You Love Me*; dir. John Reinhardt, 1935), for example, was filmed in New York with a mostly Argentinean cast, crew, and story line. Nevertheless, film critics across the continent derided the bulk of cine hispano. Viewing it through the lens of cultural nationalism, they criticized the mix of Spanish accents multinational payrolls produced (much as some transnationally produced serials are criticized today). Building on Latin American and US Spanish-language television scholar John Sinclair's work, Lisa Jarvinen sees cine hispano as the product of "a kind of diaspora in reverse"; its crew, actors, and narratives are united by a common identity defined not by push factors but rather by their common experiences in the United States.[29] Importantly, Jarvinen proposes that these films, "however odd and sometimes artificial [they] . . . seemed to critics," were often "reflective of their context."[30] Indeed, a brief scene from *Verbena trágica* (*Tragic Dance*; dir. Chares Lamont, 1939), a star-crossed love triangle set in New York's Spanish Harlem, explores dialectic diversity. Foreshadowing the film's predicament on the eve of *el día de la raza* (Columbus Day), Blanca (Luana de Alcañiz), a young Spanish married woman who is secretly pregnant with her future brother-in-law's child, discusses over the windowsill her neighbor Jensita's (Leonor Turich) own concerns about childbirth. Despite her family's financial woes, Jensita's mother is again going into labor, "With daddy jobless, another more mouth to feed. . . . I hope they are not *cuates*!" Jensita laments. "*Cuates?*" Blanca asks. "Yes, *guaguas, gemelos*! [twins]," Jensita replies. "Ah! [Blanca smiles] God willing. I will take care of your mother tonight so that you can go to the dance," she replies in support.[31] On the threshold between public and private spaces that the windowsill represents, the encounter across dialects overcomes a brief linguistic impasse, making visible the dialectic differences—as well as the bonds of solidarity—linking different Hispanic communities in the neighborhood.[32]

From Spanish Harlem to the US-Mexico border with *Cuando canta la ley* (*When the Law Sings*; dir. Richard Harlan, 1939), to *El milagro de la calle mayor* (*Miracle on Main Street*; dir. Steve Sekely, 1940), set in a Mexican neighborhood in Los Angeles, cine hispano told through melodrama "the reality of the existence" of Spanish-speaking communities in the United States.[33] Most interestingly, these films were not intended for domestic consumption only; they circulated across the continent.[34] In *Verbena*, for instance, original musical numbers—including a Spanish flamenco, a ranchera, and a bolero—betray an interest in catering to Spanish, Mexican, and Cuban spectators, respectively, among other publics. As Monsiváis explains, popular music such as tango, rancheras, and bolero was consumed across the Americas and underpins Golden Age cinema's aesthetics of suffering. The first number serves as comic relief in the film, while the other two—performed by renowned *bolerista* Sergio de Karlo—punctuate the main plot with stories of wronged male lovers. In terms of this book, cine hispano, epitomized here by *Verbena*, trafficked in new visibilities premised on migrants and their experiences, conveyed in melodramatic key. It was a melodrama expanding into new intermedial connections while redefining communal boundaries. Later iterations of melodrama reveal that the process of *making visible* and its ideological maneuvers, inherent to the melodramatic regime, is not confined to the silent period. Making visible was at the core of melodrama's origins. It persisted through the heyday of industrial cinema and continues to inform the mode today.

Current melodrama scholarship finds itself at a theoretical watershed with political implications. Several scholars have recently "unbound" melodrama from its many givens: its "excessive" nature, its generic or modal bounds, and its substitutive moral function in a post-sacred world, among other suppositions. They recognize melodrama's ability to merge aesthetic practices while providing—beyond narrative—sites of social cohesion "for a society based on economic individualism."[35] Other scholars, attentive to melodrama's recent manifestations in political populism, present a rather bleak take on the mode. Questioning melodrama's role in the political legitimacy of representation, they read melodrama as a "rhetorical genre" producing "felt legitimacy"—an ideological apparatus that, in Althusserian fashion, "hails a particular type of citizen."[36] Or, as Thomas Elsaesser recently put it, they even see melodrama as a "fully consummate failure" (*échec pleinement accompli*); the mode's leaps—from film to soap opera to reality TV to political discourse—preclude social consensus, "namely, the adjournment of *justice* and *equality*."[37] Linda Williams eloquently labels these new tendencies "melodrama run amok."[38]

To the auspicious possibilities melodrama offers—aesthetic, cultural, economic, and political—a new leap (new when considering melodrama's bicentennial history) of certain melodramatic tropes into the realm of politics pushes even farther away the fulfillment of the three promises of liberty, equality, and solidarity. As Manichean portrayals of the body politic divide the public arena into victims and perpetrators—regardless of their deeds—the modern political pact of representation, as well as its basic ideals, faces alarming skepticism, perhaps now more than ever. Reading current changes through the lens of melodrama, scholars find a disruptive force that subverts the very democratic potential melodrama represents. Reviving mid-twentieth-century readings of the mode—that is, melodrama as a product of what Adorno and Horkheimer label the "culture industry"—such scholars see melodrama as an alienating mechanism precluding the fulfillment of the three promises in the twenty-first century.

In this book, I have stressed how melodrama can be—and has been—mobilized for both liberal and illiberal ends, as it reveals *and* conceals social inequities. I have suggested that melodrama demands attention to history, as Hermann Herlinghaus aptly puts it when criticizing melodrama studies influenced by cultural critique: "Melodrama does not locate itself on the realm of the 'apolitical' or on the realm of 'authoritarian aesthetics'; we must historicize melodrama within the conflicts of modernity."[39] Because melodrama is a pervasive, yet contested, site of representation—through which diverse social actors deploy their own visualizations of society—we must not confer upon it a liberating or emancipatory function.[40] To loosely borrow from Siegfried Kracauer, we must not consider the turn to melodrama "the go-for-broke game of history," a means to create a historical continuum between the poles of remembrance and forgetting (in previous or in present times).[41] Instead, we can look at melodrama's uses critically—then and now—in the spheres of production, distribution, exhibition, and reception. At these and other interlocking dimensions, the access to representation occurs intersubjectively. Hence Jesús Martín-Barbero's insistence that we consider the *mediations* melodrama makes possible, among and across different publics: how it is perceived, how it is retold, and—through these practices of mediation—how melodrama allows a part, to those who have no part, in the discursive and exclusive constructions of a given community.[42]

One is left to wonder if the skeptical strands of academic inquiry—the ones focused on the melodrama run amok—have taken up residence in a contemporary version of the Grand Hotel Abyss. For a sardonic Georg Luckacs, it was the establishment in which "the leading German intelligentsia, including Adorno," had settled. "A beautiful hotel, equipped with every comfort, on the edge ... of nothingness, of absurdity," a place where "the daily contemplation of the abyss, between excellent meals or artistic entertainments, can only heighten the enjoyment of the subtle comforts offered."[43] Latin American scholars have fiercely resisted this position. They have countered the "academic disdain," the "class-grammar" (*gramática de clase*) that allows the lettered city to disparage popular forms.[44] In order to better understand the creative as well as the oppressive potentialities of melodrama—particularly when the mode seems to leap in and out of every medium in a dismal present—we must engage in mediations of our own. In the contemporary struggles for recognition, we must feel ourselves part of the problem. We must engage with narrative and real-life (melo)dramas in order to participate in the mode's ever-expanding, perceptual, and sense-making possibilities.

Abbreviations

For the sake of brevity, I have used acronyms to refer to some of the archives consulted in this study. In alphabetical order, these are:

AGNM	Archivo General de la Nación (México)
BLT	Biblioteca Miguel Lerdo de Tejada (México)
BNA	Biblioteca Nacional (Argentina)
BNC	Biblioteca Nacional (Colombia)
BNE	Biblioteca Nacional de España, Hemeroteca Digital
ENERC	Escuela Nacional de Experimentación y Realización Cinematográfica
FPFC	Fundación Patrimonio Fílmico Colombiano
MHDL	Media History Digital Library
NARA	National Archives II (United States)

Notes

INTRODUCTION

Epigraph. Roberto Arlt, "Contestando a la pregunta de Ghioldi," *Tribuna Libre*, 28 January 1928.
1. Quiroga, *Arte y lenguaje*, 202.
2. "Avenida de las acacias," *Corre y vuela* (Santiago), 11 September 1918, 4.
3. "Notas y comentarios," *El Hogar*, 18 December 1914.
4. Quiroga, *Arte y lenguaje*, 208.
5. One of the first film critics in Latin America, Horacio Quiroga first and foremost praised cinematic realism. With an avant la lettre Bazinian approach, Quiroga considered cinema a "window" on reality that had the potential "to create a complete sensation of truth." He was also attentive to developments in cinematic language. Thus, the "naturalness of the scene" refers here to a particular way of filmmaking epitomized, for Quiroga, by Hollywood continuity editing. Quiroga, *Arte y lenguaje*, 214, 266, 358.
6. "De todo un poco," *El Cine Gráfico*, 13 April 1917.
7. "De todo un poco."
8. Serna, *Making Cinelandia*, 2.
9. Panagia, *Rancière's Sentiments*, 9.
10. Rockhill, "Rancière's Politics of Perception," 3; Montaldo, "La desigualdad de las partes," 30.
11. See also Ospina León, "(In)visibilities."
12. Rancière, *Politics of Aesthetics*.
13. See Arroyo, Ramey, and Schuessler, *México imaginado*; Gunckel, *Mexico on Main Street*; Navistki, *Public Spectacles of Violence*; Serna, *Making Cinelandia*; and, beyond the silent period, Castro Ricarte and Mckee Irwin, *El cine mexicano se impone*; Jarvinen, *Rise of Spanish-Language Filmmaking*; Marcantonio, *Global Melodrama*; and Tierney, *New Transnationalisms*.

14. Singer, *Melodrama and Modernity*, 1.
15. Miller, *Reinventing Modernity*, 5.
16. Miller, *Reinventing Modernity*, 5.
17. Simmel, "Metropolis and Mental Life," 11.
18. "La ciudad enferma . . .," *La Película*, 5 June 1919. Interestingly, this editorial depicts cinema as a palliative against increasing stimulus, not as "one of its most robust manifestations," as many film scholars have suggested (Singer, *Melodrama and Modernity*, 93). The editorial, using pharmaceutical terms, proposes to exhibitors: "May the nerves of the public find comfort [un derivativo y un calmante] on the screen."
19. "Los afiches modernos en nuestro negocio," *El Exhibidor*, 20 July 1927.
20. "Los apóstoles de la farsa," *Películas*, April 1919.
21. *Universidad*, 7 April 1928.
22. Hershfield, *Imagining la Chica Moderna*, 12. García Canclini concurs, stating that rather than textual, "[Mexico's] cultural profile . . . is basically a visual operation"; *Culturas híbridas*, 118.
23. Sánchez, "Babilonia de Hierro," *Revista de Revistas*, May 1928.
24. Miller, *Reinventing Modernity*, 4.
25. Osborne, "Modernity Is a Qualitative," 65.
26. Sarlo, *Una modernidad periférica*, 21.
27. Ramos, *Divergent Modernities*, xl.
28. Martín-Barbero, "La telenovela desde el reconocimiento," 71. For the influence of Martín-Barbero's and Herlinghaus's notion of anachronism in Latin American communication studies, see works compiled in the latter's anthology *Narraciones anacrónicas de la modernidad*.
29. For the Brazilian case, not discussed in this book, see Schwarz, *As idéias fora do lugar*.
30. In which "traditions have not yet disappeared and modernity has not yet completely arrived." García-Canclini, *Culturas híbridas*, 1, 3.
31. Castro Gómez, *La hybris del punto cero*, ii. See also Adelman, *Sovereignty and Revolution*; Fischer, *Modernity Disavowed*; and Dussel, "Eurocentrism and Modernity."
32. In opposition to a "Eurocentric paradigm" that the Argentine Mexican philosopher finds "partial and provincial," Dussel reads the Spanish annexation of "Amerindia" as the "determining comparative advantage" of Europe—over the Ottoman Muslim world, India, and China—that, "*simultaneously would constitute* Europe as 'center' . . . over an expanding 'periphery'" in the first world-system." Dussel, *Ética de la liberación*, 51. For studies that revise coloniality and capitalism in terms of a world-system, see also Mignolo, *Darker Side of Western Modernity*; and Warwick Research Collective, *Combined and Uneven Development*. My gratitude to Krista Brune for these references.
33. Sharman, "Latin American Modernity," 493.
34. For instance, Julio Ramos's study on the autonomy of the literary field in nineteenth-century Latin America reproduces the narrative of the deficient as it claims, "In Europe, literary modernization, which entailed the autonomization of art and the professionalization of writers, was a primary social process, distinctive of those societies on the threshold of advanced capitalism. Yet in Latin

America, modernization in all respects was—and continues to be—an extremely uneven phenomenon. In these societies, 'modern' literature (if not the modern state itself) was not able to rely on institutional bases that would guarantee its autonomy." Ramos, *Divergent Modernities*, xl.

35. Osborne, "Modernity Is a Qualitative," 75.

36. Recent studies on the nineteenth century have also veered away from this tendency, examining "Latin America's role in creating republicanism, democracy, and rights in the broader Atlantic world, a creation usually credited to Europe or the United States alone." Sanders, *Vanguard of the Atlantic World*, 23.

37. Singer, *Melodrama and Modernity*, 102; and López, "Early Cinema and Modernity," 49. Recent scholarship reproduces, without fully revising, López's seminal work. See, for instance, Maite Conde's understanding of Latin American modernity. Departing from López's "fantasy or desire," but still defining it as a "project," not "emerging . . . and developing in synchronicity" with technological changes proper to Euro-America, Conde sees in the earliest films produced in Brazil "local 'copies'" of Lumière actualities. Conde, *Foundational Films*, 1–2, 4. Breaking with this tendency, Nilo Couret questions how silent film scholarship on Latin America "threatens to reduce and homogenize the differentiated experiences of modernity." See his videographic critique, "Serializing *Ramona*," 4 January 2019, https://vimeo.com/304982550.

38. Here, secularization refers to the separation of religion and the authority of the church from social life and governance. This book, however, traces processes in which the "secular age" more closely resembles Charles Taylor's definition and how these processes affect melodramatic regimes. Taylor revises the role of religion in modern societies, which he describes as pluralist societies in which believers and nonbelievers coexist. Taylor, *Secular Age*, 3.

39. Sharman, *Tradition and Modernity*, 11.

40. Miller, *Reinventing Modernity*, 6.

41. Miller, *Reinventing Modernity*, 6.

42. Sarlo, *Una modernidad periférica*, 31.

43. Harvey, *Paris*, 1.

44. García Canclini, *Culturas híbridas*, 3.

45. Miller, *Reinventing Modernity*, 30. See also Roniger and Waisman, *Globality and Multiple Modernities*.

46. Miller, *Reinventing Modernity*, 194.

47. Urrego, *Sexualidad, matrimonio y familia*, 277.

48. A premise first asserted by Peter Brooks (*Melodramatic Imagination*, 21, 50) and reproduced by Latin American scholars. See Herlinghaus, "Imaginación melodramática," 27; and Walter, "Melodrama y cotidianidad," 219.

49. Brooks, *Melodramatic Imagination*, 21. Jesús Martín-Barbero and Herman Herlinghaus have been influential in reproducing this premise in Latin American scholarship.

50. Silvestre Bonnard, "Su majestad el culebrón," *Páginas de cine*, *El Universal*, 30 July 1922.

51. The term *culebrón*, which literally means "large snake," is still commonly used to describe telenovelas across the continent.

52. Bonnard, "Su majestad el culebrón."
53. Williams, *Playing the Race Card*, 26.
54. Williams, *Playing the Race Card*, 12–3.
55. For Leah Jacobs, "situation" consists of sets of narrative conventions proper to melodrama—"striking impasses or confrontations between characters"—that arrest narrative action or challenge characters with intense circumstances, while at the same time catering to an audience eager for, and knowledgeable about, such melodramatic reversals. Jacobs, "Woman's Picture," 129–33. For the affective and revelatory power of vicarious pathos, see Terada, *Feeling in Theory*, 169. Likewise, Agustín Zarzosa considers melodrama a "distribution of the visibility of suffering." While departing from Zarzosa in important ways, my study somewhat aligns with his assessment, according to which "neither the proclamation of the moral order's existence nor the aim of equality is essential to melodrama." Zarzosa, *Refiguring Melodrama*, 20.
56. A suggestive exception would be Silvia Oroz, who locates 1950s film melodrama's origin in the sixteenth-century opera; see her *Melodrama: O cinema*. Likewise, Euro-American scholarship has recently begun to revise this Francophile tenet, considering melodrama "the culmination, not the beginning, of a sustained movement toward affective aesthetics that can be traced . . . at least as far back as the Reformation." Buckley, "Unbinding Melodrama," 22. The French Revolution directly influenced the Spanish American revolutions. Since then, melodrama has had a place in Latin American fiction. The Caraquenian Francisco de Miranda played an active role in the French Revolution as *maréchal de champ*. Napoleon and the French people acknowledged his contribution, inscribing for posterity his name on the Arc de Triomphe. Through his writing and deeds, Miranda influenced Simón Bolívar, José de San Martín, Bernardo O'Higgins, and other *libertadores* who would later carry on the independence struggles of Latin America. Equally influential, in 1794 the Bogotan Antonio Nariño translated and circulated the *Declaration of the Rights of Man and the Citizen* (1789). In tandem, as Mathew Bush notes, "From the era of the wars for independence . . . onward, melodrama has played an essential role in the process of how Latin America narrates its fictions and how it conceptually organizes and works through conflicts embedded in its very social fabric." Bush, *Pragmatic Passions*, 15. See also Phillip, *Francisco de Miranda*.
57. Brooks, *Melodramatic Imagination*, 21.
58. Jean Jacques Rousseau coined the term to describe his piece *Pygmalion*, written in 1762 and first performed in 1770. It was a novel form of theater in which "the spoken phrase is in a way announced and prepared by the musical phrase." See his "Letter to M. Burney and Fragments of Observations on Glucks' 'Alceste,'" in *Essay on the Origin of Languages*, 497.
59. Brooks, *Melodramatic Imagination*, 5, 168.
60. Day-Mayer and Mayer, "Performing/Acting Melodrama," 101.
61. Day-Mayer and Mayer, "Performing/Acting Melodrama," 27.
62. See Anker, *Orgies of Feeling*; Bush, *Pragmatic Passions*; Marcantonio, *Global Melodrama*; Singer; and Williams *Playing the Race Card* and *On the Wire*.
63. Williams, *On the Wire*, 84.

64. This study, therefore, looks at a very specific timeframe—1909 to 1927—to expound on the historical specificities of melodrama's uses. Even so, it does not disagree with more overarching claims, such as Bush's observation, in the field of literary studies, that "melodrama is the dominant narrative mode when Latin American literature speaks about politics and social development." Bush, *Pragmatic Passions*, 22.

65. Anker, *Orgies of Feeling*, 68–69.

66. Recent scholarship has questioned melodrama's origins in the French Revolution, pushing back its emergence to "at least as [far] back as the Reformation." Buckley, "Unbinding Melodrama," 22. This revision does not conflict with my reading of melodrama as a contested site of representation premised on the tenets of liberalism—which also predate the Revolution—and their visibility. Dorinda Outram contends, "Key words of the political discourse of the French Revolution, such as 'nation' or 'representation,' had already been used as early as the 1760s by the French Parlements, not in support of Enlightenment, but in their *opposition* to attempts by the Crown itself to change political and economic structures underpinned by tax inequality and privilege." Outram, *Enlightenment*, 131–33. Emphasis in original.

67. Martín-Barbero, "La telenovela desde el reconocimiento," 68; and Herlinghaus, "Imaginación melodramática," 23.

68. Martín-Barbero, "La telenovela desde el reconocimiento," 68. Although Martín-Barbero refers to melodrama as a form of interpellation, this term should not be confused with Althusser's concept of top-down subject formation (the metaphor of the passerby and the policeman). On the contrary, Martín-Barbero sees in melodrama a locus for the emergence of individual as well as group agencies at grassroots levels. Likewise, with a Gramscian perspective, he considers melodrama a genre for developing different forms of hegemony. For Althusser's theory of interpellation, see "Ideology and Ideological State Apparatuses," in *Lenin and Philosophy*, 127–87. For the concept of hegemony as a form of consensus, see Gramsci's "Hegemony, Relations of Force, Historical Bloc," in *Gramsci Reader*, 189–221.

69. Rockhill, "Rancière's Politics of Perception," 3.

70. Oroz, *Melodrama: O cinema*, 23.

71. Oroz, *Melodrama: O cinema*, 24.

72. Brooks, *Reading for the Plot*, 153.

73. "El cine y la política," *Heraldo de Mexico*, 25 September 1924, 3.

74. Sanders, *Vanguard of the Atlantic World*, 4. My gratitude to Rielle Navitski for this reference.

75. In order of appearance: Mexico, Guatemala, El Salvador, Honduras, Nicaragua, Costa Rica, Panama, Colombia, Bolivia, Peru, Chile, Venezuela, Uruguay, Cuba, and Argentina. "Septiembre, el mes de gloria," *La Prensa*, 14 September 1924.

76. "El día de la Libertad," *Heraldo de Mexico*, 20 July 1924.

77. "El día de la Libertad."

78. Honneth, *Idea of Socialism*, 11.

79. Quoted in Reich, *Saving Capitalism*, 5.

80. Piketty, *Capitalism in the Twenty-First Century*, 30.
81. Goldgel, *Cuando lo nuevo conquistó*, 16–17.
82. Paz, *Children of the Mire*, 85–88. For an exploration of Latin America as a "colonial postcolonial place," see Sharman, *Tradition and Modernity*, 86–91.
83. Pratt, *Imperial Eyes*, 188.
84. Even if producing a false sense of reciprocity, as Marx suggests in a much-quoted passage from *Capital* (280):

> The sphere of circulation or commodity exchange ... is in fact a very Eden of the innate rights of man. It is the exclusive realm of Freedom, Equality, Property, and Bentham. Freedom, because both buyer and seller of a commodity, let us say of labor-power, are determined only by their own free will. They contract as free persons, who are equal before the law. Their contract is the final result in which their joint will finds a common legal expression. Equality because each enters into relation with the other, as with a simple owner of commodities, and they exchange equivalent for equivalent. Property, because each disposes only of what is his own. And Bentham, because each looks only to his own advantage. The only force bringing them together, and putting them into relation with each other, is the selfishness, the gain and the private interest of each. Each plays heed to himself only, and no one worries about the others. And precisely for that reason, either in accordance with the pre-established harmony of things, or under the auspices of an omniscient providence, they all work together to their mutual advantage, for the common will, and in the common interest.

85. Honneth, *Idea of Socialism*, 12.
86. Gledhill, "Prologue: The Reach of Melodrama," x.
87. Honneth, *Idea of Socialism*, 25.
88. The first dimension is located in the spheres of intimacy, the family, and friendship. The second points to moral and legal principles as well as to rights in the modern state. The third dimension finds its base in community and social solidarity that acknowledge the contributions of the individual to the welfare of the group.
89. Honneth, *Struggle for Recognition*, 169.
90. Or, what Honneth defines as "disrespect." *Struggle for Recognition*, 169.
91. Streeby, *Radical Sensations*, 17.
92. Bush, *Pragmatic Passions*, 21.
93. I understand here the public sphere as a medium of civil society and therefore constantly in flux, with historically specific cultural and legal particulars. See Habermas, *Structural Transformation*.
94. On narrative film, Adorno and Horkheimer claim, "The culture industry has sardonically realized man's species being. Everyone amounts only to those qualities by which he or she can replace everyone else: all are fungible, mere specimens. As individuals they are absolutely replaceable, pure nothingness, and are made aware of this as soon as time deprives them of their sameness." *Dialectic of Enlightenment*, 116–17.
95. My reading of melodrama—as a contested site of representation—therefore departs from celebratory studies that, in due time, "defended" the cultural relevance and ubiquity of the melodramatic mode, as well as from previous, and more recent, "skeptical" takes on melodrama. As twenty-first-century studies trace melodrama's leaps—from literature to cinema, to television and other

media, and last to political populism—melodrama has again been vilified as a "rhetorical genre" that, in Althusserian fashion, "hails a particular type of citizen." It has even been understood as a "fully consummate failure" (échec pleinement accompli) vis-à-vis the political legitimacy of representation. By looking at bottom-up and top-down uses of the mode, this book evinces the many inclusive and exclusionary agendas melodrama has served through time and media. Anker, *Orgies of Feeling*, 2; and Elsaesser, "Le mélodrame," 39. My gratitude to Linda Williams for referring me to Elsaesser's article.

96. Benedict Anderson defines the nation as an "imagined political community" whose sovereign limits are defined by national borders. Anderson, *Imagined Communities*, 6–7.

97. Eugenio Xammar, "La producción cinematográfica," *Heraldo de México*, 19 March 1925, 5. In a study on Mexican cinema of the Golden Age, Ana López eloquently contends that Latin American cinema "perhaps has always been a transnational phenomenon." Lopez, "From Hollywood and Back," 6. This study builds on her observation, focused on the silent period. For a recent take on contemporary cinema along these lines, see Tierney, *New Transnationalisms*.

98. The most comprehensive annotated bibliography on Latin American scholarship of pre-, early, and silent cinema—not limited to melodrama—consists of the collective project led by Andrea Cuarterolo and Rielle Navitski, published in *Vivomatografías* (2017). The entries, organized by nation, include academic production relating to Argentina, Bolivia, Brazil, Chile, Colombia, Costa Rica, Cuba, Ecuador, El Salvador, Guatemala, Haiti, Honduras, Mexico, Nicaragua, Panama, Paraguay, Peru, Puerto Rico, Dominican Republic, Uruguay, and Venezuela. See Cuarterolo and Navitski, "Bibliografía sobre precine," 248–415.

99. Buckley, "Unbinding Melodrama," 24. See also Allen, "Passion of the Christ."

100. Urrego, *Sexualidad, matrimonio y familia*, 277.

101. Gledhill, "Prologue: The Reach of Melodrama," xiii.

102. Argentine film historian Andrea Cuarterolo rediscovered the film at the Cineteca del Friuli archive.

103. Kracauer, *History*, 75. Kracauer is not alone in theorizing the historian's involvement in the present. See Croce, *History*; and Collingwood, *Idea of History*.

104. Kracauer, *History*, 4–5.

CHAPTER 1. "FILMDOM" BEFORE AND DURING THE GREAT WAR

Epigraph. Alfonso Reyes, "Las naciones en el cine," *España*, 4 November 1915; reprinted in González Casanova, *Cine que vio Fósforo*, 128.

1. W. Stephen Bush, "Leon Gaumont on a Visit," *Moving Picture World*, 8 April 1916, 233. For Bush's influence in American film trade journals and the American early film industry, see Stromgren "Moving Picture World," 13–22.

2. "Perdiamo l'América . . .," *La Película* (Buenos Aires), 31 October 1918, 8.

3. Kristin Thompson, *Exporting Entertainment*, x. By 1914, for instance, Italy, along with Denmark, was the third largest exporter in the world. After losing their foreign film markets in the wake of the Great War, most Italian production companies went out of business after 1920. Sorlin, *Italian National Cinema*, 44.

4. Delluc, *Cinéma & Cie*, 268.

5. Thompson speculates that "had the [Great War] ended in mid-1916, the American film would have been in a much stronger position than before the war—yet it would not have been guaranteed any long-term hold on world markets." *Exporting Entertainment*, 71.

6. *Cine Gaceta*, February 1918, quoted in Purcell, *¡De película!*, 26.

7. Rafael Bermúdez Zataraín, "Memorias cinematográficas," *Rotográfico* (Mexico City), 14 March 1928. Supported by a broad examination of print sources, film historian Ángel Míquel confirms the dearth of American films in Mexico: "This rare trait of [local] exhibition in principle may seem strange, due to the relative geographical proximity with North American production centers, but it is confirmed by the almost absolute lack of journalistic accounts related to American films until 1916." "Rafael Bermúdez Zataraín," 59. See also Míquel, "Difficult Assimilation," 85–87.

8. Navitski, "Early Film Critics," 64.

9. *Exporting Entertainment*, 72–73. Laura Isabel Serna's study is the most comprehensive of such a process in a single nation, Mexico. She particularly looks at American interests in countering Mexico's initially neutral stance vis-à-vis the Great War as well as rampant piracy. *Making Cinelandia*, 28–34. In Brazil, a similar process took place. Fox and Paramount established houses in Rio de Janeiro in 1916. American distributors actively engaged the Italian and French dominance of the market. Aiming at penetrating the market, Universal opened shop with *Neptune's Daughter* (dir. Herbert Brenon, 1914) while advertising the film, in a bilingual address hinting at its European competitors, as a "capolavoro sans pareil." Melo Souza, *Imagens do passado*, 328. My gratitude to Rielle Navitski for this reference.

10. Taking into account recent market trends, Paul Schroeder-Rodríguez seconds Thompson's observations. He notes that prior to World War I, "European cinema dominated the region. . . . Hollywood's share of Latin American screen time since World War I has consistently exceeded 80 percent, oftentimes surpassing 90 percent." "Latin American Silent Cinema," 4.

11. Quoted in Serna, *Making Cinelandia*, 27.

12. In Brazil, distributors such as the Companhia Cinematográfica Brasileira, which monopolized the southeastern market in the 1910s, also welcomed the "Yankee invasion." Cheaper imports allowed the Companhia to purchase films and honor its rental agreements in São Paulo and the interior, therefore safeguarding its hold of the market. Melo Souza, *Imagens do passado*, 335.

13. *Las Últimas Noticias*, 3 March 1919, quoted in Purcell, *¡De película!*, 11.

14. Serna appropriates the term from Stuart Hall. *Making Cinelandia*, 7.

15. As I delve into later, I agree with Matthew Bush when he compellingly contends "melodrama stands historically at the foundation of the Latin American literary canon." Bush, *Pragmatic Passions*, 22.

16. Navitski, "Mediating the 'Conquering,'" 112. For Thompson, the "invasion" metaphor "would become almost universal in discussions of expanding the American film trade abroad." *Exporting Entertainment*, 49.

17. Torello, *La conquista del espacio*, 15.

18. For a seminal piece on the relation between maps and power, see Harley, "Maps, Knowledge, and Power," 277–312.

19. "Di Domenico Hmnos. & Cía," *Cine Mundial*, June 1920. The acronym SICLA, Sociedad Industrial Cinematográfica Latinoamericana or Latin American Cinematographic Industrial Society, pointed to the Di Domenicos' continental ambitions.

20. "Para la temporada de 1924," *Excelsior*, 14 November 1923.

21. "En cualquier parte del mundo donde haya ojos humanos se ve Fox," *Cine Universal*, 3 April 1920.

22. Singer, "New York," 115.

23. "Saludo," *Cine-Mundial*, January 1916, 9.

24. "Saludo," 9.

25. For a study on imperialist ambitions in "panregions" including Pan-America, see O'Loughlin and Van Der Wusten, "Political Geography of Panregions," 1–20.

26. Pan-América Cinematográfica to Isaac Manning, American Consul in Barranquilla, Colombia, 24 September 1915, NARA RG84, Consular Posts, Barranquilla, Colombia, vol. 122.

27. For a study on the "New" Monroe Doctrine under Woodrow Wilson's presidency, see Serna, "Periodistas mexicanos," 207–37.

28. The two companies dominated local distribution from 1912 to roughly 1918. Jelicié, "Entre la muerte y la risa," 20.

29. Thompson, *Exporting Entertainment*, 64, 69. British market dominance in the Southern Cone is of no surprise, given the postcolonial influence Britain has had over Argentina since its wars of independence.

30. Quoted in Thompson, *Exporting Entertainment*, 55.

31. Purcell, *¡De película!*, 76.

32. Harold B. Meyerheim, "Cinematographs in Medellin, Colombia," Consular Report, 16 August 1915, 2, NARA, RG84, Consular Posts, Barranquilla, Colombia, vol. 122.

33. Isaac A. Manning, "Cinematograph Films for Colombia," Consular Report, 25 May 1915, 1, NARA RG84, Consular Posts, Barranquilla, Colombia, vol. 122. Similar observations circulated in the United States. Quoting a studio representative, *Moving Picture World* considered South Americans "the best patrons of motion pictures anywhere in the world[.] We find that they have money and are willing to spend it, we find that they appreciate quality." W. Stephen Bush, "Light Breaking in South America," *Moving Picture World*, June 1916, 1871, quoted in Navitski, "Mediating the 'Conquering,'" 138.

34. Aughinbaugh, *Advertising for Trade*, 4, 10.

35. American Vice-Consul in Charge, letter to Harry Levey Service Corp., 22 September 1920, NARA, RG84, Consular Posts, Barranquilla, Colombia, vol. 149.

36. "Luciano Albertini," *Películas*, January 1919.

37. Consular documents stress the inability of major American companies to establish exchange houses in Colombia because of the Di Domenicos' hold on the market, as suggested in a 1920 epistolary exchange between Goldwin and consular agents. Archival records indicate that lesser-known American distribution companies experienced the same inability to pierce the market. Claude E. Guyant, American Consul, missive to Goldwyn Distribution Corporation, 4 June 1920, NARA RG84, Consular Posts, Barranquilla, Colombia, vol. 149.

38. Goldwyn Distribution Corporation to US Consul, 31 May 1920, NARA RG84, Consular Posts, Barranquilla, Colombia, vol. 149.

39. Paranaguá, *Tradición y modernidad*; and Schroeder-Rodríguez, "Latin American Silent Cinema."

40. For a study on appropriating global "junk" films that questions center/periphery conceptions of global film markets, see Askari, "Afterlife for Junk Prints."

41. This is not to deny the factor of "dumping" American material at cheap prices across the continent, an investment that American producers could recoup in the domestic market. My gratitude to Rielle Navitski for highlighting this proviso.

42. Thompson, *Exporting Entertainment*, 77.

43. "Answer to Questionnaire of Motion Picture Market of Latin America, Colombia," Consular Report to Secretary of State, 4 October 1919, NARA RG84, Diplomatic Posts, Colombia, vol. 220.

44. "Answer to Questionnaire of Motion Picture Market." American officials vied, perhaps unsuccessfully, to counter anti-US sentiment through the "important propaganda work" of screening films provided by the Department of State. The American ambassador to Colombia, Hoffman Philip, believed that "the people here would appreciate artists such as Chaplin, William Hart, Mary Pickford, Arbuckle, and Fairbanks, and public opinion would be enlightened by the presentation of war plays." Telegram to Secretary of State, 5 April 1919, NARA RG84 Diplomatic Posts, Colombia, vol. 220.

45. I further explore regional anti-US sentiment in chapter 5.

46. Data from the *Monthly Municipal Statistics Bulletin* reveal that in less than a decade film viewing increased exponentially. By December 1921, more than 2,400,000 porteño spectators had attended film screenings in 31 theaters and circuses as well as in 133 movie theaters that year. "Datos estadística municipal," *La Película*, 5 January 1922.

47. "Cinematografomanía," *La Película*, 15 September 1919. Emphasis in original.

48. Kriger, *Páginas de cine*, 124. To a lesser extent, European and local production companies also advertised in *La Película*, including Gaumont, Corporación Argentina Americana de Films, Pampa Films, and other local companies.

49. By 1927, *Revista del Exhibidor* maintained that South America was "the best market for North American films." *Excelsior*, another prominent journal, also favored American fare while discrediting local production. The journal exceptionally celebrated *Una nueva y gloriosa nación* (*Charge of the Gauchos*, 1928), a unique Argentine production shot entirely in Hollywood and directed by Albert H. Kelly. Not surprisingly, the super production that told the birth

of the Argentine nation found a warm reception in *Excelsior*, not because of the film's nationalist tenor, but because the film's producer and scriptwriter, the Spanish-born Julián de Ajuria, was one of *Excelsior*'s shareholders and owned multiple theaters that advertised in the journal. Ajuria's case epitomizes the integrated interests of local impresarios in the global circulation of moving images by the end of the silent period. I discuss Ajuria's film in chapter 5. "Sud América es el mejor mercado para el film norteamericano," *Revista del Exhibidor*, 10 September 1927, 13.

50. I have explored this discursive practice in detail in Ospina León, "Films on Paper."

51. "Las tendencias cinematográficas," *Películas*, 27 January 1917. Echoing *Películas*' rhetoric and therefore hinting at the effectiveness of the Di Domenico platform, American consular documents state that local distributors "are extremely partial to French and Italian films and are not inclined to look with favor on American productions, stating that they cannot compare in artistic qualities with the European films." Claude E. Guyant, American Consul, "Report: Market for Motion Picture Films," 7 August 1917, 1, NARA RG84 Consular Posts, Barranquilla, Colombia, vol. 129. In other Latin American film cultures, lack of realism was not cause for scorn. For instance, a Mexican critic described American serials as narratives in which "not even implausibility proved to be an obstacle" (quoted in Serna, *Making Cinelandia*, 26).

52. "Leyendo la prensa cinematográfica," *Películas*, June 1919.

53. "Crónica de Bogotá," *Cine-Mundial*, August 1919, 639–40.

54. *Películas* also promoted and published novelizations of another Italian melodramatic genre, the action-packed *Maciste* feature-lengths. For a study of Italian serials including *Maciste*, see Dall'Asta, "Italian Serial Films," 300–307.

55. "Las tendencias cinematográficas," *Películas*, 27 January 1917.

56. A rather flippant example consists of an anti-Hollywood article, "The American Danger," accompanied by illustrated ads for the Warner Brothers serial *The Lost City* (dir. E. A. Martin, 1920). *Películas*, July 1920.

57. Later this process carried over to local film production, a publication independent of the Di Domenicos suggests. A column celebrating the premier of *Como los muertos* (As the Dead; dir. Pedro Moreno Garzón and Vincenzo Di Domenico, 1925) highlights the film's distance from Hollywood stylistics: "[The film] is not infected by the mania of cinematographic sensationalism that is so seductive in the United States." "Las películas nacionales de la casa SICLA," *Mundo al día*, 25 May 1925.

58. Nicolás Díaz, "Los Desorbitados," *Cine Mundial*, June 1917, 282.

59. Hipólito Seijas, "El Menichelismo," *El Universal*, 14 October 1917. Looking at the development of local film criticism in Mexico City, Rielle Navitski considers the reception of diva films "pivotal" during the 1910s in shaping gendered conceptions of the film critic as erudite and male and spectators as middle class and female. Navitski, "Early Film Critics," 58–59.

60. To belabor this point, Ana López contends that Italian melodramas significantly influenced early narrative filmmaking in Mexico. López, "Early Cinema and Modernity," 69.

61. *El País*, 30 May 1913, 5; and *El Diario del Hogar*, 7 October 1914, 4. My gratitude to Rielle Navitski for sharing the documents from *El Diario del Hogar* cited here.

62. Gunckel, *Mexico on Main Street*, 34. Serna, *Making Cinelandia*, 171. See also Berg, *Latino Images in Film*.

63. "Notas," *Cine-Mundial*, vol. II, no. 3, March 1917, 113.

64. Rather contradictorily, editor in chief of *Cine-Mundial* Francisco García Ortega—writing in *Moving Picture World*—urged American producers to stop sending greaser films to Latin America, but not to stop making them. He suggests other markets: the United States, "Europe, [and] Africa." Francisco García Ortega, "Random Shots about Export," *Moving Picture World*, 10 March 1917, 1545, quoted in Navitski, "Mediating the 'Conquering,'" 125.

65. Serna, *Making Cinelandia*, 7.

66. García Mesa, *Cine latinoamericano*, 9.

67. General Porfirio Díaz served seven terms as Mexican president, from 1987 to 1911. He was forced from office by the series of armed conflicts that became the Mexican Revolution.

68. Fullerton, "Creating an Audience," 99, 102; see also Fullerton, *Picturing Mexico*, 105.

69. Reyes, "Hacia la industria cinematográfica," 134–35.

70. Vincenot, "Filmando a los héroes nacionales," 133.

71. López, "Early Cinema and Modernity," 56.

72. Rojas, "Cine colombiano," 8; and Nieto Ibáñez, *Barranquilla en blanco y negro*, 6.

73. Currently a matter of heated academic debate between "nationalist" and "transnationalist" film historians. See Reyes and Wood, *Cine mudo latinoamericano*, 11.

74. For recent critiques of the notion of national cinema, see Vitalli and Willemen, *Theorising National Cinema*, and, focused on Latin American contemporary cinema, Tierney, *New Transnationalisms*.

75. Ospina León, "Films on Paper."

76. López, "Early Cinema and Modernity"; and Schroeder-Rodríguez, "Latin American Silent Cinema."

77. Paranaguá, *Tradición y modernidad*, 38.

78. Finkielman, *Film Industry in Argentina*, 5–29.

79. Cuarterolo, *De la foto al fotograma*, 133. A similar process took place in Mexico City, with Salvador Toscano's "vistas" compilation film on the Centennial celebrations, *Las fiestas del centenario* (1910). See Míquel, *En tiempos de revolución*, 31–34.

80. Brooks, *Melodramatic Imagination*, 48.

81. For the role of emotion in nation-building discourse, see Anderson, *Imagined Communities*, 51, 258.

82. The list registers "A rural notable (comical)" and "The daughter of the Tequendama (4 acts, drama)" accompanied by "Corpus [Christi] procession in Bogotá 1915" and "July 18th 1915 civic procession." The same advertisement records as "works in progress," "Two noble hearts (drama)" and, based on its

title, a historical film on a Colombian founding father: "Ricaurte in San Mateo." *Olympia*, 2 October 1915.

83. *Largometrajes colombianos en cine y video*.

84. A general for the Liberal Party's rebel army, a lawyer, and a journalist, Rafael Uribe Uribe (1859–1914) fought in the civil wars of 1876, 1886, 1895, and 1899. Between wars he founded and directed two newspapers, *El trabajo* and *El Liberal*. He was murdered on 26 October 1914 by two workers, Jesús Carvajal and Leovigildo Galarza. Their motives were never fully revealed.

85. "Consecuentes," *El Cine Gráfico*, 28 January 1916. This article responds, and includes references, to several columns in Conservative Party newspapers condemning the film.

86. *El Tiempo*, 14 November 1915.

87. Suárez, *Cinembargo Colombia*, 19.

88. "Los orígenes del cine nacional," *Mundo al día*, 22 January 1924.

89. See *El Tiempo*, 14 November 1915.

90. Zarzosa, *Refiguring Melodrama*, 20.

91. Doane, *Emergence of Cinematic Time*, 155.

92. For Mary Ann Doane, the "slipperiness" associated with "the ontological status of the image" up to 1907 was related to the "largely unregulated entrepreneurship characterizing the business of cinema in its early years" in both Europe and the United States. *Emergence of Cinematic Time*, 156. Without formulating a teleological argument, but acknowledging the complex novelty of presenting local current events in narrative film, *El drama del 15 de octubre* may have triggered such contested reactions and understandings of the crime reenactment precisely because of the lack of any previous fiction film production in Colombia up to the early 1910s. As its title suggests, the film aimed at moving its spectators through melodramatic narrative rather than objectively registering historical facts.

93. In his seminal work *The Melodramatic Imagination*, Peter Brooks contends that the demise of the "traditional Sacred" and the correlative rise of the secular nation-state conditioned the possibility of the melodramatic mode (15–16). For recent critiques of this premise, in which this book also engages, particularly in chapter 3, see Allen, "Passion of the Christ," 39–42; and Buckley, "Unbinding Melodrama," 23–28. In his pivotal work *Culturas híbridas*, Néstor García Canclini stresses secularization in Latin American modernization processes (12).

94. García Riera, *Historia del cine mexicano*, 41; and Wood, "Cine mudo," 32.

95. A reference to the declaration of independence, when Miguel Hidalgo declaimed, "Death to the Spaniards and long live the Virgin of Guadalupe." Hidalgo's army used the Virgin of Guadalupe as its insignia on hats and banners. For a study of religious and nationalist discourses in Mexican identity, see Krauze, *Mexico, Biography of Power*.

96. "Hoy es el día de la Virgen de Guadalupe," *Excelsior*, 12 December 1921.

97. "Hoy es el día de la Virgen de Guadalupe."

98. Schroeder-Rodríguez, "Latin American Silent Cinema," 47.

99. Paranaguá, *Tradición y modernidad*, 46.

100. Paranaguá, *Tradición y modernidad*, 47.

101. Building on Nicola Miller's notion of "the meta-narrative of the deficient," I address this theoretical issue in the introduction. Among the vast body of literature on the topic, canonical texts reproducing the notion of modernity as rupture include Marshal Berman's *All That Is Solid Melts into Air*—an influential book for Latin American scholars—and, in Latin America, García Canclini's *Culturas híbridas*.

102. Miller, *Reinventing Modernity*, 4.

103. Ramey, "La resonancia del exilio," 124.

104. See García Riera, *Historia del cine mexicano*, 41; and Wood, "Cine mudo," 32.

105. García Blizzard, "Whiteness and the Ideal," 76.

106. Lest we forget, the United States entered the Great War in 1917 in response to U-boat warfare. Scholars dispute which is the main plot of the film: the modern star-crossed lover's story (García Blizzard, Wood) or the colonial Virgin of Guadalupe narrative (Ramey). I concur with the former. Melodramatic plotting allows for both portions of the film to "work together to resignify the religious content." García-Blizzard, "Whiteness and the Ideal," 80. See also Wood, "Cine mudo," 31.

107. Literary scholar Doris Sommer coined the term "foundational fictions" in her eponymous book. The analysis that follows differs considerably from Sommer's allegorical reading of national cohesion, however. Taking distance from Sommer's amalgamating "erotics of politics"—according to which fictional characters allegorically reconcile and bring together disparate elements of the nation—I consider in the present book that foundational fictions operate instead under what Peter Brooks defines as melodrama's "logic of the excluded middle"—that is, "the ritual . . . involv[ing] the confrontation of clearly identified antagonists and the expulsion of one of them." A model premised on expulsion rather than amalgamation best describes the stratified societies, not necessarily national, that these narratives propose. (Further, if one were to actually read Sommer's corpus, one would notice that only intramarriages, not cross-class or cross-race marriages, as well as other enduring forms of association actually take place in these novels.) Sommer, *Foundational Fictions*, 19; Brooks, *Melodramatic Imagination*, 17. For the role of the *letrado* in Latin America, see Rama, *Lettered City*.

108. Sarmiento, *Obras completas*, 208.

109. I specifically borrow from David Bolter and Richard Grusin's concept of remediation of the latter's "repurposing" function, that is, ways of borrowing narrative content from one medium to another that yield "a necessary redefinition" of medium-specific narrative conventions and content. *Remediation*, 45.

110. Navitski, *Public Spectacles of Violence*, 135. Navitski focuses on Brazil and Mexico, but as this section suggests, the effect was manifest on a broader scale.

111. "La influencia del cinematógrafo en los modernos medios de despojar al prójimo de lo que legítimamente le pertenece," *El Universal*, 31 January 1921.

112. "Ante el deber: 'El cine,'" *Acción femenina* (Buenos Aires), September 1922.

113. "Hace 25 años, 22 de diciembre (1915)," *El Tiempo*, 22 Dececember 1939, 16.

114. Mafud, "Nación y ficción," 162.

115. Abel, *Ciné Goes to Town*, 246–77.

116. In the 1910s and 1920s, nineteenth-century novels reached an unprecedented mass of readers as a result of technological imports (the rotary press) and the development of reading programs by large publishing houses. See Romero, *Libros baratos*.

117. Shumway, *Invention of Argentina*, 112.

118. "Amalia de Mármol: Dos interesantes veladas en Solís. Comentarios," *La Razón* (Uruguay), 20 February 1915, 4, quoted in Torello, *La conquista del espacio*, 61. Emphasis in original.

119. Mafud, "Nación y ficción," 160.

120. Benítez-Rojo, "Nineteenth-Century Spanish American Novel," 481.

121. Monsiváis, "El melodrama," 107; and Hershfield, *Imagining la Chica Moderna*, 123–24.

122. In chronological order, the versions were directed by Luis G. Peredo (1918), Antonio Moreno (1932), Norman Foster and Alberto Gómez de la Vega (1943), and Emilio Gómez Muriel (1969).

123. From the silent period to the present, there have been at least seven adaptations of *María* to film—and many more to soap opera and theater—in Colombia, Mexico, and Puerto Rico. In chronological order, film adaptations have been directed by Rafael Bermúdez Zataraín (Mexico, 1918), Máximo de Calvo and Alfredo del Diestro (Colombia, 1922), Chano Urueta (Mexico, 1938), Enrique Grau (Colombia, 1966), Alfonso Castro Martínez (Colombia, 1970), Tito Davison (Colombia-Mexico, 1972), and Fernando Allende (Puerto Rico, 2010).

124. Benítez-Rojo, "Nineteenth-Century Spanish American Novel," 458.

125. Literary scholar Julia Paulk, building upon Doris Sommer's work, concurs regarding how *María* was immediately accepted as "foundational fiction" at home and abroad: "*María* has never been out of publication since its first appearance in 1867, and has been so widely accepted as a narrative of nation-building that it has even 'fill[ed] the slot for foundational fiction novel in syllabi of countries such as Puerto Rico and Honduras' (Sommer 172)." "Foundational Fiction," 52.

126. Brooks, *Realist Vision*, 40.

127. Martín-Barbero, "La telenovela desde el reconocimiento," 72.

128. "María," *Anuario Teatral Argentino* (1924–1925): 65–66.

129. "La María de J. Isaacs en opera," *El Mundo al día*, 19 January 1924.

130. "Una charla en el auto Fiat," *Películas*, January 1919.

131. Miguel Rasch Isla, "La María en el cinematógrafo," *Películas*, August 1919.

132. Arias Trujillo, *Leopardos*, 11.

133. *Largometrajes colombianos en cine y video*. Extant footage is available to the general public through Luis Ospina's documentary *En busca de María* (In the search for María, 1985).

134. References to the film in Buenos Aires highlight the presence of landscapes. "La novela 'María' será adaptada a la pantalla," *Última Hora*, 24

November 1922, 3. For study of landscape in Isaacs's novel, see Alzate, "Otra amada y otro paisaje," 117–35.

135. Suárez, *Cinembargo Colombia*, 21.

136. "El estreno de la María de Isaacs," *El Tiempo*, 23 October 1922.

137. A letter archived at the FPFC, directed to Máximo De Calvo and signed by film historian Hernando Salcedo Silva in 1961, acknowledges receipt of what Salcedo Silva calls "El álbum de 'La María'" and speculates it was published in 1930. The album itself does not include a publication date. Two stills have been ripped out. Based on the texts located on the opposite page, the missing stills consist of a scene in which "María, Emma, and Efraín read Chateaubriand's novel *Atala*" and a rather mysterious picture that, based on the accompanying text, suggests a deviation from the novel: "Dreams, Dreams, Dreams."

138. The Fundación Patrimonio Fílmico Colombiano holds a series of articles published around the premier of the film in 1922. Unfortunately the articles have been cut out from their original sources and therefore lack key information such as publication titles and dates.

139. The caption reads, "After three days, the fever still withstood the doctor's efforts to fight it. The symptoms were so alarming that at certain moments not even the doctor could hide the anxiety that was taking over him. MARIA Ch. XXXVII."

140. While deeming it "primitive," film historians Hernando Martínez Pardo and Hernando Salcedo Silva consider the theatrical fixed shot to be the trademark of Colombian feature-length silent films. Martínez Pardo, *Historia del cine colombiano*, 61; and Salcedo Silva, *Crónicas del cine colombiano*, 66.

141. The epigraph, by Carmelo Hispano, reads: "The glory of Isaacs is like the glory of Bolívar: it grows with the times because both Isaacs and Bolívar, each in his own sphere and according to their degrees, are the most popular and undisputed geniuses that have magnified and dignified our America." Furthermore, with its closing expression, the epigraph alludes to José Martí's seminal essay "Our America" (first published in Mexico City, 1891), stressing the album's regional—not national—fervor.

142. Doane, *Emergence of Cinematic Time*, 155.

143. Around the 1910s, the hacienda El Paraíso was uninhabited and considerably deteriorated. At the time, multiple articles in the press exhorted readers to associate and gather funds to purchase and restore the hacienda as a nationalistic endeavor. "El escenario de 'María,'" *Lecturas Dominicales, El Tiempo*, 8 July 1923.

144. See letter to Máximo De Calvo, signed by Hernando Salcedo Silva, 1961, archived at the FPFC.

145. Two accounts in particular in Ospina's documentary feed these views: the daughter of one producer, Berta Llorente, claims that years after the film premiered and as a child, she would cut up the film's rolls to play film editor; in his turn, de Calvo's son-in-law Manuel Narvaez recollects that not knowing what to do with "all those [film] rolls," the family decided to burn them.

146. In an interview for the documentary, Narvaez affirmed that the film circulated in multiple "nations of the South."

147. Paranaguá, *Tradición y modernidad*, 39.

148. This list focuses on novels, but it is important to note that during the period theatre plays were also adapted. For a recent study, see Míquel, "Del teatro al cine."

149. Paranaguá, *Tradición y modernidad*, 39–40.

150. "La novela 'María' será adaptada a la pantalla," *Última Hora*, 24 November 1922, 3.

151. Schroeder-Rodríguez, "Latin American Silent Cinema," 20.

152. "Nobleza Gaucha," *Películas*, 2 January 1916.

153. *La Prensa*, 23 August 1915, 18, quoted in Navitski, "Silent and Early Sound Cinema," 37. See, among other historical studies, Cuarterolo, *De la foto al fotograma*, and Peña, *Cien años de cine argentino*.

154. Rielle Navitski has traced screenings in Santiago de Chile, Rio de Janeiro, Lima, and even Barcelona. Navitski, "Silent and Early Sound Cinema," 37.

155. "Una película mexicana de propaganda," *El Globo* (Mexico City), 25 February 1925, 3, quoted in Reyes, "Hacia la industria cinematográfica," 125. Emphasis added.

156. "Una película mexicana de propaganda."

CHAPTER 2. BUENOS AIRES SHADOWS

Epigraph. Pascual Contursi, *Flor de Fango* (Mud flower), music by Augusto Gentile, 1917.

1. "Sombras de Buenos Aires" *Excelsior*, 19 September 1923.

2. "Nuestro 4° Concurso Cinematográfico," *Crítica* (Buenos Aires), 28 May 1921.

3. Grand Cinematographic Contests required *Crítica* readers to fill out questionnaires, cut them out, and send them to *Crítica*'s editorial department on Sarmiento Street. The first and second contests challenged readers' cinematic proficiency with comparative questions such as "Who is the best national actor?" followed by "Who is the best foreign actor?" The third consisted of sending letters to the readers' favorite stars. Prizes ranged from seats in local theaters to small amounts of cash. For the fourth contest, readers had to fill out a coupon and send it in with a portrait of themselves attached. The lucky winners participated in *Crítica*'s acting academy—directed by famous local actors Leopoldo Torre (*Nobleza Gaucha*; dir. Eduardo Martínez de la Pera and Ernesto Gunche, 1915) and Ángel Bollano *(De vuelta al pago*; dir. José A. Ferreyra, 1919)—and were promised they would participate in a film shooting. Participants had to conceal their identity with the name of a foreign actor. Therefore, as *Crítica* advertised the contest throughout the year, readers could see (themselves) in photographs and long lists of the "selected few": distinguished by the participants' initials, droves of Mary Pickfords, Pearl Whites, Douglas Fairbanks, and William Farnums, and one Sessue Hayakawa, among other stars. Most likely Mary Pickford, the young housemaid who wishes to become a movie star in *Sombras*, winked at the many dreamers populating *Crítica*'s pages. All references in *Crítica* (Buenos Aires). "Primer Gran Concurso Cinematográfico," 17 October 1919; "Concurso de Caras," 7 February 1920; "Gran Concurso Cinematográfico," 22 November

1920; and "4° Concurso Cinematográfico: ¿Quiere ser usted artista de cine?," 17 May 1921.

4. "Producción nacional," *La Película*, 1 September 1923, 21.

5. "Modistillas porteñas," *Cine Mundial: Sección Argentina*, September 1922, 9. For a thorough account of nationalistic Argentine films prior to the 1920s, see Cuarterolo, *De la foto al fotograma*, 105–47.

6. "Una iniciativa que se debe fomentar," *Última Hora*, 1 April 1925, 4.

7. See Montaldo, *De pronto, el campo*; Cuarterolo, "Imágenes de la Argentina opulenta," 19–34; and, more recently, Suárez, "¿Gauchos de bronce o de yeso?," 64–87. For depictions of gauchos in Argentine silent cinema, see also chapter 5.

8. I refer to films such as *¡Tango!* (dir. Luis Moglia Barth) and *Los tres berretines* (Equipo Lumiton studio), both released in 1933, not the Paramount Pictures films starring Carlos Gardel. The latter focused on different, yet equally important, forms of cultural identification on local and transnational scales. See D'Lugo, "Early Cinematic Tangos," 9–23; and Navitski, "Tango on Broadway," 26–49.

9. "Y en una noche de carnaval," *La Película* (Buenos Aires), 23 July 1925, n.p.; and "La mujer de media noche," *La Película* (Buenos Aires), 15 October 1925, 16–17.

10. "Y en una noche de carnaval."

11. For a theoretical explanation of melodrama's ability to both reveal and conceal, as well as its political implications, see the introduction to this book. The processes leading to economic and gender disparity motivated by urban reform and beautification policies were not unique to Buenos Aires. Cities such as Rio de Janeiro, São Paulo, Bogotá, and Mexico City experienced similar processes. See Navitski, *Public Spectacles of Violence*, 11; and Castillo Daza, *Bogotá*, 85.

12. Karush, *Culture of Class*, 84.

13. "Ha obtenido buena aceptación el film nacional 'La costurerita que dio aquel mal paso,'" *La Película* (Buenos Aires), 16 September 1926. Carriego's poem (1910) inspired many tangos, sainete theater plays, and films. In "La costurerita," Carriego critiques female desire for upward mobility. The poem depicts a Manichean world in which innocence and goodness reside in the barrio, in contrast to the morally dangerous world of downtown. Carriego's poetry and short stories incorporated barrio life into the literary field. His contribution was key to the porteño visual regimes of the period.

14. See also the eponymous weekly novel by Josué Quesada in *La novela semanal* (Buenos Aires), 22 December 1919; the sainete by Antonio Casero, "Encarna la costurera o hasta el fin nadie es dichoso"; and the tango "La costurerita" by Leopoldo Torre Ríos and José Ferreyra, ca. 1926.

15. Other films not discussed in this chapter based on fallen woman and cross-media narratives include *La vendedora de Harrods* (The Harrods Saleswoman; dir. Francisco Defilippis Novoa, 1921), *Milonguita* (Little Milonga; dir. José Bustamante, 1922), *Buenos Aires ciudad de ensueño* (Buenos Aires Dream City; dir. José A. Ferreyra, 1922), *La muchacha del arrabal* (Barrio Girl; dir. José A. Ferreyra and Leopoldo Torres Ríos, 1922), *El guapo de arrabal*

(Barrio Tough Guy; dir. Julio Irigoyen, 1923), *Galleguita* (Little Galician Girl; dir. Julio Irigoyen, 1923); *Mientras Buenos Aires duerme* (While Buenos Aires Sleeps; dir. José A. Ferreyra, 1924); *Buenos Aires bohemio* (Bohemian Buenos Aires; dir. Leopoldo Torres Ríos, 1924); *Organito de la tarde* (Afternoon Little Organ; dir. José A. Ferreyra, 1925); *Tu cuna fue un conventillo* (Your Crib Was a Conventillo; dir. Julio Irigoyen, 1925); *Empleada se necesita* (Female Servant Wanted; dir. Leopoldo Torres Ríos, 1925); *Muchachita de Chiclana* (Little Girl from Chiclana; dir. José A. Ferreyra, 1926); *La casa del placer* (The House of Pleasure; dir. Julio Irigoyen, 1929); and *La modelo de la calle Florida* (The Model of Florida Street; dir. Julio Irigoyen, 1929).

16. Karush, *Culture of Class*, 85.
17. Gorelik, *La grilla y el parque*, 291.
18. Karush, *Culture of Class*, 85.
19. Bergero, *Intersecting Tango*.
20. Bruno, "Site-Seeing," 8.
21. In this chapter I compare two types of overcrowded tenement housing: conventillos and boardinghouses. The first consisted of family units, while the second consisted of rooms rented to individuals. See Torrado, *Historia de la familia en la Argentina moderna*, 379.
22. See Bergero, *Intersecting Tango*; and Ansolabehere, *Literatura y anarquismo*.
23. "La mosca y sus peligros," *Cine Mundial: Sección Argentina*, September 1922, 9.
24. "Filmación de películas científicas argentinas," *Última Hora*, 1 April 1920.
25. Cuarterolo, "Imágenes de la Argentina opulenta," 19.
26. Peña, *Cien años de cine argentino*, 18.
27. Losada, "La Moscau Sus Peligros," 466.
28. See, for instance, the "Novelas de Humildades" (1922), which appeared in the crime section of the first Buenos Aires tabloid newspaper, *Crítica* (1913–1962).
29. Based on surviving footage, this film seems to be one of the first attempts in Argentine cinema to explore nonlinear narrative structures and ellipses. The whole film is framed by a flashback of an aged Luis, standing with his son in front of Elvira's tomb. Apparently the novelty required guidance through intertitles. Almost at the end of the film, an expository title reads, "THE EVOCATION ENDS," cutting to the initial shot of the father and son at the graveyard.
30. Muzilli, *El trabajo femenino*, 22.
31. Brooks, *Melodramatic Imagination*, 69.
32. Karush, *Culture of Class*, 87.
33. Karush, *Culture of Class*, 89.
34. Ospina León, "Films on Paper," 39-65.
35. Singer, *Melodrama and Modernity*, 14.
36. Muzilli, *El trabajo femenino*, 6, 21.
37. Feijoo, "Las trabajadoras," 284.
38. Bergero, *Intersecting Tango*, 117.
39. Bergero, 182.
40. Muzilli, *El trabajo femenino*, 21.

41. Muzilli was among several feminist leaders who focused on stricter workplace regulations during the 1910s–1930s. On feminism in Argentina during the period see Hammond, "Working Women and Feminism in Argentina," 83.
42. Fischer, *Designing Women*, 50.
43. "La gran fiesta del Palacio Harrods," *Caras y Caretas*, September 1914, 28.
44. "Las fiestas de Navidad," *Caras y Caretas*, December 1920.
45. Muzilli, *El trabajo femenino*, 20.
46. Muzilli, *El trabajo femenino*, 21.
47. Hansen, *Babel and Babylon*, 13.
48. In his study, Nicolas Poppe suggests that in Argentina "films focusing on the lives of women became increasingly important" during the sound period. However, archival accounts such as Muzilli's and the study presented here show how porteño cinedramas already catered to such a demand. Poppe, "Siteseeing Buenos Aires," 58.
49. Tucker, "Páginas Libres," 122.
50. Initially published in the *Frankfurter Zeitung* in March 1927.
51. Conde, *Foundational Films*, 220.
52. Kracauer, "Little Shop Girls Go to the Movies," 291.
53. Kracauer, "Little Shop Girls Go to the Movies," 292. Emphasis in original.
54. Kracauer, "Little Shop Girls Go to the Movies," 292.
55. Couselo. *El Negro Ferreyra*.
56. Tucker, "Páginas Libres," 134.
57. See Romero, *Libros baratos y cultura*.
58. "El martes se estrenó 'El organito de la tarde,' obra que distribuye Argentina Program," *La Película*, 15 October 1925, 29; and "Se pasó en privado 'Perdón, viejita,'" *La Película*, 18 August 1927, 21.
59. See Jacobs, "Censorship and the Fallen Woman Cycle," 100–47.
60. I thank Laura Serna for pointing out to me the striking resemblance between both sequences.
61. Quoted in Higashi, "Cecil B. DeMille," 190.
62. Cecil B. DeMille, "Fotodrama o Arte Nuevo," *Cine-Mundial* (New York), August 1917, 385. *Cine-Mundial*, the Spanish-language version of *Moving Picture World*, circulated widely across Latin America, including Argentina, from the late 1910s up to the early 1930s.
63. Armus, "Journey from the Barrio to the City Center," 79.
64. Quoted in Bergero, *Intersecting Tango*, 121.
65. Pellarolo, *Sainetes, cabaret*, 23.
66. "'Galleguita' se ha impuesto," *Excelsior* (Buenos Aires), 1 July 1925, 29. Photograms in film ads indicate that *Galleguita* (Little Galician Girl,1925), directed by Julio Yrigoyen, also dealt with girls in cabarets. Yrigoyen began a lifelong filmmaking career, producing newsreels and institutional films on the fringes of the Argentine movie industry. Tapping into the best-grossing tendencies in the market, Yrigoyen first dipped into fiction filmmaking by capitalizing on a makeshift River Plate Chaplin (played by Carlos Torres Ríos, brother of Leopoldo Torres Ríos). Peña, *Cien años de cine argentino*, 41. During the

1920s, Yrigoyen produced films that resorted to crime mystery narrative and films that drew upon tango lyrics as a source of inspiration—a tendency introduced and mastered by José Agustín Ferreyra. Yrigoyen's company, Buenos Aires Films, was one of the most prolific and economically successful during the period. Full-page or double-page ads in trade journals distinguish Buenos Aires Film from other companies with their aggressive advertisement campaigns.

67. Sergio Piñero, "Salvemos el tango," *Martín Fierro* (Buenos Aires), 18 July and 5 August 1925. Interestingly, his diatribe taps into Colombian melodramatic literature as a way to denounce tango's excesses: "[Tango] makes superhuman efforts to achieve emotion . . . like a [José María] Vargas Vila serpentine [serpentina 'vargasviliana']."

68. "El martes se estrenó 'El organito de la tarde', obra que distribuye Argentina Program," *La Película* (Buenos Aires), 15 October 1925, 29.

69. The fact that porteño cinedrama had concerns about women's changing patterns of work does not mean that these films were exhibited for a gendered audience. In one of the film's ads, a photo of the Los Andes Theatre in Boedo shows a full house—purportedly 1,170 persons—comprised of almost as many women as men. "El organito de la tarde: el éxito de los éxitos," *Excelsior* (Buenos Aires), 21 October 1925, 16–17.

70. Monsiváis, "El melodrama," 113.

71. Monsiváis, "El melodrama," 114.

72. American scholarship has also explored the relationship between embodiment and melodrama. For a seminal essay on melodrama and other "body genres," see Williams, "Film Bodies," 2–13.

73. Given the director's propensity for borrowing from tango lyrics, the eponymous tango quoted earlier may have inspired Ferreyra's film. Vieytes, "La Vuelta al Búlin," 56.

74. "La borrachera del tango," *Revista del Exhibidor*, 20 September 1928.

75. The nude woman, framed by the man, can also be interpreted as a vamp, for Georgina Torello the "mandatory figure" in 1920s European cinema, whose body "needs to be seen, exhibited in its entirety [and] turned into the spectacle of provocative threat." La *conquista del espacio*, 148.

76. Bean, Kapse, and Horak, *Silent Cinema*, 16.

77. Bruno, "Site-Seeing," 19.

78. Singer, *Melodrama and Modernity*, 132.

79. Brooks, *Melodramatic Imagination*, 50.

CHAPTER 3. BOGOTÁ AND MEDELLÍN

Epigraph. Article 180 of the Caldas police code, quoted in Caldas Governorate to the American Consulate in Barranquilla, 13 October 1925, NARA RG84, Consular Posts, Barranquilla, Colombia, vol. 180.

1. "Arte nuevo," *Cine Colombia*, May 1924.

2. Analyzing Colombian family melodramas also highlights the role of religion and religious practices in Latin American film production, taking into account that the films studied in this chapter do not exactly match Paul Schroeder-Rodríguez's definition of the "religious film," that is, films that "celebrate the role of the

church in maintaining an idealized patriarchal order, using as a model medieval mystery and morality plays set invariably in a pastoral countryside" (see chapter 1). Instead, this chapter builds on recent studies looking at film cultures that affirmed the compatibility of material progress, modern science, and religion—the latter considered not from a theological perspective but as a "sociopolitical force and cultural determinant ... in the public sphere." Schroeder-Rodríguez, "Latin American Silent Cinema," 46; and Pérez, *Confessional Cinema*, 3.

3. Farnsworth-Alvear, *Dulcinea in the Factory*, 228.
4. See chapter 2.
5. Brooks, *Melodramatic Imagination*, 48.
6. Brooks, *Melodramatic Imagination*, 21, 50.
7. Brooks, *Melodramatic Imagination*, 15.
8. Looking at medieval painting and sculpted representations of the Passion of Christ, Richard Allen questions Brooks's account and the triumph of secularism. He proposes instead an " incipiently modern sense of selfhood that emerged within a broadly religious framework" and yielded a new "Christianity of Pathos," from which melodrama would draw its imagery of Christ as a suffering human being and a source of empathic identification—such as the imagery opening this chapter. Allen, "Passion of the Christ," 32.
9. García Canclini, *Culturas híbridas*, 12–13.
10. Paranaguá, *Tradición y modernidad*, 44.
11. Schroeder-Rodríguez, "Latin American Silent Cinema," 47.
12. Urrego, *Sexualidad, matrimonio y familia*, 277.
13. Habermas, "Awareness of What Is Missing," 18.
14. Reder and Schmidt, "Habermas and Religion," 2.
15. See also Santiago Zabala, ed., *The Future of Religion*. New York: Columbia UP, 2005.
16. Taylor, *Secular Age*, 3.
17. Habermas, "Awareness of What Is Missing," 22.
18. Concha Henao, *Historia social del cine*, 263.
19. Duque, *La aventura del cine*, 156.
20. Nieto, *Más allá de la tragedia del silencio*.
21. See the remarkably popular "Manual de Carreño," a compendium of urbanity lessons first published in 1853 and still published today. Carreño, *Manual de urbanidad*. See also Lander, "El Manual de urbanidad," 83–96.
22. It is no coincidence that leprosy motivates the story in the film. It is important to note that extant fragments of another film, *Como los muertos* (Like the Dead; SICLA, 1925), focuses on leprosy as well, just as melodramatic short stories in popular magazines did throughout the 1920s. A sociocultural factor gave salience to the disease in Colombia. Between the second half of the nineteenth century and the first decades of the twentieth, Colombia suffered collective cultural paranoia regarding the disease. Biblical mythology, overblown statistical reports, medical papers, and the popular press triggered nationwide concern over leprosy. At its peak, the result was Agua de Dios—a county-size national concentration camp, and parallel currency system, that removed sick citizens and their families from society. The main actors in this process were the state, the church, and medical practitioners. All three are influential forces in *La*

tragedia del silencio. On leprosy isolation hospitals in Colombia, see Martínez, *El lazareto de Boyacá*.

23. Concha Henao, *Historia social del cine*, 399.
24. López, "Early Cinema and Modernity," 49.
25. López, "Early Cinema and Modernity," 56.
26. See "Textos de enseñanza. Carta arzobispo Paul al ministro de Instrucción Pública," *Anales de Instrucción Pública* 12 (1888): 441–45.
27. With the approval of the church, Catholic lay associations in Colombia had the power to emit indulgences—that is, reductions of temporal punishment in purgatory for sins committed. The ability to produce indulgences, Urrego argues, granted lay associations tremendous influence in various social matters. Urrego, *Sexualidad, matrimonio y familia*, 287.
28. Film historian Concha Henao has found press articles indicating how this Inquisition-like practice included seizing and burning film journals such as *Cine-Mundial*, the Spanish version of *Moving Picture World* published out of New York. Concha Henao, *Historia social del cine*, 478.
29. Urrego, *Sexualidad, matrimonio y familia*, 276, 300.
30. For the use of religious props and shot compositions in the production of a "moral symbolic system" (*une symbolique morale*), see Lefebvre, "L'utilisation du crucifix."
31. Heliodoro González Coutin, "La tragedia del Silencio," *Cine Colombia*, May 1924.
32. The "first chapter" also includes two subplots that do not appear in the film, one alluding to Bogotá's *Muisca* cosmogonic myth and another revolving around a battle in an unspecified civil war (by the turn of the century, Colombia had had nine civil wars).
33. *El Gráfico*, 12 April 1924.
34. The premiere of the film also involved similar practices. It was "graced" by the presence of President Ospina, several secretaries, the mayor, the archbishop of Bogotá, and illustrious families, such as the Acevedo family. "La fiesta social del jueves," *El Tiempo* (Bogotá), 26 April 1924, 6.
35. "Hospital de Hortúa," *Cromos*, January 1926. Another interesting example of "material progress" appears in *El Valle del Cauca y su progreso—The Cauca Valley and Its Progress* (Colombia Film, 1925). A bilingual institutional film, *El Valle* documents industrial and infrastructural progress in the Cauca Valley region. In the film, railway bridges, industrial processes, and the "Lord of the Miracles" brick Basilica (1907) in Buga denote modernization on equal terms.
36. *El tiempo de Medellín* (Medellín), 21 November 1924, 4.
37. The Sociedad de Mejoras Públicas de Pereira was comprised of the city's industrialists and landed gentry.
38. "Pereira o Nido de Cóndores," *El Tiempo* (Bogotá), 3 September 1927, 8.
39. Quoted in Duque, *La aventura del cine*, 177.
40. Farnsworth-Alvear, *Dulcinea in the Factory*, 229.
41. Farnsworth-Alvear, *Dulcinea in the Factory*, 5.
42. Comparing São Paulo to Medellín, Paulo Antonio Paranaguá reaches a similar conclusion. To the Brazilian film historian, *Bajo el cielo antioqueño*

constitutes a "collective portrait [of] a traditional bourgeoisie" that finds in cinema "the ideal representational medium [to shape] rural tradition into urban modernity." Paranaguá, *Tradición y modernidad*, 64.

43. Palacios, *Entre la legitimidad*, 83.
44. Farnsworth-Alvear, *Dulcinea in the Factory*, 45.
45. According to film historian Álvaro Concha Henao, the film was exhibited in several Venezuelan cities. To date, no records have been found suggesting the film circulated in other countries. Concha Henao, *Historia social del cine*, 342.
46. The killers' capture and the trial sequences are examples of elaborate continuity editing techniques in the film. The first sequence contains cuts on action, exhilarating parallel editing, and close-ups on cops and killers as they reach for a gun on the floor. The second sequence, more tableau-like, complements Lina's defense at court with a flashback.
47. Suárez, *Cinembargo Colombia*, 22.
48. *La Defensa* (Medellín), October 1924, quoted in Duque, *La aventura del cine*, 175.
49. Sofía Ospina de Avarro, "Lo que es el feminismo antioqueño," *Hogar*, 16 May 1926.
50. Consular documents report on "serial films [that] have proved exceedingly popular," including serial-queen melodramas such as *The Adventures of Elaine*. E. Guyant, American consul, missive to Oceanic Film Co., 12 July 1917, NARA RG84, Consular Posts, Barranquilla, Colombia, vol. 129.
51. Singer, *Melodrama and Modernity*, 221–22.
52. See chapter 1 and Ospina León, "Films on Paper."
53. Concha Henao, *Historia social del cine*, 455.
54. Torres and Durán, "Recuperación y restauración, 54.
55. In Spanish, *miseria* denotes extreme poverty rather than emotional distress.
56. For a study centered on the rural "side" of the film, see Wood, "Erotismo, moralismo y transgresión," 33–58.
57. Urrego, *Sexualidad, matrimonio y familia*, 208.
58. Wood, "Erotismo, moralismo y transgresión," 46.
59. "En las garras del buitre," *Sal y pimienta*, 22 March 1922.
60. Don Fulano, "La pobrecita moral," *Sal y pimienta*, 20 March 1926.
61. Farnsworth-Alvear, *Dulcinea in the Factory*, 101.
62. Farnsworth-Alvear, *Dulcinea in the Factory*, 79.
63. Stevens, "Marianismo: The Other Face of Machismo," 5.
64. *Alma provinciana* reinforces Rosa's Marian purity through montage as well. In an introductory sequence, Rosa's portrait intercuts with close-ups on white roses—a cultural allusion to purity as well as a Marian allegory.
65. See Kirkpatrick, *Las Románticas*.
66. *El Colombiano* (Medellín), 12 May 1925, quoted in Duque, *La aventura del cine*, 195.
67. Comparing the film to other Peruvian and Mexican films of the period, David M. J. Wood duly notes how *Alma* expresses the "fears and contradictions" of modernization by means of "a certain stylistic nostalgia that rejects

the transition towards a North American aesthetic associated with dynamism and modernity." Wood, "Erotismo, moralismo y transgresión," 43.

68. Denning, *Mechanic Accents*, 212.

69. See Sarlo, *El imperio de los sentimientos*.

70. Particularly the articles and caricatures of the latter depict a city in constant change. In its pages, Bogotá becomes a highly eroticized visual spectacle, in which citizens of different social classes negotiate their place and agency in public and private spheres.

71. "El filipichín," *Sal y pimienta*, 8 May 1926.

72. "Las damas bogotanas y los filipichines: Diálogo en la intimidad de un tocador," *Sal y pimienta*, 8 May 1926.

73. See *Nuevo tesoro lexicográfico de la lengua española*.

74. Derrida, "Archive Fever," 9–63.

CHAPTER 4. ORIZABA, VERACRUZ

Epigraph. "El puño de hierro," in *Cine en línea* catalog, Filmoteca UNAM, 2015, https://www.filmoteca.unam.mx/cinelinea/html/puno.html.

1. Esperanza Vázquez, interview with Juan Sebastián Ospina León, June 2017.

2. Williams, *On the Wire*, 84.

3. Fernández, Wood, and Valdez, "Apuntes para una filmografía," 89–108, 90–91. On early compilation films of the Mexican Revolution see the special dossier in *Vivomatografías*, no. 2 (2016): 6–123. For repurposing practices in Uruguayan silent cinema, see Torello, "Salvar almas," 192–202.

4. Fernández, "Analytical Overview of Mexican Silent Cinema." Fernández's "film cartography" focuses on Mexican compilation films from the 1910s and 1930s through the 2000s.

5. Benjamin, "N.," in *Arcades Project*, 462 (N2a, 3).

6. In *The History of Sexuality* (1978), Michel Foucault first proposes the concept of biopolitics to describe strategies and mechanisms that multiple institutions deploy to manage human life processes while shaping the production of knowledge, power, and processes of subject formation. Taking the administration of life and populations as its subject, the function of biopolitics is, for Foucault, "to ensure, sustain, and multiply life, to put . . . life in order" (138).

7. Reyes, *Sucedió en Jalisco*, 440.

8. I elaborate the question of concurrent film versions in the next chapter.

9. In the late 1920s, films were produced in Baja California, Jalisco, Michoacán, Oaxaca, Puebla, and Yucatán. See Míquel, "Rafael Bermúdez Zataraín," 51.

10. See Estrada, "El tren fantasma"; Mayer, *William (Willie) Mayer*; Vázquez interview; Vázquez Mantecon, "El puño de hierro"; and Wood, "Recuperar lo efímero."

11. Reyes, *Sucedió en Jalisco*, 440.

12. Wood, "Recuperar lo efímero," 133.

13. Jorge de la Rosa, quoted in Wood, "Recuperar lo efímero," 139.

14. Vázquez interview.

15. Reyes, *Sucedió en Jalisco*, 440.

16. The title reads, "Restoration Data Sheet: Esperanza Vázquez: editorial restoration / Editing: Manuel Rodríguez / Technical Assistant: Antonio Valencia / Laboratory: José A. Ramírez / Restoration Coordinator: Francisco Gaytán. May 2002. *Tren Fantasma*, Filmoteca UNAM, 2002."

17. "Sinopsis del argumento del tren fantasma, puesto en escena por el Centro Cultural Cinematrográfico S.A.," box 469, exp. 31, fs. 11, 1927; and "SINOPSIS de la película cinematográfica titulada EL PUNO DE HIERRO, cuya propiedad artística y edición, son propiedad del CENTRO CULTURAL CINEMATOGRAFICO, Sociedad Anónima, Orizaba, Veracruz, México," box 472, exp. 19, fs. 8, 1927. Both boxes also contain production stills and lobby cards, which were key for Vázquez's reconstruction.

18. Vázquez interview.

19. *El tren* did screen in the United States. An advertisement suggests it was shown in Los Angeles, at the Teatro México on Main Street. *El Heraldo de México* (Los Angeles, CA), 4 November 1928. The film was also screened in Corona, California, in August 1917. See Drew and Vázquez "El Puño de Hierro," 13.

20. The film does include some dialogue intertitles. Comparing the synopsis —a third-person narration—with the film reveals that Vázquez transposed indirect discourse to direct discourse when possible. For instance, in a bullfighting sequence in which Paco Mendoza puts his life at risk to impress Elena (see plot details in the following section), the synopsis reads: "Paco tells [Elena] I will turn your laughter into tears, and faces the bull," whereas Vázquez's dialogue intertitle reads: "—I will turn your laughter into tears."

21. An introductory title reads, in Spanish only, "The lost sequence begins."

22. Compare the synopsis, "The old man they have kidnapped is Elena's uncle, no less, who was going to her wedding," with the intertitle, "Elena's uncle, who was travelling to his niece's wedding, is kidnapped by Bocachula [the head bandit]. The bandits robbed him clean in an instant."

23. Vázquez interview.

24. Coordinated by the Arts Foundation of the Ministry of Culture of Brazil (FUNARTE), the VHS series includes silent films from various Latin American countries, including Argentina, Brazil, Cuba, Mexico, Peru, and Venezuela.

25. Vázquez interview.

26. Musser, "Early Cinema of Edwin Porter," 29.

27. Musser, "Early Cinema of Edwin Porter," 30.

28. Everson, *American Silent Film*, 30.

29. Musser, "Early Cinema of Edwin Porter," 30; see also Gessner, "Porter and the Creation of Cinematic Motion," 12.

30. Fernández, Valdez, and Wood, "Apuntes para una filmografía," 89.

31. AGNM box 469, exp. 31, fs. 11, 1927.

32. "Teatro Variedades," *El Dictamen* (Veracruz), 11 February 1927.

33. "El tren fantasma," *El Dictamen* (Veracruz), 12 February 1927.

34. Advertisement in *El Heraldo de México* (Los Angeles, CA), 4 November 1928.

35. According to Navitski, American westerns were "a key point of reference for Mexican adventure melodramas of the 1920s." *Public Spectacles of Violence*, 86.

36. "Fue asaltado, saqueado y quemado el tren de Laredo," *Excelsior*, 21 March 1927; and "Una gavilla de bandoleros de las organizadas por el Episcopado Católico... asaltó el Tren que salió anteayer tarde de Guadalajara para esta Capital, quemando todos los carros y pasando a cuchillo a la mayor parte de los pasajeros de segunda," *El Universal*, 21 April 1927.

37. "La secretaría de industria considera ilegal la actitud de los huelguistas," *El Dictamen* (Veracruz), 18 February 1927.

38. "Tremenda colisión," *El Demócrata* (México City), 2 April 1926; and "Formidable choque de trenes," *El Demócrata* (Mexico City), 3 April 1926.

39. "Estrechase cada momento más el cerco a los que siguen a Núñez: Fuerzas del General Mendoza y el Coronel Núñez se disponen a atacar a los asaltantes del tren en un punto llamado San Gregorio," *El Demócrata* (Mexico City), 15 January 1926.

40. *El Demócrata* (Mexico City), 24 April 1926.

41. The bandits in the cartoon, and in *El tren*, problematically reproduce the "denigrating" image of Mexicans in late 1910s and early 1920s Hollywood westerns that generated frustration in Mexican and Hispanic Angelino audiences of the period. I return to this topic in the following chapter. For a brief history of "denigrating films" see Serna, *Making Cinelandia*, 158–71.

42. Navitski, *Public Spectacles of Violence*, 35.

43. Reyes, *Sucedió en Jalisco*, 444.

44. Vázquez's privileged access to García Moreno's family archives revealed documents in which the director describes spring mechanisms he used to stabilize the camera in railroad sequences of *El tren*. For one of *El tren*'s most thrilling sequences, in which Adolfo rescues Elena from an electric engine out of control, García Moreno also used a scale model of a railway bridge and a miniature locomotive to produce a spectacular explosion. Later press accounts I came across suggest that García Moreno did indeed experiment with different mechanisms in producing his films. An article describes him as both "director" and "inventor." "La película 'Maximiliano' se está haciendo en México," *La Prensa* (San Antonio, TX), 16 April 1933, 7. See also Vázquez and Fernández, "Gabriel García Moreno," 105.

45. Simmel, "Fashion," 543.

46. For a theoretical study on vision and modern subject formations, see Crary, *Techniques of the Observer*.

47. Goldgel, *Cuando lo nuevo conquistó*, 38.

48. The Orizaban elite's influence on the film must have been considerable, to the point that some articles gave prominence to the producers over the director. "Del estreno del Tren Fantasma en Veracruz" describes the film as "an achievement of a group of businessmen from Orizaba [who were] smartly backed [*secundados*] by the technical director Mr. Gabriel García Moreno." *El Dictamen* (Veracruz), 15 February 1927.

49. "La perfecta flapper," *El Universal Ilustrado*, 23 October 1924. The term *flapper* refers to the loose and short dresses, which purportedly flapped with the wind, that American women à la bob wore during the 1920s.

50. Hershfield, *Imagining la Chica Moderna*, 37.

51. Hershfield, *Imagining la Chica Moderna*, 6–7.

52. Hershfield, *Imagining la Chica Moderna*, 77.
53. Simmel, "Fashion," 541.
54. "La cabellera Magdalénica y el pelo 'A lo Valentino,'" *El Dictamen* (Veracruz), 27 February 1927.
55. Cabral, "Amor de hoy," *Revista de Revistas*, 3 January 1926.
56. Andrés Chazari, "Ortigas y Violetas," AGNM box 336, exp. 1, fs 159pp, 1920.
57. The pelona's power was without a doubt threatening to many men. In Mexico City streets, some men—using razors and scissors—violently attacked pelonas in 1924. Rubenstein, "War on 'Las Pelonas,'" 67–69.
58. Sluis, *Deco Body, Deco City*, 77–78. In her study, Ageeth Sluis proposes an approach akin to this book's as she considers the deco body "the site of contested and divergent notions of modernity" (61).
59. Singer, *Melodrama and Modernity*, 224.
60. Translation mine. The bilingual intertitle illogically uses the future tense in English.
61. "La toilette femenina," *Revista de Revistas*, 10 January 1926, 39.
62. See García Díaz, "La clase obrera," 179. García Díaz studies the strong unionization efforts of Orizaban workers in the 1920s and their violent conflicts with industrialists, particularly in the brewery and textile sectors. Not surprisingly, breakouts of social unrest are invisible in *El tren*. As mentioned, the film premiered around the time of the railroad workers' national strike. Film ads in newspapers aimed at attracting railroad workers, but the film itself (and the script) made no reference to unfair or exploitative working conditions in railroad companies.
63. Recall that the gentlemen of the Orizaba Rotary Club produced the film and, in press accounts, strove for prominence over the director. These men also happened to "provide" the female actresses for the film, the Ibáñez sisters. "Del estreno del Tren Fantasma en Veracruz," *El Dictamen* (Veracruz), 15 February 1927.
64. For Slius, the deco body was a "main vehicle in marketing an array of luxury products" and was "reflective of the machine age" (74, 77).
65. Zarco, *Obras completas*, 518. In a similar vein, columns on male fashion contemporary to *El tren* highlight elegance as an empowering form of distinction. An editorial in an illustrated magazine reads: "Elegance, of course, seems to us [the editor] a question of culture, a conquest of . . . the present moment." This distinction is not visual, but class based. Impervious to "bad taste," the column concludes, "the elegant man is not the one 'who looks' [elegant] but the one who by just touching him, makes one think of beautiful and immaterial things." Rafael Cardona, "De la Elegancia, Única Virtud Profana," *Revista de Revistas*, 7 February 1926.
66. "El comercio ilícito de narcóticos ha disminuido considerablemente," *El Demócrata* (Mexico City), 24 January 1926.
67. Added expository titles are clearly identified in the film by the parenthetical comment "(Taken from the synopsis)."
68. In Vázquez Mantecón, "El puño de hierro."

69. "Una inspección a las colonias de la ciudad," *El Dictamen* (Veracruz), 30 March 1927.
70. Reyes, *Sucedió en Jalisco*, 443.
71. In Vázquez Mantecón, "El puño de hierro."
72. See Cano Andaluz, La *gestión presidencial*.
73. Peredo Castro, "Entre tradición y modernidad," 284.
74. For the month of December 1924 alone, de los Reyes has tracked 111 films shown in public squares. Reyes, *Sucedió en Jalisco*, 416.
75. "La semana Antinarcótica," *Revista de Policía* (Mexico City), 25 March 1927. Title case in original.
76. "Cuatro problemas sanitarios atenderá este año la dirección gral. de Salubridad," *El Dictamen* (Veracruz), 26 January 1927.
77. Reyes, *Sucedió en Jalisco*, 437.
78. "La semana Antinarcótica."
79. "Una campaña benéfica," *Revista de Policía* (Mexico City), 30 January 1926, 5. Scrofula is a bacterial infection affecting the lymph nodes in the neck. It can cause extreme glandular swelling and is not a congenital disease. Echoing these purportedly scientific accounts, the Orizaba public hospital sequence shows children with scrofula and other ailments that affect their bodily appearance and motility.
80. Organized in pairs, the plots revolve around Carlos and Laura, two urbanites; Antonio and Esther, a gang leader and the woman he is infatuated with; Perico and Juanito, a teenager and a boy who play detective trying to catch Antonio; and El Buitre and El Tieso, two morphine dealers.
81. The public lecture sequence introduces the second plotline: Antonio, leader of the "Gang of the Bat," and his object of affection, Esther, who is involved in the morphine den's dealings. In this chapter I do not delve into their story, but it is important to note that Antonio, aka El Murciélago (the Bat), and his dark-hooded, KKK-looking gang underline the trope of masked identities in the film—a key narrative convention in my analysis.
82. The Swiss Italian architects Gaspare and Giuseppe Fossati hung the distinctive, giant medallions on the four main columns of the mosque as part of the restoration ordered by Sultan Abdülmecid between 1847 and 1849. Exceeding the limits of this book, the growing interest of Latin American periodicals in Turkey as a non-European model of conservative progress, particularly after 1923, demands further scrutiny. Through the years, references I have come across of such an interest mostly highlight Hagia Sophia and the Blue Mosque—as symbols of tradition—as well as technical achievements and Mustafa Kemal—as symbols of modern change. Historian Dudley Anderson affirms that Saturnino Cedillo, a revolutionary warlord who fought in the Revolution and the Cristero War, was "impressed" by Kemal's "achievements." See Ankerson, *Agrarian Warlord*, 141.
83. "El comercio de drogas heroicas," *El Porvenir* (Monterrey, Nuevo León), 13 March 1926. *El Porvenir* also closely followed the tightening of border patrols at the Mexico-US border to prevent drug imports from North to South. "Agentes especiales vigilarán la frontera," *El Porvenir* (Monterrey), 3 January 1926.

84. "Enérgica campaña contra las drogas en la Cd. de Chihuahua," *El Demócrata* (Mexico City), 8 February 1926.
85. "La campaña a los viciosos," *El Dictamen* (Veracruz), 21 January 1927, 7.
86. "La pipa de hachich," *El Demócrata* (Mexico City), 6 May 1923, 1.
87. "Vendedores de drogas heroicas rumbo a las islas Marías," *El Dictamen* (Veracruz), 24 January 1927.
88. Dr. Celso García Escobar, "Los narcóticos y sus funestas consecuencias," *Boletín de la Secretaría de Educación Pública* (Mexico City), 1 May 1927.
89. "El comercio ilícito de narcóticos ha disminuido considerablemente," *El Demócrata* (Mexico City), 24 January 1926.
90. "Las drogas enervantes," *Crom* (Mexico City), 15 February 1926.
91. "Cuatro problemas sanitarios."
92. "Un microbio más temible que el de la Peste Blanca caerá sobre Veracruz," *El Dictamen* (Veracruz), 26 January 1927. The ad does not refer to a specific Keaton film. However, the following day *El Dictamen* showed an ad for "El boxeador" at the Eslava theater, probably referring to *Battling Butler* (dir. Buster Keaton, 1926).
93. See Sarlo, *El imperio de los sentimentos*.
94. Film historian Carmen Elisa Gómez Gómez locates the origins of fantastic Mexican cinema—extremely popular in the 1940s, 1950s and 1960s—in *La Llorona* (dir. Ramón Peón, 1933). The elements I highlight suggest that the fantastic was already present in the silent period, however. Echoing *El puño*'s fantastic tropes, *El baúl macabro* (The Macabre Trunk; dir. Miguel Zacarías, 1936) explores "territories of a perturbing and imprecise reality," Gómez contends. Gómez Gómez, "Los géneros del cine fantástico mexicano," 111, 114.
95. For classic examples of these tropes—merging the melodramatic and the fantastic while premised on dreams, hallucinations, and physicians—see Horacio Quiroga's short stories "El almohadón de plumas" (1907) and "La mancha hiptálmica" (1917).
96. Todorov, *Introducción a la literatura fantástica*, 86.
97. Todorov, *Introducción a la literatura fantástica*, 23. For Todorov, the first choice would "demote" the fantastic story to a mere story of the marvelous genre.
98. Callahan, "Screening Musidora," 63.
99. Such elaborate narrative arcs, combining real with unreal worlds, are not foreign to Latin American silent cinema. The Argentine film *Hasta después de muerta* (dir. Ernesto Gunche and Eduardo Martínez de la Pera, 1916) uses a similar framework; the bulk of the film consists of an "evocation." See chapter 2.
100. Callahan, "Screening Musidora," 63.
101. Navitski, *Public Spectacles of Violence*, 91.

CHAPTER 5. SOUTH TO NORTH

Epigraph. "Latin-Americans Wideawake; Know and Want Best Pictures," *Moving Picture World*, 29 December 1923, 791.
1. "Nuestra Opinión," *Cine-Mundial*, January 1928, 35. Emphasis in original.

2. "Nuestra Opinión." Producing films technically on a par with Hollywood's was a consistent concern in porteño trade journals. Five years before *Charge*'s release, journals harshly critiqued the "local effort" in filmmaking as not comparable "in spirit, technique, and craft to foreign [American] productions." "Lo que significa hasta ahora el esfuerzo de la cinematografía local," *Excelsior*, 29 November 1923, 1.

3. "La nueva tendencia de los productores yanquis respecto a las películas hispano-americanas," *Heraldo de México*, 29 May 1927, 10.

4. Curubeto, *Babilonia gaucha*, 182.

5. "Cast and Staff of 'Belgrano' Set," *Hollywood Vagabond*, 3 March 1927.

6. Schroeder-Rodríguez, "Latin American Silent Cinema," 20. This was a concern that by the 1920s transcended the Latin American region; see Maltby, "Introduction: 'The Americanisation of the World,'" 2–20.

7. I appropriate the expression from P. David Marshall who, building on Dyer, considers stars and celebrities forms of cultural exegesis. As discursive constructions, in this chapter I consider how they can also performatively shape social formations and disrupt hierarchical arrangements. Marshall, Introduction to *Celebrity Culture Reader*, 2–3.

8. "A space exists when one takes into consideration vectors of direction, velocities, and time variables. Thus space is composed of intersections of mobile elements. It is . . . articulated by the ensemble of movements deployed within it." Michel de Certeau, *Practice of Everyday Life*, 117.

9. Further archival research is needed to assess the film's reception in other countries. In Mexico, the film premiered under the title *Siempre Vencedor* (Forever vanquisher). In Spain and Italy it went by *La carga de los gauchos* and *La carica dei gauchos*, respectively; in England by *The Beautiful Spy*; and in Germany by *Belgrano der Freiheitsheld* (Belgrano, hero of freedom). Zylberman, "Films argentinos," 369; and Cuarterolo, "Filmar la América," 8.

10. Film historian Andrea Cuarterolo, who discovered the film at the Cineteca del Friuli, is currently contrasting this copy to another version she unearthed at the Deutsche Kinemathek.

11. The cast was entirely American, except for the actor playing the gaucho Juan López (Paul Ellis), whom porteño trade journals recognize as the Argentine actor Benjamín Ingénito. "El domingo próximo se exhibirá en privado 'Una nueva y gloriosa nación,'" *Revista del Exhibidor*, 20 April 1928.

12. Ajuria associated with the Italian-born Mario Gallo to produce *La revolución de mayo* (The May Revolution, 1909), discussed in chapter 1, and the lost *El fusilamiento de Dorrego* (Dorrego's Execution, 1910). Di Núbila, *La época de oro*, 16.

13. De Ajuria also produced the canonical film *Nobleza Gaucha* (Gaucho Nobility; dir. Eduardo Martínez de la Pera and Ernesto Gunche, 1915). During the 1910s, and appropriated by porteño letrados, the gaucho accrued cultural capital in identity discourses.

14. Ajuria, *El cinematógrafo como espejo del mundo*, 19.

15. Cuarterolo, *De la foto al fotograma*, 132.

16. European immigrants to Argentina, particularly Spanish and Italian, popularized the expression "hacer la América" as early as the nineteenth century. A

US equivalent would be "the American Dream." In this section, however, I use the expression to highlight how "América" in this context transcends national frameworks and, understood as the search for personal success, allows for complex networks and exchanges between film cultures across borders. For the experience of Italian immigrants and their senses of belonging, see Baily, "'Hacer la América,'" 57–68.

17. Ajuria, *El cinematográfo como espejo del mundo*, 23.
18. Ajuria, *El cinematográfo como espejo del mundo*, 214.
19. Finkielman, *Film Industry in Argentina*, 81.
20. "En Broadway," *Cine-Mundial*, April 1927, 271. Andrea Cuarterolo proposes a more modest budget, of $300,000. Cuarterolo, "Una Nueva y Gloriosa Nación," 182.
21. Benson, *Ben-Hur*.
22. For shifting world markets before and during the Great War, see chapter 1.
23. And eventually expanded its business to Spain.
24. Ajuria, *El cinematográfo como espejo del mundo*, 214.
25. Mitre, "Speech before the National Congress" (1860), quoted in Ajuria, *El cinematográfo como espejo del mundo*, 214. Ajuria's memoirs are sprinkled with quotations by other Argentine figures, such as Domingo Faustino Sarmiento, and excerpts of the Argentine Constitution.
26. Quoted in Finkielman, *Film Industry in Argentina*, 72.
27. Finkielman, *Film Industry in Argentina*, 71.
28. To date, Bushman had made an outstandingly prolific career, which began in the early 1910s. Logan had appeared in several supporting roles in the 1920s.
29. "Bushman to Portray South American Historical Figure," *Motion Picture News*, 25 February 1927, 665.
30. In Hollywood, Benoît was entrusted with the cinematography of *The Wonder Man* (dir. John G. Adolfi, 1920), *What's a Wife Worth?* (dir. Christy Cabanne, 1921), *Live and Let Live* (dir. Cabanne, 1921), *West of Broadway* (dir. Robert Thornby, 1926), and *Pals in Paradise* (dir. George B. Seitz, 1926).
31. Press advertisements highlighted the breadth of the production, bewildering readers with large numbers. With an air of exoticism, an ad boasted: "2000 Thoroughbred Pampas horses! 5000 Blue-hooded Gauchos, embattled infantry! 1500 Tons of muskets, cannons and other implements of warfare! 600 High-explosive shells discharged in artillery barrages! . . . 30 cameras grinding at one time on great battle panoramas! . . . 100 Argentine beauties, selected from thousands of that nation's most dazzling girls at the fateful ball! "Charge of the Gauchos," *Variety*, 19 September 1928, 19.
32. The film also circulated under the title *The Beautiful Spy*, highlighting Logan's leading role.
33. Bordering with Bolivia, Paraguay, and the north of Chile, Salta is located in the northernmost part of Argentina, about two thousand kilometers from Buenos Aires, therefore making the timely rescue impossible.
34. Cuarterolo, "Una Nueva y Gloriosa Nación," 14.
35. Cuarterolo, "Una Nueva y Gloriosa Nación," 17, 29.

36. *El Pueblo*, May 1928, quoted in Ajuria, *El cinematógrafo como espejo del mundo*, 677.

37. An article in *Motion Picture News* describes, by apposition, "the role of Belgrano, 'the George Washington of South America.'" The article also mentions a production "now being made with a new Technicolor process" in which Bushman plays the role of Washington. Ajuria may have chosen to associate on-screen Belgrano and Washington, drawing on American audiences' acquaintance with the star's concomitant role. "Bushman to Portray South American Historical Figure," 665.

38. Lugones, *El Payador*, 21. See also Ludmer, *Gaucho Genre*.

39. "Buenos Aires Film estrenará el mes próximo 'De nuestras pampas,'" *Excelsior*, 24 October 1923, 23. In addition to "country ambiance" films, *cinedrama porteño* dominated local film production. See chapter 2.

40. "Mi alazán tostao," *La Película*, 20 September 1923, 20.

41. An ad for *La chacra de Don Lorenzo* (*Don Lorenzo's Country House*; Buenos Aires Film, 1929) summarizes the film while itemizing gaucho practices therein: "A beautiful *campero* poem. The most human drama that cinematography has ever produced. All the sentiment that an agonizing lineage [the gaucho] and the example that a gaucho gives to his children in the face of tragic adversity. Great country party—horse taming—cattle branding—rodeo—counterpoint *payada*." "La Chacra de Don Lorenzo," *La Película*, 12 September 1929, 24.

42. Their market appeal reached such a degree that in Italy a production company, Italo Argentina Films, was created for the sole purpose of producing gaucho-themed films, according to trade journals. Further inquiry is needed on this company, which purportedly produced at least one film with clear porteño influence, *Civilizzati and selvaggi* (Civilized and savages). Further, the company purportedly drew from porteño letrados for its films such as Domingo Faustino Sarmiento, José Ingenieros, and the Uruguayan Zorrilla de San Martín, an article claims. "¡En Italia se editarán películas gauchescas!," *La Película*, 20 October 1921, 11.

43. "Nobleza gaucha y su quince aniversario," *Excelsior*, 12 August 1925, 27. A noteworthy exception, *Nobleza Gaucha* was so popular that it was used in ads to block-book Hollywood productions, not the other way around. A full-page illustrated ad by the distribution company American Film celebrates *Nobleza*'s tenth anniversary and, in smaller type, advertises the Hollywood films *Mother Eternal* (dir. Ivan Branson, 1921), *The Old Nest* (dir. Reginald Barker, Goldwyn, 1921), and *Be My Wife* (dir. Max Linder, 1921), among others. "El décimo aniversario del esterno nacional más grande de Sud América," *Excelsior*, 12 August 1925, 29.

44. Ansolabehere, *Literatura y anarquismo en Argentina*, 19. See also Prieto, *El discurso criollista*; and Andrea Cuarterolo's analysis of *Nobleza Gaucha* (Gaucho nobility; dir. Eduardo Martínez de la Pera and Ernesto Gunche, 1915) in *De la foto al fotograma*, 135–47.

45. "La opinión del Presidente de la República," facsimile in Ajuria, *El cinematógrafo como espejo del mundo*, lámina 1.

46. "Carta del Dr. Antoino Dellepiane," facsimile in Ajuria, *El cinematógrafo como espejo del mundo*, lámina 3.

47. Rojas famously described serialized novels as "paper alkaloids." "Ricardo Rojas, el eminente escritor nacionalista, decano de nuestra Facultad de Filosofía y Letras, opina sobre la inundación literaria de la gran ciudad cosmopolita," *La Razón*, 14 May 1923, 4.

48. "Autógrafo del Dr. Ricardo Rojas," facsimile in Ajuria, *El cinematógrafo como espejo del mundo*, lámina 2. A facsimile of the missive with further comment praising Ajuria also circulated in trade journals. "El rector de la Universidad de BS. As. hace el elogio de 'Una nueva y gloriosa nación,'" *Revista del Exhibidor*, 30 April 1928, 10.

49. "El rector de la Universidad de BS. As. hace el elogio de 'Una nueva y gloriosa nación.'"

50. "De 'La Prensa,'" transcription in Ajuria, *El cinematógrafo como espejo del mundo*, 671.

51. War Secretary, missive to Ajuria, facsimile in Ajuria, *El cinematógrafo como espejo del mundo*, lámina 4.

52. War Secretary, missive to Ajuria.

53. Advertisements and articles on *Charge* run in *Revista del Exhibidor* throughout 1928.

54. "Se hará una profusa reclame a la producción Ajuria 'Una nueva y gloriosa nación,'" *Revista del Exhibidor*, 30 December 1927.

55. Both ads and articles constituting the campaign hyperbolically praise the film but at the same time point to its expanded circulation in the Southern Cone. An article indicates, as "a record difficult to surpass," that the film was shown in fifty theaters in Argentina, Uruguay, and Chile combined. "'Una nueva y gloriosa nación' se viene exhibiendo entre los aplausos del público," *Revista del Exhibidor*, 30 May 1928, 13.

56. "'Una nueva y gloriosa nación' en el Uruguay y Chile," *Revista del Exhibidor*, 10 June 1928, 8.

57. *La Vanguardia*, 7 September 1927.

58. Don Q., "Estrellas y estrellados," *Cine-Mundial*, May 1927, 415.

59. Bertellini, "Manipulation and Authenticity," 76.

60. "Pictorial Section," *Exhibitors Herald*, 29 September 1928, 29.

61. Film Booking Offices of America, Inc., would later become RKO Pictures.

62. "Hollywood Happenings," *Film Daily* (New York),10 April 1927.

63. *Film Daily Yearbook* (New York: The Film Daily, 1929), 289.

64. "Alphabet Guide to Features," *Motion Picture News*, 29 September 1928, 968. Other reviews describe the film as "wholesome romance" and "gay romance." Respectively, "One Showman to Another" and "FBO's Product Announcement," *Exhibitors Herald*, 19 May 1928.

65. "New Pictures," *Exhibitors*, 15 September 1928, 46.

66. "War—for Loot and Liberty," *Exhibitors*, 15 September 1928.

67. "What the Picture Did for Me," *Exhibitors*, 2 February 1929, 71.

68. "What the Picture Did for Me," *Exhibitors*, 2 March 1929, 58.

69. "The Box Office Record," *Exhibitors*, 4 May 1929, 55.

70. "The Box Office Record," *Exhibitors*. Comments registered March 6 and November 29, respectively.

71. "Charge of the Gauchos," *Variety* (New York), 10 October 1928, 26.

72. "Charge of the Gauchos."

73. A discrepancy when compared to the film's record—six reels—in the Library of Congress's *Motion Picture Catalog of Copyright Entries, 1912–1935* (1951), 125.

74. "What the Picture Did for Me," *Exhibitors*, 13 July 1929, 76.

75. "What the Picture Did for Me," *Exhibitors*, 5 January 1929, 59.

76. The statistical record "The Check-Up" offers a bird's-eye view of the film's poor reception. Averaging reports received from exhibitors "in every part of the country on current features," it catalogs films in four categories: poor, fair, good, and big. The column offers a percentage yielding the average rating on a feature, obtained by rating the categories as poor, 20 percent; fair, 40 percent; good, 70 percent; and big, 100 percent. *Charge* yields a percentage of 52 percent. *Moving Picture News*, 9 February 1929, 440–41.

77. Cuarterolo, "Una Nueva y Gloriosa Nación," 181.

78. Malpasutti was an Italian writer, dramaturge, scriptwriter, and nobleman. Associated with Gabriele D'Annunzio, his name, without a doubt, elevated the cultural status of the film in local film circuits.

79. Cuarterolo, "Una Nueva y Gloriosa Nación," 19.

80. Ajuria, *El cinematógrafo como espejo del mundo*, lámina 9–31.

81. Anderson, *Imagined Communities*, 4. As early as 1914, Latin American film critics recognized cinema's ability to produce "collective emotional states" through the "aesthetic inherent to action." Alfonso Reyes, "El cine y el folletín," *España*, 25 November 1915; reprinted in González Casanova, *El cine que vio Fósforo*, 135.

82. Hansen, "Fallen Women, Rising Stars," 12.

83. Bertellini, in "Manipulation and Authenticity," studies this phenomenon regarding Valentino's effect in Argentine and Italian publics.

84. Marcantonio, *Global Melodrama*, 62.

85. Gledhill, "Prologue: The Reach of Melodrama," xii.

86. Finkielman, *Film Industry in Argentina*, 84.

87. Finkielman, *Film Industry in Argentina*, 84.

88. "Nuestra Opinión," *Cine-Mundial*, January 1928, 35.

89. Theodore Roosevelt, "Charter Day Address," *University of California Chronicle* 13 (1911): 139. The address was presented on 23 March.

90. "8000 Cheer Roosevelt in Greek Theatre," *San Francisco Call*, 24 March 1911. "Happenings on the Pacific Slope: Roosevelt Aids University Day," *Los Angeles Times*, 24 March 1911, 13. "'I Took Canal Zone'—T.R.," *Washington Post*, 24 March 1911, 4.

91. "La adquisición del canal de Panamá: averiguación propuesta," *La Prensa*, 8 April 1911, 11.

92. "Alrededor de la cuestión de Panamá: la declaración de Roosevelt. Investigación pedida," *La Prensa*, 13 April 1911.

93. Clyde Peirce, "The Panama Canal Libel Cases," *Indiana Magazine of History* 33, no. 2 (1937): 171–86, 171. The suit revolves around a Wall Street firm backed by American investors close to Roosevelt. Purportedly, the firm secretly bought a large stake of the worthless shares of the French company that had failed to build the canal in the 1880s. The US government supposedly paid

$40 million to the liquidator of the French company for the rights to continue the project. Pultizer's newspaper alleged that $12 million had been paid instead to a shell company fronting for J. P. Morgan, thus massively enriching Roosevelt's associates. See also Kantaris, "Space, Politics, and the Crisis of Hegemony," 93.

94. "Conferencia de Roosevelt," *El Diario*, 27 March 1911.

95. "Seamos fuertes porque el coloso del norte quiere tener por lindero el Canal de Panamá," *Opinión* (Veracruz), 19 November 1911. The article taps into late nineteenth-century anti-US rhetoric, particularly José Martí's 1891 essay "Nuestra América," to which I return later.

96. "Notas editoriales," *El Trabajo* (Popayán), 3 June 1911, 2.

97. Bertellini, *Divo and duce*, 7, 20.

98. Marshall, Introduction to *Celebrity Culture Reader*, 2–3.

99. After a formal protest against Roosevelt's boast by Colombian officials on 28 March, some American periodicals did demand government action, while converting the affair into sensationalist headlines. "The Stain on Our Flag," *Independent* 71 (1911): 347–55. Leander Chamberlain, "A Chapter of National Dishonor," *North American Review* 675 (1912): 145–74.

100. "Colombia and Mexico," Consular Report, 4 March 1919, 1, NARA RG84, Diplomatic Posts, Colombia, vol. 220. The report includes quotations from several newspapers, some of which explicitly deploy animosity against the American president: "Today the serene spirit of Colombia . . . brings to bear the weight of its eternal censure against Mr. Theodore Roosevelt."

101. Evidenced in records of the American Department of State, first unearthed in 1982 by historian Jorge Orlando Melo at the National Archives in Washington DC. Suárez and Arbeláez, "Garras de Oro," 56. In a recent study, Leydi Paola Bolaños Florido quotes a letter written by F. L. Herron, then president of the MPPDA, who, based on "a reliable source," claims that a copy of the film circulated in Japan, with Japanese and English subtitles, and that seven other copies were circulated in Central American and South America. My own archival research at NARA did not find this letter. Bolaños Florido, "La censura de *Garras de Oro*," 21.

102. Favoring instead his account of community building through print media in "homogenous, empty time." Anderson, *Imagined Communities*, 24.

103. Anderson, *Imagined Communities*, 51, 258. These narratives carry such emotional import that Anderson asks himself—without offering a definitive answer—why they generate "such colossal sacrifices" as the willingness, in many, to die for their own country (7).

104. Anker, *Orgies of Feeling*, 2, 87.

105. Bolaños Florido, "La censura de *Garras de Oro*," 4.

106. In English in intertitles.

107. Emphasis in original.

108. Colombia actually received $5 million in compensation.

109. See Gaudreault, "Narration and Monstration in the Cinema," 29–36.

110. Burch, *Life to Those Shadows*, 154.

111. Elssaesser, "New Film History," 115.

112. Martí lived in the United States, where he wrote a prolific corpus of chronicles on American politics, education, and culture.

113. Martí, "The Washington Pan-American Congress," *La Nación* (Buenos Aires), 19–20 December 1889, reproduced in *Inside the Monster*, 341.
114. Martí, "Coney Island," *La Pluma* (Bogotá), 3 December, 1881, reproduced in *Inside the Monster*, 165.
115. Anderson, *Imagined Communities*, 51.
116. Anderson, *Imagined Communities*, 171.
117. Quoted in Palacios and Safford, *Colombia*, 517.
118. *Oxford English Dictionary*, s.v. "Monster."
119. Moraña, *El monstruo como máquina de guerra*, 23. On arrests of narrative flow, see also Gunning's seminal essay on the cinema of attraction and the avant-garde: Tom Gunning, "Cinema of Attraction."
120. Bolaños Florido, "La censura de *Garras de Oro*," 19–20.
121. Assia Djebar, *L'amour, la fantasia*, 84. For a reflection on the "weak ontologica frontier" between fiction and documentary in early cinema and the indexical sign, see Doane, *The Emergence of Cinematic Time*, 155.
122. Moraña, *El monstruo como máquina de guerra*, 22–23. Emphasis in original. In her groundbreaking study on the monstrous in Western thought and Latin American narrative, Moraña highlights links between the monster and melodrama, as the former "appeals [to] the individual's proclivity for the ludic, the oneiric, the melodramatic, and the sinister" (25).
123. All consulted documents are from NARA, RG 59, General Records of the Department of State, boxes 7298 and 7299.
124. Samuel H. Piles, head of the US Legation in Bogotá, missive to US Secretary of State, 4 February 1928.
125. American Legation in Panama, telegram to Department of State, 22 December 1927.
126. Department of State, telegram to American Legation in Panama, 23 December 1927.
127. Department of State, telegram to American Legation in Panama, 4 January 1928.
128. Samuel H. Piles, telegram to Department of State, 1 January 1928.
129. Piles, missive to US Secretary of State, 4 February 1928. The territories comprising the Republic of Colombia are divided into departments.
130. "Se impide la proyección de una cinta nacional," *El Tiempo* (Bogotá), 10 February 1928, 1.
131. "La censura y la historia," *El Tiempo*, 11 February 1928, 3, quoted in Concha Henao, *Historia social del cine en Colombia*, 313. English and emphasis in original.
132. "De Ibagué," *El Tiempo*, 6 March 1928, 7.
133. Alfred Burri, American Consul in Barranquilla, missive to Samuel Piles, 23 March 1928.
134. Department of State, telegram to American Legation in Panama, 4 January 1928.
135. Samuel H. Piles, missive to US Secretary of State, 14 January 1928.
136. Piles, missive to US Secretary of State, 4 February 1928.
137. The letter also indicates Navia was defrauded by other stockholders of Cali Film. Piles gathers Navia's telegram to the American Legation is his way

of seeking "revenge" on his business partners. For this melodramatic subplot of the film's material history, see Suárez and Arbeláez, "Garras de Oro," 57.

138. In the late 1910s and early 1920s, the soviet filmmaker and theorist Lev Kuleshov conducted editing experiments to prove that cinematic meaning derives from the ordering of shots. For a critical take on his findings, see Prince and Hensley, "The Kuleshov Effect," 59–75.

139. Martínez Pardo, *Historia del cine colombiano*, 61. See also Salcedo Silva, *Crónicas del cine colombiano*, 66.

140. Buenaventura, "Colombian Silent Cinema," 63.

141. Suárez and Arbeláez, "Garras de Oro," 61.

142. In Arbeláez, *Garras de Oro: Herida*. My gratitude to Ramiro Arbeláez for providing a copy of his documentary.

143. In intertitles he appears under the pseudonym P. P. Jambrina.

144. Ospina León, "Garras de Oro: Herida," 208.

145. An expository title describing how *The World*'s editorial circulates in New York City reads: "Por la ciudad monumental **corrìa** la hoja combativa, desde la *street* **mastodòntica** de las mil y una ruedas, hasta." Emphasis in original; misspelled Spanish in bold. Arbeláez concurs with this observation. Ospina León, "Garras de Oro: Herida," 211.

146. See Suárez and Arbeláez, "Garras de Oro."

147. To elaborate on this point, it is worth noting that the flag at the end of Paterson's story, held by one of his children, consists of a tricolor flag similar to but not entirely concordant with the Colombian flag.

148. Resorting to scholars in Italy, Arbeláez contends Zanussi played Paterson's girlfriend and Lady Justice. Ospina León, "Garras de Oro: Herida," 213. A brief column in *El Correo del Cauca* advertises Lucia Zanussi in the film—*Quo Vadis?* (dir. Gabriellino D'Annunzio, 1924) and *Maciste in Hell* (dir. Guido Brignone, 1925)—without specifying her role. Quoted in Suárez, *Critical Essays on Colombian Cinema*, 31.

149. See also Ospina León, "Films on Paper."

150. Appositely, the fact that Colombian impresarios did not resort to more developed Latin American film industries in Argentina, Brazil, or Mexico suggests that South-to-South exchanges between Latin American film industries and cultures developed in earnest during the early sound period.

151. "Cali, 20," *Mundo al día*, 21 April 1925, 6. Colombia Film hired an Italian troupe consisting of a director, two cameramen, and the actresses Gina Buzaki and Lyda Restivo to produce the now-lost *Suerte y Azar* (Luck and Chance; dir. Camilo Cantinazzi, 1925) and *Tuya es la culpa* (Yours is the Guilt; dir. Camilo Cantinazzi, 1926). The Di Domenicos later hired Lyda Restivo, aka Mara Meva, for their production *El amor, el deber y el crimen* (Love, Duty, and Crime; dir. Pedro Moreno Garzón and Vincenzo Di Domenico, 1926). Meva is at the roots of a fraught attempt to jump-start a local star system, which demands further scrutiny.

152. Salcedo Silva, *Crónicas del cine colombiano*, 114.

153. Notarial Registration, Document no. 1156, 23 October 1925, located by Arbeláez, quoted in Suárez, *Critical Essays on Colombian Cinema*, 209.

154. 6th Orphan Film Symposium, NYU, 26–29 March 2008, http://www.nyu.edu/orphanfilm/orphans6/.

155. 6th Orphan Film Symposium.

156. On the concept of rhizome, see Gilles Deleuze and Félix Guattari's introduction to *A Thousand Plateaus*; for a Caribbean exploration of the concept, see Glissant, *Introduction à une poétique du divers*.

157. See a similar argument in Schroeder-Rodríguez, "Latin American Silent Cinema."

158. See Oroz, *Melodrama: O cinema*.

159. Buenos Aires trade journals highlight the roles and skill of certain Mexican stars in Hollywood films, particularly Dolores del Río. "Artistas Unidos estrena hoy la super-producción titulada 'Ramona', con Dolores del Río de protagonista," *Revista del Exhibidor*, 10 June 1928. It was only in the 1940s that commercial Latin American film industries would begin to exchange in earnest crews and talent to cater to transnational Spanish-speaking audiences. See, for instance, Moguillansky, *Cines del sur*.

CONCLUSION

Epigraph. Quoted in Purcell, *¡De película!*, 11.

1. Rockhill, "Rancière's Politics of Perception," 3.
2. Iturriaga, *La masificación del cine en Chile*, 271.
3. Brooks, *Melodramatic Imagination*, 21, 50.
4. For a recent study of *Canta* as a "conservative" melodrama, see Tompkins "Ideología en dos melodramas," 102–5, 111–12.
5. Torello invites us to reconsider local modes of exhibition and the chronologies with which we construe the standardization of viewing practices on a global scale. Rather than examining these slide shows as somewhat lagging or tardy vis-à-vis other regions, Torello reads therein "resistant forms" and "sovereignty gestures" through which a local film culture defined itself. *La conquista del espacio*, 80, 99.
6. Aimaretti, "Vuelve Wara Wara," 317; and Sala and Romero Zapata, "Wara Wara," 5.
7. Aimaretti, "Vuelve Wara Wara," 318.
8. See España, *Cine argentino*; Oroz, *Melodrama: O cinema*; and Schroeder-Rodríguez, "Latin American Silent Cinema.".
9. Schroeder-Rodríguez, "Latin American Silent Cinema," 74. For the radical drop of imported virgin film stock by kilograms, see España, *Cine argentino*, 194.
10. Monsiváis, "El melodrama," 116.
11. López, "Film and Radio," 317.
12. Navitski, *Public Spectacles of Violence*, 249.
13. España, *Cine argentino*, 203.
14. Peña, *Cien años*, 56–7.
15. Kriger, *Cine y Peronismo*, 18; Losada, *Projected Nation*, 26.
16. Félix-Didier and Levinson, "Building a Nation," 51.

17. Montaldo, *De pronto, el campo*, 117; and Lusnich, *El drama social-folclórico*, 156.

18. Navitski, *Public Spectacles of Violence*, 249.

19. Wu, "Consuming Tacos," 177.

20. Contemporary directors following Fernández's and Figueroa's conventional formulae of Mexicanness include Julio Bracho, Alejandro Galindo, Fenando de Fuentes, Foberto Galvadón, Ismael Rodríguez, and later on Tito Davison. Like Gabriel García Moreno, most of these directors worked in Hollywood during the early sound era. And some, such as Fernández, gained international fame by receiving French film criticism's approval as auteurs. Tierney, *Emilio Fernández*, 2, 13.

21. Schroeder-Rodríguez, "Latin American Silent Cinema," 74. I refer to internationally acclaimed art-house films of the early 2000s labeled *nuevo cine* (demonym) and their renowned authors, such as Lucrecia Martel of the nuevo cine argentino. For a study of "new" Argentine police procedurals as a mainstream response to art-house cinema, see Navitski, "Last Heist Revisited," 359–80.

22. Examples include regional surveys, for example, King, *Magical Reels*, and Paranaguá, *Tradición y modernidad*, as well as nation-bound studies, for example Di Núbila, *Historia del cine argentino* and more recently Finkielman, *Film Industry in Argentina*; García Riera, *Historia documental del cine mexicano* (Guadajalara: Universidad de Guadalajara, 1992); and Salcedo Silva, *Crónicas del cine colombiano*, among others.

23. Pérez Melgosa, "Cosmopolitan Nationalisms," 137.

24. Lusnich, Aisemberg, and Cuarterolo, *Pantallas transnacionales*. This volume includes indexes of Argentine films screened in Mexico and vice versa between 1925 and 1959.

25. Peredo Castro, *Cine y propaganda*, 36.

26. Reyes, "De Nobleza Baturra a El Charro," 245.

27. See Jarvinen, "Mass Market for Spanish-Language Films"; and Avila, "El Espectáculo," 31–51, 80–97.

28. Schroeder-Rodríguez, "Latin American Silent Cinema," 77.

29. Jarvinen, "Mass Market for Spanish-Language Films," 83.

30. Jarvinen, "Mass Market for Spanish-Language Films," 93.

31. The film suggests Jensita's family is of Mexican origin; the Mexican flag flanks her window while American flags and flags from several Latin American nations (including Brazil) decorate other windows facing the street. Importantly, the terms Jensita uses stress the diverse environment she inhabits. *Cuate* in Mexico and Central America denotes close friend, but in Mexico it is also used to denote twins. To denote baby, *guagua* is used in South America, particularly in Argentina, Bolivia, Colombia, Ecuador, and Peru. Using both terms, the dialogue suggests Jensita draws from different dialects to try to convey her message to her Hispanic peer. Ultimately she opts for *gemelos*, a more standardized term for twins. For the historical uses of these terms, see *Nuevo tesoro lexicográfico de la Real Academia Española*, http://buscon.rae.es/ntlle/SrvltGUILoginNtlle.

32. At the end of the film, after Mateo (Fernando Soler) kills his rival for Blanca's love, Pat the policeman (Lou Hicks) seems to impose barriers upon the

diverse Hispanic community. Dispersing the crowd, he says in Spanish—with a thick American accent—"No one can enter!" But once inside the apartment, his kindness reveals he also partakes in community life. Sympathizing with Mateo, he shares the community's pain, thus expanding the ethnic boundaries of Spanish Harlem. "I am sorry Mateo. But you have to come with me," he says in Spanish. "Yes, Patty," Mateo complies.

33. Jarvinen, "Mass Market for Spanish-Language Films," 91.

34. Jarvinen mentions screenings in Chile, Mexico, and Puerto Rico.

35. Gledhill, "Prologue: The Reach of Melodrama," xv. See important contributions to the field in Gledhill and Williams's anthology *Melodrama Unbound*.

36. Anker, *Orgies of Feeling*, 2. See also Althusser's seminal essay "Ideology and Ideological State Apparatuses," in *Lenin and Philosophy and Other Essays*.

37. Elsaesser, "Le mélodrame," 35. In contrast, recall Elsaesser's foundational essay on 1940s and 1950s Hollywood family melodrama, originally published in 1972. There, he conferred on the mode "subversi[ve] or escapis[t] functions" dependent on "historical and social context." Unlike his current take on the mode, in his previous assessment Elsaesser saw in mid-twentieth century Hollywood conventions "the very signs of the characters' alienation, [which] serve to formulate a devastating critique of the ideology that supports [American cinema]." "Tales of Sound and Fury," 72, 85.

38. Williams, "Beyond Genre: The Modalities of Melodrama" (keynote speech, Swiss Association for North American Studies, University of Lausanne, 3 November 2018). Williams also includes in her list Jonna Eagle's *Imperial Affects*, which examines how melodramatic conventions in American political discourse and action-based films "prim[e] expectations of violence as both exciting and virtuous" in support of the project of American Empire. Eagle, *Imperial Affects*, 2–3.

39. Herlinghaus, "La imaginación melodramática," 35.

40. Herlinghaus would concur that melodrama "works with what is 'good' and what is 'bad,' but it is neither good or bad; in the sense that melodrama's validity takes shape in scenarios where melodrama's *intermedial logic* shows links between anthropological dimensions, psychological situations, conflicts of social legitimacy and desire, and communicative expression." "Imaginación melodramática," 42. Emphasis in original.

41. Kracauer, "Photography," 61. For a sophisticated reading of this essay, see Koch, "Surface and Self-Representation," 26–47.

42. Martín-Barbero, "Laberintos narrativos," 449–50; and Bush, *Pragmatic Passions*, 21.

43. Lukacs, *Theory of the Novel*, 22.

44. Martín-Barbero, "Laberintos narrativos," 447. See also the canonical work by Ángel Rama, *La ciudad letrada*.

Works Cited

Abel, Richard. *The Ciné Goes to Town: French Cinema 1896–1914*. Berkeley: University of California Press, 1998.
Adelman, Jeremy. *Sovereignty and Revolution in the Iberian Atlantic*. Princeton, NJ: Princeton University Press, 2006.
Adorno, Theodor W., and Max Horkheimer. *Dialectic of Enlightenment*. Translated by Edmund Jephcott. Stanford, CA: Stanford University Press, 2002.
Agrasanchez, Rogelio. *Mexican Movies in the United States: A History of the Films, Theaters and Audiences, 1920–1960*. Jefferson, NC: Mcfarland, 2011.
Aimaretti, María. "¡Vuelve Wara Wara! Arqueología y biografía de un film silente boliviano que regresa." *Vivomatografías*, no. 2 (2016): 299–324.
Ajuria, Julian de. *El cinematógrafo como espejo del mundo: Arte, ciencias, teatro, cultura, lujo y belleza a través del lente mágico*. Buenos Aires: Guillermo Kraft, 1946.
Allen, Richard. "The Passion of the Christ and the Melodramatic Imagination." In *Melodrama Unbound: Across History, Media, and National Cultures*, edited by Christine Gledhill and Linda Williams, 31–47. New York: Columbia University Press, 2018.
Allen, Robert C. "The Role of the Star in Film History (Joan Crawford)." In *Film Theory and Criticism*, edited by Leo Braudy and Marshall Cohen, 606–19. New York: Oxford University Press, 2009.
Althusser, Louis. *Lenin and Philosophy and Other Essays*. Translated by Ben Brewster. New York: Monthly Review Press, 1971.
Alzate, Carolina. "Otra amada y otro paisaje para nuestro siglo XIX: Soledad Acosta de Samper y Eugenio Díaz Castro frente a *María*." *Lingüística y Literatura* 59 (2011): 117–35.
Anderson, Benedict. *Imagined Communities: Reflections on the Origin and Spread of Nationalism*. London: Verso, 2016.

Anker, Elisabeth R. *Orgies of Feeling: Melodrama and the Politics of Freedom.* Durham, NC: Duke University Press, 2014.
Ankerson, Dudley. *Agrarian Warlord: Saturnino Cedillo and the Mexican Revolution in San Luis Potosi.* DeKalb: Northern Illinois University Press, 1985.
Ansolabehere, Pablo. *Literatura y anarquismo en Argentina (1879–1919).* Buenos Aires: Beatriz Viterbo Editora, 2011.
Arbeláez, Ramiro. *Garras de Oro: Herida abierta en un continente.* Cali: Universidad del Valle, 2015.
Arias Trujillo, Ricardo. *Los Leopardos: Una historia intelectual de los años 1920.* Bogotá: Universidad de Los Andes, 2013.
Armus, Diego. "The Journey from the Barrio to the City Center: Tísicas, Milonguitas, and Costureritas in Buenos Aires, 1910–1940." *Salud Pública* 1, no. 1 (2005): 79–96.
Arroyo, Claudia, James Ramey, and Michael Schuessler, eds. *México imaginado: Nuevos enfoques sobre el cine (trans)nacional.* Mexico City: CONACULTA, Universidad Autónoma Metropolitana, 2011.
Askari, Kaveh. "An Afterlife for Junk Prints: Serials and Other Classics in Late-1920s Tehran." In *Silent Cinema and the Politics of Space*, edited by Jennifer M. Bean, Anupama Kapse, and Laura Horak, 99–120. Bloomington: Indiana University Press, 2014.
Aughinbaugh, William Edmund. *Advertising for Trade in Latin-America.* New York: Century, 1922.
Avila, Jacqueline. "El Espectáculo: The Culture of the *Revistas* in Mexico City and Los Angeles, 1900–1940." In *Cinema Between Latin America and Los Angeles*, edited by Colin Gunckel, Jan-Christopher Horak, and Lisa Jarvinen, 31–51. New Brunswick, NJ: Rutgers University Press, 2019.
Baily, Samuel. "'Hacer la América': los italianos ganan dinero en New York y Buenos Aires, 1880–1914." *Estudios Migratorios Latinoamericanos* 14, no. 38 (1998): 57–68.
Bean, Jennifer, Anupama Kapse, and Laura Horak, eds. *Silent Cinema and the Politics of Space.* Indianapolis: Indiana University Press, 2014.
Benítez-Rojo, Antonio. "The Nineteenth-Century Spanish American Novel." In *The Cambridge History of Latin America Literature*, edited by Roberto González Echavarría and Enrique Pupo-Walker, 417–89. New York: Cambridge University Press, 1996.
Benjamin, Walter. *The Arcades Project.* Translated by Howard Eiland and Kevin McLaughlin. Cambridge, MA: Belknap Press, 2002.
Benson, Scott, dir. *Ben-Hur: The Making of an Epic.* Turner Home Entertainment, 1993.
Berg, Charles Ramírez. *Latino Images in Film: Stereotypes, Subversion, and Resistance.* Austin: University of Texas Press, 2002.
Bergero, Adriana J. *Intersecting Tango: Cultural Geographies of Buenos Aires, 1900–1930.* Pittsburgh, PA: University of Pittsburgh Press, 2008.
Berman, Marshal. *All That Is Solid Melts into Air.* New York: Viking Penguin, 1988.
Bertellini, Giorgio. *The Divo and the Duce: Promoting Film Stardom and Political Leadership in 1920s America.* Oakland: University of California Press, 2019.

———. "Manipulation and Authenticity: The Unassimilable Valentino in 1920s Argentina." In *Cosmopolitan Visions: Transnational Horizons of Latin American Film Culture, 1896–1960*, edited by Rielle Navitski and Nicholas Poppe, 73–97. Bloomington: Indiana University Press, 2017.

Bolaños Florido, Leidy Paola. "La censura de *Garras de Oro* y la propagación de la antiamericanización en los años veinte: Un asunto internacional." *Secuencia*, no. 106 (2020): 1–38.

Bolter, Jay David, and Richard Grusin. *Remediation: Understanding New Media*. Cambridge, MA: MIT Press, 2000.

Bordwell, David, Janet Staiger, and Kristin Thompson. *The Classical Hollywood Cinema: Film Style & Mode of Production to 1960*. New York: Columbia University Press, 1985.

Bratu Hansen, Miriam. "Fallen Women, Rising Stars, New Horizons: Shanghai Silent Films as Vernacular Modernism." *Film Quarterly* 54, no. 1 (2000): 10–22.

Brooks, Peter. *The Melodramatic Imagination: Balzac, Henry James, Melodrama and the Mode of Excess*. New Haven, CT: Yale University Press, 1996.

———. *Reading for the Plot*. Cambridge, MA: Harvard University Press, 1992.

———. *Realist Vision*. New Haven, CT: Yale University Press, 2005.

Bruno, Giuliana. "Site-Seeing: Architecture and the Moving Image." *Wide Angle* 19, no. 4 (1997): 8–24.

Buckley, Matthew. "Unbinding Melodrama." In *Melodrama Unbound*, edited by Christine Gledhill and Linda Williams, 15–30. New York: Columbia University Press, 2018.

Buenaventura, Juan G. "Colombian Silent Cinema: The Case of *Garras de Oro*." Master's thesis, University of Kansas, 1992.

Burch, Noël. *Life to Those Shadows*. Berkeley: University of California Press, 1990.

Bush, Matthew. *Pragmatic Passions: Melodrama and Latin American Social Narrative*. Madrid: Iberoamericana Editorial Vervuert, 2014.

Callahan, Vicki. "Screening Musidora: Inscribing Indeterminacy in Film History." *Camera Obscura* 16, no. 3 (2001): 58–81.

Cano Andaluz, Aurora. *La gestión presidencial de Plutarco Elías Calles*. Mexico City: UNAM, 2006.

Carreño, Miguel Antonio. *Manual de urbanidad y buenas maneras*. Bogotá: Panamericana, 2003.

Castillo Daza, Juan Carlos. *Bogotá: El tránsito a la ciudad moderna 1920–1950*. Bogotá: Universidad Nacional de Colombia, 2003.

Castro Ricarte, Maricruz, and Robert Mckee Irwin. *El cine mexicano se impone: Mercados internacionales y penetración cultural en la época dorada*. Mexico City: Universidad Nacional Autónoma de México, 2012.

Castro-Gómez, Santiago. *La hybris del punto cero: Ciencia, raza e ilustración en la Nueva Granada (1750–1816)*. Bogotá: Editorial Pontificia Universidad Javeriana, Instituto Pensar, 2005.

Certeau, Michel de. *The Practice of Everyday Life*. Berkeley: University of California Press, 1984.

Collingwood, Robin George. *The Idea of History*. Oxford: Oxford University Press, 1994.

Concha Henao, Álvaro. *Historia social del cine en Colombia*. Tomo I, 1897–1929. Bogotá: Publicaciones Black María Escuela de Cine, 2014.
Conde, Maite. *Foundational Films: Early Cinema and Modernity in Brazil*. Oakland: University of California Press, 2018.
Couret, Nilo. "Serializing Ramona: Provincializing Early Cinema Spectatorship in Cuba." *Vivomatografías*, no. 4 (2018): 136–42.
Couselo, Jorge Miguel. *El Negro Ferreyra: Un cine por instinto*. Buenos Aires: Editorial Freeland, 1969.
Crary, Jonathan. *Techniques of the Observer: On Vision and Modernity in the 19th Century*. Cambridge, MA: MIT Press, 1992.
Croce, Benedetto. *History: Its Theory and Practice*. New York: Russel and Russel, 1960.
Cuarterolo, Andrea. *De la foto al fotograma: Relaciones entre cine y fotografía en la Argentina (1840–1933)*. Montevideo: CdF Ediciones, 2012.
———. "Filmar la América." *Radar*, August 25, 2013.
———. "Imágenes de la Argentina opulenta: Una lectura de Nobleza Gaucha (1915) desde el proyecto fotográfico de la Sociedad Fotográfica Argentina de Aficionados." In *Civilización y barbarie en el cine argentino y latinoamericano*, edited by Ana Laura Lusnich, 19–34. Buenos Aires: Editorial Biblos, 2005.
———. "Una Nueva y Gloriosa Nación (Albert Kelley, 1928): Entre la 'ficción orientadora' y la 'fantasía histórica.'" *Imagofagia*, no. 8 (2013): 1–32.
———. "Una Nueva y Gloriosa Nación (The Charge of the Gauchos/La Carica Dei Gauchos/The Beautiful Spy)." In *Le Giornate del cinema muto: Catalogo*, edited by Caherine A. Surowiec. Pordenone, Italy: Cineteca del Friuli, 2013.
Cuarterolo, Andrea, and Rielle Navitski, eds. "Bibliografía sobre precine y cine silente latinoamericano." *Vivomatografías*, no. 3 (2017): 248–415.
Curubeto, Diego. *Babilonia gaucha: Hollywood en la Argentina, la Argentina en Hollywood*. Buenos Aires: Planeta, 1993.
Dall'Asta, Monica. "Italian Serial Films and 'International Popular Culture.'" *Film History* 12, no. 3 (2000): 300–307.
Dávalos, Federico, and Esperanza Vázquez. *Carlos Villatoro: Paisajes en la vida de un hombre de cine*. Mexico City: Universidad Autónoma de México, 1999.
Day-Mayer, Helen, and David Mayer. "Performing/Acting Melodrama." In *Melodrama Unbound across History, Media, and National Cultures*, edited by Christine Gledhill and Linda Williams, 99–113. New York: Columbia University Press, 2018.
Deleuze, Gilles, and Felix Guattari. *A Thousand Plateaus: Capitalism and Schizophrenia*. Translated by Brian Massumi. Minneapolis: University of Minnesota Press, 1987.
Delluc, Louis. *Cinéma & Cie: Confidences d'un spectateur*. Paris: Grasset, 1919.
Denning, Michael. *Mechanic Accents: Dime Novels and Working-Class Culture in America*. London: Verso, 1998.
Derrida, Jacques. "Archive Fever: A Freudian Impression." *Diacritics* 25, no. 2 (1995): 9–63.

Di Núbila, Domingo. *Historia del cine argentino*. Buenos Aires: Cruz de Malta, 1959.

———. *La época de oro: Historia del cine argentino*. Vol. I. Buenos Aires: Ediciones del Jilguero, 1998.

Djebar, Assia. *L'amour, la fantasia*. Paris: Livre de poche, 2001.

D'Lugo, Marvin. "Early Cinematic Tangos: Audiovisual Culture and Transnational Film Aesthetics." *Studies in Hispanic Cinemas* 5, nos. 1–2 (2008): 9–23.

Doane, Mary Ann. *The Emergence of Cinematic Time: Modernity, Contingency, the Archive*. Cambridge, MA: Harvard University Press, 2002.

Drew, William M., and Esperanza Vázquez. "El Puño de Hierro: A Mexican Silent Film Classic." *Journal of Film Preservation* 10, no. 66 (2003): 10–22.

Duque, Pilar. *La aventura del cine en Medellín*. Bogotá: Universidad Nacional de Colombia, El Ancora Editores, 1992.

Dussel, Enrique. *Ética de la liberación en la edad de la globalización y la exclusión*. Madrid: Trotta, 1998.

———. "Eurocentrism and Modernity (Introduction to the Frankfurt Lectures)," *Boundary 2* 20, no.3 (1993): 65–76.

Dyer, Richard. *Stars*. London: BFI, 1998.

Eagle, Jonna. *Imperial Affects: Sensational Melodrama and the Attractions of American Cinema*. New Brunswick, NJ: Rutgers University Press, 2017.

El'Gazi, Leila. "Cien años de la llegada del cine a Colombia." *Credencial Historia*, April 1997, 6–7.

Elsaesser, Thomas. "Le mélodrame: Entre globalisation de l'empathie et standardisation de l'intime." In *Le mélodrame filmique revisité/Revisiting Film Melodrama*, edited by Dominique Nasta, Muriel Andrin, and Anne Gailly, translated by Anne Gailly, 31–47. Brussels: P.I.E. Peter Lang, 2014.

———. "The New Film History as Media Archeology." *Cinémas: Revue d'études cinématographiques* 14, nos. 2–3 (2004): 75–117.

———. "Tales of Sound and Fury: Observations on the Family Melodrama." In *Imitations of Life: A Reader on Film and Television Melodrama*, edited by Marcia Landy, 68–91. Detroit, MI: Wayne State University Press, 1991.

España, Claudio. *Cine argentino: Industria y clasicismo 1933/1956*. Vol. II. Buenos Aires: Fondo Nacional de las Artes, 2000.

Estrada, Óscar, dir. *Historias Recuperadas*. Episode "El tren fantasma." Aired in 2005 on TV-UNAM. Betacam video.

Everson, William. *American Silent Film*. New York: Da Capo Press, 1998.

Farnsworth-Alvear, Ann. *Dulcinea in the Factory: Myths, Morals, Men, and Women in Colombia's Industrial Experiment, 1905–1960*. Durham, NC: Duke University Press, 2000.

Feijoo, María del Carmen. "Las trabajadoras porteñas a comienzos de siglo." In *Mundo urbano y cultura popular: Estudios de historia social argentina*, edited by Diego Armus, 283–311. Buenos Aires: Editorial Sudamericana, 1990.

Félix-Didier, Paula, and Andrés Levinson. "The Building of a Nation: *La Guerra Gaucha* as Historical Melodrama." In *Latin American Melodrama*, edited by Darelene J. Sadlier, 50–63. Chicago: University of Illinois Press, 2009.

Fernández, Itzia. "Analytical Overview of Mexican Silent Cinema Through Film Compilation." Presentation at Society for Cinema and Media Studies, Toronto, 14–18 March 2018.

Fernandez, Itzia, David Wood, and Daniel Valdez. "Apuntes para una filmografía: De las practicas del reempleo (found footage o metraje reencontrado)." *Nuevo Texto Crítico* 28, no. 1 (2016): 89–108.

Finkielman, Jorge. *The Film Industry in Argentina: An Illustrated Cultural History*. Jefferson, NC: McFarland, 2004.

Fischer, Lucy. *Designing Women: Cinema, Art Deco, and the Female Form*. New York: Columbia University Press, 2003.

Fischer, Sibylle. *Modernity Disavowed: Haiti and the Cultures of Slavery in the Age of Revolution*. Durham, NC: Duke University Press, 2004.

Foucault, Michel. *The History of Sexuality*. Vol. 1. Translated by Robert Hurley. New York: Pantheon Books, 1978.

Fullerton, John. "Creating an Audience for the 'Cinématographe': Two Lumière Agents in Mexico, 1896." *Film History* 20, no. 1 (2008): 95–114.

———. *Picturing Mexico: From the Camera Lucida to Film*. New Barnet, Herts, UK: John Libbey, 2014.

García Blizzard, Mónica. "Whiteness and the Ideal of Modern Mexican Citizenship in Tepeyac (1917)." *Vivomatografías*, no. 1 (2015): 72–95.

García Canclini, Néstor. *Culturas híbridas: Estrategias para entrar y salir de la modernidad*. Buenos Aires: Paidós, 2008.

García Díaz, Bernardo García. "La clase obrera textil orizabeña durante los años veinte." *Investigación Económica* 41, no. 162 (1982): 179–95.

García Mesa, Héctor. *Cine latinoamericano (1896–1930)*. Caracas: Consejo Nacional de la Cultura, 2014.

García Riera, Emilio. *Historia del cine mexicano*. Mexico City: Secretaría de Educación Pública, 1986.

———. *Historia documental del cine mexicano*. Guadajalara: Universidad de Guadalajara, 1992.

Gaudreault, André. "Narration and Monstration in the Cinema." *Journal of Film and Video* 39, no. 2 (1987): 29–36.

Gessner, Robert. "Porter and the Creation of Cinematic Motion: An Analysis of 'The Life of an American Fireman.'" *Journal of the Society of Cinematologists* 2 (1962): 1–13.

Gledhill, Christine. "Prologue: The Reach of Melodrama." In *Melodrama Unbound across History, Media, and National Cultures*, edited by Linda Williams and Christine Gledhill, ix–xxv. New York: Columbia University Press, 2018.

Gledhill, Christine, and Linda Williams, eds. *Melodrama Unbound*. New York: Columbia University Press, 2018.

Glissant, Édouard. *Introduction à une poétique du divers*. Paris: Gallimard, 1996.

Goldgel, Víctor. *Cuando lo nuevo conquistó américa: Prensa, moda y literatura en el siglo XIX*. Buenos Aires: Siglo XXI Editores, 2013.

Gómez Gómez, Carmen Elisa. "Los géneros del cine fantástico mexicano." In *Miradas al cine mexicano*, edited by Aurelio de los Reyes, 2:109–31. Mexico: IMCINE, 2016.

González Casanova, Manuel. *El cine que vio Fósforo: Alfonso Reyes y Martín Luis Guzmán*. Mexico City: Fondo de Cultura Económica, 2003.

González Coutin, Heliodoro. "La tragedia del silencio." *Cine Colombia*, May 1924.

González Marín, Jesús Daniel. "¿Es que no sabes que eres un hombre? Star System y masculinidades en cinco actores del cine mexicano." In *Miradas al cine mexicano*, edited by Aurelio de los Reyes, 1:369–91. Mexico City: IMCINE, 2016.

Gorelik, Adrián. *La grilla y el parque: Espacio público y cultura urbana en Buenos Aires, 1887–1936*. Buenos Aires: Universidad Nacional de Quilmes, 2001.

Gunckel, Colin. *Mexico on Main Street: Transnational Film Culture in Los Angeles before World War II*. New Brunswick, NJ: Rutgers University Press, 2015.

Gunning, Tom. "The Cinema of Attractions: Early Cinema, Its Spectator, and the Avant-Garde." *Wide Angle* 8, nos. 3–4 (1986): 63–70.

Gramsci, Antonio. *The Gramsci Reader: Selected Writings 1914–1935*. Edited by David Forgas. New York: New York University Press, 2000.

Habermas, Jürgen. "An Awareness of What Is Missing." In *An Awareness of What Is Missing: Faith and Reason in a Post-Secular Age*, translated by Ciaran Cronin, 15–23. Cambridge, UK: Polity, 2011.

———. *The Structural Transformation of the Public Sphere*. Cambridge, MA: MIT Press, 1962.

Hammond, Gregory. "Working Women and Feminism in Argentina, 1900–1920." *Latin Americanist* 63, no. 1 (2019): 73–88.

Hansen, Miriam. *Babel and Babylon: Spectatorship in American Silent Film*. Cambridge, MA: Harvard University Press, 1994.

Hansen, Miriam Bratu. "Fallen Women, Rising Stars, New Horizons: Shanghai Silent Film as Vernacular Modernism." *Film Quarterly* 54, no. 1 (2000): 10–22.

Harley, Brian. "Maps, Knowledge, and Power." In *The Iconography of Landscape: Essays on the Symbolic Representation, Design, and Use of Past Environments*, 277–312. New York: Cambridge University Press, 1988.

Harvey, David. *Paris, Capital of Modernity*. New York: Routledge, 2005.

Herlinghaus, Hermann. "La imaginación melodramática: Rasgos intermediales y heterogéneos de una categoría precaria." In *Narraciones anacrónicas de la modernidad: Melodrama e intermedialidad en América Latina*, edited by Herman Herlinghaus, 21–60. Santiago: Editorial Cuarto Propio, 2002.

———. *Narraciones anacrónicas de la modernidad: Melodrama e intermedialidad en América Latina*. Santiago: Editorial Cuarto Propio, 2002.

Hershfield, Joanne. *Imagining la Chica Moderna: Women, Nation, and Visual Culture in Mexico, 1917–1936*. Durham, NC: Duke University Press, 2008.

Higashi, Sumiko. "Cecil B. DeMille and the Lasky Company: Legitimating Feature Film as Art." *Film History* 4, no. 3 (1990): 181–97.

Honneth, Axel. *The Idea of Socialism: Towards a Renewal*. Cambridge, UK: Polity, 2017.

———. *The Struggle for Recognition: The Moral Grammar of Social Conflicts*. Translated by Joel Anderson. Cambridge, MA: MIT Press, 1996.

Iturriaga, Jorge. *La masificación del cine en Chile, 1907–1932: La conflictiva construcción de una cultura plebeya*. Santiago: LOM Ediciones, 2015.

Jacobs, Lea. "Censorship and the Fallen Woman Cycle." In *Home Is Where the Heart Is*, edited by Christine Gledhill, 100–147. London: BFI, 1987.

———. "The Woman's Picture and the Poetics of Melodrama." *Camera Obscura*, no. 31 (1993): 121–47.

Jarvinen, Lisa. "A Mass Market for Spanish-Language Films: Los Angeles, Hybridity, and the Emergence of Latino Audiovisual Media." In *Cinema between Latin America and Los Angeles: Origins to 1960*, edited by Colin Gunckel, Jan-Christopher Horak, and Lisa Jarvinen, 80–97. New Brunswick, NJ: Rutgers University Press, 2019.

———. *The Rise of Spanish-Language Filmmaking: Out from Hollywood's Shadow, 1929–1939*. New Brunswick, NJ: Rutgers University Press, 2012.

Jelicié, Emiliano. "Entre la muerte y la risa: La circulación de los films de guerra en la Argentina y la figura de Max Linder (1914–1918)." *Vivomatografías*, no. 4 (2018): 8–47.

Kantaris, Geoffrey. "Space, Politics, and the Crisis of Hegemony in Latin American Film." In *The Routledge Companion to Latin American Cinema*, edited by Marvin D'Lugo, Ana M. López, and Laura Podalsky, 92–104. New York: Routledge, 2017.

Karush, Matthew B. *Culture of Class: Radio and Cinema in the Making of a Divided Argentina, 1920–1946*. Durham, NC: Duke University Press, 2012.

King, John. *Magical Reels: A History of Cinema in Latin America*. London: Verso, 1990.

Kirkpatrick, Susan. *Las Románticas: Women Writers and Subjectivity in Spain, 1835–1850*. Berkeley, University of California Press, 1989.

Knight, Alan. "¿Fue un éxito la Revolución mexicana?" In *La revolución cósmica: Utopías, regiones y resultados, México 1910–1940*. Mexico City: Fondo de Cultura Económica, 2015.

Koch, Gertrud. "Surface and Self-Representation: 'The Mass Ornament' and *Die Angestellten*." In *Siegfried Kracauer: An Introduction*, 26–47. Princeton, NJ: Princeton University Press, 2000.

Kracauer, Siegfried. *History: The Last Things Before the Last*. Translated by Paul Oskar Kristeller. Princeton, NJ: Markus Wiener, 2013.

———. "The Little Shop Girls Go to the Movies." In *The Mass Ornament: Weimar Essays*, translated by Thomas Levin, 291–306. Cambridge, MA: Harvard University Press, 1995.

———. "Photography." In *The Mass Ornament: Weimar Essays*, translated by Thomas Levin, 47–64. Cambridge, MA: Harvard University Press, 1995.

Krauze, Enrique. *Mexico, Biography of Power: A History of Modern Mexico 1810–1996*. New York: HarperCollins, 1997.

Kriger, Clara. *Cine y peronismo: El estado en escena*. Buenos Aires: Siglo XXI Editores, 2009.

———. *Páginas de cine*. Buenos Aires: Archivo General de la Nación, 2003.

Lander, María Fernanda. "El Manual de urbanidad y buenas maneras de Manuel Antonio Carreño: Reglas para la construcción del ciudadano ideal." *Arizona Journal of Hispanic Cultural Studies*, no. 6 (2002): 83–96.

Largometrajes colombianos en cine y video, 1915–2004. Bogotá: Fundación Patrimonio Fílmico Colombiano, 2005.

Lefebvre, Thierry. "L'utilisation du crucifix comme accessoire de film." In *Une invention du diable? Cinéma des premiers temps et religion*, edited by Roland Cosandey, André Gaudreault, and Tom Gunning, 212–22. Lévis, Switzerland: Les presses de l'Université Laval, Éditions Payot Lausanne, 1990.

López, Ana. "From Hollywood and Back: Dolores Del Rio, a Trans(National) Star." *Studies in Latin American Popular Culture*, no. 17 (1998): 5–32.

López, Ana M. "Early Cinema and Modernity in Latin America." *Cinema Journal* 40, no. 1 (2000): 48–78.

———. "Film and Radio Intermedialities in Early Latin American Sound Cinema." In *The Routledge Companion to Latin American Cinema*, edited by Marvin D'Lugo and Laura Podalsky, 316–27. New York: Routledge, 2017.

López Díaz, Nazly Maryith. *Miradas esquivas a una nación fragmentada: Reflexiones en torno al cine silente de los años veinte y la puesta en escena de la colombianidad*. Bogotá: Alcaldía Mayor de Bogotá, Cinemateca Distrital, 2006.

Losada, Matt. "La Mosca y Sus Peligros: Science, Affect and the Microscopic Sublime." *Revista de Estudios Hispánicos* 46, no. 3 (2012): 465–480.

———. *The Projected Nation: Argentine Cinema and the Social Margins*. New York: State University of New York, 2018.

Ludmer, Josefina. *The Gaucho Genre*. Durham, NC: Duke University Press, 2002.

Lugones, Leopoldo. *El Payador*. Buenos Aires: Huemul, 1978.

Lukacs, Georg. *Theory of the Novel*. Translated by Anna Bostock. Cambridge, MA: MIT Press, 1971.

Lusnich, Ana Laura. *El drama social-folclórico: El universo rural en el cine argentino*. Buenos Aires: Biblos, 2007.

Lusnich, Ana Laura, Alicia Aisemberg, and Andrea Cuarterolo, eds. *Pantallas transnacionales: El cine argentino y mexicano del período clásico*. Buenos Aires: Ediciones Imago Mundi, 2017.

Maciel, David. *El bandolero, el pocho y la raza: Imágenes cinematográficas del chicano*. Mexico City: Siglo XXI, 2000.

Mafud, Lucio. "Nación y ficción: Mariano moreno y la revolución de mayo en el contexto previo al centenario de la independencia." In *Cine mudo latinoamericano: Inicios, nación, vanguardias y transición*, edited by Aurelio de los Reyes and David M. J. Wood, 153–74. Mexico City: Universidad Autónoma de México, Instituto de Investigaciones Estéticas, 2015.

Maltby, Richard. "Introduction: 'The Americanisation of the World.'" In *Hollywood Abroad: Audiences and Cultural Exchange*, edited by Melvyn Stokes and Richard Maltby, 2–20. London, BFI, 2004.

Marcantonio, Carla. *Global Melodrama: Nation, Body, and History in Contemporary Film*. New York: Palgrave Macmillan, 2015.

Marshall, P. David. Introduction to *The Celebrity Culture Reader*, edited by P. David Marshall, 1–16. New York: Routledge, 2006.

Martí, José. *Inside the Monster by José Martí*. Edited by Philip S. Foner. Translated by Elinor Randall. New York: Monthly Review Press, 1975.

Martín-Barbero, Jesús. "La telenovela desde el reconocimiento y la anacronía." In *Narraciones anacrónicas de la modernidad: Melodrama e intermedialidad en América Latina*, edited by Herman Herlinghaus. Santiago: Editorial Cuarto Propio, 2002.

———. "Laberintos narrativos de la contemporaneidad." In *Heterotropías: Narrativas de identidad y alteridad latinoamericana*, edited by Carlos A. Jáuregui and Juan Pablo Dabove, 447–59. Pittsburgh, PA: Instituto Internacional de Literatura Iberoamericana, University of Pittsburgh Press, 2003.

Martínez, Abel Fernando. *El lazareto de Boyacá: lepra, medicina, Iglesia y Estado, 1869–1916*. Tunja: Universidad Pedagógica y Tecnológica de Colombia, 2006.

Martínez Pardo, Hernando. *Historia del cine colombiano*. Bogotá: Editorial América Latina, 1978.

Marx, Karl. *Capital*. Translated by Ben Fowkes. Vol. I. New York: Vintage, 1976.

Mayer, Roberto L. *William (Willie) Mayer*. Mexico City: Editorial Herder, 2017.

Melo Souza, José Inácio de. *Imagens do passado: São Paulo e Rio de Janeiro nos primórdios do cinema*. São Paulo: Editora Senac, 2003.

Mignolo, Walter. *The Darker Side of Western Modernity*. Durham, NC: Duke University Press, 2011.

Miller, Nicola. *Reinventing Modernity in Latin America: Intellectuals Imagine the Future, 1900–1930*. New York: Palgrave Macmillan, 2008.

Miquel, Ángel. "Del teatro al cine: Enrique Borrás en la Ciudad de México, 1908–1915." *Vivomatografías*, no. 4 (2018): 48–63.

———. "A Difficult Assimilation: American Silent Movies and Mexican Literary Culture." *Film History* 29, no. 1 (2017): 84–109.

———. *En tiempos de revolución: El cine en la Ciudad de México, 1910–1916*. Mexico City: Filmoteca UNAM, 2012.

———. "Rafael Bermúdez Zataraín y El Magazine Fílmico." *Vivomatografías*, no. 3 (2017): 46–70.

Moguillansky, Marina. *Cines del sur: La integración cinematográfica entre los países del Mercosur*. Buenos Aires: Editorial Imago Mundi, 2016.

Monsiváis, Carlos. "El melodrama: 'No te vayas mi amor que es inmoral llorar a solas.'" In *Narraciones anacrónicas de la modernidad: Melodrama e intermedialidad en América Latina*, edited by Herman Herlinghaus, 105–23. Santiago: Editorial Cuarto Propio, 2002.

Montaldo, Graciela. *De pronto, el campo*. Rosario: Beatriz Viterbo Editora, 1994.

———. "La desigualdad de las partes." *A Contracorriente* 7, no. 1 (2009): 14–44.

Mora Forero, Cira. "Los Acevedo." *Cuadernos de cine colombiano*, June 2003, 10–17.

Moraña, Mabel. *El monstruo como máquina de guerra*. Madrid: Iberoamericana/Vervuert, 2017.

Musser, Charles. "The Early Cinema of Edwin Porter." *Cinema Journal* 19, no. 1 (1979): 1–38.

Muzilli, Carolina. *El trabajo femenino*. Buenos Aires: Rosso y Cía, 1916.

Navitski, Rielle. "Early Film Critics and Fanatical Fans: The Reception of the Italian Diva Film and the Making of Modern Spectators in Postrevolutionary Mexico." *Film History* 29, no. 1 (2017): 57–83.

———. "The Last Heist Revisited: Reimagining Hollywood Genre in Contemporary Argentine Crime Film." *Screen* 53, no. 4 (2012): 359–80.

———. "Mediating the 'Conquering and Cosmopolitan Cinema': US Spanish-Language Film Magazines and Latin American Audiences, 1916–1948." In *Cosmopolitan Film Cultures in Latin America, 1896–1960*, edited by Nicholas Poppe and Rielle Navitski, 112–46. Bloomington: Indiana University Press, 2017.

———. *Public Spectacles of Violence: Sensational Cinema and Journalism in Early Twentieth-Century Mexico and Brazil*. Durham, NC: Duke University Press, 2017.

———. "Silent and Early Sound Cinema in Latin America: Local, National, and Transnational Perspectives." In *The Routledge Companion to Latin American Cinema*, edited by Marvin D'Lugo, Ana M. López, and Laura Podalsky, 31–43. New York: Routledge, 2018.

———. "The Tango on Broadway: Carlos Gardel's International Stardom and the Transition to Sound in Argentina." *Cinema Journal* 51, no. 1 (2011): 26–49.

Nieto, Jorge. *Más allá de la tragedia del silencio*. Bogotá: FOCINE, 1987. DVD.

Nieto, Jorge, and Diego Rojas. *Tiempos del Olympia*. Bogotá: Fundación Patrimonio Fílmico Colombiano, 1991.

Nieto Ibáñez, José. *Barranquilla en blanco y negro: El cine silente y parlante llega a la ciudad 1908–1935*. Vol. 3. Barranquilla, Colombia: Editorial Mejoras, 2009.

Nuevo tesoro lexicográfico de la lengua Española. http://ntlle.rae.es/ntlle/SrvltGUILoginNtlle.

O'Loughlin, John, and Herman Van Der Wusten. "Political Geography of Pan-regions." *Geographical Review* 80, no. 1 (1990): 1–20.

Oroz, Silvia. *Melodrama: O cinema de lagrimas da America Latina*. Rio de Janeiro: Rio Fundo Editora, 1992.

Osborne, Peter. "Modernity Is a Qualitative, Not a Chronological, Category." *New Left Review*, no. 192 (1992): 52–85.

Ospina León, Juan Sebastián. "Films on Paper: Early Colombian Cinema Periodicals, 1916–1920." In *Cosmopolitan Visions: Transnational Horizons of Latin American Film Culture, 1896–1960*, edited by Rielle Navitski and Nicholas Poppe, 39–65. Bloomington: Indiana University Press, 2017.

———. "Garras de oro: Herida abierta en un continente; Entrevista a Ramiro Arbeláez." *Vivomatografías*, no. 2 (2015): 203–17.

———. "(In)visibilities: Iñárritu's Cinema and the Melodramatic Regime." *JCMS* 59, no. 2 (2020): 43–61.

Outram, Dorinda. *The Enlightenment*. Cambridge, UK: Cambridge University Press, 2006.

Palacios, Marco. *Entre la legitimidad y la violencia: Colombia 1875–1994*. Bogotá: Norma, 2003.

Palacios, Marco, and Frank Safford. *Colombia: País fragmentado, sociedad dividida, su historia*. Bogotá: Editorial Norma, 2002.
Panagia, Davide. *Rancière's Sentiments*. Durham, NC: Duke University Press, 2018.
Paranaguá, Paulo Antonio. *Tradición y modernidad en el cine de América Latina*. Madrid: Fondo de Cultura Económica, 2003.
Paulk, Julia C. "Foundational Fiction and Representations of Jewish Identity in Jorge Isaacs' María." *Hispanófila*, no. 162 (2011): 43–59.
Paz, Octavio. *Children of the Mire: Modern Poetry from Romanticism to the Avant-Garde*. Translated by Rachel Phillips. Cambridge, MA: Harvard University Press, 1991.
Pellarolo, Sirena. *Sainetes, cabaret, minas y tangos*. Buenos Aires: Corregidor, 2010.
Peña, Fernando. *Cien años de cine argentino*. Buenos Aires: Biblos, 2012.
Peredo Castro, Francisco. *Cine y propaganda para Latinoamérica: México y Estados Unidos en la encrucijada de los años cuarenta*. Mexico City: Centro de Investigaciones sobre América Latina y el Caribe, Universidad Autónoma de México, 2011.
———. "Entre tradición y modernidad: El cine mexicano en su evolución y contradicciones discursivas (1896–1956)." In *Historia sociocultural del cine mexicano: Aportes al entretejido de su trama (1896–1966)*, edited by Francisco Peredo Castro and Federico Dávalos, 271–347. Mexico City: Universidad Autónoma de México, 2016.
Pérez, Jorge. *Confessional Cinema: Religion, Film, and Modernity in Spain's Development Years, 1960–1975*. Toronto: University of Toronto Press, 2017.
Pérez Melgosa, Adrián. "Cosmopolitan Nationalisms: Transnational Aesthetic Negotiations in Early Latin American Sound Cinema." In *The Routledge Companion to Latin American Cinema*, edited by Marvin D'Lugo, Ana M. López, and Laura Podalsky, 135–49. New York: Routledge, 2017.
Phillip, John Sheridan. *Francisco de Miranda: Forerunner of Spanish-American Independence*. San Antonio, TX: Naylor, 1960.
Piketty, Thomas. *Capitalism in the Twenty-First Century*. Cambridge, MA: Harvard University Press, 2014.
Poppe, Nicholas. "Siteseeing Buenos Aires in the Early Argentine Sound Film *Los Tres Berretines*." *Journal of Cultural Geography* 26, no. 1 (2006): 49–69.
Pratt, Mary Louise. *Imperial Eyes: Travel Writing and Transculturation*. New York: Routledge, 1992.
Prieto, Adolfo. *El discurso criollista en la formación de la Argentina moderna*. Buenos Aires: Editorial Sudamericana, 1988.
Prince, Stephen, and Wayne E. Hensley. "The Kuleshov Effect." *Cinema Journal* 31, no. 2 (1992): 59–75.
Purcell, Fernando. *¡De película! Hollywood y su impacto en Chile, 1910–1950*. Santiago: Taurus, 2012.
Quiroga, Horacio. *Arte y lenguaje del cine*. Buenos Aires: Editorial Losada, 1997.
Rama, Ángel. *La ciudad letrada*. Hanover: Ediciones del Norte, 1984.
———. *The Lettered City*. Translated by John Charles Chasteen. Durham, NC: Duke University Press, 1996.

Ramey, James. "La resonancia del exilio y la conquista en el cine indigenista mexicano." In *México imaginado: Nuevos enfoques sobre el cine (trans)nacional*, edited by Claudia Arroyo, James Ramey, and Michael Schuessler, 124–25. Mexico City: CONACULTA, Universidad Autónoma Metropolitana, 2011.

Ramos, Julio. *Divergent Modernities: Culture and Politics in Nineteenth-Century Latin America*. Translated by John D. Blanco. Durham, NC: Duke University Press, 2001.

Rancière, Jacques. *The Politics of Aesthetics*. Translated by Gabriel Rockhill. London: Continuum, 2004.

Reder, Michael, and Josef Schmidt. "Habermas and Religion." In *An Awareness of What Is Missing: Faith and Reason in a Post-Secular Age*, translated by Ciaran Cronin, 1–14. Cambridge, UK: Polity, 2011.

Reich, Robert B. *Saving Capitalism*. New York: Alfred A. Knopf, 2015.

Reyes, Alfonso. "El cine que vio Fósforo: Alfonso Reyes y Martín Luis Guzmán." In *El cine que vio Fósforo: Alfonso Reyes y Martín Luis Guzmán*, edited by Manuel González Casanova, 159–60. Mexico City: Fondo de Cultura Económica, 2003.

Reyes, Aurelio de los. "De Nobleza Baturra a El Charro: Desintegración de la comedia ranchera." In *Miradas al cine mexicano*, edited by Aurelio de los Reyes, 1:241–82. Mexico City: IMCINE, 2016.

———. "Hacia la industria cinematográfica en México." *Vivomatografías*, no. 2 (2015): 124–51.

———. *Sucedió en Jalisco o los Cristeros: Cine y sociedad en México 1896–1930*. Mexico City: Universidad Nacional Autónoma de México, 2014.

Reyes, Aurelio de los, and David M. J. Wood, eds. *Cine mudo latinoamericano: Inicios, nación, vanguardias y transición*. Mexico City: Universidad Autónoma de México, Instituto de Investigaciones Estéticas, 2015.

Rockhill, Gabriel. "Jacques Rancière's Politics of Perception." In *The Politics of Aesthetics*, by Jacques Rancière, translated by Gabriel Rockhill, 1–6. London: Continuum, 2004.

Rojas, Diego. "Cine colombiano: Primeras noticias, primeros años, primeras películas." *Credencial Historia*, April 1997, 8–10.

Romero, Luis Alberto. *Libros baratos y cultura de los sectores populares*. Buenos Aires: Centro de Investigaciones Sociales sobre el Estado y la Administración, 1986.

Roniger, Luis, and Carlos H. Waisman, eds. *Globality and Multiple Modernities: Comparative North American and Latin American Perspectives*. Brighton: Sussex University Press, 2002.

Rousseau, Jean Jacques. *Essay on the Origin of Languages and Writings Related to Music*. Edited by John T. Scott. Hanover, NH: Dartmouth College Press, 1998.

Rubenstein, Anne. "The War on 'Las Pelonas': Modern Women and Their Enemies, Mexico City, 1924." In *Sex in Revolution: Gender, Politics, and Power in Modern Mexico*, edited by Mary Kay Vaughan, Gabriela Cano, and Jocelyn H. Olcott, 57–80. Durham, NC: Duke University Press, 2006.

Sala, Jorge, and Rodrigo Romero Zapata. "Wara Wara (José María Velasco Maidana, 1930): Alegoría cinematográfica del nacimiento de una nación." *Imagofagia*, no. 8 (2013): 1–17.

Salcedo Silva, Hernando. *Crónicas del cine colombiano, 1897–1950*. Bogotá: Carlos Valencia Editores, 1981.
Sanders, James E. *The Vanguard of the Atlantic World: Creating Modernity, Nation, and Democracy in Nineteenth-Century Latin America*. Durham, NC: Duke University Press, 2014.
Sarlo, Beatriz. *El imperio de los sentimientos: Narraciones de circulación periódica en la Argentina*. Buenos Aires: Siglo XXI, 2011.
———. *Una modernidad periférica: Buenos Aires 1920 y 1930*. Buenos Aires: Ediciones Nueva Visión, 2003.
Sarmiento, Domingo Faustino. *Obras completas: Artículos críticos y literarios, 1841–1842*. Vol. 1. Buenos Aires: Editorial Luz del Día, 1948.
Schroeder-Rodríguez, Paul A. "Latin American Silent Cinema: Triangulation and the Politics of Criollo Aesthetics." *Latin American Research Review* 43, no. 3 (2008): 33–58.
Schwarz, Roberto. *As idéias fora do lugar*. São Paulo: Companhia das Letras, 2014.
Serna, Ana María. "Periodistas mexicanos: ¿Voceros de la nueva Doctrina Monroe?" *Estudios Mexicanos* 26, no. 2 (2010): 207–37.
Serna, Laura Isabel. "Cinema on the US-Mexico Border: American Motion Pictures and Mexican Audiences, 1896–1930." In *Land of Necessity: Consumer Culture in the United States-Mexico Borderlands*, edited by Alexis McCrossen, 143–66. Durham, NC: Duke University Press, 2009.
———. *Making Cinelandia: American Films and Mexican Film Culture before the Golden Age*. Durham, NC: Duke University Press, 2014.
Serna, Laura Isabel, and Rielle Navitski. "Ephemerata." *Film History* 29, no. 1 (2017): 140–77.
Sharman, Adam. "Latin American Modernity, . . . and Yet." *Bulletin of Latin American Research* 30, no. 4 (2011): 488–501.
———. *Tradition and Modernity in Spanish American Literature: From Darío to Carpentier*. New York: Palgrave Macmillan, 2006.
Shumway, Nicholas. *The Invention of Argentina*. Berkeley: University of California Press, 1991.
Simmel, Georg. "Fashion." *American Journal of Sociology* 62, no. 6 (1957): 541–58.
———. "The Metropolis and Mental Life." In *The Blackwell City Reader*, translated by Gary Bridge and Sophie Watson, 11–19. Oxford: Wiley-Blackwell, 2002.
Singer, Ben. *Melodrama and Modernity: Early Sensational Cinema and Its Contexts*. New York: Columbia University Press, 2001.
———. "New York, Just Like I Pictured It." *Cinema Journal* 35, no. 3 (1996): 104–28.
Sluis, Ageeth. *Deco Body, Deco City: Female Spectacle and Modernity in Mexico City, 1900–1939*. Lincoln: University of Nebraska Press, 2016.
Sommer, Doris. *Foundational Fictions: The National Romances of Latin America*. Berkeley: University of California Press, 1993.
Sorlin, Pierre. *Italian National Cinema: 1886–1996*. New York: Routledge, 1996.

Stevens, Evelyn P. "Marianismo: The Other Face of Machismo." In *Confronting Change, Challenging Tradition: Women in Latin American History*, edited by Gertrude M. Yeager, 3–17. Wilmington, DE: SR Books, 1994.

Streeby, Shelley. *Radical Sensations: World Movements, Violence, and Visual Culture*. Durham, NC: Duke University Press, 2013.

Stromgren, Richard L. "The Moving Picture World of W. Stephen Bush." *Film History* 2, no. 1 (1988): 13–22.

Suárez, Juana. *Critical Essays on Colombian Cinema and Culture: Cinembargo Colombia*. Translated by Laura Chesak. New York: Palgrave Macmillan, 2012.

Suárez, Juana, and Ramiro Arbeláez. "Garras de Oro (The Dawn of Justice—Alborada de Justicia) The Intriguing Orphan of Colombian Silent Films." Translated by Laura Chesak. *The Moving Image* 9, no. 1 (2009): 54–82.

Suárez, Nicolás. "¿Gauchos de bronce o de yeso?" *Vivomatografías* 4 (2018): 64–87.

Taylor, Charles. *A Secular Age*. Cambridge, MA: Belknap Press of Harvard University Press, 2007.

Terada, Rei. *Feeling in Theory: Emotion after the "Death of the Subject"*. Cambridge, MA: Harvard University Press, 2001.

Thompson, Kristin. *Exporting Entertainment: America in the World Film Market, 1907–1934*. London: British Film Institute, 1986.

Tierney, Dolores. *Emilio Fernández: Pictures in the Margins*. Manchester, UK: Manchester University Press, 2012.

———. *New Transnationalisms in Contemporary Latin American Cinemas*. Edinburgh: Edinburgh University Press, 2019.

Todorov, Tzvetan. *Introducción a la literatura fantástica*. Translated by Silvia Delpy. Mexico City: Premia, 1981.

Tompkins, Cynthia Margarita. "Ideología en dos melodramas fundacionales chilenos: *El húsar de la Muerte* (Pedro Sienna, 1925) y *Canta y no llores corazón* (Juan Pérez Berrocal, 1925)." *Vivomatografías*, no. 4 (2018): 88–115.

Torello, Georgina. *La conquista del espacio: Cine silente uruguayo (1915–1932)*. Montevideo: Yaugurú, 2018.

———. "Salvar almas: Entrevista a Nelson Carro." *Vivomatografías* 1 (2015): 192–202.

Torrado, Susana. *Historia de la familia en la Argentina moderna (1870–2000)*. Buenos Aires: Ediciones la Flor, 2003.

Torres, Rito, and Jorge Durán. "Recuperación y restauración de nuestra Alma Provinciana." *Journal of Film Preservation*, no. 65 (2002): 53–57.

Tucker, Laura. "Páginas Libres: Inclusion and Representation in Early Argentine Cinematic Practices." *Revista de Estudios Hispánicos* 48, no. 1 (2015): 121–45.

Urrego, Miguel Ángel. *Sexualidad, matrimonio y familia en Bogotá, 1880–1930*. Bogotá: Fundación Universidad Central-DIUC, 1997.

Vázquez, Esperanza, and Xóchitl Fernández. "Gabriel García Moreno: Inventor in Hollywood, Innovator in Mexico." In *Hollywood Goes Latin*, edited by María Elena de las Carreras and Jan-Christopher Horak, 105–12. Bloomington: Indiana University Press, 2019.

Vázquez Mantecón, Álvaro, dir. *Historias Recuperadas*. Episode "El puño de hierro." Aired December 16, 2005, on TV-UNAM.

Venturini, Adolfo H. "The Earliest-Known Extant Motion Picture of Anesthesia in the World Was Filmed in Buenos Aires." *Journal of Anesthesia History* 1, no. 2 (2015): 55–57.

Vieytes, Mari. "La Vuelta al Bulín." In *Mosaico Criollo*, 55–58. Buenos Aires: Museo del Cine, 2009.

Vincenot, Emmanuel. "Filmando a los héroes nacionales: El homenaje a Antonio Maceo en 'La última jornada del titán de bronce' (Max Tosquella, 1930)." In *Cine mudo latinoamericano: Inicios, nación, vanguardias y transición*, edited by Aurelio de los Reyes and David M. J. Wood, 133–52. Mexico City: Universidad Autónoma de México, Instituto de Investigaciones Estéticas, 2015.

Vitalli, Valentina, and Paul Willemen, eds. *Theorising National Cinema*. London: BFI, 2006.

Walter, Monika. "Melodrama y cotidianidad: Un acercamiento a las bases antropológicas y estéticas de un modo narrativo." In *Narraciones anacrónicas de la modernidad: Melodrama e intermedialidad en América Latina*, translated by Hermann Herlinghaus, 199–244. Santiago: Editorial Cuarto Propio, 2001.

Warwick Research Collective. *Combined and Uneven Development*. Liverpool: Liverpool University Press, 2015.

Williams, Linda. "Film Bodies: Gender, Genre, and Excess." *Film Quarterly* 44, no. 4 (1991): 2–13.

———. *On the Wire*. Durham, NC: Duke University Press, 2014.

———. *Playing the Race Card: Melodramas of Black and White from Uncle Tom to O. J. Simpson*. Princeton, NJ: Princeton University Press, 2002.

———. "'Tales of Sound and Fury' or, the Elephant of Melodrama." In *Melodrama Unbound Across History, Media, and National Cultures*, edited by Christine Gledhill and Linda Williams, 205–18. New York: Columbia University Press, 2018.

Wood, David M. J. "Cine mudo, ¿cine nacional?" In *México imaginado: Nuevos enfoques sobre el cine (trans)nacional*, edited by Claudia Arroyo, James Ramey, and Michael Schuessler, 29–51. Mexico City: CONACULTA, Universidad Autónoma Metropolitana, 2011.

———. "Erotismo, moralismo y transgresión sexual en tres películas mudas latinoamericanas." In *Placeres en imagen: Fotografía y cine eróticos 1900–1960*, edited by Ángel Míquel, 33–58. Mexico: Universidad Autónoma del Estado de Morelos, 2009.

———. "Recuperar lo efímero: Restauración del cine mudo en México." In *El patrimonio de los siglos XX y XXI*, edited by Louise Noelle, 125–57. Mexico City: Universidad Autónoma de México, 2011.

Wu, Harmony. "Consuming Tacos and Enchiladas: Gender and Nation in *Como Agua Para Chocolate*." In *Visible Nations: Latin American Cinema and Video*, edited by Chon Noriega, 174–93. Minneapolis: University of Minnesota Press, 2000.

Zabala, Santiago, ed. *The Future of Religion*. New York: Columbia University Press, 2005.

Zarco, Francisco. *Obras completas: Crónicas de teatro y de la ciudad, la moda*. Vol. 19. Mexico City: Centro de Investigación Científica Ingeniero Jorge L. Tamayo, 1994.

Zarzosa, Agustín. *Refiguring Melodrama in Film and Television: Captive Affects, Elastic Sufferings, Vicarious Objects*. Lanham, MD: Lexington Books, 2013.

Zylberman, Dana. "Films argentinos estrenados en México (1912–1959)." In *Pantallas transnacionales: El cine argentino y mexicano del período clásico*, edited by Ana Laura Lusnich, Alicia Aisemberg, and Andrea Cuarterolo, 369–85. Buenos Aires: Ediciones Imago Mundi, 2017.

Index

Acevedo, Arturo, 85–86; *Bajo el cielo antioqueño* (Under the Antioquia Sky,1925), 90–96; *La tragedia del silencio* (The Tragedy of Silence, 1924), 80–82, 85–86, 196–97n22
adjectival modernity, 6–10
advertising. *See* marketing; specific film titles
affect, role in melodrama, 9–10, 12, 16–18; *El drama del 15 de octubre* (The October 15th Drama; Di Domenico; 1915), 40; *La revolución de mayo* (The May Revolution; dir. Mario Gallo, 1909), 39; nationalism, emotional narratives of, 152; power to upend status quo, 161–62; profound emotional legitimacy, 149–50
agile reconstruction, 114
AGNM (Archivo General de la Nación), 109
Ajuria, Julián de, 23, 137, 139–50, 141*fig*, 163
Ajuria Productions Company, 146–47
Alippi, Elías, 75
Alma provinciana (Soul of the Province; dir. Félix J. Rodríguez, 1926), 96–107, 99*fig*, 101*fig*, 102*fig*, 107*fig*, 198–99n67
Altamirano, Ignacio Manuel, 41
Amalia (1914), 1–2, 45
ambiente campero, 144–45
American film. *See* Hollywood; United States
Amnesia (dir. Ernesto Vollrath, 1921), 51

Amor de perdição (Doomed Love), film adaptations of, 51
Anderson, Benedict, 149–50, 151, 152, 155, 181n96
Ángel Urrego, Miguel, 84
Arango de Mejía, Alicia, 92
Arbeláez, Ramiro, 159
Archivo General de la Nación (AGNM), 109
Argentina: *Amalia* (1914), 45; Centenario films, 38; department stores, working women and consumer culture, 63–71; film culture, history of, 166–70; films about Buenos Aires, 55–57, 56*fig*; gaucho genre, 20, 168, 207n41–42; Julián de Ajuria's transnational ambitions, 139–42; *La revolución de mayo* (The May Revolution; dir. Mario Gallo, 1909), 38–39; melodramatic mass culture, 58–59; *Nobleza Gaucha* (Gaucho Nobility, 1915), 52, 60–61, 144; porteño cinedrama, 20; tenement housing, overcrowding and (moral) disease, 60–63; *Una nueva y gloriosa nación* (Charge of the Gauchos; dir. Albert H. Kelly, 1928), 23, 137, 140–50, 141*fig*, 184–85n49. *See also* Buenos Aires
Argentine Photographic Society of Enthusiasts, 61
argentino imagery, 144–45
Arniches, Carlos, 51

235

Index

arrabal (slums and marginal neighborhoods), 55–57, 56fig, 60–63
atonement: *Alma provinciana* (Soul of the Province; dir. Félix J. Rodríguez, 1926), 97–98, 104–5; *Bajo el cielo antioqueño* (Under the Antioquia Sky; dir. Arturo Acevedo, 1925), 90–93; *La tragedia del silencio* (The Tragedy of Silence; dir. Arturo Acevedo, 1924), 82, 87–88; narrative story arcs, 73, 82, 107
Aughinbaugh, William Edmund, 31
Aura o las violetas (Aura or the Violets; dir. Pedro Moreno Garzón and Vicente Di Domenico, 1924), 51

"Babylon of Steel," 6, 7fig
bachelor apartments (garçonnières): *La borrachera del tango* (Tango Inebriation; dir. Edmo Cominetti, 1928), 76–78; porteño cinedrama, site-seeing in, 59; sexual economies and male displacement, 71–78
Bajo el cielo antioqueño (Under the Antioquia Sky; dir. Arturo Acevedo, 1925), 82, 83fig, 90–96, 104
bandoleros, 116
barrio emotion (emoción arrabalera), 57, 60–63
barrio identity, 59, 60–63
Benítez-Rojo, Antonio, 46
Benjamin, Walter, 110
Benoît, Georges, 142
Bergero, Adriana, 59
Bermúdez Zataraín, Rafael, 34, 45–47
Bernat, J., 54
Biblioteca Miguel Lerdo de Tejada (BLT) (México), 7fig, 117fig, 131fig
Biblioteca Nacional (BNA) (Argentina), 29fig, 58fig, 66fig
Biblioteca Nacional (BNC) (Colombia), 81fig, 99fig, 101fig, 102fig
Biblioteca Nacional de España, Hemeroteca Digital (BNE), 5fig
biopolitics, *El puño de hierro*, 127–30, 135–36, 164, 199n6
Blanca Podestá Company, 46
BLT (Biblioteca Miguel Lerdo de Tejada) (México), 7fig, 117fig, 131fig
BNA (Biblioteca Nacional) (Argentina), 29fig, 58fig, 66fig
BNC (Biblioteca Nacional) (Colombia), 81fig, 99fig, 101fig, 102fig
BNE (Biblioteca Nacional de España, Hemeroteca Digital), 5fig

boardinghouses. *See* tenement housing
Bogotá, 4, 6; *Alma provinciana* (Soul of the Province; dir. Félix J. Rodríguez, 1926), 96–107, 99fig, 105–8, 107fig, 198–99n67; battle for Latin American markets (1910–1920s), 28, 32–33; *El drama del 15 de octubre* (The October 15th Drama; Di Domenico; 1915), 39–40; film culture, overview, 20–21; Gabriel Veyre, films by, 37; *La tragedia del silencio* (The Tragedy of Silence; dir. Arturo Acevedo, 1924), 80–82, 85–86, 196–97n22; *María* (1867), film adaptation, 47–51, 49fig; melodrama narratives of, 12; religion and film, overview, 80–85, 81fig, 83fig
bolero, 167
Bolivia, 166
Bon Bernard, Fernand, 36
Bonel, Alí, 97
Bonnard, Silvestre, 11
"The Bourgeois King" (Ruben Darío, 1880), 123
Brazil: battle for Latin American markets (1910–1920s), 32–33, 182n9, 182n12; film industry (1930s–1950s), 167–68
Brooks, Peter, 12, 20–21, 82, 84, 187n93, 188n107
Brunner, José Joaquín, 9
Bruno, Giuliana, 59
Buenaventura, Juan G., 159, 160
Buenos Aires, 4, 6; argentino imagery, 144–45; battle for Latin American markets (1910–1920s), 32–33, 182n9; cabaret culture, 72; cabarets and bachelor apartments, sexual economies and male displacement, 71–78; Corporación Argentina Americana de Films, 28; department stores, working women and consumer culture, 63–71; department stores in, 65, 66fig; gaucho genre, 20; *Hasta después de muerta* (Even after Death; dir. Eduardo Martínez de la Pera and Ernesto Gunche, 1916), 62; *La borrachera del tango* (Tango Inebriation; dir. Edmo Cominetti, 1928), 75–78; *La chica de la calle Florida* (The Girl of Florida Street; dir. José A. Ferreyra, 1922), 68–71; *Melenita de oro* (José Ferreyra, 1923), 74–75; melodrama, uses and usefulness of, 67–68; modernization of, 9; *Nobleza Gaucha* (Gaucho Nobility, 1915), 52; porteño cinedrama, 20; tango, influence on film, 72–74, 74fig; *¡Tango!*

(dir. Luis Moglia Barth, 1933), 78; tenement housing, overcrowding and (moral) disease, 60–63. *See also* Argentina
Buenos Aires Film, 194–95n29; *La costurerita que dio aquel mal paso* (The Little Seamstress Who Stumbled; dir. José A. Ferreyra, 1926), 57; screen writing contest (1922), 54; *Sombras de Buenos Aires* (Buenos Aires Shadows; dir. Julio Irigoyen, 1923), 54–55
Bush, Matthew, 17, 178n56, 179n64
Bushman, Francis X., 139, 141*fig*, 142

cabarets: cabaret culture, 72; *La borrachera del tango* (*Tango Inebriation*; dir. Edmo Cominetti, 1928), 75–78; *La vuelta al bulín* (dir. José Ferreyra, 1926), 74; *Melenita de oro* (dir. José Ferreyra, 1923), 74–75; porteño cinedrama, site-seeing in, 59, 75; sexual economies and male displacements, 71–78; tango, influence on film, 72–74, 74*fig*; ¡*Tango!* (dir. Luis Moglia Barth, 1933), 78
Cabiria (dir. Giovanni Pastrone, 1914), 31
Cali, Santiago de, 22
Cali Film, 160, 161
Canta y no llores, corazón (Sing and do not cry; dir. Juan Pérez Berrocal, 1925), 165
Caras y Caretas (1893–1939), 4, 5*fig*, 65
Caribbean: battle for Latin American markets (1910–1920s), 28; Gabriel Veyre, films by, 37
Carretero, Andrés, 71–72
Carrillo, Roberto Arroyo, 41
Castelo Branco, Camilo, 51
Catholic Church: *Alma provinciana* (Soul of the Province; dir. Félix J. Rodríguez, 1926), 103–4, 198–99n67; *Bajo el cielo antioqueño* (Under the Antioquia Sky; dir. Arturo Acevedo, 1925), 90–96; Colombia, Hegemonía Conservadora (Conservative Hegemony), 86–87, 108; Colombia, industry and moral fortitude, 90–96; Colombia, overview of religious influence on film, 80–85, 81*fig*, 83*fig*, 107–8, 197n27; Cristero war (1926-1929), 116; la moral visual regime and, 21, 82, 85, 100, 164; *La tragedia del silencio* (The Tragedy of Silence; dir. Arturo Acevedo, 1924), 85–89, 196–97n22; marriage, virtue of, 85–89; sacralization of society, 84–85
celebrity culture: Theodore Roosevelt, media economy and, 151; transnational films, overview of, 137–39; transnational star power, 22–23, 142, 151, 162–63
censorship: Catholic religious practices, 80, 87; critiques of double standards in, 100, 102*fig*; greaser films, 35
Centenarios, 38
Central America, 28, 160
chanchadas (musical comedies), 168
Charge of the Gauchos. *See Una nueva y gloriosa nación* (Charge of the Gauchos; dir. Albert H. Kelly, 1928)
The Cheat (Lasky production company, 1915), 70
Chejade, Miguel, 52
chica moderna (modern girl), 122
Chile, 1, 26, 27, 52, 146, 165
Cine Colombia, 80, 81*fig*, 88
cine hispano, 169–70
Cinematográfica Colombia, 80
Cine-Mundial, 28, 30, 33–36, 70, 146–47, 186n64
Cine Universal, 28, 29*fig*
class divisions: *Alma provinciana* (Soul of the Province; dir. Félix J. Rodríguez, 1926), 96–107, 99*fig*, 101*fig*, 102*fig*, 107*fig*, 198–99n67; in Argentina, 58–59; *Bajo el cielo antioqueño* (Under the Antioquia Sky; dir. Arturo Acevedo, 1925), 91–96; in Colombia, 82; fashion and urban modernity, 121–26, 124*fig*; filipichín characters, 106–7, 107*fig*; melodrama, cross-class reach of, 14–15; *Perdón, viejita* (Forgive Me Dear Mother; dir. José A. Ferreyra, 1927), 68; print media, serialized melodrama, 14; tenement housing, overcrowding and (moral) disease, 60–63; visual regimes of, 105. *See also* social inequality and mobility
Colombia: *Bajo el cielo antioqueño* (Under the Antioquia Sky; dir. Arturo Acevedo, 1925), 82, 83*fig*; battle for Latin American markets (1910–1920s), 28, 30–33, 183n33, 184n37, 184n44; Compañía Filmadora de Medellín (Medellín Filmmaking Company), 90; feminist movement in, 94–95; film techniques of mid-1920s, 159–60; Gabriel Veyre, films by, 37; *Garras de Oro* (Talons of gold; dir. P. P. Jambrina, 1926), 23, 159–61; Hegemonía Conservadora (Conservative Hegemony), 86–87, 108; industry and moral fortitude, 90–96; *La tragedia del silencio* (The Tragedy of Silence; dir. Arturo Acevedo, 1924), 80, 85–89,

Colombia (continued)
  196–97n22; leprosy in, 196–97n22;
  María (1867), 45–51 49*fig*; religion
  and film, overview, 80–85, 81*fig*, 83*fig*,
  107–8, 195–96n2; sacralization of
  society, 21. *See also* Bogotá; Medellín
Colombia Film, 80, 161
Colombian Film Heritage Foundation, 161
colonialism: *Alma provinciana* (Soul of the
  Province; dir. Félix J. Rodríguez, 1926),
  98; *Bajo el cielo antioqueño* (Under the
  Antioquia Sky; dir. Arturo Acevedo,
  1925), 94, 95; cinematic colonization,
  26; Colombia, social structure in, 47,
  93, 94, 95, 98; modernization, effect on,
  8; Spanish American revolutions, 16;
  *Tepeyac: Adaptación cinematográfica
  de una tradición mexicana* (*Tepeyac:
  Cinematographic Adaptation of a
  Mexican Tradition*, 1917), 41–43
comedia ranchera (ranch comedies), 167,
  168–69
Comminetti, Edmo, 20
Compañía Filmadora de Medellín (Medellín
  Filmmaking Company), 90
compilation films, 22, 110, 135, 160
"Coney Island" (1881, José Martí), 155–56
Conservative Hegemony (Hegemonía
  Conservadora), 86–87, 108
consumer society: cabaret culture, 71–72;
  cinema audiences, marketing to, 31, 55,
  71; department stores, working women
  and consumer culture, 63–71; fashion
  and urban modernity, 121–26, 124*fig*
conventillo, 60, 62–63, 193n21; *El drama
  del 15 de octubre* (The October 15th
  Drama; Di Domenico; 1915), 73–74,
  74*fig*; *Perdón, viejita* (Forgive Me Dear
  Mother; dir. José A. Ferreyra, 1927), 68
Corporación Argentina Americana de
  Films, 28
cosmopolitan nationalist aesthetic, 168–69
Cota, Pilar, 41
Couselo, Jorge Miguel, 67
Cristero war (1926-1929), 116
Crítica, 54
Crítica Free Academy, 54, 191n3
critics. *See* film critics; specific film titles
Cuando canta la ley (When the Law Sings;
  dir. Richard Harlan, 1939), 170
Cuarterolo, Andrea, 143–44, 149
Cuba, 36–37, 170
culebrón, 11, 177n51
cultural dispositif, 156–57
cultural imperialism, 26, 36, 52
culture industry, 171

Dalla, Maga, 97
Darío, Ruben, 123
de Alcañiz, Luana, 169
de Alencar, José, 50–51
de Calvo, Máximo, 47–51, 49*fig*
de Karlo, Sergio, 170
de la Pera, Eduardo Martínez, 52, 60–61
del Diestro, Alfredo, 51
Dellepiane, Antonio, 145
Delluc, Louis, 25–26
de los Reyes, Aurelio, 22, 36, 110, 111–12,
  115, 127
de los Ríos, Manuel, 118, 129
DeMille, Cecil B., 31, 70
Denmark, 35
Denning, Michael, 105
Department of State, U.S., 23; in Colombia,
  30–31, 32, 183n33, 184n37, 185n51;
  Garras de Oro (Talons of gold; dir.
  P. P. Jambrina, 1926), 152, 157–59;
  Latin American film market, assessment
  of, 30–31, 183n33, 184n37, 184n44,
  185n51, 198n50
department stores: *La chica de la calle
  Florida* (The Girl of Florida Street; dir.
  José A. Ferreyra, 1922), 68–71; as palaces of consumption, 65, 66*fig*; *Perdón,
  viejita* (Forgive Me Dear Mother; dir.
  José A. Ferreyra, 1927), 68; porteño
  cinedrama, site-seeing in, 59, 63; working women and consumer culture, 63–71
dialectical images, 110, 136
Dialectic of Enlightenment (Adorno, Horkheimer, 1944), 18, 180n94
Díaz, Belisario, 32
Díaz, Porfirio, 36
Díaz Quesada, Enrique, 51
Dicenta, Joaquín, 51
Di Domenico, Francesco and Vincenzo:
  control of Colombian film industry, 28,
  31, 32, 34, 160–61; *El drama del 15 de
  octubre* (The October 15th Drama; Di
  Domenico; 1915), 39–40; *María* (1867),
  film adaptation, 47
Diego, Juan, 40–43
distributors: Di Domenico "protectionist"
  circuit, 160–61; Latin American industry
  pioneers, 19, 26–30, 32, 34, 36, 37–43,
  52–53, 165; political pressure to suppress *Garras de Oro* (Talons of Gold)
  in U.S. market, 152, 157; transnational

films, classification challenges of, 147;
    transnational systems, bias in, 138–39
Djebar, Assia, 156
drama de arrabal, 55
drama of recognition, 12–13
drug abuse policy, *El puño de hierro*, 127–34,
    131fig, 135–36
Durán, Jorge, 96–97
Dussel, Enrique, 8

economic enterprise, film as, 126
El buitre (The Vulture, 1926), 136
El Demócrata, 130, 131fig
El día que me quieras (The Day You Love
    Me; dir. John Reinhardt, 1935), 169
El drama del 15 de octubre (The October 15th Drama; Di Domenico; 1915),
    39–40, 187n92
El Hogar, 1, 123
Ellis, Paul, 144
El milagro de la calle mayor (Miracle on
    Main Street; dir. Steve Sekely, 1940), 170
El organito de la tarde (Evening Little
    Barrel Organ, 1925), 73–74, 74fig
El Payador (1916), 144
El pobre Valbuena (Poor Valbuena, 1916), 51
El puño de hierro, 109–10, 127–34, 131fig,
    134–37, 203n79; film recovery and
    restoration, 111–15
Elsaesser, Thomas, 171
El tren fantasma (The Phantom Train; dir.
    Gabriel García Moreno, 1926), 21–22,
    134–37, 201n41; as fast-action melo-
    drama, 115–26, 120fig; film recovery
    and restoration, 111–15; film restoration,
    109–10; plot summary, 118–19, 121
El Universal, 11
En busca de María (In Search of María;
    Ospina; 1985), 50
ENERC (Escuela Nacional de Experimen-
    tación y Realización Cinematográfica),
    74fig
equality, liberal promise of, 14–18
Escobar, Álvaro, 74, 75
Escuela Nacional de Experimentación y
    Realización Cinematográfica (ENERC),
    74fig
esteem, types of recognition, 17
Europe: battle for Latin American markets
    (1910–1920s), 30, 31, 32–33; film mar-
    kets, post-World War I, 25–27; France,
    Lumière films, 36–37; French Revolution,
    12, 13, 14–15, 84, 178n56, 179n66. *See
    also* Italy

exhibitors: Di Domenico "protectionist"
    circuit, 160–61; Latin American industry
    pioneers, 19, 26–30, 32, 34, 36, 37–43,
    52–53, 165; political pressure to sup-
    press *Garras de Oro* (Talons of Gold)
    in U.S. market, 152, 157; transnational
    films, marketing challenges of, 147–48
*Exhibitors Herald and Moving Picture
    World*, 147–48, 149
Exporting Entertainment (Thompson), 25

fallen women narratives, 164; *Bajo el
    cielo antioqueño* (Under the Antioquia
    Sky; dir. Arturo Acevedo, 1925), 92;
    department stores, working women
    and consumer culture, 63–71; *El drama
    del 15 de octubre* (The October 15th
    Drama; Di Domenico; 1915), 73–74,
    74fig; *La borrachera del tango* (Tango
    Inebriation; Edmo Cominetti, 1928),
    75–76; *Perdón, viejita* (Forgive Me Dear
    Mother; dir. José A. Ferreyra, 1927), 68;
    porteño cinedrama, 20, 55–57, 56fig;
    tango, influence on film, 72–74, 74fig;
    ¡Tango! (dir. Luis Moglia Barth, 1933),
    78; use of costume and body language
    to represent debasement, 69
fantastic genre, 133–34, 135, 204n94
Farah, Felipe, 75
Farnsworth-Alvear, Ann, 91, 100, 103
fashion, 121–26, 124fig, 135–36, 164,
    202n65
fast-action melodrama, 115–26, 117fig,
    120fig
feminism: *Bajo el cielo antioqueño* (Under
    the Antioquia Sky; dir. Arturo Acevedo,
    1925), 94–95; chica moderna (modern
    girl), 122; in Colombia, 94–95; fashion
    and urban modernity, 121–26, 124fig
Fernández, Emilio (el indio), 168
Ferreyra, José, 20, 57, 60, 62–63, 67; *La
    chica de la calle Florida* (The Girl of
    Florida Street, 1922), 68–71; *La costu-
    rerita que dio aquel mal paso* (The Little
    Seamstress Who Stumbled; 1926), 57;
    La vuelta al bulín (1926), 74; *Melenita
    de oro* (1923), 74–75; *Perdón, viejita*
    (Forgive Me Dear Mother; 1927), 68
feuilleton, 14
fiction films: Bogotá, first films in, 39; film
    d'art, 50; foundational fictions, 45,
    46–47, 50–51, 188n107, 189n125;
    happiness literature, 105–6; history and
    fiction, blurred lines between, 143–44,

240 | Index

fiction films (continued)
146; *La revolución de mayo* (The May Revolution; dir. Mario Gallo, 1909), 38–39; melodramatic efficiency, 73; pathos, blurring of fact and fiction, 40; sensationalism and, 116; serial-queen melodrama, 95–96
Figueroa, Gabriel, 168
filipichín characters, 106–7, 107f
film á these (social problem film), 104–5
film critics: Latin American industry pioneers, 37–43, 52–53, 185n59; *Una nueva y gloriosa nación* (Charge of the Gauchos; dir. Albert H. Kelly, 1928), reception in U.S., 146–49. *See also* specific film titles
film culture: Golden Age of Latin American Cinema, 166–70; importing entertainment, 25–27; multidirectional and transnational connections, 18–24; negotiated readings, film market development and, 27; use of melodrama, national contexts and, 3–4. *See also* transnational film culture
Film Daily, 147
Film Daily Yearbook, 147
film d'art: *Amalia* (1914), 45; foundational fictions, use of, 50–51, 188n107, 189n125; literary works, film adaptations of, 44–45; *María* (1867), 45–52; rise of melodrama, 43–53; *Santa* (1903), 45
filmic cartographies, 28–30
filmmaking, as artisanal endeavor, 2–3
Filmoteca UNAM, 109, 112
film preservation, restoration, and appropriation: agile reconstruction, 114; compilation films, 110; dialectical images, 110, 136; *El puño de hierro*, 109–15, 127–34, 131fig; *El tren fantasma* (The Phantom Train; dir Gabriel García Moreno, 1926), 111–26, 117fig, 120fig; overview of, 21–22, 109–11, 134–36; parallel editing, 115, 119, 131–32, 134–35
Finkielman, Jorge, 150
Fisher, Lucy, 65
flapper, 201n49
follentín de arrabal, 55
folletines, 44
Foucault, Michel, 199n6
foundational fictions, 46–47, 50–51, 188n107, 189n125
Fox Film, 26, 28, 29fig, 146–47, 182n9; battle for Latin American markets (1910–1920s), 33; *Una nueva y gloriosa nación* (Charge of the Gauchos; dir. Albert H. Kelly, 1928), 137
FPFC (Fundación Patrimonio Fílmico Colombiano), 49fig, 83fig, 107fig, 154fig, 190n137
France: Lumière films, 36–37. *See also* French Revolution
Francy, Nedda, 75–76
fraternity, liberal promise of, 15–18
Fray Mocho (Buenos Aires), 58fig
freedom, liberal promise of, 16–18
French Revolution, 12, 13, 14–15, 84, 178n56, 179n66
Fullerton, John, 36
Fundación Patrimonio Fílmico Colombiano (Colombian Film Heritage Foundation) (FPFC), 48, 49fig, 82, 83fig, 107fig, 154fig, 190n137

Gallo, Mario, 38–39, 51
Gamboa, Federico, 45, 50
García-Blizzard, Mónica, 42
García Canclini, Néstor, 8, 9, 20–21, 84
García Mesa, Héctor, 36
García Moreno, Gabriel, 21–22, 110, 113, 118–19, 131, 136
García Ortega, Francisco, 186n64
garçonnières (bachelor apartments): *La borrachera del tango* (Tango Inebriation; Edmo Cominetti, 1928), 76–78; porteño cinedrama, site-seeing in, 59; sexual economies and male displacement, 71–78
Gardel, Carlos, 78, 169
Garras de Oro (Talons of gold; dir. P. P. Jambrina, 1926), 23, 138, 151–63, 154fig, 209–10n93; anti-American sentiment in, 152–53, 155–57; as orphan film, 161; plot summary, 153–55, 154fig; political pressure to suppress in U.S. market, 152, 156–60; popular reception of film, 158–59; sequences and intertitles, use of, 159–61; transnational production of, 159–61
Gath & Chavez department store, 65, 66fig
gaucho genre, 168; *El Payador* (1916), 144; identity politics and gaucho figure, 144–45, 168; *Nobleza Gaucha* (Gaucho Nobility; dir. Eduardo Martínez de la Pera and Ernesto Gunche, 1915), 52, 60–61, 144; overview of, 20, 207n41–42; *Una nueva y gloriosa nación* (Charge of the Gauchos; dir. Albert H. Kelly, 1928), 23, 137, 139–50, 141fig, 184–85n49
Gaumont, Léon, 25

Index | 241

gender inequalities: *Alma provinciana* (Soul of the Province; dir. Félix J. Rodríguez, 1926), 96–107, 99*fig*, 101*fig*, 102*fig*, 107*fig*; *Bajo el cielo antioqueño* (Under the Antioquia Sky; dir. Arturo Acevedo, 1925), 93, 94–95; cabarets and bachelor apartments, sexual economies and male displacement, 71–78; Colombia, feminist movement in, 94–95; department stores, working women, 63–71; fashion and urban modernity, 121–26, 124*fig*; female body, functions in melodrama, 70–71, 76–77, 98–103, 101*fig*, 102*fig*, 195n75; female consumption, critiques of, 66–67; *Hasta después de muerta* (Even after Death; dir. Eduardo Martínez de la Pera and Ernesto Gunche, 1916), 61–62; labor practices, 100, 103; moral judgment of female characters, 62–63; porteño cinedrama, 55–57, 56*fig*, 62–63; serial-queen melodrama, 95–96; working conditions for women, 63–65. *See also* fallen women narratives
género chico (short plays with music), 168–69
Gish, Lillian, 11–12
Gledhill, Christine, 16, 22, 150
Glücksmann, Max, 30, 45
Goethe Institut, 161
Golden Age of Latin American Cinema, 166–70
Goldwyn Distribution Co., 26, 31
Gómez, Argentino, 61
Gonzáles, Carlos E., 40–43
Good *vs*. Evil, 12
Gorelik, Adrián, 59
greaser films, 35–36, 52, 186n64
The Great Train Robbery (dir. Edwin S. Porter, 1903), 115
Griffith, D. W., 11–12, 31
Guido, Elena, 69
guilt: *La tragedia del silencio* (The Tragedy of Silence; dir. Arturo Acevedo, 1924), 87–88; as narrative arc, 82, 107
Guimérá, Ángela, 51
Gunche, Ernesto, 52, 60–61

Habermas, Jürgen, 85
Hansen, Miriam, 66, 150
happiness literature, 105, 133
Harlan, Richard, 170
Harrods department store, 65
Hasta después de muerta (Even after Death; dir. Eduardo Martínez de la Pera and Ernesto Gunche, 1916), 61–62

Hayakawa, Sessue, 70
Hegemonía Conservadora (Conservative Hegemony), 86–87, 108
Heraldo de México, 14, 15
Herlinghaus, Herman, 8, 171
Hershfield, Joanne, 122
Hispanic Caribbean, 22
historical accuracy, in films, 22, 36–37, 121, 143–44, 145, 146
historical artifacts, film as, 110–11
Hollywood: battle for Latin American markets (1910–1920s), 27–36, 29*fig*, 182n7, 182n9, 182n12, 183n33, 184n37, 184n44; cine-hispano, Spanish-language filmmaking, 169–70; film culture of, 146–49; film exports to Argentina, data on, 142; *Garras de Oro* (Talons of gold; dir. P. P. Jambrina, 1926), 138; global dominance of, 25–27; greaser films, 35–36, 52, 186n64; hybrid film culture with Mexico, 169; influence of Latin American cinema on, 167–70; transnational celebrity culture, 22–23; two-way exchanges, North and South, 163, 164–65; *Una nueva y gloriosa nación* (Charge of the Gauchos; dir. Albert H. Kelly, 1928), 137, 140–50, 141*fig*, 184–85n49
Honneth, Axel, 15, 16, 17
humor, use of, 106, 168–69; comedia ranchera (ranch comedies), 167, 168–69; musical comedies (chanchadas), 168
Hybrid Cultures (García Canclini), 84

Ibáñez, Angelita, 121
Ibáñez, Clara, 118
illness, 203n79; *El puño de hierro*, 127–34, 131*fig*; *La tragedia del silencio* (The Tragedy of Silence; dir. Arturo Acevedo, 1924), 86, 196–97n22; suspicions of government and medical community, 132–33; tenement housing, overcrowding and (moral) disease, 60–63
immigrants: anti-immigrant sentiment, drug use policy and, 130; barrios and tenement housing, immigrant narratives and, 55–56, 60–63; Latin American film pioneers, 37, 38, 39, 43, 47, 139
Incendio (Fire; dir. Carlos del Mudo, 1926), 165–66
indigenous populations, 166
industrialization: *Bajo el cielo antioqueño* (Under the Antioquia Sky; dir. Arturo

industrialization (*continued*)
Acevedo, 1925), 90–96; fashion and urban modernity, 121–26, 124*fig*
infrastructure projects as metaphor for modernity, 89; *Bajo el cielo antioqueño* (Under the Antioquia Sky; dir. Arturo Acevedo, 1925), 90–96; Colombia, industry and moral fortitude, 90–96
interpellation, 13, 179n68
intersubjectivity, 16–18
intertitles: film preservation and reconstruction, 109–10, 111–14, 127, 133, 135, 160; film techniques of mid-1920s, Colombia, 159–60; literacy challenges, 143
intimate distances, 59; cabaret culture, 72; department stores, working women and consumer culture, 63–71; tenement housing, overcrowding and (moral) disease, 60–63
invisibilities. *See* visibility / invisibility
Iracema (dir. Capellaro, 1917), 51
Isaacs, Jorge, 45–46, 48–49, 50
Italy: battle for Latin American markets (1910–1920s), 32–36, 182n3; Di Domenico "protectionist" distribution and exhibition circuit, 160–61; *Garras de Oro* (Talons of gold; dir. P. P. Jambrina, 1926), production of, 159–61
Iturriaga, Jorge, 165

Jacobs, Leah, 178n55
Jaramillo, Rosa, 92
Jarvinen, Lisa, 169
Juan José (1910), 51
Juan sin Ropa (dir. José Quiroga, 1919), 142

Karush, Mathew, 59
Kelley, Albert, 147
Kelly, Albert H., 23
Kracauer, Siegfried, 23–24, 66–67, 171
Kuleshov, Lev, 212n138
Kuleshov effect, 159, 160, 212n138

La borrachera del tango (*Tango Inebriation*; dir. Edmo Cominetti, 1928), 75–78
La chica de la calle Florida (The Girl of Florida Street; dir. José A. Ferreyra, 1922), 68–71, 75, 76
La costurerita que dio aquel mal paso (The Little Seamstress Who Stumbled; dir. José A. Ferreyra, 1926), 57
Lafuente, Jorge, 69

Lamont, Charles, 169–70
la moral visual regime, 21, 82, 85, 164; *Alma provinciana* (Soul of the Province; dir. Félix J. Rodríguez, 1926), 96–107, 99*fig*, 101*fig*, 102*fig*, 107*fig*, 198–99n67; *Bajo el cielo antioqueño* (Under the Antioquia Sky; dir. Arturo Acevedo, 1925), 90–96; Colombia, industry and moral fortitude, 90–96; criticisms of, 100; *La tragedia del silencio* (The Tragedy of Silence; dir. Arturo Acevedo, 1924), 89, 196–97n22. *See also* morality; religion
La mosca y sus peligros (The Fly and Its Dangers; dir. Eduardo Martínez de la Pera and Ernesto Gunche, 1920), 60, 61
La Película (1919-1950), 32–33, 192n13
La Prensa, 15, 145
La revolución de mayo (The May Revolution; dir. Mario Gallo, 1909), 38–39
Latin America: anti-U.S. sentiment, 151–52, 155–57; battle for markets (1910–1920s), 27–36, 29*fig*; Di Domenico "protectionist" distribution and exhibition circuit, 160–61; film industry pioneers, 19, 26–30, 32, 34, 36, 37–43, 52–53, 165; film markets, post-World War I, 26–27; French Revolution, influence of, 12, 13, 14–15, 84, 178n56, 179n66; Lumière films, influence of, 36–37; political pressure to suppress *Garras de Oro* (Talons of Gold) in U.S. market, 152, 157; transnational promotion of Latin American authors, 50–51. *See also* specific city and country names
Latin American Industrial Cinematographic Society (SICLA), 28
La tragedia del silencio (The Tragedy of Silence; dir. Arturo Acevedo, 1924), 80, 85–89, 196–97n22
La vuelta al bulín (José Ferreyra, 1926), 74
legal recognition, 17
leprosy, 86, 87–88, 196–97n22
Lesser Antilles, 28
letrados, 44, 50, 72, 155–56
liberal philosophy, 3, 10, 13, 180n84; Medellín society, film portrayal of, 95, 96; melodrama and unfulfilled promises, 12, 14–18, 152, 164–72
liberty, liberal promise of, 15–18, 180n84
Library of Congres (LOC) paper prints, 115
Life of an American Fireman (dir. Edwin S. Porter, 1902), 115
lighting choices, 69–70
Liss, Lidia, 69

literary works, film adaptations of, 44–45, 189n116; *Amalia* (1914), 45; *María* (1867), 45–52; *Santa* (1903), 45; transnational promotion of Latin American authors, 50–51
Logan, Jacqueline, 142
López, Ana, 36–37, 86, 167, 181n97
López Isaza, Alberto, 87
love, types of recognition, 17
Luckacs, Georg, 172
Lugones, Leopoldo, 144
Lumière films, 36–37

male identity displacement, 76–78
María (1867), 45–47, 189n123, 189n125
marianismo, 104
marketing: consumer culture, rise of, 68; for *El tren fantasma* (The Phantom Train; dir Gabriel García Moreno, 1926), 115–18, 117fig; regional and local advertising, 90; serial-queen melodrama, 95–96; transnational films, classification challenges of, 147; transnational films, cultural differences, 31; transnational marketing systems, bias in, 138–39; *Una nueva y gloriosa nación* (Charge of the Gauchos; dir. Albert H. Kelly, 1928), 139, 144, 145–46, 184–85n49. *See also* specific film titles
Market Society, 15
Mármol, José, 45, 50
marriage, virtue of, 85–89, 104, 105
Martí, José, 155–56
Martín-Barbero, Jesús, 6, 8, 9, 13, 18, 46, 172, 179n68
Martínez Pardo, Hernando, 159
Martínez Velasco, Alfonso, 159
Martín Fierro, 72–73
Marx, Karl, 180n84
masked identities, 12, 127–34, 131fig, 203n81
Mayer, William, 111–12
Maynham, Harold, 92
Medellín: *Bajo el cielo antioqueño* (Under the Antioquia Sky; dir. Arturo Acevedo, 1925), 82, 90–96; Colombia, industry and moral fortitude, 90–96; Compañía Filmadora de Medellín (Medellín Filmmaking Company), 90; feminist movement in, 94–95; film culture, overview, 20–21; industrialization of, 91; melodrama narratives of, 12; religion and film, overview, 80–85, 81fig, 83fig, 107–8. *See also* Colombia

Media History Digital Library (MHDL), 64fig
Mejía, Gonzalo, 90, 92, 94
Melenita de oro (José Ferreyra, 1923), 74–75
"Melenita de Oro" (Samuel Linning, 1922), 72
melodrama: affect, role of, 9–10, 12, 16–18, 39, 40, 149–50, 152, 161–62; cited in critical film reviews, 1–2, 14; costume and body language, use of, 69; as drama of recognition, 12, 164–72; fast-action melodrama, 115–26, 117fig, 120fig; female body, functions in film, 70–71, 76–77, 98–103, 101fig, 102fig, 195n75; Golden Age of Latin American Cinema, 166–70; iteration and repetition as connection to everyday life, 46, 48; lighting choices, 69–70; meanings of, 11–18, 84, 178n58, 180n94; miscommunication in transnational films, 150; modern change and, 10; narrative conventions in, 178n55; nationalist films as a rhetorical strategy, 152, 170–71; origins of, 12, 178n56, 179n66; production company styles of, 2; tango, embodied and embodying effect of, 73–74; as tool to relate to modern change, 2–4, 176n18; types of recognition elicited by, 17–18, 180–81n95, 180n94 (*See also* recognition); underside of, 17–18; uses and usefulness in film, 67–68
The Melodramatic Imagination: Balzac, Henry James, Melodrama, and the Mode of Excess (Brooks, 1976), 12
melodramatic regime, 3
mélodrame, 12, 13
Menichelli, Pina, 35
menichellismo, 35
metanarrative of the deficient, 6–10, 176–77n34
"The Metropolis and Mental Life" (Simmel, 1903), 4
Metzger, R. C., 147–48
mexicanidad, 168
Mexico: battle for Latin American markets (1910–1920s), 35, 182n7; *El puño de hierro*, 127–34, 131fig; *El tren fantasma* (The Phantom Train; dir Gabriel García Moreno, 1926), 115–26, 117fig, 120fig; film culture, history of, 166–70; film recovery and restoration, 111–15; greaser films, 35–36, 52, 186n64; hybrid film culture with Hollywood, 169; mexicanidad, 168; *México ante los ojos*

Mexico (*continued*)
del mundo (Mexico Before the Eyes of the World, ca. 1925), 52; *Santa* (1903), 45; *Tepeyac: Adaptación cinematográfica de una tradición mexicana* (*Tepeyac: Cinematographic Adaptation of a Mexican Tradition*, 1917), 40–43. *See also* Orizaba (Mexico)
México ante los ojos del mundo (Mexico Before the Eyes of the World, ca. 1925), 52
Mexico City, 6, 7fig; drug abuse policy, 130, 131fig; film culture, overview, 21–22; film markets, post–World War I, 26–27; Gabriel Veyre, films by, 36
MHDL (Media History Digital Library), 64fig
migration, transnational, 9
Miller, Nicola, 6
Míquel, Ángel, 182n7
miscegenation, 166
mise-en-scène, 159–60
Mitre, Bartolomé, 142
modernidad, use of term, 4
modernity and modernization: adjectival modernity, 6–10; *Alma provinciana* (Soul of the Province; dir. Félix J. Rodríguez, 1926), 96–107, 99fig, 101fig, 102fig, 107fig, 198–99n67; *Bajo el cielo antioqueño* (Under the Antioquia Sky; dir. Arturo Acevedo, 1925), 90–96; in Bogotá, 80–82, 81fig; chica moderna (modern girl), 122; Colombia, Hegemonía Conservadora (Conservative Hegemony), 86–87, 108; Colombia, industry and moral fortitude, 90–96; colonialism, impact of, 6; department stores, working women and consumer culture, 63–71; *El tren fantasma* (The Phantom Train; dir Gabriel García Moreno, 1926), 21–22; fashion as symbol of, 121–26, 124fig; as a felt experience, 9–10; infrastructure projects, imagery of, 89; Latin American state formation and, 84; *La tragedia del silencio* (The Tragedy of Silence; dir. Arturo Acevedo, 1924), 86–89, 196–97n22; meanings of, 4–10, 5fig, 7fig; melodrama and modern change, 10, 164–72; metanarrative of the deficient, 6–10, 176–77n34; modernity, use of term, 8; modernization, use of term, 9; multiple-modernities perspective, 10; porteño cinedrama, 20; public backlash against narrative cinema, 44–45; *Puño de hierro* (Iron Fist; dir. Gabriel García Moreno, 1927), 21–22; religion, social role of, 85; sacralization of society, 10, 20–21, 84–85; Second Industrial Revolution and, 9; tango, influence on film, 72–74, 74fig; traditional Sacred, loss of, 78, 84; traditional Sacred, persistence of, 40–43, 84; transportation, railroad images, 118–19
moderno, use of adjective, 4, 5fig
Monsiváis, Carlos, 9, 73–74, 167, 170
monsters and monstration, 155–56, 160
morality: *Alma provinciana* (Soul of the Province; dir. Félix J. Rodríguez, 1926), 96–107, 99fig, 198–99n67; *Bajo el cielo antioqueño* (Under the Antioquia Sky; dir. Arturo Acevedo, 1925), 90–96; censorship, 80, 87, 100, 102fig; cinema as threat to moral values, 44–45; Colombia, Hegemonía Conservadora (Conservative Hegemony), 86–87, 108; Colombia, industry and moral fortitude, 90–96, 195–96n2; conventillo as space of innocence, 62–63; department stores, working women and consumer culture, 63–71; female body as object of value, 70–71, 76–77, 98–103, 101fig, 102fig, 195n75; *La tragedia del silencio* (The Tragedy of Silence; dir. Arturo Acevedo, 1924), 85–89, 196–97n22; marianismo, 104–5; marriage, virtue of, 85–89; melodrama and character virtue, 13; *Perdón, viejita* (Forgive Me Dear Mother; dir. José A. Ferreyra, 1927), 68; post-Sacred world, 78, 84; sacralization of society, 10, 20–21, 84–85; *Santa* (1903), 45; tango, influence on film, 72–74, 74fig; tenement housing, overcrowding and (moral) disease, 60–63. *See also* porteño cinedrama; religion
Morera, Eduardo, 75
Mundo al día, 39–40
Museum of Modern Art, New York, 115, 161
music, role in Latin American cinema, 167
musical comedies (chanchadas), 168
Musuraca, Nicholas, 142
Muzilli, Carolina, 65–66

Naranjo, Juan B., 82, 83fig, 92
narrative cinema: Centenarios, 38; in Colombia, 85–89; conventions in melodrama, 178n55; *Dialectic of Enlightenment* (Adorno and Horkheimer), on the culture industry, 180n94; gaucho genre,

identity politics and, 144–45; Latin American pioneers in, 43, 52–53, 165; *La tragedia del silencio* (The Tragedy of Silence; dir. Arturo Acevedo, 1924), 85–89, 196–97n22; *Tepeyac: Adaptación cinematográfica de una tradición mexicana* (*Tepeyac: Cinematographic Adaptation of a Mexican Tradition*, 1917), 42–43
nation, definition of, 181n96
national film culture: film d'art, rise of melodrama, 43–52; foundational fictions, 46–47, 188n107, 189n125; Latin American pioneers in, 43–44, 52–53, 165; local film production, 37–43; national cultural hegemony, competition for, 18. *See also* nationalist frameworks
National Film Heritage Foundation, 96
nationalist frameworks, 36–43, 167–71; cosmopolitan nationalist aesthetic, 168–69; *El drama del 15 de octubre* (The October 15th Drama; Di Domenico; 1915), 39–40; emotional legitimacy and, 149–50; Gabriel Veyre, films by, 36–37; *Garras de Oro* (Talons of gold; dir. P. P. Jambrina, 1926), 151–62, 209–10n93; *La revolución de mayo* (The May Revolution; dir. Mario Gallo, 1909), 38–39; *María* (1867), film adaptation, 48–49; *Tepeyac: Adaptación cinematográfica de una tradición mexicana* (*Tepeyac: Cinematographic Adaptation of a Mexican Tradition*, 1917), 40–43; *Una nueva y gloriosa nación* (Charge of the Gauchos; dir. Albert H. Kelly, 1928), 23, 139–50, 141*fig*, 184–85n49
National Pictures, 33
nation-state, 15–16
Navitski, Rielle, 44, 118
Nervo, Amado, 51
Nettles and violets, 123, 124*fig*
New Latin American Cinema, 168–69
New York Commercial, 31
New York World, 23
Nido de Cóndores (Nest of Condors, 1926), 90
Nielsen, Asta, 35
Nobleza Gaucha (Gaucho Nobility; dir. Eduardo Martínez de la Pera and Ernesto Gunche, 1915), 52, 60–61, 144
Noriega, Manuel, 51
Noriega Hope, Carlos, 11
novela cinematográfica: defined, 88; *La tragedia del silencio* (The Tragedy of Silence; dir. Arturo Acevedo, 1924), 88–89, 196–97n22

O Guaraní (The Guarani; dir. Vittorio Capellaro, 1916 and 1926), 51
Ojede, Ignacio, 129
opiate abuse, 127–36, 131*fig*, 164
orientalism, 130, 131*fig*
Orizaba (Mexico), 135–36, 203n79; drug abuse policy, 130; *El puño de hierro*, 127–34, 131*fig*; *El tren fantasma* (The Phantom Train; dir Gabriel García Moreno, 1926), 115–26, 117*fig*, 120*fig*; fashion and urban modernity, 121–26, 124*fig*; film culture, overview, 21–22; labor unrest in, 202n62; melodrama narratives of, 12, 110–11; modernization of, 118
Oroz, Silvia, 178n56
orphan films, 161
Osborne, Peter, 6
Ospina, Luis, 50, 159
Ospina, Pedro Nel, 80, 86, 87, 164
Outram, Dorinda, 179n66

Panama, 85; *Garras de Oro* (Talons of gold; dir. P. P. Jambrina, 1926), 23, 151–62, 209–10n93; Theodore Roosevelt, on taking of Panama, 151, 209–10n93
Panama Isthmus, 12
Pan-América Cinematográfica, 30
Pantallas Transnacionales, 168
parallel editing, 115, 119, 131–32, 134–35
Paramount Pictures, 33, 182n9
Paranaguá, Paulo Antonio, 51
Parodi, Elvira, 61
Parravacini, Florencio, 61
paternalism, 91; *Bajo el cielo antioqueño* (Under the Antioquia Sky; dir. Arturo Acevedo, 1925), 94; female labor, "protective" role of factory owners, 103
pathos, 196n8; *El drama del 15 de octubre* (The October 15th Drama; Di Domenico; 1915), 40
patriarchy: *Alma provinciana* (Soul of the Province, dir. Félix J. Rodríguez, 1926), 97; *Bajo el cielo antioqueño* (Under the Antioquia Sky; dir. Arturo Acevedo, 1925), 92, 93; family melodrama, 107–8, 196n2; *María* (1867), 46, 48; melodrama narratives and, 12
patrimony: film d'art, 44; film reconstruction and, 135
patronatos (boardinghouses), 103

Películas, 6, 32–36
Pellarolo, Sirena, 72
pelona figure, 122–26, 124*fig*
Perdón, viejita (Forgive Me Dear Mother; dir. José A. Ferreyra, 1927), 68
Peredo, Luis G., 45
Peredo Castro, Francisco, 168
Pérez Monfortt, Ricardo, 127
periodicals. *See* print media; specific periodical titles
personal-emotional recognition, 17
personalization of the social, 22–23
Piketty, Thomas, 15–16
Piles, Samuel H., 157–60, 161
Piñero, Sergio, 72–73
Polanyi, Karl, 15
politics: biopolitics, 127–30, 135–36, 164, 199n6; Colombia, Hegemonía Conservadora (Conservative Hegemony), 86–87, 108; *El drama del 15 de octubre* (The October 15th Drama; Di Domenico; 1915), controversy over, 39–40; *Garras de Oro* (Talons of gold; dir. P. P. Jambrina, 1926), 137–39, 151–62, 209–10n93; geopolitical impact of melodrama, 23, 138, 151, 162, 163, 164–65, 168–69; melodrama and, 14, 170–71; nationalist films as rhetorical strategy, 152, 170–71; tenement housing, overcrowding and (moral) disease, 60–63; Theodore Roosevelt, on taking of Panama, 151, 209–10n93
Ponce, Jaime, 114–15
porteño cinedrama, 20, 33; *Amalia* (1914), 45; ambiente campero genre, 144–45; cabarets and bachelor apartments, sexual economies and male displacement, 71–78; conventillo as space of innocence, 62–63; department stores, working women and consumer culture, 63–71; *El organito de la tarde* (*Evening Little Barrel Organ*, 1925), 73–74, 74*fig*; female body, functions of in film, 70–71, 76–77, 98–103, 101*fig*, 102*fig*, 195n75; gaucho genre, identity politics and, 144–45; *Hasta después de muerta* (Even after Death; dir. Eduardo Martínez de la Pera and Ernesto Gunche, 1916), 61–62; intimate distances, creation of, 59; *La borrachera del tango* (*Tango Inebriation;* Edmo Cominetti, 1928), 75–78; *La chica de la calle Florida* (The Girl of Florida Street; dir. José A. Ferreyra, 1922), 68–71; *La costurerita que dio aquel mal paso* (The Little Seamstress Who Stumbled; dir. José A. Ferreyra, 1926), 57; *La vuelta al bulín* (José Ferreyra, 1926), 74; lighting choices in, 69–70; *Melenita de oro* (José Ferreyra, 1923), 74–75; *Nobleza Gaucha* (Gaucho Nobility; dir. Eduardo Martínez de la Pera and Ernesto Gunche, 1915), 144–45; overview of, 55–57, 56*fig*, 78–79, 195n69; *Perdón, viejita* (Forgive Me Dear Mother; dir. José A. Ferreyra, 1927), 68; porteño and Hollywood film cultures, differences of, 146–49; sound cinema, changes in, 167–68; tango, influence on film, 72–74, 74*fig*; ¡*Tango!* (dir. Luis Moglia Barth, 1933), 78; tenement housing, overcrowding and (moral) disease, 60–63; use of costume and body language, 69; uses and usefulness of melodrama, 67–68
Porter, Edwin S., 115
Posada, Antonio José, 51
post-Sacred narrative form, 10, 78, 84
Pratt, Mary Louise, 16
preservation. *See* film preservation, restoration, and appropriation
press material. *See* marketing
print media: battle for Latin American markets (1910–1920s), 32–36; *Caras y Caretas* (1893–1939), 4, 5*fig*; *El tren fantasma* (The Phantom Train; dir Gabriel García Moreno, 1926), 115–18, 117*fig*; humor magazines, 106; *La tragedia del silencio* (The Tragedy of Silence; dir. Arturo Acevedo, 1924), 88, 196–97n22; modernity, representations of, 4–6, 5*fig*; national and transnational film culture, 18–24; novela cinematográfica, 88; porteño cinedrama, weekly novel themes in, 55–57, 56*fig*; response to Roosevelt's taking of Panama, 151, 209–10n93; response to suppression of *Garras de Oro* (Talons of gold; dir. P. P. Jambrina, 1926), 157–60; *Revista Cromos* (1916–present), 4; serialized melodrama, feuilleton, 14; technological advances in, 4. *See also* specific publication titles
profound emotional legitimacy, 149–50
prophylaxis campaigns, 127–28, 132, 136
prostitutes (public women), 71–78; cabaret culture, 72; *El drama del 15 de octubre* (The October 15th Drama; Di

Domenico; 1915), 73–74, 74fig; types of, 71–72
public health, 196–97n22, 203n79; *El puño de hierro*, 127–34, 131fig; *La tragedia del silencio* (The Tragedy of Silence; dir. Arturo Acevedo, 1924), 86, 196–97n22; suspicions of government and medical community, 132–33; tenement housing, overcrowding and (moral) disease, 60–63
Puebla, Mexico, 26
Pulitzer, Joseph, 151, 153, 209–10n93
Puño de hierro (Iron Fist; dir. Gabriel García Moreno, 1927), 21–22
Purcell, Fernando, 30

Quiroga, Horacio, 1–2, 175n1
Quo Vadis? (dir. Enrico Guazzoni, 1913), 31

racism: denigrating films (images), 201n41; greaser films, 35–36, 52, 186n64; miscegenation, *Wara Wara* (dir. José María Velasco Maidana, 1930), 166; press criticism of Hollywood stereotypes, 158; *Tepeyac: Adaptación cinematográfica de una tradición mexicana* (*Tepeyac: Cinematographic Adaptation of a Mexican Tradition*, 1917), 42–43
Ramos, José Manuel, 40–43
Ramos, Julio, 6, 9, 176–77n34
ranchera films, 167, 168–69, 170
Rancière, Jacques, 14
recognition: contemporary uses of melodrama, 13; drama of recognition, 12–13, 16–17, 164–72; female body, functions in melodrama, 70–71, 76–77, 98–103, 101fig, 102fig, 195n75; gaucho figure, identity politics and, 144–45; liberal philosophy and, 15–17; misrecognition, 17, 70; nationalist films, identity formation and, 43, 126, 152, 162; of rights in society, 70; subjugating recognition, individuals as means of utility, 16; types of, 13, 17–18, 180–81n95, 180n94; visibility regimes and, 16–17; *Way Down East* (dir D. W. Griffith, 1920), 12
reduzione, 139
Reinhardt, John, 169
religion: *Bajo el cielo antioqueño* (Under the Antioquia Sky; dir. Arturo Acevedo, 1925), 82, 83fig, 90–96; cinema as threat to moral values, 44–45; Colombia, industry and moral fortitude, 90–96; Colombia, overview of religious influence on film, 80–85, 81fig, 83fig, 107–8,

195–96n2, 197n27; Hegemonía Conservadora (Conservative Hegemony), Colombia, 86–87, 108; *La tragedia del silencio* (The Tragedy of Silence; dir. Arturo Acevedo, 1924), 80, 85–89, 196–97n22; marianismo, 104–5; marriage, virtue of, 85–89; secular society, rise of, 84–85, 177n38, 196n8; social role of, 85; *Tepeyac: Adaptación cinematográfica de una tradición mexicana* (*Tepeyac: Cinematographic Adaptation of a Mexican Tradition*, 1917), 40–43; traditional Sacred, loss of, 78, 84; traditional Sacred, persistence of, 40–43, 84
restoration. *See* film preservation, restoration, and appropriation
revista (multi-act popular entertainment), 169
Revista de Revisats, 7fig
Reyes, Alfonso, 10
rights, types of recognition, 17
Rio de Janeiro, 51, 182n9
Rodríguez, Félix, 96–107
Rodríguez, Manuel, 113, 115
Rojas, Diego, 50
Rojas, Ricardo, 145
Roldán, Emma, 51
Roosevelt, Theodore, 151–62, 209–10n93
Rousseau, Jean Jacques, 178n58

sacralization of society, 10, 20–21, 84–85
sainete (one-act plays), 55, 75–78
Salcedo Silva, Hernando, 49, 161
Sal y pimienta (Salt and Pepper), 98
samba, 167
San Martín, José, 38–39
Sansono contro i filistei (Samson against the Philistines; dir. Domenico Gaido, 1918), 31
Santa (1903), 45
Santiago de Chile, 26, 27
Santos, Francisco, 51
Santos Discépolo, Enrique, 78
Sarlo, Beatriz, 6, 9, 105, 133
Sarmiento, Domingo Faustino, 44
Sáyago, Fernando, 40–43
Schaeffer Gallo, Carlos, 75
Schroeder-Rodríguez, Paul, 169
Schwarz, Roberto, 8
scientific themes, 60–61
scrofula, 203n79
secularization of society, 84–85, 177n38, 196n8
Sekely, Steve, 170

self-esteem, 17
self-inflicted punishment, 87–88, 196–97n22
self-respect, 17
serial-queen melodrama, 63, 64fig, 95–96, 125–26
Serna, Laura, 36
Serra Roxlo, Guillermo, 46
sexual exploitation: *Alma provinciana* (Soul of the Province; dir. Félix J. Rodríguez, 1926), 98; cabarets and bachelor apartments, sexual economies and male displacement, 71–78; female body as object of value, 70–71, 76–77, 98–103, 101fig, 102fig, 195n75; female labor, sexual dangers and, 100, 103; film portrayals of, 69–70; *Hasta después de muerta* (Even after Death; dir. Eduardo Martínez de la Pera and Ernesto Gunche, 1916), 61–62; *La borrachera del tango* (Tango Inebriation; Edmo Cominetti, 1928), 75–78; porteño cinedrama, 20; working women and consumer culture, 63–71
Sharman, Adam, 8, 9
SICLA (Latin American Industrial Cinematographic Society), 28
silent film, overview of, 19–20
Simmel, Georg, 4
Sinclair, John, 169
Singer, Ben, 4, 20–21, 28, 29fig, 78
social esteem, 17
social inequality and mobility: *Alma provinciana* (Soul of the Province; dir. Félix J. Rodríguez, 1926), 96–107, 99fig, 101fig, 102fig, 107fig, 198–99n67; in Argentina, 58–59; *Bajo el cielo antioqueño* (Under the Antioquia Sky; dir. Arturo Acevedo, 1925), 91–96; in Colombia, 82; department stores, working women and consumer culture, 63–71; female body as object of value, 70–71, 76–77, 98–103, 101fig, 102fig, 195n75; filipichín characters, 106–7, 107fig; *La borrachera del tango* (Tango Inebriation; Edmo Cominetti, 1928), 75–78; melodrama, role in revealing, 12–18, 164–72, 180n94; porteño cinedrama, 55–57, 56fig; silent film culture portrayals of, 3; social problem film (film á these), 104–5; tenement housing, overcrowding and (moral) disease, 60–63; visual regimes of, 105. See also class divisions
social instability, porteño cinedrama, 20
social problem film (film á these), 104–5

Sociedad General Cinematográfica, 30, 140, 145–46
socioculture separation, 59; in Colombia, 82; department stores, working women and consumer culture, 63–71; *Perdón, viejita* (Forgive Me Dear Mother; dir. José A. Ferreyra, 1927), 68; tenement housing, overcrowding and (moral) disease, 60–63. See also class divisions; social inequality and mobility
Sombras de Buenos Aires (Buenos Aires Shadows; dir. Julio Irigoyen, 1923), 54–55, 57
Sommer, Doris, 188n107
Southern Cone, 28
South-to-North exchanges, 138–39, 162–63, 168–69. See also *Una nueva y gloriosa nación* (Charge of the Gauchos; dir. Albert H. Kelly, 1928)
South-to-South exchanges, 52, 138–39, 162–63, 168–69, 212n150
Spanish American revolutions, 16
star power. See celebrity culture
State Department. See Department of State, U.S.
Stevens, Evelyn P., 104
studio cinema, 168–69
Suárez, Juana, 93, 159

tableaux vivants, 38–39; Catholic imagery, use of, 82–84, 83fig
tango, 167; cabaret culture, 72; influence on film, 72–74, 74fig, 192n13; *La borrachera del tango* (Tango Inebriation; Edmo Cominetti, 1928), 75–78; *La vuelta al bulín* (José Ferreyra, 1926), 74; *Melenita de oro* (José Ferreyra, 1923), 74–75; site-seeing, 75
tango songs, 55–57, 56fig
¡Tango! (dir. Luis Moglia Barth, 1933), 78
Taylor, Charles, 85, 177n38
tenement housing, 193n21; overcrowding and (moral) disease, 60–63; porteño cinedrama, site-seeing in, 59
Tepeyac: Adaptación cinematográfica de una tradición mexicana (Tepeyac: Cinematographic Adaptation of a Mexican Tradition, 1917), 40–43
Tesouros do Cinema Latino-Americano (1998), 114
Thompson, Kristin, 25, 26, 31, 182n3
Tierra baja (Lowland, 1912), 51
Torcuato de Alvear, Marcelo, 145
Torello, Georgina, 27–28, 166

Torres, L., 54
Torres, Rito, 96–97
traditional Sacred: *Bajo el cielo antioqueño* (Under the Antioquia Sky; dir. Arturo Acevedo, 1925), 90–96; *La tragedia del silencio* (The Tragedy of Silence; dir. Arturo Acevedo, 1924), 89; loss of, 78, 84; persistence of, 40–43, 84; *Tepeyac: Adaptación cinematográfica de una tradición mexicana* (*Tepeyac: Cinematographic Adaptation of a Mexican Tradition*, 1917), 40–43. *See also* Catholic Church; religion
transnational film culture, 181n97; battle for Latin American markets (1910–1920s), 27–36, 29fig; celebrity culture, 22–23; cosmopolitan nationalist aesthetic, 168–69; film promotional strategies and audience reception, 145–49; *Garras de Oro* (Talons of gold; dir. P. P. Jambrina, 1926), 138, 151–63, 209–10n93; Golden Age of Latin American Cinema, 166–70; Hollywood-style films, different interpretations of, 150; importing entertainment, 25–27; Julián de Ajuria's transnational ambitions, 139–42; literacy challenges on intertitles, 143; literary works, film adaptations of, 44–45; *María* (1867), 45–52; marketing and distributions systems, bias in, 138–39; Mexico-Hollywood hybrid film culture, 169; miscommunication in transnational films, 150; nationalist films, national identity formation and, 152–53; New Latin American Cinema, 168–69; overview of, 18–24; porteño cinedrama, 55–57, 56fig; privilege of North-to-South consumption, 137–39; two-way exchanges, 162–63; *Una nueva y gloriosa nación* (Charge of the Gauchos; dir. Albert H. Kelly, 1928), 23, 137, 140–50, 141fig, 184–85n49; visual imagery choices for transnational appeal, 143–44. *See also* film culture
transnational migration, 9
transportation technologies, images of modernity, 118–19
Turich, Leonor, 169
Turkey, 203n82
two-way exchanges, film cultures and, 162–63

Una nueva y gloriosa nación (Charge of the Gauchos; dir. Albert H. Kelly, 1928), 23, 137, 140–50, 141fig, 163, 184–85n49; Buenos Aires premiere, 150; critical and popular reception of, 145–49; historical discrepancies in, 143, 145, 146; intertitles, transnational challenges, 143; plot description, 142–43; visual imagery choices for transnational appeal, 143–44
United States: anti-American sentiment in Latin America, 151–52, 155–57; battle for Latin American markets (1910–1920s), 27–36, 29fig; cine hispano, 169; *Garras de Oro* (Talons of gold; dir. P. P. Jambrina, 1926), 151–62, 209–10n93; greaser films, 35–36, 52, 186n64; Hollywood, global dominance of, 25–27; marketing and distribution systems, bias in, 138–39; transnational celebrity culture, 22–23; transnational contexts, challenges with, 164–65; *Una nueva y gloriosa nación* (Charge of the Gauchos; dir. Albert H. Kelly, 1928), 23, 140–50, 141fig, 184–85n49. *See also* Department of State, U.S.; Hollywood
Universal Studios, 26
urbanization, 4–6, 5fig; *Alma provinciana* (Soul of the Province; dir. Félix J. Rodríguez, 1926), 96–107, 99fig, 101fig, 102fig, 107fig, 198–99n67; *Bajo el cielo antioqueño* (Under the Antioquia Sky; dir. Arturo Acevedo, 1925), 90–96; Colombia, industry and moral fortitude, 90–96; *El tren fantasma* (The Phantom Train; dir Gabriel García Moreno, 1926), 21–22; fashion and urban modernity, 121–26, 124fig; *La tragedia del silencio* (The Tragedy of Silence; dir. Arturo Acevedo, 1924), 89, 196–97n22; porteño cinedrama, 20, 78–79; *Puño de hierro* (Iron Fist; dir. Gabriel García Moreno, 1927), 21–22; secular society, rise of, 84, 196n8
urban / rural divide, 93–94, 168; *Alma provinciana* (Soul of the Province; dir. Félix J. Rodríguez, 1926), 96–107, 99fig, 101fig, 102fig, 107fig, 198–99n67
urban themes and outcasts, 168; *Alma provinciana* (Soul of the Province; dir. Félix J. Rodríguez, 1926), 96–107, 99fig, 198–99n67; Buenos Aires, films about, 55–57, 56fig; cabarets and bachelor apartments, sexual economies and male displacement, 71–78; department stores, working women and consumer culture, 63–71; *El organito de la tarde* (Evening

urban themes and outcasts (*continued*)
Little Barrel Organ, 1925), 73–74, 74*fig*; *La borrachera del tango* (*Tango Inebriation*; Edmo Cominetti, 1928), 75–78; *La chica de la calle Florida* (The Girl of Florida Street; dir. José A. Ferreyra, 1922), 68–71; porteño cinedrama, 20, 55–57, 56*fig*, 78–79; *Sombras de Buenos Aires* (Buenos Aires Shadows; dir. Julio Irigoyen, 1923), 54–55; tango, influence on film, 73–74, 74*fig*; tenement housing, overcrowding and (moral) disease, 60–63; urban space as contested space, 59
Uribe Uribe, Rafael, 39–40
Uruguay, 27–28, 166

Valencia, Hortensia, 129
Valencia, Octavio, 129
Valente Cervantes, 26–27
vampiric tableau, 76–77, 78, 122, 195n75
Vargas Vila, José María, 51
Variety, 149
Vázquez, Esperanza, 109, 112–15, 119, 121, 127, 133, 134–35
Velasco, Martínez, 161
Venezuela, 85
Veracruz: drug abuse policy, 130; *El puño de hierro*, 127–34, 131*fig*; *El tren fantasma* (The Phantom Train; dir Gabriel García Moreno, 1926), 116
Vera Cruz Studio, 168
Verbena trágica (*Tragic Dance*; dir. Chares Lamont, 1939), 169–70
Veyre, Gabriel, 36–37, 43
Vianna, José, 51
Villatoro, Carlos, 118
Vincenot, Emmanuel, 36
Virgin of Guadalupe, 40–43
visibility / invisibility: drama of recognition, 12–18; of emerging social actors, 67, 106, 123; monsters and monstration, 155–56, 160; morality, drama of, 21; nationalist films, identity formation and, 152; pathos, use of, 40; private spaces, 76; role of melodrama in, 2–3, 12–13, 16–17, 164–72, 179n66; of suffering, 40, 82, 178n55. *See also* recognition
visual regimes: *Alma provinciana* (Soul of the Province; dir. Félix J. Rodríguez, 1926), 96–107, 99*fig*, 101*fig*, 102*fig*, 107*fig*, 198–99n67; argentino imagery, 144–45; *Bajo el cielo antioqueño* (Under the Antioquia Sky; dir. Arturo Acevedo, 1925), 90–96; Colombia, industry and moral fortitude, 90–96; criminality, imagery of, 116–18, 117*fig*; fashion and urban modernity, 106–7, 121–26, 124*fig*; filipichín, 106–7, 107*fig*; *Garras de Oro* (Talons of gold; dir. P. P. Jambrina, 1926), 23, 159–61; intimate distances, 59; *La tragedia del silencio* (The Tragedy of Silence; dir. Arturo Acevedo, 1924), 87–88, 89, 196–97n22; melodrama and, 3, 14, 17, 21, 163; modernity and, 53, 79, 115–16, 135–36; monsters and monstration, 155–56, 160; nationalist films, 37–38, 40, 41–42, 43, 47; religious imagery and morality, 21, 82, 85, 89, 103–4, 107–8; social order, depiction of, 105–7, 161–62; transnational contexts, challenges of, 137, 143–44, 152, 161–62, 164–65; *Una nueva y gloriosa nación* (Charge of the Gauchos; dir. Albert H. Kelly, 1928), 143–44, 164–65; urban spaces, 61
Vitagraph, 33

Wara Wara (dir. José María Velasco Maidana, 1930), 166
Ward, Fannie, 70
Warner Brothers, 33
waste basket films, 30, 31
Way Down East (dir D. W. Griffith, 1920), 11–12, 17
white slavery, porteño cinedrama, 20, 69
Williams, Linda, 11
Wood, David, 98, 112, 198–99n67
World War I, impact on global film industry, 25–27
"A Wretched Passerby" *El Demócrata* (1926), 116–18, 117*fig*

Yrigoyen, Julio, 194–95n29

Zanussi, Lucia, 160
Zarco, Francisco, 126
Zarzosa, Agustín, 178n55

Founded in 1893,
UNIVERSITY OF CALIFORNIA PRESS
publishes bold, progressive books and journals
on topics in the arts, humanities, social sciences,
and natural sciences—with a focus on social
justice issues—that inspire thought and action
among readers worldwide.

The UC PRESS FOUNDATION
raises funds to uphold the press's vital role
as an independent, nonprofit publisher, and
receives philanthropic support from a wide
range of individuals and institutions—and from
committed readers like you. To learn more, visit
ucpress.edu/supportus.

www.ingramcontent.com/pod-product-compliance
Lightning Source LLC
Chambersburg PA
CBHW030535230426
43665CB00010B/899